Young Children
with Disabilities
in Natural Environments

Young Children with Disabilities *in* Natural Environments

Methods & Procedures

by

Mary Jo Noonan, Ph.D., & Linda McCormick, Ph.D.

University of Hawaii at Manoa

·P·A·U·L·H·
BROOKES
PUBLISHING C⁰®

Baltimore • London • Sydney

KH

Paul H. Brookes Publishing Co.
Post Office Box 10624
Baltimore, Maryland 21285-0624

www.brookespublishing.com

"Paul H. Brookes Publishing Co." is a registered trademark of
Paul H. Brookes Publishing Co., Inc.

Typeset by Integrated Publishing Solutions, Grand Rapids, Michigan.
Manufactured in the United States of America by
Sheridan Books, Inc., Chelsea, Michigan.

The cases described in this book are fictionalized accounts based on
the authors' clinical and research experience that do not represent the
lives of specific individuals, and no implications should be inferred.

Library of Congress Cataloging-in-Publication Data

Noonan, Mary Jo.
  Young children with disabilities in natural environments : methods &
  procedures / by Mary Jo Noonan, Linda McCormick.
     p.   cm.
  Includes bibliographical references and index.
  ISBN-10: 1-55766-861-2 (pbk.)
  ISBN-13: 978-1-55766-861-5 (pbk.)
  1. Children with disabilities—Education (Early childhood) 2. Early
  childhood special education. 3. Autism. I. McCormick, Linda. II. Title.

LC4019.3.N66 2006
371.9'0472—dc22   2005034129

British Library Cataloguing in Publication data are available from the
British Library.

3/6/08

Contents

About the Authors

Mary Jo Noonan, Ph.D., Professor of Special Education at the University of Hawaii at Manoa, Wist Hall, Room 120, 1776 University Avenue, Honolulu, Hawaii 96822-2463

Dr. Noonan coordinates the Graduate Teacher Preparation Program for Students with Severe Disabilities and the Ph.D. in Education Program, Exceptionalities Specialization, at the University of Hawaii at Manoa. She has been the director of several early childhood special education grants as well as teacher education and leadership training grants. She has worked extensively as a consultant throughout the Pacific Basin region and is the author of many articles and chapters concerning early childhood special education and teaching students who have severe disabilities.

Linda McCormick, Ph.D., Professor of Special Education at the University of Hawaii at Manoa, Wist Hall, Room 120, 1776 University Avenue, Honolulu, Hawaii 96822-2463

Dr. McCormick coordinates the Early Childhood Special Education Teacher Training Program at the University of Hawaii at Manoa. Prior to 1979, when she joined that faculty, she had had experience as a teacher-counselor working with children with behavior disorders, as state coordinator of infant and preschool services, as director of outpatient programs for children under the Tennessee Department of Mental Health, and as a member of the faculties of Peabody College (Vanderbilt University) and the University of Alabama at Birmingham. Her areas of research and expertise include early intervention and early childhood special education, language intervention, inclusion/co-teaching, and severe disabilities. She has conducted workshops in the Pacific Basin and Taiwan and has served as principal investigator for numerous research and personnel preparation grants with an emphasis on early intervention.

Foreword

Congress passed the Education of the Handicapped Act Amendments of 1986 (PL 99-457) to mandate services for eligible children ages 3 through 5 and to provide for statewide systems of early intervention for eligible infants and toddlers ages birth through 2. This reauthorization also contained a new description of a service delivery setting: natural environments. The law stated that the natural environment for children was the home or places in which other children participated—places that are natural or normal for children who do not have disabilities (§ 634[16][A]). One reason for this emphasis was to ensure that young children with disabilities and their families would be included in everyday home and community activities and that, by law, early intervention services would not be delivered in places that would isolate the child with disabilities or his or her family from everyday life.

In 1993, Mary Jo Noonan and Linda McCormick published the first edition of *Early Intervention in Natural Environments: Methods and Procedures*. In this textbook, they integrated the concept of natural environments into intervention practices and then took the field a step further by illustrating how natural environments should be the context for children learning functional skills across developmental domains. This framework was a fresh perspective for those practitioners who were struggling to provide optimal services for young children and their families.

Now, 13 years later, Noonan and McCormick have produced an even fresher perspective on service delivery for young children with disabilities in natural environments. This textbook encompasses more than a decade of new research findings in early intervention research while maintaining its focus on functional learning for children and a partnership with families. Other key service delivery components, such as policy collaborative teaming and cultural competence, also are featured prominently. Separate chapters focus on children with autism, positive behavior supports, social competence, and transitions. These complement the solid instructional foundation provided by chapters on policy, assessment, curriculum, instruction, program planning, and monitoring/evaluation and provide a comprehensive resource for both preservice and in-service personnel training systems.

This textbook is timely as it emphasizes evidence-based strategies focused on improved outcomes for families and their children. New federal reporting requirements for states serving young children with disabilities (ages birth through 5 years) mandate that evidence on child and family outcomes is reported on a yearly basis. The information, content, methods, and procedures contained in this textbook will facilitate both the reporting of data and the implementation of strategies to ensure positive outcomes. The textbook makes a valuable contribution to the field of early childhood intervention for this reason, and also because it is well organized, thoughtfully written, and comprehensive.

It is a privilege to write this foreword to a textbook of this quality. As someone who has been involved in personnel preparation in early childhood intervention for almost 30 years, I am pleased when a training tool comes along to make my job easier. I feel that my colleagues in personnel preparation, as well as service providers (both future and current), will benefit enormously from this book. I have long admired the dedication of Mary Jo Noonan and Linda McCormick to effective early childhood intervention service delivery, which is evident throughout the book. Also evident are the intervention research and evaluation skills they have refined through their work with children and families over their long involvement in the field. This textbook represents an opportunity for the field to focus on improvements: for providers, systems of service delivery, and, ultimately, the children and families who are served through intervention.

Mary Beth Bruder, Ph.D.
Professor and Director
A.J. Pappanikou Center for
Excellence in Developmental
Disabilities Education, Research and Service
University of Connecticut

REFERENCES

Education of the Handicapped Act Amendments of 1986, PL 99-457, 20 U.S.C. §§ 1400 *et seq.*
Noonan, M.J., & McCormick, L. (1993). *Early intervention in natural environments: Methods and procedures.* Pacific Grove, CA: Brooks/Cole Publishing Co.

Preface

The field of early intervention/early childhood special education has been radically altered since the mid-1990s. Most significant have been the advances in developing and maintaining partnerships with families and socially integrating young children with and without disabilities with one another in inclusive programs. Personnel preparation programs in the field have multiplied, but there continues to be a national shortage of professionals with the skills and competencies to meet the unique needs of infants and young children with disabilities and their families.

Effective procedures are those that have a high probability of producing desired outcomes. This book is intended as a practical guide to effective procedures for practitioners in early intervention/early childhood special education (pre- and in-service early interventionists, teachers, and family members). It draws from more than 40 years of research and demonstration efforts designed to develop and model teaching strategies to support the development and learning of infants and young children with disabilities in inclusive settings. Each chapter provides basic information and instructions for implementing early intervention practices and procedures for infants, toddlers, and preschoolers with disabilities and their families. Guidelines are current, empirically validated, and functional. They are designed to be used with individual children and groups in a range of inclusive classroom, home, and community settings.

Chapter 1 provides a brief overview of the history of early intervention perspectives and policies, the legislation affecting practices and services for infants and young children with disabilities and their families, and current trends in the field.

Chapter 2 addresses the importance of professionals working cooperatively and harmoniously with one another and with families. Skills for collaborative teaming are discussed in the context of considering the effects of cultural diversity on professionals' relationships and how the culture of special education influences our beliefs and values.

Chapter 3 describes types and approaches to assessment, with particular attention on the assessment requirements of the Individuals with Disabilities Education Act (IDEA) of 1990 (PL 101-476) and its amendments and approaches that are pertinent to the development and implementation of the individualized family service plan (IFSP) and the individualized education program (IEP). This chapter also provides ways to write high-quality goals and objectives.

Chapter 4 describes the naturalistic curriculum model. Specifically, it offers ways to develop curriculum from a child's unique natural experiences, using minimally intrusive instructional methods.

Chapter 5 describes program planning and monitoring/evaluation procedures. The chapter addresses the following questions: 1) How do we decide what to teach? 2) Who should teach? 3) Where should the teaching occur? and 4) Was the teaching effective?

Chapter 6 discusses the specific steps for implementing systematic instruction. Also discussed are prompting procedures—steps to take in identifying and providing naturally occurring prompts and motivational variables during assessment and instruction.

Chapter 7 focuses on the importance of culturally relevant instruction and strategies to support young children who are learning English as a second language. The importance of understanding a child's culture is discussed. It is argued that identifying a child's learning styles and preferences has the potential to increase the effectiveness of instruction.

Chapter 8 begins with an introduction to the current diagnostic criteria used with individuals with autism. The remainder of the chapter focuses on the learning characteristics of children with autism and how to use the eight general instructional procedures discussed in this text to affect their learning.

Chapter 9 describes environmental structuring to promote engagement, communication, interaction, and play in inclusive settings. It also provides methods for adapting common classroom procedures and activities to increase the participation of young children with disabilities in routine activities.

Chapter 10 provides directions for implementing the positive behavior support model for serious challenging behaviors. Positive behavior support techniques are implemented to prevent challenging behavior and to teach appropriate replacement behaviors.

Chapter 11 describes procedures for group instruction. Specifically, it describes strategies for facilitating participation in groups: quick pacing, selective attention, partial/adaptive participation, group interaction, and group responding. Techniques for using group arrangements to support the instruction process are also described.

Chapter 12 draws from research investigating peer-related social competence and friendships and social communication of young children with disabilities in inclusive settings. The focus of the procedures is twofold: 1) how to help children become members of groups and socially competent and 2) how to facilitate and support communication with peers.

Chapter 13 discusses independent skills for meaningful participation in natural settings. The criteria for selecting instructional procedures to facilitate participation in natural settings are that the procedures be nonintrusive, naturalistic, easily incorporated into daily activities and designed to facilitate generalization. The meaning of and procedures for facilitating functional independence also are discussed.

Chapter 14 describes the important transitions of early childhood, contrasting the IDEA Part B and Part C provisions related to transition. Also discussed are the Division for Early Childhood recommended practices for transition, preparation of young children for kindergarten, and the STEPS (Sequenced Transition to Education in the Public Schools) model.

Each chapter begins with a chapter focus and concludes with study questions designed to help students focus on key concepts. The text is replete with instructional strategies and techniques for implementing the recommended practices, as well as detailed examples. As noted earlier, the focus is on empirically based procedures applicable to infants and young children with disabilities in natural and inclusive settings. Our hope is that this text illustrates that high-quality inclusive early intervention and early childhood special education are eminently feasible.

Acknowledgments

We would like to express our gratitude to Heather Shrestha, Editorial Director, and Trish Byrnes, Book Production Editor, at Paul H. Brookes Publishing Co. for their support in producing this book and their careful attention to detail. We also extend our thanks to the reviewers who graciously gave of their time and expertise.

1

Perspectives, Policies, and Practices

Linda McCormick

arly identification and intervention are essential to maximize skill development and reduce or alleviate the need for special services when a child with a disability enters school. Fortunately, in addition to an increase in early intervention services, important legislation has been enacted that expands the availability of curricula, teaching techniques, and qualified personnel in this area. The challenge now is to achieve widespread implementation of validated practices and procedures.

This book provides basic information and instructions for implementing early intervention practices and procedures with infants, toddlers, and preschoolers with disabilities and their families. This chapter offers a brief overview of the history of early intervention perspectives and policies, the legislation affecting practices and services for infants and young children and their families, and current trends in the field. Following the historical overview is a summary of recommended practices for early childhood special education. The recommended practices are elaborated on in the remainder of the text.

HISTORY OF CONCERN FOR EARLY INTERVENTION

Early childhood special education (ECSE) is a relatively young field with a distinguished "family history." In addition to roots in general early childhood education (ECE), compensatory education, and special education for school-age children, ECSE draws from theory and methods in psychology, human development, nursing, and sociology (Peterson, 1987). Innumerable people in these fields committed their professional careers to understanding and affecting the course of development of young children. We briefly summarize the contributions of some of these individuals to give some sense of the beginnings of ECSE.

Contributors

The roots of early childhood special education can be traced back to European and American contributors. Europeans, the earliest contributors, were mostly physicians who explored how children learn. The American contributors who followed studied the effects of the environment on early development.

European Contributions   Itard, Montessori, and Piaget are probably the best known of the European progenitors of ECSE. Jean-Marc Itard (1775–1838), a French physician and authority on diseases of the ear, is credited with developing and implementing the first intervention procedures for children with disabilities. Itard's thesis, which was extremely radical for his time, was that learning potential is affected by both the environment and physiological stimulation. He had an opportunity to test his theory and his sensory-training approach with a child who was found wandering around the outskirts of a village in the province of Aveyron, France. The child was naked, his face and neck were heavily scarred, and he neither spoke nor responded to speech. Itard disagreed with Paris physicians who insisted that the boy (later named Victor) was not "wild" as he had been described, but rather "mentally deficient" (Humphrey, 1962). They argued that the child's state was due to having survived alone in the woods for 7 or more years and that he could not be educated.

Itard devoted the next 5 years to an intensive one-to-one education program (similar to what would be described in a present-day individualized education program [IEP]) for Victor. His goals for the boy were

- To interest him in a social life
- To improve his awareness of environmental stimuli
- To extend the range of his ideas (e.g., introduce him to games, culture, and so forth)
- To teach him to speak
- To teach him to communicate with symbols such as pictures and written words (Humphrey, 1962)

Victor did not make the progress that Itard had hoped for. After 5 years he was able to carry out only simple commands, and he could read and speak only a few words. He demonstrated affection for his caregivers but his behavior did not approach typical behavior. Itard maintained that his sensory-training approach would have been successful if Victor had been a few years younger. Indeed this may have been the case, but many modern readers of Itard's personal account of his work with Victor conclude that the child most likely had mental retardation or autism (French, 2000).

What is important about this effort is that it was the first attempt to provide an enriched environment to compensate for severe developmental delays. It did away with the paralyzing sense of hopelessness and inertia that kept the medical profession and everyone else from trying to do anything constructive for children with significant developmental delays (Kanner, 1967). Edouard Sequin, Itard's student, later improved on and extended Itard's sensory-training approach, earning fame in Europe and elsewhere for his nonverbal intelligence test, which had its roots in Itard's work.

A century later, in Italy, another physician, Maria Montessori (1870–1952), drew on the work of Itard, Sequin, and others. Her earliest work was with children who had mental retardation and lived in an institution in Rome. She provided these children with mental stimulation, meaningful activities, and opportunities to develop self-esteem. Many of the children were able to pass standardized tests for sixth-grade students in the Italian public schools. Somewhat later she opened a school called Children's House for young children living in Rome's tenements.

Montessori's method, which she called a *prepared environment*, stresses the development of initiative and self-reliance. Children are encouraged to pursue independently the things that interest them. She believed that children pass through a series of sensitive periods when they are especially attuned to a particular aspect of learning. She designed learning activities and materials to match these sensitive periods. Montessori's method continues to be used in programs throughout the United States and elsewhere in the world. (For further reading on the Montessori method, see Montessori, 1964.)

Jean Piaget (1896–1980), a Swiss philosopher and psychologist, spent much of his wide-ranging and prolific career listening to and watching children. At the core of Piaget's work is the belief that looking carefully at how knowledge develops in children will elucidate the nature of knowledge in general. Fields of science that grew out of his work include developmental psychology, cognitive theory, and genetic epistemology. Although Piaget was not an educator, his influence on education has been profound and pervasive.

Piaget's work provided new insights into children's thinking processes and products. Among his most important contributions was the notion that the thinking and reasoning processes of children are not quantitatively different from those of adults; rather, they are *qualitatively* different. From infancy, children are "little scientists" who constantly create and then test their theories of the world in every interaction.

Although not always acknowledged, early childhood programs in this country draw on Piaget's ideas. The most important are the notions that 1) qualitative shifts occur in children's thinking over time, 2) children gradually move in the direction of greater logic and less egocentrism with age, 3) learning comes through assimilation and accommodation, and 4) learning is necessarily an active process that results from questioning and exploring.

American Contributions   Toward the middle of the 20th century, Americans began to consider the possible effects of the environment on children's cognitive development, thus stimulating concern for services for young children with special needs. It began with a classic research study in Iowa in the 1930s that actually came about as a result of an unforeseen event (Skeels & Dye, 1939). Dr. Harold Skeels, a psychologist, was asked by the superintendent of an orphanage to find a placement for two little girls, ages 18 months and 2 years. Born out of wedlock to mothers with mental retardation, their IQs were 35 and 46 respectively. The state found temporary space for the girls on wards in a state institution with women identified as mentally deficient. Life on the wards was very different from life in the orphanage, where there was only minimal attention to children's physical concerns and little contact with adults. To the amazement of the professional community, the little girls showed dramatic IQ gains when they were retested 2 years later: Their intellectual functioning was near typical. They were subsequently placed in foster homes.

Skeels and his colleague Harold Dye were intrigued. They arranged to move 13 more children from the orphanage to the state institution. These children were under age 3, and all but two were classified as having mental retardation (average IQ 64; classification criteria were less stringent then.) Each child was placed on a ward with adolescent women with mental retardation and assigned a surrogate mother out of this group. The teenage "mothers" were trained in how to hold, feed, talk to, and play with the children and given toys and educational materials for the children. When retested 18–36 months later, the children who had been assigned to the surrogate mothers had made a mean gain of 27.5 IQ points. All of these children were subsequently adopted. A comparison group of 12 children remained in the orphanage. All but two of these children functioned in the typical range. The average IQ of these two children was 86. When retested 18–36 months later, the children who remained in the orphanage showed a mean loss of 26.2 IQ points.

If these findings had been taken seriously at the time, early intervention efforts might have begun in the 1940s. However, because of the strong belief at that time in the importance of nature over nurture, the findings were largely ignored. Sadly, many of the most influential psychologists of the time even ridiculed the study, arguing that children suffering from an irreversible condition such as mental retardation could not possibly show IQ gains, and that the data "obviously" reflected a statistical rather than an educational phenomenon (Goodenough & Maurer, 1961).

Skeels's follow-up data, collected some 25 years later, were as remarkable as his earlier findings. Eleven of the 13 children in the experimental group had married, and only one of the marriages had ended in divorce. The 10 "intact" marriages had produced nine children, all of typical intelligence. The group's median educational level was 12th grade, and some of them had attended college. All were employed in business or domestic service or working as homemakers. Of the children who remained in the orphanage, one had died and four others were still institutionalized. Their median educational level was third grade. All but one of the seven adults who were not institutionalized were working as skilled laborers.

Other American researchers in the 1940s who tipped the scales in the direction of recognizing the importance of a stimulating environment were Rene Spitz, William Goldfarb, Samuel Kirk, J. McVicker Hunt, and Benjamin Bloom. Rene Spitz (1945, 1946a, 1946b) compared infants from a foundling home in which there was little stimulation or social attention with infants in a nursery attached to a reformatory for delinquent girls. The infants in the nursery environment were cared for by their mothers, who were described in reformatory records as, for example, "socially maladjusted," "mentally retarded," "physically disabled," "psychopathic," or "criminal." The infants in the foundling home showed progressive declines in developmental abilities (from a mean developmental quotient [DQ] of 131 to a mean DQ of 72) over a period of 8–10 months, as well as weight loss, withdrawal, excessive crying, and an extreme susceptibility to infection. The mean DQ of the infants in the reformatory nursery remained at approximately the same level despite their having what Spitz described as undesirable genetic backgrounds.

William Goldfarb (1945, 1949, 1955) also compared groups of infants in two different environments: those institutionalized for a few months and those institutionalized for the first 3 years of life. Those institutionalized for their first 3 years showed delays in virtually all aspects of development. They were socially immature and unpopular with peers, and they demonstrated hyperactivity, short attention spans, and poor academic performance. Children who were institutionalized for only a few months appeared to develop typically.

Samuel Kirk (1958) initiated an important research study that looked at the impact of early intervention on children with disabilities. Specifically, he measured the effect of 2 years of preschool experience on the social and cognitive development of 43 institutionalized children with IQs ranging from 40 to 85. His results showed gains of between 10 and 30 points for the experimental group who attended either preschool or nursery school and substantial losses for children in the control group who received no intervention. These differences between the groups were maintained over a period of years. None of the control group left the institution, but almost half of the experimental children were placed in foster homes.

In addition to this early research, two books by respected writers strengthened arguments for the benefits of early intervention. J. McVicker Hunt (1961) published *Intelligence and Experience,* an extensive review of the accumulated research by Spitz, Goldfarb, and others. Hunt's two major recommendations, which would be accepted as common sense today, were greeted with surprise when the book was published. They were 1) to focus intervention on the early years because these years are the most critical for later development and 2) to optimize young children's interactions with the environment to accelerate intellectual development.

Benjamin Bloom's (1964) classic work *Stability and Change in Human Characteristics* presented an extensive review of longitudinal studies in human development. He agreed with Hunt that the data supported several conclusions regarding the role of early experience. First, human characteristics are shaped by early experiences. Second, environment and early experiences are critical because human development is cumulative. Third, initial learning is easier than attempting to replace inappropriate behaviors, once learned, with new ones.

Transactional Perspectives   What has emerged since the 1960s is a transactional perspective that stresses the bidirectionality of influences in child–adult interactions (Sameroff & Chandler, 1975). Developmental outcomes at any point in time are seen as a result of a continuous dynamic interplay among a child's behavior, adult responses to the child's behavior, and environmental variables that may influence both the child and the adult. A change in the child will trigger a change in the environment, which in turn will affect the child, and so forth.

Another transactional perspective arguing that developmental processes and outcomes are multiply determined—a joint function of the characteristics of the environment *and* of the developing organism—is the ecological model (Bronfenbrenner, 1979). Urie Bronfenbrenner's notions about early intervention place the emphasis on ecological systems, specifically the interdependence of the many formal and informal social subsystems (e.g., the immediate family, the extended family, networks of friends and neighbors, churches, agencies, policy-making groups) in a child's life and how they affect one another and the child. Child behavior and development are considered to be highly influenced by the different subsystems and relations between the subsystems in which children are participating members (Bronfenbrenner, 1992). Ecological theory has influenced the design of early intervention programs for children at risk as well as children with disabilities, both nationally and internationally. Table 1.1 provides a summary of the historical contributions noted above.

This brief history of influences on ideas and approaches to early intervention shows how the field has moved beyond appreciation of the effects of both nature and nurture to concern for their interactions with each other. Research on brain development builds on the tradition of the transactional perspective, providing new and provocative data concerning nature and nurture (Shonkoff & Phillips, 2000). Thanks to technological advances that allow neuroscientists

Table 1.1. Historical contributions to early intervention concepts

Time frame	Contributors	Contributions	Significance
1800s	Jean-Marc Itard	Demonstration: Intervention with Victor	First systematic instruction
	Edouard Sequin	Demonstration: Extension of Itard's work	Argued for training of sensory and motor skills
Early 1900s	Maria Montessori	Demonstration: Prepared environment	Stimulating/meaningful learning activities and materials to match sensitive periods
Middle 1900s	Jean Piaget	Theory: Cognitive theory and genetic epistemology	Insights regarding children's learning processes/products
	Harold Skeels	Research: IQ gains resulting from early stimulation	Attention to the importance of nurture in the nature–nurture debate
	Rene Spitz	Research: IQ and other benefits of early stimulation	Effects of lack of stimulation on physical and mental development
	William Goldfarb	Research: IQ and other developmental benefits of early stimulation	Effects of lack of stimulation on social and adaptive development
	Samuel Kirk	Research: Preschool versus no early intervention	Effects of preschool experience on IQ
	J. McVicker Hunt	Book: *Intelligence and Experience*	Importance of early years and optimizing early interactions as critical
	Benjamin Bloom	Book: *Stability and Change in Human Characteristics*	Initial learning easier than trying to replace inappropriate behaviors
	Arnold Sameroff	Research/theory: Transactional model	Bidirectional influences—a change in the child triggers a change in the environment
Late 1900s	Urie Bronfenbrenner	Theory: Ecological model	Need to focus intervention on the environment as well as the child

to see inside an infant's brain, we are learning that experience affects the very structure of the growing child's brain. These findings further strengthen arguments for early intervention and support for infants and their caregivers (Siegel, 1999; Shonkoff & Phillips, 2000; Thompson, 2001). As noted at the beginning of this chapter, the discipline of ECSE evolved in the 1970s from the merger of special education, general early childhood education, and compensatory education that had begun in the 1960s. In 1973 the Division for Early Childhood was established with the Council for Exceptional Children (CEC). (Soon thereafter, the new division began publishing the *Journal of the Division for Early Childhood*, which has been renamed the *Journal of Early Intervention*.)

Changing Policies

Public policy is government action that reflects the current values and concerns of the people. It is interpreted and enforced by legislative actions and the judicial system. Public policy ultimately stimulates and guides services. The federal legislation since the 1970s (beginning with the 1972 amendments to the Head Start legislation) reflects the shift of attitudes about the effects of both biological and environmental factors on children's overall development and the growing body of knowledge documenting the effects of early intervention on children with disabilities. The following will briefly summarize the most significant legislation (listed in Table 1.2) for young children with disabilities.

Table 1.2. Major legislation affecting services for young children with special needs

1968	PL 90-538, the Handicapped Children's Early Education Assistance Act (HCEEAA) established the Handicapped Children's Early Education Program (HCEEP).
1972	PL 92-424 amended the Economic Opportunity Act to extend Head Start services to children with disabilities.
1975	PL 94-142, the Education for All Handicapped Children Act, was passed, establishing Preschool Incentive Grants and state grant awards that could include 3- through 5-year-olds.
1986	PL 99-457 amended PL 94-142, requiring states to provide a free and appropriate public education to preschoolers (Section 619) and providing incentives for serving infants and toddlers and their families (Part H).
1990	PL 101-476 renamed the Education for All Handicapped Children Act as the Individuals with Disabilities Education Act (IDEA).
1990	PL 101-336, the Americans with Disabilities Act (ADA), was signed into law giving all individuals with disabilities (including infants and preschoolers) the right to equal access and reasonable accommodations in public and private services.
1991	PL 102-119 reauthorized and amended IDEA Part H (services for infants and toddlers and their families) and Section 619 of Part B for preschool children.
1997	PL 105-17 reauthorized IDEA, restructuring it into four parts: Part H was redesignated to Part C and all services for preschoolers were included in Part B.
2004	PL 108-446 reauthorized IDEA and authorized Local Education Agencies (LEAs) to use up to 15 percent of IDEA funds for supportive services to help students who have not yet been identified with disabilities but who require additional academic and behavioral supports to succeed in general education settings.

Handicapped Children's Early Education Assistance Act The efforts of many parents and professionals paid off in 1968 when the Handicapped Children's Early Education Assistance Act (HCEEAA) (PL 90-538) was passed into law. The appropriation accompanying this law provided funds for demonstration projects to identify effective procedures and models for serving infants and young children with disabilities and their families. Initially these projects were called the Handicapped Children's Early Education Program (HCEEP) or First Chance Projects; they are now the Early Education Programs for Children with Disabilities (EEPCD). These projects developed and disseminated a variety of intervention procedures across the country, providing a much-needed knowledge base for services and practices for families with infants and young children with disabilities.

Head Start Legislation The pioneering efforts of the researchers and writers described in the previous section were catalysts for attitudinal changes and substantial later research that provided the roots for the compensatory education movement that began in the 1960s. Head Start was funded under the Elementary and Secondary Education Act (ESEA) passed in 1965. The program was conceived by the Kennedy and Johnson administrations in the early 1960s as a part of the War on Poverty campaign. As one of several compensatory education programs, it was designed to prepare children for success in school by providing stimulating education programs; by improving the children's nutrition, health care, and social and emotional development; and by improving parental attitudes toward education. Head Start was originally a summer program, but it was soon expanded to year-round programming. In the first summer more than 561,000 children were enrolled.

The original Head Start legislation made no mention of young children with disabilities. Seven years later, the 1972 amendments to that legislation established a requirement that Head Start programs reserve at least 10% of their enrollments for preschoolers with disabilities.

Education for All Handicapped Children Act Passage of the Education for All Handicapped Children Act of 1975 (PL 94-142) marked the beginning of an unprecedented alliance of professionals and parents. Part B of this law mandates a free and appropriate public education (FAPE) for all children with disabilities from ages 3 to 21. Educational services are to be provided in the least restrictive environment (LRE), and an individualized education program (IEP) must be in effect for all eligible children. Although this legislation was an important milestone in the history of education for children with disabilities, it left some gaping loopholes. The law allowed an exception to the FAPE requirements for 3- through 5-year-olds if children without disabilities in this age range were not served by the state's public schools. Schools were required to identify and evaluate young children with suspected disabilities; however, if providing services ran counter to state law or judicial ruling regarding services for preschoolers, then the schools did not have to develop services for these preschoolers with disabilities. Many states used this loophole to avoid serving this population.

Education of the Handicapped Act Amendments of 1986 Passage of the Education of the Handicapped Act Amendments of 1986 (PL 99-457) was a major achievement for proponents of early childhood special education. It amended and extended Part B of the Education for All Handicapped Children Act (PL 94-142) to rectify the shortcomings concerning preschoolers, and it established a new program (Part H) that provided for comprehensive services for infants and toddlers with special needs and their families. Although participation in the Part H program for infants and toddlers at risk for and with disabilities was not mandatory, the monetary incentives were so strong that every state, the District of Columbia, Puerto Rico, and the territories indicated an intention to develop the recommended early intervention system. The funds supported planning, development, *and* implementation of services for children from birth to age 3 who were identified as *developmentally delayed.* The definition of *developmentally delayed* was left to the discretion of the states and other governmental entities.

Part H required that each child be given a multidisciplinary assessment. If the child was determined to be eligible for services, an individualized family service plan (IFSP) would be required before the child and family could begin receiving services.

The new section of Part B states that any preschool child who is eligible for special education and related services is entitled to all the rights and protections guaranteed to school-age children. These rights and protections include FAPE, placement in the LRE, multidisciplinary evaluation, procedural safeguards, due process, and confidentiality of information.

Individuals with Disabilities Education Act The Individuals with Disabilities Education Act (1DEA) of 1990 (PL 101-476) reauthorized the Education for All Handicapped Children Act. The term *handicapped* was replaced by the term *disabilities*, and "people first" language (e.g., "children with disabilities," "woman with mental retardation") was used to show greater respect and sensitivity for individuals with disabilities and their families. In 1991, there was another reauthorization (PL 102-119) that changed the specific language in Part B and Part H with respect to eligibility, related services, IFSPs for preschoolers, LRE, and funding.

In 1997, IDEA was reauthorized once again and signed into law as PL 105-17. This was the most substantial revision of IDEA since 1975. There was no equivocation or weakening of the strong congressional preference for "full inclusion" of children with disabilities in general education early childhood classrooms. The 1975 mandates were reaffirmed and federal statutory requirements for inclusion were strengthened. Schools now were accountable not only for conducting an IEP and a placement process that fairly considered placement in a general class but also for providing services in the general education class that would make inclusion effective. The specific mandate for early intervention programs was that services must—to the maximum extent appropriate—be provided *in natural environments,* including home and community settings in which children with disabilities participate.

In the 1997 reauthorization, Congress recognized that IDEA had been successful in ensuring FAPE and improved education results for students with disabilities. The need for improvement in some areas was also recognized, resulting in important changes, including

- Giving students greater access to the general education curriculum
- Strengthening roles and opportunities for parents to participate in their children's education
- Providing special education and related services, aids, and supports in general education classrooms "whenever appropriate"
- Providing incentives to help children before they become labeled
- Giving the child's regular education teacher a central role in the IEP process
- Reducing paperwork requirements that do not improve educational results

Almost all publicly funded programs have eligibility criteria, and early intervention programs are no exception. IDEA recognizes three groups of infants and toddlers as potentially eligible to receive early intervention services: 1) children who have a developmental delay, 2) children who have a diagnosed physical or mental condition that has a high probability of resulting in a developmental delay, and 3) children who are at risk of experiencing substantial delays if not provided with early intervention.

The 1997 IDEA amendments provided a notable change in the age limit for an eligibility requirement; namely, the possibility of using the eligibility category *developmental delay* as an alternative to a specific disability label for children through age 9 (previously this eligibility category was only applicable for 3 through 5-year-olds). States therefore have the option of continuing to use the categories designated for children ages 6 through 21, or they may choose to serve children who they deem to be "developmentally delayed." If they choose the eligibility category of developmental delay, they must formulate a definition for eligibility in this category and determine the age population for which it will be used (only for preschoolers or for children through ages 6, 7, 8, or 9). Most states define *developmental delay* in terms of standard deviation (sd) or delay expressed as a percentage of the chronological age. Some states allow qualitative criteria and "professional judgment."

The most recent reauthorization of IDEA was in 2004 (PL 108-446), which includes the following changes that apply to infants and young children with disabilities:

- The family's early intervention program (Part C) service coordinator (or other representative of the early intervention program) is to be invited to participate in the IEP meeting to facilitate a smooth transition from Part C to Part B services. (Chapter 14 discusses transition planning and implementation.)

- States may apply for a program giving parents of children receiving early intervention services (under Part C) the option of continuing those services (and not receiving a FAPE) until the child is eligible for kindergarten.

- The IEP team must consider the materials described in the individualized family service plan (IFSP) when developing the IEP for a child transitioning from an early intervention program to kindergarten.

- Parents whose child is served under Part B and the child's teacher may agree to make minor changes in the child's IEP during the school year without reconvening the IEP team.

- Quarterly reports to parents on the progress their child is making toward meeting IEP goals and objectives and how that progress is being measured are required.

Americans with Disabilities Act (ADA) (PL 101-336)   The ADA is civil rights legislation for people with disabilities. It was patterned on Section 504 of the Rehabilitation Act of 1973. This legislation, passed in 1990, ensures the right of people with disabilities to participate in society and to have the same access to facilities and information as people without disabilities. The provisions of ADA have special relevance to young children with disabilities and their families. The law guarantees that children with disabilities cannot be excluded from "public accommodations" because they have a disability. "Public accommodations" include private preschools, child care centers, school-age child care programs, after-school programs, and family child care.

The ADA is essentially a mandate for inclusion. The basic requirements are straightforward:

- Child care homes and centers must make reasonable modifications to their policies and practices to include children with disabilities *unless* doing so would constitute a *fundamental alteration of the program.* The phrase *reasonable modifications* means changes that can be carried out without much difficulty or expense. Examples of such modifications are changing policies and/or procedures, removing physical barriers, training staff, and providing adaptive equipment.

- Centers must provide *auxiliary aids and services* as needed for effective communication with children with disabilities, when doing so would not constitute an *undue burden.* Auxiliary aids and services include devices or services to help children communicate (e.g., sign language, interpreters, large-print books). Undue burden means changes that would result in significant difficulty or expense to the program.

- Centers cannot exclude children with disabilities from their programs unless their presence would pose a direct threat to the health or safety of others or require a fundamental alteration of the program. *Direct threat* means that the child's condition poses a significant threat to the health or safety of other children or the staff. Child care providers must evaluate children on an individual basis; they cannot determine risk based on their own personal assumptions about a child.

By opening the doors of community child care and recreational programs, ADA gave young children with disabilities opportunities similar to those available to children without disabilities. If children with disabilities can participate with reasonable accommodations, they may not be denied access solely on the basis of their disability.

INCLUSION MODELS

In this section, we consider what the terms *natural environment, least restrictive environment (LRE)*, and *access to the general education curriculum* as used in IDEA actually mean for the delivery of services to infants and young children with disabilities. Initially, many educational agencies thought that the LRE requirement did not apply to preschool children unless school-funded early childhood opportunities were available. Others thought that locating a segregated preschool class in a general elementary school was sufficient to meet the LRE requirement for preschoolers. The LRE requirement has been substantially revised and clarified since it was first set forth in PL 94-142 (Smith & Rapport, 2001). The 1997 amendments moved the concept of LRE beyond simplistic responses to the mandate in the direction of meaningful inclusion for infants and young children with disabilities.

Natural Environment

The term *natural environment* is used in Part C of IDEA (1997) to refer to inclusive environments for children from birth to age 3. IDEA requires that states develop policies and procedures to ensure that, to the maximum extent appropriate, early intervention services are provided in natural environments and occur elsewhere only if early intervention cannot be achieved satisfactorily in a natural environment. *Natural environment* is defined as "a setting that is natural or typical for the child's age peers who have no disabilities" (34 C.F.R. 303.18) (IDEA 1997). Early intervention services are defined as "developmental services that   to the maximum extent appropriate are provided in natural environments, including home and community settings in which children without disabilities participate" (IDEA 1997, §1432). The specifics as to how these requirements should be addressed are left up to each state.

Examples of natural environments include those that provide children with opportunities such as playing in a sandbox, splashing in a puddle or pool of water, making mud pies, constructing a fence with blocks, and watching a parade, to name just a few. Services are provided in a variety of community settings (e.g., storytime at the library, playgroups at the park, children's gyms) as well as child care programs and nursery schools that include peers without disabilities. Program locations are selected on the basis of their compatibility with the family's cultural values, the intensity of services that the child needs, and geographical accessibility for the family.

The individualized family service plan (IFSP) must identify the natural environment in which special services are to be provided and justify the extent, if any, to which the services will not be provided in the natural environment. An exception occurs only when the child's IFSP team (including the parents) determines that the goals and objectives related to the child's development cannot be achieved satisfactorily through intervention in environments that are natural for his or her same-age peers.

Part B of IDEA 2004 primarily focuses on services for school-age children. This part uses the terms *LRE, be involved,* and *make progress* in the general education curriculum to refer to inclusive environments. That the law and the regulations take into account the significant differences between services for 3 through 5-year-olds and those for school-age children is evident in several age-related adaptations. The section of the law governing the IEP requires the IEP to state "how a child's disability affects the child's involvement and progress in the general curriculum." A distinction is made for preschool children: "For preschool children, as appropriate, how the disability affects the child's participation in appropriate *activities*" (34 C.F.R. 300–347). Another age-related adaptation in the regulations is a statement to the effect that community-based settings with same-age peers who are typically developing must be available for preschool children.

Preschool Models

Guralnick (2001) described four inclusion models for preschool-age children. These options parallel the special education continuum of LREs described by Taylor (1988). Keep in mind when reading about these different models that although all of the program types consider themselves to be inclusive, *access to the general education curriculum* and *planned participation* between children with and without disabilities varies substantially across program types (Guralnick, 2001).

The first model is *full inclusion.* In this model, children with disabilities are full participants in general education early childhood classrooms. They participate in all activities in the general early childhood curriculum with their peers without disabilities. When necessary, activities are adapted to promote participation of the children with disabilities, and their IEPs are developed in a way that goals and objectives can be accomplished within the general early childhood curriculum. This model is sometimes called a *consultant model* or an *itinerant teacher model* because support is provided on an intermittent or continuing basis through consultation and teaming by related services specialists and other specialized staff. Special education and related services are fully integrated into the ongoing curriculum. The early childhood educator has primary responsibility for the entire program and all of the children.

Guralnick calls the second model a *cluster model.* This model is similar to the *co-teaching model* described by Friend and Cook (1996); McCormick, Noonan, and Heck (1998); and Reinhiller (1996). The difference in the cluster, or co-teaching, model and the full inclusion model is that rather than including one or two children in a general early childhood classroom, two classes (a class of children with disabilities and a class of children without disabilities) and their respective teachers join together in the same classroom. A defining characteristic of this model is that the two teachers share all planning and teaching responsibilities.

The third model is the *reverse inclusion model.* In this model, a relatively small group of children without disabilities is included in a special education class staffed by early childhood special educators. This model has many variations across programs in terms of structure, curriculum, and educational philosophy. Efforts are made to include all children in all activities.

In the fourth model, the *social inclusion model,* children have substantially fewer opportunities to get to know one another or participate in common activities. Although housed in the same general location, the early childhood program and the early childhood special education program are maintained in separate classrooms with different curricula, different program philosophies, and separate staffs. The two classes may be on the playground together before school and at recess, and they may come together for art activities or free play.

RECOMMENDED PRACTICES

Successful inclusion is enormously complex. The first and perhaps the most important requirement is that the participants in the process must believe in it: research confirms that teachers' beliefs and attitudes affect what they do and how they do it (Lieber et al., 1997; Peck, Furman, & Helmstetter, 1993). Every one involved must truly believe that inclusion is beneficial for children with and without disabilities.

Second, teachers must have the skills necessary to provide specialized instruction in inclusive settings; that is, they must be skilled in using the individualized instructional techniques and curricula that have proven to be effective in producing positive developmental and behavioral outcomes in inclusive settings (Odom, 2000). One consequence of the broad acceptance of the importance of early intervention and the growing recognition of the benefits of inclusive education programs is a strong research base describing empirically validated practices and procedures (e.g., Guralnick, 2001; Odom, 2000; Strain, 1990; Strain, McGee, & Kohler, 2001).

Specialized Instructional Techniques and Curricula

In successful inclusive preschool programs, implementing a child's IEP goals does not supplant the classroom curriculum or restrict the child's participation in classroom activities. Specialized instruction ensures that the teaching and practice of individual goals and objectives is in the context of meaningful and interesting activities. Naturalistic intervention is specialized instruction provided in the context of naturally occurring routines and events. Instructors facilitate learning and ensure the mastery of functional skills that have immediate application across settings. Specialized instructional techniques include

- Milieu teaching and enhanced milieu teaching (EMT) (Hemmeter & Kaiser, 1994; Kaiser, 1993; Kaiser, 2000; Rogers-Warren & Warren, 1980)

- Activity-based intervention (Losardo & Bricker, 1994)

- Embedded and distributed time delay trials (Halle, Marshall, & Spradlin, 1979; Wolery, 2001)

- High-probability procedures (Santos, 2001)

Strategies included in these approaches are 1) embedding learning opportunities into ongoing classroom activities; 2) expanding on the child's preferences and interests in identifying materials and activities; 3) arranging the physical space and materials to maximize engagement; 4) devising strategies to encourage proximity to peers; 5) analyzing and teaching the separate steps in complex tasks; 6) providing scaffolding and support through feedback, prompts, and other forms of assistance to ensure success; and 7) providing special equipment such as adaptive equipment or technology as required to ensure the participation of all children. Specialized instructional techniques are described and discussed in Chapters 7, 8, 9, 11, 12, and 13.

Culturally Relevant Instruction

The term *culture* refers to the many different factors—race, ethnicity, religion, geographic location, income status, gender, and occupation—that shape our sense of group identity (McCormick, 2003a). The way individuals think, feel, perceive, and behave reflects their cultural group membership. Cultural variations in children's behavior represent different ways of arriving at universal developmental accomplishments. Children may whimper or scream when hungry, struggle for autonomy with tantrums or passive resistance, or play with blocks or dolls—all in the course of achieving typical milestones. The ideas of their social world will ultimately shape their development by penetrating their age/stage potential and their personal characteristics. Culture affects how children learn and solve problems (as well as the kinds of problems they will solve), how they organize their environment, which language they learn, and how they spend their leisure time.

Family cultural practices and native languages create unique challenges for all teachers, especially those who are seeking to include children with disabilities in natural environments. Culture affects the ability of families and educators to gather and exchange information, their expectations for their children, and their beliefs concerning disability issues and the value of education. Similarly, as culture affects how families and educators view child rearing, learning and education, and disabilities, it also affects their views about inclusion.

Recognizing each child as a unique individual and each family as a unique family—and being as accepting and responsive to differences in language, social class, heritage, ethnic origins, geographic location, and religion as to the differing abilities and interests of children and their families—is the first and most important requirement for culturally relevant instruction (Hanson, Gutierrez, Morgan, Brennan, & Zercher, 1997; Hanson et al., 1998). Culturally relevant instruction is *specifically* described and discussed in Chapter 7, but the concept of culturally relevant instruction is embedded in discussions of instructional procedures throughout this book.

Learning Outside the Classroom

IDEA mandates delivery of early intervention services in children's natural environments—places that do not isolate the child with disabilities or his or her family from mainstream community life. At the broadest level, natural environments are places where there are activities that include children who do not have disabilities. Part C of IDEA 1997 calls for a move away from discipline-specific services. Foremost among the many challenges associated with providing services for infants and toddlers with disabilities and their families in natural environments is the difficulty faced by early intervention professionals (e.g., early interventionists, therapists, nurses) who must shift from discipline-specific assessment and intervention provided in clinics or rehabilitation facilities to family-centered, team-based services delivered within a child's natural environments. Service providers must 1) consult with parents, other service providers, and representatives of appropriate community agencies to ensure the effective provision of services in that area; 2) train parents and others regarding the provision of those services; and 3) participate in team assessment of the child and the child's family and in the development of the integrated goals and outcomes for the IFSP (303.12.12[c]).

Early intervention in natural environments does not mean simply changing the location of services; that is, providing the same types of services in the home and community settings that were previously provided in a clinic (Bruder, 2001; Dunst, 2001). It means using the "development-enhancing potential" (Bruder, 2001, p. 221) of the environments. Dunst (2001) describes the rich array of family, neighborhood, and community activities that enhance children's development as *participatory learning opportunities* (PLOs).

The same is true for preschool-age children. What occurs outside the classroom and school environment is a significant contributor to their "quality of life." The range of important and enduring relationships they develop from participating in family and neighborhood life and community settings provide the context for concept acquisition, skill development, and social and cultural expectations. All of the interventions in this book can be implemented in home as well as community environments.

Supported Inclusion for Children with Autism

Strain, McGee, and Kohler (2001, p. 345) outlined the myths that have perpetuated the contention that children with autism should be served in segregated educational settings. The word *myths* as used in this context refers to conclusions about early intervention for children with autism that 1) have no empirical support, 2) often contradict the available data, 3) are based on the misconception that any success (even when using inappropriate practices) demonstrates the superiority of the practice, and 4) have become institutionalized and memorialized simply because they appear in the writings of respected professionals, funding patterns, and service delivery policies and practices.

The myths that are used to keep young children with autism in segregated environments include the following:

- *Young children with autism need readiness training.* The contention is that children with autism need to achieve certain developmental milestones and learn to comply with simple motor-imitation tasks (taught using the most directive, adult-driven teaching methods) before they are moved from segregated to inclusive settings.

- *Young children with autism can only acquire important developmental skills if provided with tutorial, one-to-one instruction.* The contention is that this is the only way young children with autism can make necessary developmental gains.

- *Young children with autism are overstimulated in typical general education environments.* The contention is that young children with autism need segregated settings with reduced (uninteresting?) stimuli.

- *Young children with autism need behavioral control procedures that can only be provided in segregated settings.* The contention is that intervention directed toward reducing challenging behaviors cannot be implemented in typical general education environments.

Most important to keep in mind is that there are no data supporting the superiority of segregated settings for young children with autism.

For children with autism, the inclusion option likely to achieve the "maximum feasible benefits" is *supported inclusion* (Strain, et al., 2001, p. 345). Supported inclusion is defined as "provision of resources needed to ensure maximum learning in the context of natural environments" (Strain et al., p. 345). Achievement of positive outcomes with these children depends on the type and intensity of support they receive in their educational settings and in other community settings. The first and most essential requisite if young children with autism are to receive the maximum benefits from inclusion is planned *intensive* social and communication intervention, and this intervention *must* include typically developing peers as well as the child with autism. Specific procedures for implementing this instruction are provided in Chapter 8. Chapters 6, 9, 10, 11, and 12 also offer procedures for children with autism.

Family-Centered Intervention

Family systems theory shifts the focus of attention from the child in isolation to the child as one element of a system—the family system. Turnbull and colleagues (1983) have helped us integrate the tenets of this theory into practice. They suggested the following attitudes for professionals working with families: 1) view each family as unique in terms of membership characteristics, culture, and style; 2) recognize that families are systems with constantly shifting components and boundaries; 3) be aware that families (collectively and individual family members) fulfill many and varied functions to support the continued growth and development of the child; and 4) understand that families experience many changes that produce different amounts of stress for each family member.

Early intervention professionals made significant progress in the 1990s in the conceptualization and implementation of family-centered practices (Bailey & McWilliam, 1990; Dunst, Johanson, Trivette, & Hamby, 1991; Turbiville, Turnbull, Garland, & Lee, 1996). These practices focus on enhancing the well-being of the family as a whole in addition to the well-being of the child. They include 1) treating families with dignity and respect, 2) being sensitive to family cultural and socioeconomic diversity, 3) providing families with choices that defer to their priorities and concerns, 4) ensuring that families have the information they need to make decisions, 5) introducing a range of informal community resources as parenting and family supports, and 6) using helpful practices that empower parents and enhance their competency (Dunst et al., 1991).

The assumptions underlying family-centered intervention—that families should be the decision makers where their children are concerned and that the goals and priorities they identified should drive the intervention process—are now basic tenets of early intervention. These assumptions are redefining parent–professional relationships. Being partners with families means that professionals in early intervention programs must understand cultural diversity, human relations, and communication and must be able to put that understanding into practice. In addition to their basic responsibilities for conducting assessment and providing and evaluating intervention, professionals must be able to build trust, resolve conflicts, and actively participate in planning with families (especially how to link up with needed services). Family-centered intervention is specifically discussed in Chapters 2 and 3.

Integrated Therapy

Integrated therapy, also called *integrated intervention*, is special instruction, facilitation, and support provided in the context of ongoing activities and routines in natural environments. When this concept was first introduced, it was a radical departure from the traditional therapy model in which therapists and other specialists removed the child to a separate clinic or therapy room for intervention. In the mid-1990s, research demonstrated the superiority of integrated therapy (McWilliam, 1996a). In addition to the research, other factors that contributed to the shift from separate therapy to integrated therapy were 1) the lack of generalization of skills learned in isolated therapy settings, 2) recognition of the potentially negative effects of removing children from natural environments to receive therapy (i.e., it deprives children of whatever activities are in process and marks them as "different" in the eyes of their peers), and 3) fragmentation and overlap of services (i.e., therapists, parents, and teachers were often unaware of what other team members were working on with the child).

Integrated therapy for young children with disabilities has many implications for the way therapists and other professionals work with one another and with families. It requires professionals to individualize within a developmentally appropriate practice framework; to learn to consult, collaborate, and coordinate with families as well as other professionals; and to coordinate a wide range of community services from a variety of agencies and programs. McWilliam (1996b) is very specific about the preparation that teachers need to fulfill their role in integrated therapy. Both early childhood special education (ECSE) teachers and general early childhood education (ECE) teachers need to know how to adapt classroom activities to incorporate suggestions from therapists and other specialists and how to embed individualized interventions into classroom routines. These skills are discussed in Chapters 6, 9, 12, and 13.

Teaming and Parent-Professional Partnerships

From the first days and weeks of implementing the initial legislation for children with disabilities, it was clear that collaboration and communication were the keystones of effective intervention and successful programs. This basic requirement for effective services has been referred to as the *collaboration imperative* (McCormick, 2003a). The teaming approach that has evolved as the best organizational structure for people concerned with providing quality early intervention services is the transdisciplinary team model. In a transdisciplinary team model, professionals work closely together to plan, implement, and evaluate intervention.

Characteristics of the transdisciplinary team model include joint functioning, continuous staff development, and role release (Lyon & Lyon, 1980). Joint functioning means that team members perform required functions together whenever possible. Arena assessment, which will be described in Chapter 2, is an example of joint functioning. Continuous staff development means that team members commit to helping one another learn new skills. Role release involves sharing or releasing some functions traditionally associated with a specific discipline. It occurs when a team member assists other team members to perform functions that were typically part of the assisting team member's role. For example, the speech therapist may provide training and support to enable the teacher to develop and implement a plan to increase one child's spontaneous requesting behavior. Establishing and maintaining a collaborative team requires people who are an effective cooperative learning group (Thousand &

Villa, 2000). This means that members must interact face to face on a frequent basis and have a mutual "we are all in this together" feeling of positive interdependence. They must be committed to developing small-group interpersonal skills such as trust building, communication, leadership, creative problem solving, decision making, and conflict management, and they must agree to set aside time regularly to assess and discuss the team's functioning and to set goals for improving relationships and accomplishing tasks more effectively. Finally, team members must agree on methods for holding one another accountable for agreed-on responsibilities.

A positive, trusting, and respectful relationship with the family and child is a basic requirement in early intervention. That families place great value on working with competent, caring professionals is a consistent finding in the early intervention literature (Dinnebeil, Hale, & Rule, 1996; Park, Turnbull, & Park, 2001). The issue is how to prepare professionals to be partners with parents. Preservice students in the key early intervention disciplines should have direct experience working with families and on transdisciplinary teams before they graduate. In addition, families should be involved in preparing students in early childhood special education and related fields at the university level. To be good family partners, professionals must be skilled in human relationships and able to communicate confidently, effectively, and confidentially with families from different cultures who have different worldviews and different expectations for their children. Also, as noted above, early interventionists must be knowledgeable about and able to link families to local and state resources. Chapter 2 provides specific suggestions for developing and maintaining partnerships with parents.

Ecological Assessment

Almost 3 decades ago, Brown and colleagues (1979) described procedures drawn from the tenets of ecological theory that could be used to generate functional goals and objectives for students with severe and multiple disabilities. They called this assessment the *ecological inventory*. Since that time, it has been widely used with children of all ages and disabilities. The ecological inventory process is especially helpful for generating functional goals and objectives and for individualizing instruction and planning needed adaptations. It is used with families to identify goals and objectives for intervention with infants and toddlers and with teachers to plan for preschool-age children. The ecological inventory is beneficial for planning intervention in natural environments. It helps the team address the following critical intervention decisions:

• What are the intervention goals and objectives?

• Where should intervention be provided?

• How should intervention be provided?

• When should intervention be provided?

• How can intervention be evaluated?

Ecological assessment (such as the ecological inventory) differs from traditional assessment in that it considers the child's behavior in relation to environmental expectations (rather than in relation to the performance of the population used in standardizing the test). The environments where the child is expected to function are examined to determine what the child needs to learn and what adaptations need to be made to facilitate participation in the activities and routines of the environments. The product of an ecological assessment is a list of functional goals and objectives for the child's specific environments (e.g., home, family child care setting, community recreation site, preschool) and ideas for necessary adaptations of activities and/or materials. For children with more severe disabilities, skill objectives may then be listed in a task analysis for task analytic assessment. Task analytic assessment allows evaluation of the child's performance on each component of the skill. Instructions for implementing ecological assessment and other types of authentic assessment are provided in Chapters 3, 5, and 10.

Positive Behavior Support

Positive behavior support (PBS) is the application of positive behavioral interventions and procedures to reduce problem behaviors and replace them with socially adaptive behavior. Initially developed as an alternative to aversive interventions used with students who engaged in extreme forms of self-injurious behavior and aggression, it is now used with a wide range of students in a variety of contexts (Sugai, Horner, & Sprague, 1999). In fact, the 1997 amendments of IDEA require use of PBS as the preferred strategy for dealing with challenging behaviors of students with disabilities. The IEP team may consider other strategies in addition to PBS, but the regulations state that PBS *must* be considered when a child's behavior is judged to impede his or her learning or that of others. The Division for Early Childhood (DEC) concurs with the importance of using PBS procedures (Division for Early Childhood [DEC], 1999). PBS practices have been thoroughly researched and validated (e.g., Carr, 1977; Carr & Durand, 1985; Repp & Horner, 1999).

Implementation of PBS varies according to the age of the child, the context of intervention, and the nature of the challenging behavior. However, there is a subset of procedures common to all applications: They all begin with a functional behavioral assessment (FBA). The purpose of FBA procedures (informant assessment, observations, and experimental analysis) is to identify the events that are causing and maintaining the challenging behavior and thereby determine the function of the behavior.

In addition to FBA, procedures common to PBS applications include 1) environmental arrangement (manipulation of antecedent conditions to reduce or prevent the likelihood that the problem behaviors will occur), 2) teaching new social and communication skills so that the child will no longer need to use the challenging behaviors to obtain desired outcomes, and 3) careful redesign of existing consequences to eliminate the events that are maintaining the challenging behaviors and to replace them with more acceptable social and communication behaviors. Thus, the focus of FBA is on adjusting social and environ-mental variables (e.g., routines, responses, instructions) and improving learning environments. Finally, PBS emphasizes decision making based on analysis of data collected through a range of procedures and from a variety of sources. In addition to analysis of observable behaviors, intervention design considers a multitude of cognitive, biophysical, developmental, and physical/environmental variables that have the potential to affect the current functioning of the child. Procedures to implement PBS are described in Chapter 10.

Assistive Technology

The issues surrounding assistive technology—what to get, where to get it, how to use it, how to pay for it, and how to evaluate its usefulness and effectiveness in helping a child achieve success in school and independence in daily living—are major challenges for families and people who care for and about children with disabilities. Fortunately, they are challenges that are much closer to being met than ever before. Assistive technology options that were unheard of in the 1990s are now available to all children with disabilities.

Assistive technology in special education refers to any devices and/or ser-vices that are necessary for a child to benefit from special education or related services and to be educated in the least restrictive environment. The item, piece of equipment, or product system may be constructed, acquired commercially, modified, or customized. Assistive devices range from pens and papers, to com-puters, to hearing aids, to calculators, to software, to powered scooters, to adap-tive eating utensils, to custom-fitted wheelchairs. The only requisite is that the device must increase, maintain, or improve the functional capabilities of the child with disabilities. Assistive technology service is any service that directly assists a child with a disability in the selection, acquisition, or use of an assis-tive technology device. This includes assessment of the child's technology needs; purchasing, leasing, or otherwise providing for the acquisition of assis-tive technology devices; coordinating and using other therapies, interventions, and services with assistive technology devices; training or technical assistance for the child (and the child's family, if needed); and training for professionals and others in the child's environments. Any infant or toddler who is eligible for early intervention and any child who is eligible for special education and re-lated services is entitled to receive assistive technology.

The use of technology with infants and very young children presents a special challenge. Professionals in the early childhood field are only just begin-ning to realize the range and variety of potential uses for high-tech and low-tech devices, and an initial database is beginning to accumulate. Technology has great potential for curricular applications in the areas of motor develop-ment, communication/language development, social interaction, adaptive be-havior, daily life skills, plans, and emerging literacy. Procedures for application of assistive technology in these areas for infants, toddlers, and preschoolers with disabilities are discussed throughout the book, but especially in Chapters 12 and 13.

Transition Planning

As change is inevitable, so is the need for successful transitions. Early interventionists have learned that specialized planning can significantly reduce families' feelings of vulnerability and the disruptions for children that are inherent in transitions in the preschool years (Noonan & Kilgo, 1987). The goals of transition planning are 1) to ensure continuity of service, 2) to minimize disruption of the family system, and 3) to promote children's functioning in natural environments (DEC Task Force on Recommended Practices, 1993). The important transition periods for infants and young children with disabilities in early childhood are from the hospital (e.g., the neonatal intensive care unit) to community-based early intervention services; from early intervention services to preschool; and, finally, from preschool to kindergarten.

A major goal in early intervention is continuity of services, sometimes referred to as a *seamless system* of services delivery. The challenges in providing a seamless system are immense (Sainato & Morrison, 2001). Legislative mandates related to transition services (e.g., eligibility differences for children from birth to age 3 years and for children ages 3 through 6 years) present a challenge, as do differences in the regulatory systems of the involved programs and services. In many states, responsibility for services for children from birth to age 3 years and responsibility for services for 3- through 6-year-olds reside with different governmental departments. This means that transition difficulties for families are often multiplied because there is more involved than just movement from one program to another: Transitions are across departments and agencies with very different philosophies and separate operating structures. A related issue is differences in the theoretical orientation, preparation, and experience of staff. The issues surrounding preschool transitions, factors affecting transitions, and competencies for transition planning and coordination are described in Chapter 14.

SUMMARY

This chapter has provided an introduction to the history of early intervention and policies affecting services for infants and young children with disabilities and their families. At present, relatively little research has considered characteristics of effective early intervention programs and team-based service delivery models that provide services in natural environments. What *is* known from the considerable research over the past several decades is the competency base that early intervention providers and ECSE teachers must have to be effective in inclusive settings (Bruder, 1997, 2000a, 2001; Winton, McCollum, & Catlett, 1997). The skills and knowledge that make up this competency base are outlined in this chapter under the heading Recommended Practices. All of these topics are addressed at length in later chapters.

••••••••••••••••••••• STUDY QUESTIONS •••••••••••••••••••••

1. Describe the contributions of each of the following to the field of early intervention: Itard, Sequin, Montessori, Piaget, Skeels, Spitz, Goldfarb, Kirk, Hunt, Bloom, Sameroff, and Bronfenbrenner.

2. Describe the legislation that has most affected services for infants and young children with disabilities and their families.

3. Describe the major contributions of PL 99-457.

4. What is the definition of *developmental delay*?

5. Describe the relevance of ADA to inclusion of young children with disabilities.

6. Discuss how the LRE requirement has affected services for infants and young children with disabilities and their families.

7. List and describe the four inclusion models for preschool-age children.

8. What are the characteristics of specialized instructional techniques?

9. What are the characteristics of culturally relevant instruction?

10. What are "natural environments" for infants and preschoolers?

11. What are the myths concerning inclusion for young children with autism?

12. What is *supported inclusion*?

13. How does the family systems theory relate to family-centered intervention?

14. Describe the factors that account for the shift from separate therapy to integrated therapy.

15. Describe the transdisciplinary team model.

16. What is ecological assessment?

17. Describe implementation of positive behavioral support.

18. List possible low-tech and high-tech assistive devices for infants and young children with disabilities.

19. Describe legislative mandates related to transition services for infants and young children with disabilities.

2

Professional and Family Partnerships

Linda McCormick

• FOCUS OF THIS CHAPTER • • • • • • • • • • • • • • • • • • •

- Characteristics of successful inclusion
- Teaming models
- Procedures for effective teaming
- Communication skills associated with successful collaboration
- Partnerships with families
- Culture of special education
- Cultural values in parenting
- Cultural reciprocity

T he ability of service providers to work cooperatively and harmoniously with one another and with families may be the single most important contributor to the success of early intervention (EI) and early childhood special education (ECSE) programs. It is also the major challenge. A national study by Smith and Rose (1993) found that the major barriers to developing inclusive environments for young children were service providers' lack of respect for differing views and resistance to collaboration. Because cross-cultural competence and collaboration are essential to establishing and maintaining necessary partnerships, there has to be the same commitment to developing these attitudes and skills as to acquiring knowledge and skills for child assessment, intervention, instruction, and program evaluation. The first part of this chapter addresses the importance of professionals working cooperatively and harmoniously with one another and with families, paying particular attention to skills for collaborative interpersonal relationships and teaming. The chapter then considers the effects of cultural diversity on professionals' relationships with families, with an emphasis on how the culture of special education influences our beliefs and values.

WORKING WITH OTHERS

Why are interpersonal relationships so important in early intervention and early childhood special education? They are important because partnerships are important, and partnerships are important because no one person (infant specialist, ECSE teacher, ECE teacher, parent, therapist, or physician) can meet the complex needs of infants and young children with disabilities and their families.

Those inclusive programs that do not survive over time are marked by partnership difficulties—what Peck, Furman, and Helmstetter described as "acrimonious professional relationships" (1993, p.105) and "struggles over control of time, activities, and programs for individual children" (p. 197). Lieber and colleagues (1997) also identified partnership problems as the major cause of unsuccessful programs. Partnership problems occurred when staff 1) had significant philosophical differences and 2) lacked the skills for effective negotiation and collaboration. Successful programs in their study were notable for having "a philosophy jointly agreed upon by the major participants" and "a sense of well-being" among the participants (p. 79).

Differences in philosophical perspectives (theoretical beliefs and practices) were once thought to be the sole source of conflicts between ECE teachers and ECSE professionals (Carta, Schwartz, Atwater, & McConnell, 1991). Certainly, there is ample justification for this assumption because there are basic differences in the philosophical underpinnings and, hence, the practices of the two fields. In line with the guidelines for developmentally appropriate practice set forth by the National Association for the Education of Young Children (NAEYC) (Bredekamp & Copple, 1997), most ECE teachers believe that children discover principles and construct knowledge and meaning from their own experiences in their environments. They view their role as facilitating and guiding children through the discovery and construction processes. In contrast, ECSE teachers arrange the environment to ensure that there are opportunities for children to practice newly acquired skills. When children have specific skill deficits, ECSE teachers generally provide direct instruction.

Ideas have changed. Although many (Minke, Bear, Deemer, & Griffin, 1996) continue to cite the philosophical differences between ECE and ECSE teachers to explain observed relationship difficulties (Minke et al., 1996), research suggests otherwise. A survey of ECE and ECSE professionals by Kilgo and colleagues (1999) found substantial agreement in the beliefs the two groups held about recommended practices and procedures.

So if a lack of shared philosophical beliefs and differences in practices is not the cause of conflicts and dissatisfaction in inclusive settings, then what is? This is the question that Minke and colleagues asked in a survey of teachers in inclusive situations. The teachers responded that it helps to have similar philosophies but that a "shared work ethic" is more critical. What is needed in co-teaching arrangements, they said, are "'real partnerships' in which both teachers trust, support, respect, and cooperate with each other." (p. 176) As others have done, these teachers compared the co-teaching partnership with a marriage, noting that it "cannot work without mutual respect and affection" (p. 176).

The difficulties that plague teacher–teacher relationships are also evident in teachers' interactions with other service providers (e.g., audiologists, nurses, nutritionists, physicians, occupational therapists, family therapists, physical therapists, psychologists, social workers, speech–language pathologists) Interactions sometimes become tense, noncommunicative, and even explosive. Here again are differing philosophical perspectives that, although perhaps not the sole cause of relationship problems, certainly contribute to communication difficulties. Most service providers in early intervention settings have a medical orientation. Services provided by professionals trained in a traditional medical perspective tend to focus on providing individual therapy with an emphasis on remediation of identified deficits. The professional's job is to identify and diagnose a child's difficulties. Then a remedy is prescribed and applied to fix the problem. In contrast, because they are acculturated in an educational model, ECSE teachers concentrate on family preferences and the functional needs and desires of the children (Sandall, Hemmeter, Smith, & McLean, 2005). This is appropriate in EI programs because most problems of infants and young children with disabilities cannot be fixed. The focus is on maximizing opportunities for optimum growth and development and maintaining extant skills and abilities.

In addition to dozens of books and articles, there are numerous standards in DEC Recommended Practices recognizing the importance of collaboration and teamwork (Sandall et al., 2005). Still, the goal of true collaboration among professionals and partnerships with families is not easily achieved. Learning to collaborate and function as a team takes work, skill, commitment, and perseverance.

Friend (2000) noted the following myths and misinterpretations associated with collaboration and team building that alert us to some of the pitfalls:

Myth #1: Everyone is doing it. Don't believe this for a minute. Most schools and programs claim that their staff functions collaboratively, but few actually have true collaboration (as described subsequently). People may engage in some sort of shared effort, but in most cases a directive leader defines the group's tasks. Alternately, colleagues may meet to report on assigned tasks and share information about what they are doing. Neither of these examples (a group with a directive leader or a "show and tell" group) is truly a collaborative team.

Myth #2: More is better. People often assume that if something is good, more of it will be better. Where collaboration is concerned, more is *not* necessarily better, and it may very well be worse. Collaboration demands time, and time is a limited resource. If collaboration demands too much time it may impair the overall functioning of the program.

Myth #3: It's about feeling good and liking others. Feeling good and liking others may be desirable benefits of collaboration, but these rewards are not the major reason for collaboration, which is to provide more effective services.

Myth #4: It comes naturally. Many professionals assume that because they have good social skills, a great deal of experience in social settings with other adults, and teaching skills, effective collaboration will "just happen." Unfortunately, this is not the case. In most circumstances, successful collaboration requires a specific set of skills. A subset of these skills may come naturally to some people, but most require professional preparation *and practice.*

Effective collaborators truly believe that sharing and cooperating with one another maximizes their effectiveness. They believe that the more perspectives differ, the better the decision making—that decision making is enriched and improved by different viewpoints. Thus, at the most basic level, collaboration is sharing. It is sharing 1) information, knowledge, and skills; 2) classroom and/or center space; 3) ideas and creativity; 4) resources (e.g., time, materials, equipment); and, most important, 5) responsibilities.

Team Models

A team is a small assembly of people with a common purpose and shared goals. Teaming models provide a framework for how the group will communicate and make decisions. The three team models most often employed in early intervention and special education settings are the *multidisciplinary model*, the *interdisciplinary model*, and the *transdisciplinary model* (McCormick & Goldman,

1979). A fourth model, the *collaborative team model* (sometimes called the cooperative team model) combines the best features of the other three.

The *multidisciplinary model* is most often seen in medical settings. Professionals of different disciplines implement their respective discipline functions with minimal—if any—coordination, collaboration, or communication with one another. Professionals assess and attempt to remediate those aspects of the child's needs that fall within their disciplines' unique province (occupational therapy, physical therapy, speech–language pathology, and so on). This model has individual accountability but little, if any, sharing of information, joint planning, or *team* accountability.

The *interdisciplinary model* evolved in response to dissatisfaction with the lack of communication and the fragmented services in teams functioning with the multidisciplinary model. With the interdisciplinary model, communication occurs across disciplines: Professionals usually develop joint intervention goals and a unified intervention plan. The problem lies with implementing the intervention recommendations. Intervention recommendations are given to the person responsible for providing direct services, but they do not include a feedback loop. Information flows one way; there is no provision for monitoring and, if necessary, modifying the intervention recommendations if they do not prove to be practical and effective.

The *transdisciplinary model* is preferred over the interdisciplinary model because it provides a framework for professionals to share information and skills with one another *and* with the family (McWilliam, 2000a; Sandall et al., 2005). As discussed in Chapter 1, the important characteristics of this model are joint functioning, continual staff development, and role release (Lyon & Lyon, 1980). *Joint functioning* means that whenever possible, team members perform required services together. Arena assessment is an example of joint functioning (Wolery & Dyk, 1984). In arena assessment, one person designated as assessment facilitator engages the child in specific activities while other team members observe and record their assessment of the child's performance. *Continuous staff development* means that team members help one another learn new skills. This emphasis on continual opportunities for skill development is particularly important: It means that team members are always learning new skills.

Role release occurs when professionals on the team assist the direct service provider in performing a function that is typically part of the assisting team member's role. For instance, a speech therapist might help a teacher practice several of the children's therapy goals (e.g., asking and answering "wh" questions, using three-word sentences) at sharing time in morning circle. At some point, most team members release their direct service roles to function as consultants to the direct service provider.

The *collaborative team model* includes the best features of the other models (Rainforth, York, & MacDonald, 1992; Thousand & Villa, 2000). Collaborative teams in EI/ECSE settings include service providers, family members, and members of relevant community agencies.

Teaming Procedures

The following procedures are essential (e.g., Johnson & Johnson, 1989; Napier & Gershenfeld, 1993) for members of a transdisciplinary or collaboration team to work effectively together:

- Discussing and agreeing on
  - Reasons for their existence
  - Ground rules (e.g., how barriers and conflicts will be handled)
  - Logistics of meeting times and locations
- Setting clear and measurable goals that require the team to work together if the goals are to be accomplished
- Trusting one another and practicing open communication and active listening
- Sharing ideas and feelings in an atmosphere of nonjudgmental acceptance so that all team members feel that their contributions are valued
- Sharing leadership and consensual decision making
- Using constructive conflict resolution techniques (e.g., paraphrasing one another's ideas and feelings as accurately as they can and without making value judgments)
- Sharing accountability
- Keeping records to monitor the effectiveness of decisions and activities

In effective teams, the members avoid 1) strategy incongruence, 2) advice overflow, 3) credibility problems, and 4) confused problem ownership (Johnson, Pugach, & Hammitte, 1988). *Strategy incongruence* occurs when participating professionals, because of their philosophical differences, set forth very different approaches to solving a problem. Recall the discussion earlier in this chapter about philosophical differences among professionals. If the ECE and ECSE teachers on the team hold differing views on classroom management, problems may arise in collaborating to develop classroom rules. Where teachers and therapists are concerned, strategy incongruence occurs because teachers view the problem from an educational perspective and therapists see it from a medical perspective. The solution is for everyone to keep an open mind and work to understand one another's perspectives. Ultimately, there must be consensus to incorporate the strategies that best support the children and their families.

Advice overflow occurs when a consultant or a team member begins giving unsolicited advice. There are usually two reasons for advice overflow: One team member believes that he or she is ultimately responsible for the direction and outcome of the collaboration, or a member considers him- or herself to be the expert regarding the problem being discussed. Too much advice can lead to the collaboration's failure. If the advice leads to a successful outcome, a dependency on (and sometimes resentment toward) the advice giver may occur. If the advice does not prove successful, distrust and blame result. Advice overflow is problematic because it is basically unilateral decision making rather than team problem solving.

Credibility problems occur when participants have not established credibility with one another. If a solution recommended by a member who sets him- or herself up as an expert does not bring about the desired outcome, the other people on the team may no longer view that person as having the expertise needed to contribute to the team's goals. Conversely, if the outcome does not occur as the expert has planned, he or she may view the direct service provider as not having the skills to successfully implement the recommended strategy. Professionals can guard against credibility conflicts by making it very clear that they recognize one another's expertise.

Confused problem ownership occurs when team members take more responsibility than the direct service provider (typically the ECE teacher or the ECSE teacher). When the direct service provider no longer feels a commitment to the decision-making process, he or she will likely shift attention to other problems. Solutions may be generated, but without teacher input and support, they are likely to fail. There must be mutual ownership of problems as well as mutual ownership of recommended solutions.

Communication Skills Communication skills are essential to all activities associated with successful collaboration. The two types of communication skills are 1) task-oriented skills and 2) relationship-oriented skills. Task-oriented skills include the ability to

- Clearly identify and define the problem at hand
- Determine potential strengths in the situation
- Keep an open mind to alternative solutions
- Develop appropriate goals and objectives
- Search for and analyze relevant information from different sources
- Interpret and clarify planning and implementation issues
- Combine and summarize related constructs and ideas
- Elicit input and consensus from others

Task-oriented communication skills facilitate problem solving and decision making. They are focused on clarifying the problem(s) and generating solutions. In contrast, relationship-oriented skills involve interpersonal communication competencies. They assist cooperation and collaboration and include the ability to

- Stimulate the participation of others
- Reconcile opposing positions in a positive manner
- Compromise for the sake of productive discussion
- View differences as negotiable
- Solicit and make use of feedback

- Clarify perceptions and feelings
- Communicate understanding and acceptance of the opinions of others
- Translate technical concepts into understandable terms
- Communicate accessibility, responsiveness, and honest concern
- Establish an atmosphere of trust, respect, and acceptance

The barriers to effective collaboration at the interagency and program levels are essentially the same. They include 1) competitiveness, 2) parochial interests, 3) lack of communication skills, 4) resistance to change, 5) concerns about confidentiality, 6) inadequate knowledge about other agencies and programs, 7) negative attitudes, and 8) political naiveté. Doing things "the way we've always done them" is always easier than trying new solutions, but the price an agency or a program-level team pays for this attitude may be high in terms of collaboration.

Parent Partnerships

A parent partnership is an association between a family member and one or more professionals who function collaboratively with agreed-on roles in pursuit of a common goal (Dunst & Paget, 1991). Research on parent partnerships has looked at it from the perspectives of both the parents and the service providers (e.g., Dinnebeil et al., 1996; Harrison, Lynch, Rosander, & Borton, 1990; Park et al., 2001). High-quality partnerships are characterized by good communication skills, facilitative interpersonal factors, professional expertise, and practice of certain values and attitudes.

The same communication and group-process skills noted above for collaborative team interactions apply to partnerships with parents. Most notably, these include good listening skills, openness to suggestions, and responsiveness. In successful partnerships, the two sides communicate openly and honestly about where they stand and how they feel. They listen to understand, not just to hear. Ideas and feelings are shared in an atmosphere of nonjudgmental acceptance.

A study by Dinnebeil et al. (1996) helps us define "facilitative interpersonal factors," the second characteristic of high-quality partnerships. These researchers surveyed 1,400 parents and service coordinators. Specifically, they asked those surveyed to describe the variables that the other person in the partnership brings to the relationship that either enhance or interfere with collaboration. The respondents identified interpersonal practices such as honesty and tact as well as establishing a positive atmosphere as the most important contributors to successful partnerships. Interpersonal courtesies such as keeping appointments, being on time, being organized and prepared, and following through were also highly valued.

The respondents referred to professional expertise as "expert power." They defined that as the extent to which a person is perceived as having the specialized knowledge necessary for a task or goal and identified it as among the most important variables in successful collaborative relationships. In another study by Park and colleagues (2001) of partnerships between professionals and Korean American parents, respondents reported a similar finding. The parents noted that they appreciated professionals with good teaching skills, knowledge about planning for their children's future, and resourcefulness. They wanted professionals to encourage their children's potential and not emphasize what their children could *not* do. They wanted professionals who were skilled at teaching academics and at decreasing challenging behaviors and who could teach them how to help their children catch up academically. Thus, although a service provider may be caring, committed, and enthusiastic, he or she is not viewed as an effective collaborator unless parents perceive the individual to be knowledgeable and competent in his or her field.

Dinnebeil and colleagues (1996) found that where values and beliefs are concerned, parents considered it essential for service providers to hold *and practice* a belief in family-centered practices. They considered it central to an effective collaborative relationship that service providers are willing to carry through on commitments as well as to provide assistance with regard to family-centered practices.

This section has considered barriers to professional collaboration, team models, procedures for effective teaming (notably communication skills), and characteristics of a high-quality partnership with parents. The remainder of the chapter deals with the culture of the profession of special education, cultural values in parenting, and cultural reciprocity.

CULTURAL DIVERSITY AND CULTURAL COMPETENCE

Culture can be defined broadly to include differences in economic status, sexual orientation, gender, and lifestyle (Hains, Lynch, & Winton, 2000), or more narrowly to include only ethnic, racial, and linguistic differences (Nieto, 2000). The beliefs, values, and attitudes that are transmitted to young children through socialization are the core of culture. Differences in socialization depend on various sociocultural factors such as child-rearing practices, family styles, sociolinguistic patterns, the family's economic status, how long the family has lived in the United States, and the conditions of the family's immigration.

Membership in a particular cultural group does not necessarily *determine* behavior. It does, however, make some types of behavior more probable than others because members of a common culture typically have similar responses and tend to interpret events in similar ways. Cultural values and personal beliefs are far more than just the background for our relationships with others— they are the central operating system that will ultimately overshadow efforts to alter our behavior or influence our practices (Harry, 1998). Cultural factors vary widely across groups: Commonly held beliefs, values, and attitudes become yardsticks against which people judge and compare the behaviors and attitudes of others.

Cultural diversity in the United States grows larger each year (U.S. Bureau of the Census, 1996; Children's Defense Fund, 1998). By 2030, the non-Hispanic White population will be in the minority of the U.S. population under 18 (U.S. Department of Education, 1999). Administrators and teachers recognize the implications of this population shift, but in general they are ill-prepared to deal with them (e.g., schools lack language interpreters, teachers are unfamiliar with the cultural backgrounds of their students). Data from a national survey in 1999 indicate that less than 20% of America's teachers who work with culturally diverse students feel well prepared to meet the needs (learning a new language, coming to school with educational gaps, and so forth) of these children (U.S. Department of Education, 1999).

Cultural and ethnic diversity is nowhere more apparent than with the children and families served in early intervention services, preschools, and other community programs (Christensen, 1992). That diversity is *not*, however, reflected in the service providers for these programs or in the student population in the relevant personnel preparation programs.

Cultural diversity has the potential to increase relationship difficulties and conflicts and disrupt and inhibit collaboration between professionals and families (Hains et al., 2000). The cultural diversity in EI/ECSE settings, in effect, compounds the collaboration difficulties. The differences in background, race, and ethnicity between professionals and families can be addressed in two ways, and both are being pursued. One way is for preservice programs (college programs training early childhood professionals) to recruit students from a wide range of cultures and linguistic backgrounds. The second way is to promote the cultural competence of preservice students as well as personnel in EI/ECSE settings.

Cross-cultural competence (or *intercultural competence*) is substantially more than acknowledging the beliefs and practices of different cultures. It is an appreciation of diversity and the ability to relate and communicate effectively with individuals who do not share one's ethnicity, culture, language, or other salient variables (Hains et al., 2000; Hanson, 2004). It is respecting each family's values, traditions, and beliefs regarding child rearing and development, its communication and decision-making styles, and its views on assistance from people outside the family. It is viewing ethnic, cultural, and/or linguistic diversity as an asset while at the same time recognizing the difficulties inherent in immigration and the process of acculturation (Lynch & Hanson, 2004). Most important, cross-cultural competence is translating respect and understanding into actions that create and maintain an environment supportive of each person's participation.

DEC's recommended practices for personnel competence emphasize the importance of addressing cultural and ethnic diversity in didactic program content and through field experiences to prepare professionals to work effectively with culturally diverse families (Sandall et al., 2005). Preparation in cross-cultural competence assists people to 1) feel comfortable and effective in their interactions and relationships with families whose cultures and life experiences differ from their own, 2) interact in ways that enable families from different cultures and life experiences to feel positive about the interactions and the interventionists, and 3) accomplish the goals that each family and interventionist establish (Brislin, Cushner, Cherrie, & Yong, 1986).

Harry (2002) recommended adopting a broad conceptual framework that goes beyond the needs of specific cultural groups to avoid stereotyping. Another reason for adopting a broad conceptual framework is the impossibility of dealing with the infinite range of differences both within and among cultural groups. Lynch (2004) identified three essential components of preparation for "cross-cultural competence": 1) self-examination and values clarification; 2) general knowledge of the values, beliefs, and behaviors that may be encountered in cross-cultural interactions; and 3) ability to apply principles of effective cross-cultural communication, both verbal and nonverbal, at both interpersonal and systems levels. Kalyanpur and Harry (1999) emphasized the importance of understanding the underpinnings of the culture of special education in the United States, especially the potential effects of this culture on relationships with families.

The Culture of Special Education

Banks (1997a, 1997b) described culture as a multitiered structure of macro and micro levels. The United States has a national culture that may be conceptualized as an overarching framework at the macro level. At the micro level there are many ethnic cultures, subsocieties, and institutions. Microcultural groups participate to varying degrees in the macroculture, while retaining varying amounts of their separate cultural traditions. All individuals have characteristics of their macroculture, their original or primary microculture, as well as the other microcultural groups to which they belong. The pattern of identity that emerges incorporates factors such as race, ethnicity, nationality, language, social class, geographical location, and professional or personal interest groups (Harry, 2002).

Most people readily recognize and cite their macroculture and their primary microcultural affiliations (the race, ethnicity, nationality, language, social status, and geographical location with which they identify). However, people often fail to recognize the influence of a variety of professional or personal interest groups to which they belong. Examples of such interest groups include parents, musicians, golfers, teachers, nurses, and so forth. Some have specific and well-defined beliefs and practices; others have only implicit beliefs and values. Most of us do not think of these groups as cultures.

Special education is an example of a professional group that constitutes a microculture. Membership in the culture of special education influences cultural identity and, in turn, interactions with others (Kalyanpur & Harry, 1999). Understanding how this occurs is critical if we are to be sensitive to how discrepancies may separate us and affect our ability to be open to the values of other groups. In *Culture in Special Education*, Kalyanpur and Harry (1999) provided a thorough and comprehensive discussion of the cultural underpinnings of special education—what it means to share membership in the culture of special education and how that membership influences relationships with other professionals and families. Understanding these variables helps us to recognize our professional acculturation, how it occurs, and its potential effects. In turn, this awareness helps us to be more open to the value positions held by others.

Personnel preparation programs in all disciplines, including special education, explicitly teach the policies and practices of their field (Bowers, 1984; Skrtic, 1991, 1995). When they demonstrate that they have internalized these policies and practices, students are certified as competent by their department and their institute of higher education. At this point in special education, students are admitted to the professional community and licensed to teach.

The beliefs and values underlying the policies and practices of the field are not made explicit for students during the training period. However, they are embedded in all of the journal articles and textbooks that students read and in every class lecture or discussion. Over the course of the professional preparation period, these beliefs or core values become inculcated or taken for granted in the consciousness of preservice students to the extent that they are experienced as "the natural order of things" (Bowers, 1984, p. 36). Instead of being critically examined and reflected on throughout this period and continuously thereafter, these beliefs and values come to be accepted as the way things are intended to be.

The first question we need to ask is: What are the core values of the cultural foundation of special education policy and professional knowledge? Kalyanpur and Harry (1999) believed that they are *individualism, choice, and equity*. These core values are reflected in the six basic principles of IDEA: zero rejection, nondiscriminatory assessment, free and appropriate public education (FAPE), least restrictive environment (LRE), due process, and parent participation. We next must ask: What are the beliefs underlying the core values and what effect can they have on working with families?

The belief underlying the core value of *individualism* is that all children have the right to a meaningful education that is appropriate to their abilities. The assumption is that an education will maximize each child's potential to get a job and become an independent, productive adult. This assumption is most apparent in the due process requirement of IDEA, which states that children with disabilities have the right to protection under the law. Parents of children with disabilities must be told their rights specific to their child's education. The belief underlying the core value of *choice* is that everyone has the right to the pursuit of happiness and to choose how they want to attain it. In IDEA, the right to choice is most evident in the principles of LRE and parent participation. The belief underlying the core value of *equity* is reflected in three of the basic principles of IDEA: zero rejection, nondiscriminatory assessment, and parent participation. Thus, beliefs determine core values that in turn affect legislation and practice.

As noted above, the core values are rarely stated explicitly, but they are inculcated in the course of each teacher's professional preparation program. Over time they come to be taken for granted as the natural order of things and are assumed to be universal values. When families and professionals share these values, problems are minimized. When there is a common frame of reference, relationships have a high probability of being harmonious with minimal dissonance and generally straightforward communication. What many do not realize, however, is that the core values—individualism, choice, and equity—are *not* universal values. Some cultures in our multicultural society (and thus in our classrooms and early intervention programs) have very different concepts of self, choice, equity, and status.

It is useful to consider some examples of the disparity between the core values and defining features of special education and the values of other cultures (Kalyanpur & Harry, 1999). For example, the concept of *individualism*, which means that the individual (not society) comes first, is antithetical to the beliefs of most Asian American families. Of course, there is considerable diversity across the 28 different Asian groups in the United States (Asian American Heritage, 1995; Chung, 1992) but even taking that considerable diversity into consideration, most members of Asian American communities share a subset of common values. They are often troubled and confused by the belief in individual rights that underlies many Western cultures and, more specifically, special education policy and practices. It is contrary to their beliefs in 1) group orientation, 2) strong family ties, 3) emphasis on education, and 4) respect for authority and the elderly. Traditional Asian families place more value on the family unit than on the individual. Individual needs are considered to be subservient to those of the family and the community. Many Asian families consider harmonious interpersonal relationships, interdependence, and mutual obligations or loyalty essential for peaceful coexistence with family and others.

Where the Asian community is concerned, people have duties and responsibilities, not *rights*. Thus, it is easy to understand why Asian families, particularly those who have immigrated to the United States, may have difficulty with the concept of individualism and, hence, with claiming their child's right to an appropriate education. Even when made aware of their rights, they may not be as assertive as necessary or understand the importance of protest when their child's rights are violated (Dentler & Hafner, 1997).

The concept of *choice* is also perplexing to many Asians. This value is baffling because some societies do not believe in allowing individuals freedom of choice in all matters. For example, some cultural groups do not believe that their adolescent children should choose their own friends, their occupations, and/or their marriage partners. Families from these cultures are mystified by the array of special education program and service options for their children with disabilities.

Equity, the third core value of special education policy and practices, is as ingrained in the American collective conscience as individualism and choice. Here again, difficult as it is for many to accept and understand, equity is not a universal value. Some cultures believe that human beings are inherently *unequal* by reason of birth, caste, skin pigmentation, and economic and social status (Miles & Miles, 1993). They accept that some people should dominate others because of their backgrounds and status (e.g., education, age). There are traditions and expectations in these cultures to prevent the abuse of power in hierarchical structures. Those in more privileged positions are expected to fulfill certain obligations toward those who are less privileged. Families in these cultures expect professionals to protect, assist, and support their clients or students because the professionals have higher status. They find it difficult if not impossible to view themselves as equals and partners with professionals in making educational decisions (Kalyanpur & Harry, 1999).

Other families (e.g., African American parents) have different reasons for not feeling comfortable participating in decision making with professionals. Their own negative experiences in educational settings lead them to view the power dynamics between themselves and educational professionals as inherently unequal. The silence of these parents should not be taken as consent. Silence could have any number of meanings; for example that the parents 1) do not expect their contributions to be respected, 2) view compliance and deferring to authority as the only way to get along, and/or 3) do not agree with what is occurring.

The reason for highlighting the values that underlie special education policies and practices and professional knowledge is to point out the potential for difficulties inherent in interactions with families. Professionals in special education need to be aware of and question the influence that the assumptions of our field have on our beliefs and our practices in order to avoid egocentrism and to achieve cross-cultural competence. We must continuously reflect on our values and beliefs and how they are affecting our interactions with and respect for the values, traditions, and beliefs of the families we serve. Cross-cultural competence—learning to think, feel, and act in ways that acknowledge, respect, and incorporate ethnic, cultural, and linguistic diversity—is a lifelong goal to begin working toward during professional preparation.

Cultural Values in Parenting

Children and their families bring their heritage, their experiences, their personalities, their talents, their skills, and their values and beliefs to EI/ECSE environments (Hanson & Zercher, 2001). The challenge for professionals is providing services that respect and support these perspectives and are at the same time consistent with best practices and the legal mandates of IDEA.

Family-centered practices are at the core of best practices in EI/ECSE. To be truly family centered they must be delivered in a way that supports the ability of parents to parent their child and that facilitates the child's learning without intimidating or dishonoring the family's cultural, religious, or familial traditions. Family-centered practices treat families with dignity and respect. They are culturally and socioeconomically sensitive to family diversity, offer choices for families in relation to their priorities and concerns, fully disclose information to families to help them in decision making, assist families in accessing a range of informal community resources as sources of parenting and family supports, and provide help in ways that are empowering and that enhance competency (Dunst, 1997).

How should (or how *can*) professionals respond when families' perspectives and visions of their children's social pathways differ from the state of the art in the field of special education? This was the key question that a 4-year study by Harry (1998) sought to answer. She examined the role of culture and social class on the social pathways established by seven culturally diverse families for their children with disabilities. Harry noted that when she began her study she was relieved to hear the parents expressing a wish for a normal life for their children. She assumed they meant that they "wanted their children to lead lives that mirrored those of typically developing children, including concepts such as choice, friendship, independence, and equality of opportunity" (p. 58).

Over the 4 years of the study, it became apparent that Harry was mistaken. Major discrepancies were found between the parents' visions of a normal life for their children and the values espoused by the field of special education. The parents' visions for their children (those with and without disabilities) had to be understood through their cultural/acculturation and socioeconomic status. Sometimes parents' visions for their children with disabilities were based on different assumptions than those held for their other children. Parents viewed the friendships of their children (those with and without disabilities) as evolving more within the family than with peers outside the family circle (the typical American vision). Personal choice did not rank highly as a value for *any* family member and was even more restricted for the individual with a disability. Parents valued equality of opportunity for their children without disabilities, but generally valued it less for their child with a disability. Independence did not mean a life apart from the family, even for their typically developing children, and especially not for the child with a disability.

The children in Harry's study ranged in age from 8 to 18. The families were Indian (from Central America), Caucasian (from Palestine), African Caribbean (from Trinidad), African American, and American Chinese/Caucasian. It is interesting to compare her findings with those of Denney and colleagues (2001), who considered the beliefs and goals of Mexican families whose infants were in the neonatal intensive care units of two hospitals. Denney and colleagues were especially interested in the families' views about caregiving and development for their infants with prematurity, low birth weight, and/or intensive health care needs.

The Mexican families were extremely frustrated with the caregiving practices of the hospitals, many of which were in conflict with the families' beliefs. Parental stress associated with fear for their infants' small size or medically intensive birth history was amplified by their limited access to information about how to care for their infants. This information was not readily available because the physicians and nurses were not bilingual and access to translators was limited. In addition, the Mexican immigrant families had different expectations about caregiving customs. The two hospital caregiving practices that caused them the most concern were 1) the practice of having infants fully exposed and unswaddled (because physicians and nurses need to have quick access to intravenous catheters, ventilators, and monitoring equipment) and 2) the practice of giving mothers cold liquids and foods after birth. Based on their family beliefs and traditions in Mexico, parents believed that newborn babies should be dressed warmly, wrapped, and covered with blankets, and that leaving babies unswaddled placed them at risk for illness. They also believed that cold foods and liquids decreased the mother's ability to produce breast milk.

Other interesting findings from this study were 1) the importance of viewing extended family members as potential caregivers and including them in medical treatment decisions and training opportunities and 2) the view that the desire to have infants sleep in the parents' room is associated with a larger socialization goal of interdependence and emotional relatedness. The belief in the desirability of interdependence and emotional relatedness that is presumed to be nurtured by close physical proximity with infants contrasts with the mainstream Euro American belief that infants should be socialized from birth to become independent (Hanson, 2004). Parents begin this socialization by arranging for their infant to sleep in a separate room.

What can we learn about cultural competency from the experiences of these early intervention programs in hospital settings? First is the importance of ensuring that parents have regular access to information (in their language) about the ongoing medical status and caregiving needs of their children. A second insight comes from the different expectations about caregiving customs. Professionals must work to become as familiar as possible with the cultural values and socialization practices of the ethnically and linguistically diverse families they serve. Whenever possible, differences in caregiving practices should be modified or, if modifications are not possible, families should be given a thorough explanation of the reasons for the practices. Finally, service providers should give families an opportunity to say whom they want included in making treatment decisions and training for the infant's home care. For example, they may want extended family members to be included.

The major recommendation coming from studies that have examined the experiences of Asian and Latino immigrant families with children with disabilities is that service providers must work to gain an awareness of the individual familial beliefs, values, customs about health and child rearing, and communication preferences (e.g., Denney et al., 2001; Harry, 1998). Family preferences must guide the course of relationships with families of children with disabilities. Each family system is unique. Some families will have an extended base of support while others will include only the immediate family and depend on external support networks such as neighbors. Trusting relationships will develop if service providers embrace diversity and are open to and accepting of different opinions and beliefs.

Cultural Reciprocity

Kalyanpur and Harry (1999) argued that awareness of individual differences, although important, is "only the scaffolding for building collaborate relationships" (p. 118). Professionals need to go beyond awareness to reflect on their practices and question the assumptions of the field. (The importance of questioning the assumptions of the field of special education was discussed in the last section.) This section describes "the process of cultural reciprocity" (Kalyanpur & Harry, 1999, p. 115), a process for building effective parent–professional collaboration. The key features of this process are self-awareness, understanding and acceptance, internalization, treating each situation as unique, and empowerment.

Self-Awareness   Cultural reciprocity requires a constant and nonjudgmental awareness of one's own worldview—beliefs, values, and biases (religious, moral, political, social, and cultural)—as well as that of others. Drawing from Schön (1983), Kalyanpur and Harry (1999) asserted the importance of a reflective posture that recognizes our fallibility and that being experts in our field does not mean that we have all (or for that matter *any*) of the answers. What we want to transmit to families is that we are committed to working with them as partners to find answers.

Understanding and Acceptance   Cultural reciprocity is understanding the cultural values that underlie our assumptions and the responses of others to these assumptions. We need to continuously question ourselves: Why do we expect people and/or events to be one way rather than another? What is the basis of our beliefs about how people should behave and how events should occur? Why do others hold their particular expectations? What is the basis of *their* beliefs and expectations? As we answer these questions we are clarifying embedded assumptions. Ultimately this leads to a higher level of awareness of differences.

Internalization   Kalyanpur and Harry (1999) insisted that the basic values of reciprocity, respect, and collaboration must be internalized if the "posture of cultural reciprocity" is to become a way of life for professionals (p. 113). It should not be viewed as a strategy applicable only to specific contexts such as parent–professional interactions: It applies to all human interactions at every level.

Treating Each Situation as Unique   Coming from a posture of cultural reciprocity means that professionals understand each family's unique reasons for its behavior. It is recognizing that there are no stereotypical solutions for the challenge of building effective parent professional collaboration. Just as every person is appreciated as a unique individual, every situation and every family must be appreciated and treated as unique.

Empowerment   Inherent in the posture of cultural reciprocity is the requirement that parties engage in a dialogue and that all participants learn from this dialogue. Through these interactions, service providers will learn about the cultures of the families with whom they interact, and they will learn more about themselves and about their own culture.

Kalyanpur and Harry (1999) cautioned against viewing the posture of reciprocity as a bag of tricks to be pulled out at times of conflict. It is a value to be internalized and applied throughout our lives in all contexts. Also, they remind us that it is a mistake to think that only professionals from minority cultures can work with families from minority cultures. There is no evidence that professionals are any more successful in establishing collaborative relationships with families who belong to their culture than those who do not. Harry (1992) and Ladson-Billings (1994) found the best examples of parent–professional collaborative relationships with professionals who had little or no affiliation with the culture of families.

SUMMARY

This chapter has provided an introduction to three areas that embrace fundamental beliefs and values in the field of EI/ECSE: 1) the importance of collaboration and partnerships with other professionals and families, 2) teamwork, and 3) cultural reciprocity. These concepts and practices are at the very core of recommended practices in the field and are essential to the delivery of high-quality services to infants and young children and their families. Although collaboration and teamwork are often challenging, professionals can learn skills that promote effective communication and build interpersonal connections. The chapter also considered cultural diversity and cultural competence from the perspective of working with families. (Chapter 7 considers cultural diversity from the perspective of the child. Specifically, that chapter describes environmental arrangements and instructional approaches for children from culturally and linguistically diverse backgrounds.) The cultural reciprocity model was presented as a strategy for professionals to learn about families' cultural values and to build trusting relationships.

•••••••••••••••••••• **STUDY QUESTIONS** ••••••••••••••••••••

1. Discuss the role of collaboration in inclusive programs.

2. What are four myths associated with collaboration and team building?

3. Describe the four team models.

4. Describe characteristics of the transdisciplinary team model that make it different from the other models.

5. Describe the effects of strategy incongruence, advice overflow, credibility problems, and confused problem ownership on effective teaming.

6. Identify the two types of communication skills requisite for collaborative team interactions and the skills for each type of communication.

7. What do parents consider important for high-quality partnerships?

8. Provide a definition of culture.

9. What are two ways to address the differences in background, race, and ethnicity between professionals and the families they serve?

10. What are the characteristics of a teacher or other service provider who has cross-cultural competence?

11. Discuss the cultural underpinnings (the core values) of the field of special education and how they affect professionals' interactions with families.

12. How should professionals respond when a family's perspectives and visions for their child differ from the "state of the art" in the field of special education?

13. Describe the key features of cultural reciprocity.

3

Assessment and Planning: The IFSP and the IEP

Linda McCormick

- IDEA assessment requirements
- Assessment purposes
- Assessment approaches
- Developing the IFSP
- Developing the IEP
- Writing goals and objectives

C hapter 1 reviewed the requirements of IDEA (the original legislation as well as IDEA 1997 and 2004). Key requirements that have always been in this legislation include nondiscriminatory assessment and an individually designed educational plan. For infants (ages birth to 3), the educational plan is the individualized family service plan (IFSP); for school-age children (ages 3 and above), it is the individualized education program (IEP). This chapter will review various types and approaches to assessment, with particular attention on assessment approaches that are pertinent to IFSP and IEP development. IFSP and IEP components and procedures will be discussed in detail, with attention to their similarities and differences.

In 1997, Congress changed several key components of the Individuals with Disabilities Education Act (IDEA) (PL 105-17) to improve educational opportunities for students with disabilities. In 2004, IDEA was reauthorized once again, and among the changes that maintain in that legislation are

- Giving students greater access to the general education curriculum
- Strengthening the roles and opportunities of parents as participants in their children's education
- Providing special education and related services, aids, and supports in the general education classroom "whenever appropriate"
- Supporting high-quality professional preparation and in-service education
- Offering incentives to help children before they become labeled
- Focusing resources on teaching and learning
- Reducing paperwork requirements that do not improve educational results

The number of sections in IDEA 2004 was reduced from nine to four (A–D). Part A describes the purposes and policies underlying the legislation (e.g., the goals of equal opportunity, full participation or inclusion, independent living, economic self-sufficiency). Part B sets out and provides for the obligations of the states, requirements for states' participation in IDEA, procedural safeguards, and monitoring and enforcement. Part C contains requirements for the identification and provision of early intervention services for infants and toddlers with disabilities and their families (and procedural safeguards). Part D includes provisions for research, teacher training, resource centers, parent training and information centers, and state improvement grants.

Both the 1997 and the 2004 IDEA amendments maintain the guarantees of the previous versions, most notably that children with disabilities shall be assessed by a multidisciplinary team; have a family service plan or an education program; and receive a free, appropriate public education in the least restrictive educational environment. Accountability systems, outcome measures or benchmarks, and goals are emphasized for children of all ages.

The major statutory change in the 1997 legislation regarding early intervention was to strengthen the "natural environment" language. Part C stipulates that early intervention services for infants and toddlers are to be delivered in "natural environments," which are defined as "settings that are natural or typical for the child's age peers who have no disabilities" (34 C.F.R. 303.18). If there is a decision to provide services in other than natural environments, a clear justification in writing for that decision must be supplied.

The parents' role in assessment and services for eligible children birth through age 2 was also strengthened. The definition of "parent" was amended to give adoptive parents the same status as "natural" parents. Also, the role of foster parents was clarified. Foster parents may act as parents if 1) the natural parents' parental rights have been extinguished under state law; 2) the foster parents have an ongoing, long-term parental relationship with the child; 3) the foster parents are willing to make the decisions required of parents under IDEA; and 4) the foster parents have no interests that would conflict with the child's interests.

As noted in Chapter 1, major changes in IDEA 2004 are the requirements that 1) the family's Part C service coordinator (or other representative of the early intervention program) must be invited to participate in the IEP meeting, 2) the information in the IFSP must be considered when developing the IEP, 3) parents have the option of continuing to receive early intervention services for their preschool-age children in some states, 4) parents and teachers may agree to make minor changes in a child's IEP during the school year without reconvening the IEP team, and 5) parents must receive quarterly reports on their child's progress toward meeting IEP goals and objectives.

ASSESSMENT

IDEA guarantees all students with disabilities the right to an unbiased evaluation of their education strengths and needs. This evaluation is intended to determine whether there is a disability, whether special education and related services are needed (because of the disability), and, if so, what kind of special education and related services the student will receive. IDEA provides specific guidelines to ensure that the assessment process is unbiased and nondiscriminatory. (See Table 3.1 for IDEA eligibility categories.)

Assessment Purposes

The major reasons for assessment are *screening, diagnosis* and/or *eligibility determination, intervention planning,* and *monitoring and evaluation.* Assessment at each of these decision points asks different questions.

For example, *screening* asks the question: Is there a possibility that this child has a problem? Screening programs typically utilize brief, inexpensive measures that can be administered in a short time with relatively little effort. The purpose is to identify children who should receive more comprehensive assessment and, possibly, intervention. IDEA requires screening activities called *Child Find* to identify children who may need comprehensive assessment and

Table 3.1. IDEA (PL 105-17) eligibility categories

- Specific learning disabilities
- Speech or language impairments
- Mental retardation
- Serious emotional disturbance
- Multiple disabilities
- Hearing impairments
- Orthopedic impairments
- Other health impairments
- Visual impairments
- Autism
- Deafblindness
- Traumatic brain injury

intervention. There is even a prescreening effort to locate infants, toddlers, and preschool children who should participate in a more thorough formal screening process.

Diagnosis asks the questions: Is there a significant problem? What is the nature and extent of the problem? Comprehensive diagnostic assessment of infants and toddlers considers medical issues and sensory and motor functioning as well as cognitive, motor, communication, social/play, and self-care/adaptive development. Methods for answering these questions include observations, interviews, case history, informal tests, and norm-referenced tests (described below).

Eligibility determination may be done in conjunction with diagnosis but it asks different questions: Is the child eligible for services under IDEA? If yes, to what disability category will the child be assigned, and where will the child be served? Preschoolers with disabilities may be eligible for services under any of the categories of disabilities specified in Part B for school-age children (see Table 3.1). In addition, preschool and young children (ages 3 through 9) may be eligible under the more general designation of *developmental delay* (or a similar term selected by the state).

Intervention planning asks "what" and "how" questions. For example, What do we need to teach this child? What are appropriate instructional goals and objectives? What are the child's strengths relative to the demands or expectations in his or her natural environments? Examples of "how" questions are: How will we teach this child? How should we arrange the environment to facilitate learning? Intervention planning uses observations of the child in his or her natural environments, interviews with the family and other caregivers, and information from other professionals who know the child. This assessment should be closely linked to the actual curriculum and daily activities and routines in the child's preschool program. The information generated by this assessment is used to develop goals and objectives, plan instruction, arrange the learning environment, and adapt materials.

Monitoring answers two important questions: Is the child making progress in the program? Is the programming effective? The basic steps in the process are 1) determining what behavior to measure, 2) defining the behavior in observable terms, and 3) selecting an appropriate system for recording and summarizing the data. *Evaluation* may be summative or formative. Summative evaluation takes place after the service has been provided to determine whether the goals and objectives have been achieved. Formative evaluation takes place before and during instruction and intervention to determine if the services are being provided as planned and whether they are effective. The purpose of formative evaluation is to identify strengths and weaknesses in the intervention/ instructional process. The information generated by formative evaluation is used to make decisions about whether programming should continue as provided or whether there is a need to modify or completely change the intervention/ instructional process.

Assessment Approaches

The two traditional approaches to assessment, *norm-referenced tests* and *criterion-referenced tests*, have very different purposes and characteristics.

Norm-Referenced Tests   Norm-referenced tests compare the child's achievements with those of same-age peers. They are used primarily for making diagnostic, eligibility, and placement decisions. The basis for selection of items for inclusion on norm-referenced tests is the percentage of children who master a particular skill at a certain age and whether an item correlates well with the total test. For the results of these tests to be comparable across children, they must be administered under standardized procedures. In other words, all children taking the test must have an identical experience, with exactly the same amount of assistance and the same directions, materials, and scoring criteria.

Everyone who administers norm-referenced tests must not only recognize the importance of strict adherence to standardized procedures but also its limitations where children with disabilities are concerned. Rigid application of standardized procedures may result in invalid conclusions because the child's disability often affects his or her ability to respond. Imagine asking a child with little arm control to point to a picture or stack blocks to match those of a model as a way to assess his or her cognitive skills! Another limitation where very young children with disabilities (and many without disabilities) are concerned has to do with attending to and following directions. Young children are easily distracted and often reluctant to follow directions. Finally, norm-referenced tests do not consider the effects of environmental variables or instructional strategies (Losardo & Notari-Syverson, 2001).

Sandall et al. (2000) counseled vigilance when using norm-referenced instruments with infants and young children with disabilities. They suggested using only those tests that are appropriately reliable and valid and that include children who are similar to those being tested in the standardization population.

Criterion-Referenced Tests   Criterion-referenced tests provide highly specific information regarding a child's level of performance relative to a specific set of skills. Selection of items is based on their importance to school performance or daily living. The resulting scores indicate which portion of the specific domain or subject area the child has mastered. Curriculum-based assessment (sometimes called curriculum-*referenced* assessment) is a special form of criterion-referenced assessment. The major difference is that the criteria are drawn from the objectives of the curriculum. Assessment of the child's performance relative to the predetermined sequence of curriculum objectives indicates how well the child has mastered what has been taught; that is, whether the child is benefiting from the instruction. If the child is not learning, adjustments can be made.

Developmental tests are a type of criterion-referenced test where the items are developmental skills derived from surveys of large numbers of children and normal development research. The developmental milestones become the criteria against which a child's performance is measured. One limitation of these assessments is the practice of targeting the first items that a child fails as primary intervention targets. Wolery (2004) advised care when using this practice. His reasons were that 1) the items on many of these tests were not developed or intended as instructional goals, 2) it cannot be assumed that adjacent items are necessarily related to the same skill, 3) the sequence of items is not necessarily the best teaching sequence (especially for children with sensory and physical disabilities), and 4) many of the sequences have large gaps between items. In addition, the practice of targeting the first items that a child fails does not consider prerequisite skills and the relationship of skills across developmental domains. The process of developing intervention goals is clearly more complex than teaching the first items that a child fails on a test.

When these instruments are administered, the resulting score indicates the child's developmental functioning levels in the different domains (cognitive, motor, social, language, and so forth). If a child's skills are delayed in relation to typical milestones in a developmental domain, it is customary to target the next skills in the sequence as intervention goals.

Targeting and teaching skills in the order in which they occur (*or are thought to occur*) in typical development is called the developmental stage model. Although this model has some appeal for children with minimal delay in a single domain, it may not be the best approach for children with more severe and pervasive delays. When we use it with young children with disabilities, we make two assumptions: 1) that the development of young children with disabilities is essentially the same as that of children without disabilities and 2) that children with disabilities are simply functioning at an earlier stage of development (Goodman, 1992; Goodman & Bond, 1993; Guess & Noonan, 1982). There is no empirical support for either of these assumptions.

Relying on data concerning developmental milestones as the sole source of goals and objectives may even have negative consequences (Guess & Noonan, 1982). Service providers may spend too much valuable intervention time (the child's and their own) trying to teach developmental skills when the nature of the child's disabilities preclude attaining typical milestones. Another possible drawback is that preoccupation with typical development sequences may lead service providers to restrict children's experiences, thus denying them the same interesting and attractive activities offered to children without disabilities. In fact, so much time and effort may be directed toward trying to teach the skills observed in younger, typically developing children that service providers leave the child with little time to socialize and participate with peers in developmentally appropriate learning opportunities. There is no intent here to discredit criterion- or curriculum-referenced tests. The point is that the team should look carefully at the results before automatically including failed items as intervention goals or objectives (Wolery, 2004). Table 3.2 suggests some questions that should be asked about the items.

The shift in assessment practices over the past decade reflects what we have learned about the complex and holistic nature of development and the role of context and culture in learning (Barrera, 1996; Greenspan & Meisels, 1996; Gutierrez-Clellen, 1996; Losardo & Notari-Syverson, 2001; Meltzer, 1994; Thorp, 1997). Recent scientific research on brain development in the early years (Shonkoff & Phillips, 2001) and contemporary conceptual models of early development (Guralnick, 1997) underscored the fact that the developmental process is much more complex and dynamic than originally conceived. There are

Table 3.2. Questions to consider when developing intervention goals from criterion- and curriculum-referenced test results

1. What were the items that the child failed designed to measure?
2. Are the items that the child failed important constructs or skills that the child needs to acquire?
3. Do separate items that the child failed represent classes of important behaviors?
4. What do the failed items say about the child's overall competence in the across skill areas?
5. Why are these skills important to this infant or child?
6. Is this an essential skill for the infant or child to function in present and future environments?
7. What are the prerequisites for this skill and does the child have these prerequisite abilities?
8. How does performance of the skill relate to other skills in this domain or other developmental domains?
9. Is this skill an important prerequisite to other skills?
10. Should the focus of instruction for this skill be on acquisition, fluency, maintenance, or generalization?

Source: Wolery, 2004.

multiple and diverse biological and environmental factors that are continuously interacting with one another in a reciprocal fashion.

In summary, some limitations of traditional assessment approaches include 1) the unnatural separation of development domains, 2) the view that behavior is relatively stable over time, and 3) the limited scope of test items. Tests tended to focus on the separate developmental domains as if each were detached from and impervious to the others. In reality, developmental areas are interrelated and interdependent: Development is holistic and integrated. Further, traditional assessment approaches virtually ignored the association between contextual differences and variations in performance. The implication was that behavior can be separated from the context of daily experiences, family influences, and sociocultural experiences. Assessment results told us nothing about the settings, tasks, and activities in which the children were likely to learn best. Finally, traditional instruments were limited in that they provided no information about some very important behavior, such as social and emotional behavior and communication.

Alternative Assessment Approaches   Losardo and Notari-Syverson (2001) identified three categories of *alternative assessment approaches:* embedded, authentic, and mediated models. These approaches use observations and communication with children and families across daily activities. Embedded approaches include observations of children's behavior in natural contexts (with different persons, using different materials, and in multiple environments). Ecological assessment (described in Chapter 5) is an example of an embedded assessment approach.

Authentic assessment approaches document the child's abilities by preserving examples of performance. The focus is on documenting the changes brought about through instruction. Portfolio assessment (described in Chapter 5) is another example of an authentic assessment approach. Mediated assessment approaches use guided teaching (scaffolding) to gather information about the child's responsiveness to instruction. These approaches are characterized by guided support for the purpose of gauging the child's learning potential—not what the child has learned but what the child is capable of learning (Palincsar, Brown, & Campione, 1994). The focus is on process and learning potential over mastery. Dynamic assessment is an example of mediated assessment. Alternative assessment approaches are most likely to be used for intervention planning and intervention.

Whichever alternative assessment approach is used to identify intervention goals and objectives, *functionality* is a critical concern for children with severe disabilities. Functionality is judged by the extent to which skills facilitate a child's participation and independence in daily living and recreational activities. In a functional approach, assessment is likely to be organized around basic skills such as achieving mobility, feeding oneself, toileting, dressing, imitating peers, responding to directions, making choices, playing with toys, and taking turns. The idea is to identify age-appropriate goals that can have immediate usefulness and benefits for the child. Age-appropriate goals lead to participation in activities and demonstration of skills that are appropriate for same-age peers without disabilities. An example of a violation of the precept of age appropriateness would be asking a preschooler with disabilities to play with infant toys (e.g., stacking rings) or to play Pat-a-cake. Engaging with materials, toys, or activities that are not age appropriate is stigmatizing.

Child-centered planning comes under the heading of authentic assessment. Child-centered planning—also called MAPS (McGill Action Planning System) (Vandercook, York, & Forest, 1989), person-centered planning (Mount, 1992), or personal-futures planning—is more than a procedure for gathering information. It is a comprehensive planning process that goes beyond traditional assessment to involve all the people who have an interest in the child. Basic to this procedure is the belief that 1) planning for a child's future should be in the hands of the people who love the child and 2) a child who needs services should be thoroughly understood by the people who will provide those services. Attention is directed away from traditional test results and diagnostic labels facilitating the child's participation in natural environments with his or her peers without disabilities. The outcome of the process is a positive and realistic picture of the child that appreciates his or her unique characteristics and leads to a shared vision for the future. Child-centered planning is often incorporated as part of another authentic assessment approach.

The goals and ideas generated by the child-centered planning process provide a measure of social validity that expands and supplements the objective measures of behavior from which IFSP and IEP goals are typically derived. The concept of *social validity*, first introduced by Wolf (1978), refers to whether the goals and focus of intervention are in line with the values and desires of the consumers and participants. Child-centered planning ensures social validity. It is a means of eliciting the contributions and views of the consumers (the immediate and extended family, peers of the child with disabilities [when appropriate], and friends and neighbors of the family) and participants in the early intervention process (related services providers, community preschool staff, early intervention staff, and special education personnel). The vision that comes out of the child-centered planning process is the yardstick against which to measure the validity of the goals and objectives, the intervention procedures, and the outcomes of intervention.

PLANNING

IDEA provides for two types of individualized plans: the individualized family service plan (IFSP) and the individualized education program (IEP). Which plan is developed depends on the age of the child. Part B of IDEA states that eligible children up to age 6 may have an IFSP (*if* the state, the family, and the local service program want one), but most states provide an IFSP only for eligible children under age 3 and their families. When children transition to preschool at

Table 3.3.   Comparison of the IDEA requirements for the IFSP and the IEP

An IFSP must include	An IEP must include
A statement of the child's present level of development in these areas: physical (including vision, hearing, and health status), cognitive, communication, psychosocial, and adaptive behavior.	A statement of the child's present levels of educational performance. For preschool children, a description of how the disability affects the child's participation in age-appropriate activities.
A statement of family strengths, resources, concerns, and priorities related to the child's development.	
A statement of the major outcomes expected to be achieved for the child and family.	A statement of annual goals and short-term objectives detailing what the child is expected to learn over a specific time with criteria to determine if the goals/objectives have been achieved.
A statement of the frequency, intensity, and method of delivering the early intervention services necessary to produce desired outcomes for the child and family.	A statement of the special education and related services to be provided to help the child reach the goals and objectives.
A statement of the natural environments where services will be provided or a statement explaining why services will not be provided in natural environments.	The extent of time to which the child will participate with nondisabled peers in the general education setting, including district and state assessments and an explanation of the time the student will *not* participate with nondisabled peers.
Projected dates for the initiation of services and anticipated duration of services.	Projected dates that the special education program and other services will begin and anticipated duration of services.
The name of a service coordinator responsible for implementation of the IFSP and coordination with other agencies/professionals.	
Steps to be implemented to ensure successful transition (a transition plan) to preschool services provided by the public schools.	A transition plan (at age 14) stating the student's needs and agency responsibilities.
Written consent from the parents or legal guardians.	Date for evaluation of performance (review at least annually or as often as progress is reported for children without disabilities).

age 3, they are reevaluated and an IEP is developed. Table 3.3 provides a comparison of the federal requirements for the IFSP and the IEP. The remainder of this chapter describes the requirements for these plans as set forth in IDEA, and the major activity of the IFSP or IEP meeting, which is development of meaningful and functional goals and objectives.

The Individualized Family Service Plan (IFSP)

The IFSP differs from the IEP in that it revolves around the family as the only constant in a child's life. It is not a product so much as a *process* and a context for establishing and maintaining a productive and supportive professional–family relationship. There is continuous gathering, sharing, exchanging, and expanding of information as the family makes decisions about which early intervention services they want and need for their child and themselves. This continues throughout intervention to ensure effective early intervention in accordance with the law. The IFSP specifies desired outcomes for the child based on the child's development and needs but it may also include outcomes for the family. Families may identify their resources, priorities, and concerns related to enhancing their child's development, but this is optional. Other ways that the IFSP differs from the IEP include the focus on natural environments, inclusion of the services of multiple community agencies, and the assignment of a service coordinator for every family. (The service coordinator is described below.)

The form used for the IFSP differs across states and programs. The appearance and organization of this form is not important. What matters is that it includes all of the information as specified by IDEA (shown in the first column of Table 3.3).

The transition requirement was strengthened in the 1997 IDEA reauthorization. Note that there are specific directions for the transition plan. The IFSP must indicate the steps to be taken to support the transition of the child from Part C to preschool services under Part B if those are appropriate, or other services that may be available, if appropriate. There is no presumption that the child will transition to preschool special education. (Transition is discussed at length in Chapter 14.)

Developing the IFSP   The goal of the ongoing IFSP process is to enable families to make informed choices about the services they want and need for their children and themselves. What does it take for families to make informed choices and feel empowered to act on them? Most notably, they must have a trusting relationship and clear communication with EI service providers. From the first contact (by phone or in person), the EI professionals (not the family) are responsible for building this relationship.

Ultimately, the IFSP is only as good as the information from which it is constructed. The family members and the support network are the primary sources of this information. Family information gathering is most effective when EI providers understand and respect the value system and the unique perspective and beliefs of the family. It is important to be knowledgeable about the impact of cultural, environmental, and social factors (e.g., background, socioeconomic status, education) on the families' views and beliefs about disability, parenting, child-rearing practices, and early intervention services.

Banks, Santos, and Roof (2003) provided some suggestions for gathering information from families. They suggested beginning the first meeting by acknowledging and thanking the people present for taking the time to attend the meeting. Next, establish rapport and make sure that family members understand the purpose of the questions they will be asked. Explain why the information the families provide is so valuable in planning intervention and answer their questions about the IFSP process. Most important is to communicate to the families that they are important and that what they have to say will be decisive in the planning process.

Begin with open-ended questions such as "What does your child seem to enjoy the most?" and "What are you most concerned about right now?" to get a feeling for the family's concerns, resources, and priorities. Request details in a sensitive manner, realizing that questions may seem threatening, demeaning, or an invasion of privacy to some families. Observations may use a tool such as the Home Observation for Measurement of the Environment (HOME) (Caldwell & Bradley, 1984), but informal report writing is preferred by many families and EI professionals because it seems less intrusive and threatening. The important thing is for EI providers to consider the family's viewpoint first, rather than their own (Banks et al., 2003).

Formal procedures (interviewing, observation, and surveys) are designed to assist identification of family needs and strengths, thus aiding prioritization of intervention services. They are not intended to be used as a norm-referenced instrument or to generate a quantitative score. Among the survey instruments available to gather information from families are the "Family Needs Scale" (Dunst, Cooper, Weeldreyer, Snyder, & Chase, 1988), the "Family Interest Survey" (Bricker, 1993), and the "Family Needs Survey" (Bailey & Simeonsson, 1990). They should be used with great care. Some families find formal survey instruments impersonal and evaluative. Others are comfortable with them as an efficient means of recording information. Some may even prefer to fill out their own survey forms. The majority of families are most at ease with conversations (called "Talk Story" in Hawaii) as a means of accruing the information needed for planning.

Following the initial evaluation and assessment process, a meeting is scheduled. This meeting should include the family, the service coordinator (described below), at least one member of the evaluation team, and any others that the family or service providers want to invite. The purpose of this meeting is to make decisions about which services are needed. These service decisions are then documented on the IFSP. Table 3.4 shows early intervention services that are authorized by Part C. If there is a need for services that are *not* authorized by Part C, those services are described on the IFSP, but separate funding sources must be sought. If the family will be charged for some services (which is allowable under the law), this should also be noted on the IFSP.

Service Coordination   Congress created the professional service coordinator (initially called case manager) because of concern that families would need help advocating for their children, plotting a course through the maze of early intervention service providers, and coordinating services across agencies. The selection of a service coordinator is central to the IFSP process because this person will assist the family in accessing services and ensure that they receive the rights, procedural safeguards, and services that are authorized under the state's early intervention program.

Part C is very specific about the service coordinator's responsibilities (34 C.F.R. 303.23). The service coordinator helps parents access and coordinate ser-

Table 3.4. Part C early intervention services

Early intervention services may include any one or some combination of the following services:
- Assessments to identify
    the child's strengths and developmental needs
    the family's concerns, priorities, and resources
- Assistive technology, including specially designed or altered adaptive assistive devices
- Audiology testing and referral
- Family training and counseling, as requested
- Health services to enable the child to benefit from other early intervention services
- Medical services for the purpose of diagnosis or evaluation—provided by a licensed physician to determine developmental status and the need for early intervention services
- Nursing services as necessary to enable a child to benefit from early intervention services
- Nutrition assessment and development and monitoring of a plan to address the child's nutritional needs
- Occupational therapy services to help the child learn skills for play and daily living and design and provide assistive devices
- Physical therapy to identify and help prevent or reduce movement problems
- Psychological assessment and counseling for the child, parents, and family regarding child development, child behavior, parent training, and educational services
- Service coordination to provide information and assist in obtaining needed services and resources in the community
- Social work assessment in the home and family environment and individual and family group counseling and other activities to build social skills
- Special instruction to assist the child in learning new skills
- Speech/language pathology that includes identification, referral, and provision of services to assist development of language and communication
- Transportation services as necessary to enable the child and family to receive early intervention services
- Vision assessment and referral for medical or other professional services necessary for habilitation or rehabilitation

vices and assistance among agencies. Examples of service coordination activities include

- Coordinating and monitoring evaluations and assessments
- Ensuring that parents actually receive the early intervention services described in their IFSP in a timely manner
- Coordinating and monitoring the provision of early intervention and other services (e.g., medical services) so that there are no gaps or unnecessary overlaps in services
- Continuously seeking and helping the parents find appropriate services, service providers, and environments that will benefit the child's development
- Facilitating and participating in the development, review, and evaluation of the IFSP
- Informing families of the availability of advocacy services
- Facilitating the development of a transition plan

Because the law permits some discretion in developing service coordination systems, there is a great deal of variation across states. In some states, service coordinators have no responsibilities other than service coordination. In other states, any or all of the professionals on the early intervention team may assume the responsibilities of service coordination in addition to their specific early intervention functions. Which professional works with a particular family depends on the needs of the child and the wishes of the family. Minimum qualifications for service coordinators include knowledge and understanding of 1) infants and toddlers with special needs and their families, 2) early intervention legislation, and 3) the nature and scope of services available under the state's early intervention program.

Expected Outcomes   The EI service providers and the family collaborate to develop a list of expected outcomes. The purpose of the expected outcomes is twofold: to increase the family's capacity to support the child, and to increase the child's participation in valued activities in natural environments. As noted above, desired outcomes for the child are based on the child's development and needs. Expected outcomes may be developed for the family if they choose to identify their resources, priorities, and concerns related to enhancing their child's development.

Outcome statements should not be confused with traditional assessment-driven therapeutic goal statements. Outcome statements reflect the team's shared vision for the child and the status of planning for achievement of that vision. They are written in the family's own words. Most statements will be altered or expanded numerous times in response to changes in the child's physical and developmental status and the family's preferences, resources, and challenges. Thus, they should be viewed as tentative.

Rosenkoetter and Squires (2000) described a thinking process that can aid in developing meaningful outcomes for children and their families. They also suggest some questions that team members can use to evaluate their outcome statements and help them choose those with the greatest impact on development. What follows draws heavily from their data and experiences.

The first step, after team members have gotten to know one another, is to begin to discuss 1) developmental priorities for the child, 2) the family's concerns regarding issues that affect the child's development, and 3) preferences for initial intervention activities. The next step is to gather information about the environments in which the child and the family spend their time and the activities they do or wish to do in those environments. In addition to a variety of locations in the home (e.g., kitchen, playroom, backyard, bedroom), most families identify a number of community settings (e.g., library storytime, family child care placement, homes of relatives, a cooperative playgroup) where they spend time daily, semiweekly, or weekly. Actual and/or desired activities in these different locations should also be discussed. For example, if the parents identify breakfast in the kitchen as an activity, the discussion would focus on the family's breakfast routine and the child's present behavior at breakfast. Then the parents describe what they would like the child to do at breakfast, and the EI service providers (e.g., occupational therapist, service coordinator) may suggest methods for achieving those desired behaviors.

The format for outcome statements is straightforward. It begins with a statement of what the child will do (as a result of the intervention) followed by the rationale (why this is important for the family and for the child's development). For example, Jace, a 3-year-old with Down syndrome, will sit in his highchair and feed himself finger foods (dry cereal, pieces of fruit) so that the family can enjoy breakfast together and Jace can become more independent.

The next step is for the team to list what various people will do to achieve the outcomes and when and where intervention will take place. This is basically the implementation plan. In the case of Jace, teaching will occur at breakfast (and conceivably at other meals in the kitchen), and the people responsible will be the family members who are present at mealtimes. The EI service providers participate by teaching family members how to physically shape Jace's fingers around a food particle and guide it to his mouth.

The final step is for the team to decide how they will know if each outcome has been achieved. The evaluation plan should be appropriate to the setting and phrased so that it is meaningful. Using the example of Jace at breakfast, data collection can be as simple as jotting notes on a pad or calendar kept on the kitchen table. The parent may estimate the percentage of his breakfast that Jace is feeding himself independently or count the number of bites that he eats on his own.

Rosenkoetter and Squires (2000) suggested asking the following questions as a way to revisit the thinking process involved in developing each outcome:

- Is this outcome important to the family's long-term aims for their child and the family support agenda?
- Is this outcome doable within the family's daily routines and considering their other responsibilities and commitments?
- Are the strategies for accomplishing the outcome the least intrusive and the most natural?
- Who will pay for or provide the intervention and what programmatic actions are needed to locate funding and enlist the commitment of others?
- Is the outcome written in language that the family might use?

In addition to outcomes that focus on the child in daily activities, there may be other types of outcomes focused on activities that family members identify as important to the family's functioning. These might include accessing information for decision making and financial planning or locating and building relationships with possible community supports. Other outcomes might focus on improving the family's health, safety, and quality of life (e.g., securing and moving to affordable housing, earning a GED). Finally, there may also be outcomes that specify agency or administrative activities. Among these are outcomes that identify needs for additional assessment, equipment and materials (both ac-

Table 3.5. Guidelines for IFSP development

Focus on the family.

Emphasize two points at the beginning of the relationship: (1) that the intervention team and the family are a partnership and (2) that the family's concerns, priorities, and resources will guide the IFSP process.

Identify the family's environments.

Ask about the family's environments and the people, activities, and routines in those environments. Analyze the teaching/learning possibilities of family activities and routines. (Ecological Assessment is described at length in Chapter 5.)

Engage in functional assessment.

Try to get an accurate picture of the child's strengths, preferences, interests, and needs. Plan to observe the child in his or her natural environments to verify and complete the picture.

Review and respond to family questions.

Review all the available information and respond to each family member's concerns about the child. Plan for assembling additional information if needed.

Decide expected outcomes.

Collaborate to develop statements of activities that will increase the family's capacity to support the child and the child's participation in valued activities in natural environments.

Assign people and strategies to address the outcomes.

The team (including the family) should decide and assign members the responsibilities for intervention services to accomplish the mutually agreed upon outcomes. Team members' responsibilities should depend on the needs of the situation, not the traditional functions associated with a specific discipline.

Decide on an implementation plan.

Collaborate to decide on specific interventions and strategies to bring about the desired outcomes. Select interventions that will promote generalization of outcomes, target several skills during one activity, promote independence, and resemble typical interactions. (These interventions are described in Chapters 7–13.)

Plan ongoing and periodic evaluations.

Evaluations should consider the rate and the quality of progress toward expected outcomes. Most important is whether the intervention strategies are resulting in developmental gains and increased participation in natural environments.

Source: Bruder, 2000b.

quisition and training for their use), transportation, and training and technical assistance.

The IFSP is reviewed *at least* every six months, or more frequently, to be sure that it continues to meet the needs of the child and family. There is a meeting at least once a year at which parents review their child's outcomes and the early intervention services to decide whether changes are needed. Table 3.5, based on Bruder (2000b), provides a summary of the guidelines for IFSP development discussed in this section.

The Individualized Education Program (IEP)

The purpose of the IEP is to ensure that eligible students ages 3 through 21 receive an appropriate and individualized special education and related services. At the most basic level, the IEP is an agreement between the parents and the school specifying what the child's needs are and what the school system will do to address those needs. A student's IEP team (sometimes called the IEP committee) may include professionals (e.g., teachers, administrators, language interventionists, nurses, school psychologists, physical therapists, and/or occupational therapists), community members (e.g., child care providers, social workers), and family members (e.g., parents, grandparents, siblings, aunts, uncles).

The major components of the IEP are 1) evaluation information indicating whether the student has a disability and whether he or she needs special education services and related services; 2) appropriate annual goals and short-term objectives, with criteria, procedures, and schedules that will be used to determine whether the objectives are met; 3) a statement of the appropriate special education placement and the specific related services that the student will receive; and 4) a declaration of the amount of time the student will be in the general classroom with supplementary aids and services. A general outline of the information that must be included in the IEP as compared with the IFSP is shown in the second column of Table 3.3. Specifically, the IEP must include

- A statement of the student's present level of education performance, including

  - How the disability of the student affects his or her involvement and progress in the general curriculum (ages 6 through 21)

  - How the disability affects his or her participation in appropriate activities (ages 3 through 5)

- A statement of measurable annual goals, including benchmarks or short-term objectives related to 1) meeting needs resulting from the disability in order to progress in the general education curriculum and 2) meeting the student's other disability-related needs

- A statement of the special education and related services and supplementary aids and services to be provided and the program modifications or supports for school personnel so that the student can 1) advance appropriately toward meeting annual goals, 2) be involved and progress through the general curriculum and participate in extracurricular activities, and 3) be educated and participate with other students (with and without disabilities) in extracurricular and other nonacademic activities

- An explanation of the extent, if any, to which the student will *not* participate with students without disabilities in general education classes and extracurricular activities

- A statement of individual modifications in the administration of state- or district-wide assessments of student achievement that are needed for the child to participate in the assessments

- The projected date for beginning services and program modifications and the anticipated frequency, location, and duration of each service

- A transition plan that includes

- A statement of the student's needs related to transition services (beginning age 14 and each year thereafter)
- A statement of needed transition services, including interagency responsibilities for needed linkages (beginning age 16)
- A statement that the student has been informed of his or her rights that will transfer to the student from the parents when the student comes of age at 18

- A statement of how the student's progress toward annual goals will be measured and how the parents will be regularly informed of the student's progress

The IEP requirements listed above should align meaningfully. For example, annual goals and related services should address the child's present levels of performance. There are also special factors that must be considered when the IEP is developed. These include

- Positive behavioral interventions, strategies, and supports if a child's behavior impedes his or her learning or that of others
- The child's language needs as they relate to the IEP (when there is limited English proficiency)
- Instruction in the use of braille for a child who is blind or visually impaired (unless the team decides that braille is not appropriate for the child)
- The child's language and communication needs if the child is deaf or hard of hearing, including opportunities for direct instruction in the child's communication mode and communication with peers and professionals in that mode
- The need for assistive technology devices and services

The requirement that the IEP must be finalized prior to actual placement is a problem where preschoolers are concerned. If the child is not yet in his or her placement, as is often the case with preschoolers, members of the IEP team do not yet know what the child's strengths and needs are relative to the expectations of the preschool setting. Bateman (1992) and others have commented on this, noting that the IEP is written at the wrong time and for the wrong purpose. Thus, the validity and appropriateness of the goals and objectives on a child's *first* IEP may be in question if 1) assessment focused exclusively on establishing eligibility for services and the type of services needed (rather than the child's specific instruction and support needs), 2) the goals and objectives were developed by persons unfamiliar with the child's daily functioning *in natural environments*, and/or 3) the goals and objectives were generated by persons other than those responsible for the child's daily instructional activities.

When one or more of these three conditions is not met, a second IEP meeting should be called a few weeks after placement to revise and/or rewrite the goals and objectives. This meeting can include all the service providers in the child's preschool setting. Procedures for decision making related to planning intervention, including development of intervention goals and objectives, are described in Chapter 5. This process is called ecological assessment and planning (Grisham-Brown & Hemmeter, 1998; McCormick & Noonan, 1996; 2002).

Developing the IEP   IDEA stresses the need to 1) link specific IEP goals with supports (accommodations and necessary modifications), 2) involve general education teachers on the IEP team, and 3) increase parent involvement. IEPs are not intended to be filed away for periodic monitoring; rather, they are intended to serve as a guide for instruction. Each child's IEP should be functional and individualized for that child, and it should be possible to teach *and evaluate* the skills that are identified as goals and objectives in the context of developmentally appropriate activities and routines.

The end product of a well-grounded assessment process is goals and objectives that identify functional and age-appropriate skills that are linked directly with learning and development. Ideally, the IEP is discipline-free and jargon-free in the sense that any service provider (e.g., teacher, paraeducator, therapist, family member) could readily understand and implement it on a daily basis (Capone & Hull, 1994). Intervention areas are not assigned to disciplines. It is a misconception that social, cognitive, and academic skills "belong" to specific service providers (McCormick, 2003b). It is a mistake to think of speech, language, and communication as "belonging" to speech–language pathologists, motor skills as "belonging" to occupational or physical therapists, and social and cognitive skills as "belonging" to teachers. Such assignments of responsibility give the mistaken impression that the different disciplines have totally separate and distinct knowledge bases. In reality, there is enormous overlap in both research and practice across disciplines. More important, where accountability is concerned it is inappropriate to hold a single professional solely responsible for a child's progress in one area. There should be pooling of expertise so that each goal reflects a holistic view of the child and the consensus of the whole team as to the child's intervention needs.

In addition to other goals, the team formulates long-term health goals and objectives and identifies backup staff members (e.g., nurse) to assist with required services for children with chronic health needs. Included under the heading of "chronic health needs" are children with asthma, diabetes, and cystic fibrosis as well as those who require health-related procedures such as gastrostomy tube feedings, nebulizer treatments, administration of oxygen, and suctioning a tracheostomy (Presler & Routt, 1997). The specific health-related needs of children who require ongoing support and technology for survival as well as needs regarding equipment and staff training should be described in the IEP.

After passage of the first version of IDEA in 1975, there was some controversy as to precisely which related services and supplementary aids and services local education agencies should be responsible for providing. The issue was how to determine whether a particular service was a "related service" or a "medical service." In 1984, the Supreme Court clarified the school's responsibilities in medical management (*Irving Independent School District v. Tatro*, 1984). The guidelines that grew out of that decision state that any services that can be performed by an individual other than a physician (e.g., a school nurse or some other qualified person or layperson)—thus enabling the child to attend school with peers—should be available to the child within the school setting (Greismann, 1990). Sometimes a school or personal nurse is available to administer health-related procedures. If not, the ECSE teacher and assistant should be trained by professional health personnel to assume primary responsibility for ongoing support.

WRITING IEP GOALS AND OBJECTIVES

Goals are short statements identifying the desired outcome of intervention or instruction (Wolery, 2004). Each goal describes a behavior(s) that the child can *reasonably* be expected to accomplish in a 12-month period. Examples of broad goals generated through the ecological assessment process for children in an inclusive preschool setting are: "Jace will participate in the morning circle routine," "Anisa will eat and drink independently at snack time and at lunch," "Anthony will play on the wheel toys and the playground equipment." Goals should be positive and active (such as the above examples) rather than negative (e.g., "Sarah will not grab toys and other objects from peers") or passive ("Bryan will wait quietly in the lunch line").

Objectives provide information about what to teach, where and how to teach it, and how to judge that what has been taught has in fact been learned. An objective has three important components: 1) the behavior, 2) the conditions under which the behavior will be taught, and 3) the criterion for judging when the behavior has been learned. In other words, an objective states the behavior the child needs to learn, the activity or activities during which the child will learn and demonstrate the behavior, and the standard for achievement of the desired learning.

Some writers recommend expanding objectives to include information about intervention/instruction. Grisham-Brown and Hemmeter (1998) suggested adding a list of activities from relevant environments that will serve as contexts for instruction *and* a list of possible adaptations and/or instructional strategies to the traditional objectives format. They provide the following example of an expanded objective statement:

> When involved in an activity (described following) and given choices between two objects, Kendall will indicate her preference by looking at the desired object for 5 seconds across three activities for 3 days.
>
> Example activities include
>
> > *Home:* Mealtime (choice between two snacks), bedtime (choice between two books)
> > *School:* Center time (choice between centers), snack time (choice between crackers and bananas)

Community: Playground (choice between two pieces of play equipment), feeding the ducks (choice between feeding the ducks bread or crackers) (pp. 6–7)

Possible adaptations are 1) providing multisensory cues (i.e., visual, verbal, and tactile) prior to asking the child to make choices, 2) using concrete objects that clearly represent the activity, and 3) using things with high color contrast such as red objects on a black background.

The target skill in this example is "making choices." Including a variety of different choice-making activities across the child's environments (home, school, community) has two advantages: There are frequent opportunities for practice, and programming for generalization is embedded in the instructional process.

Recommended practices require identifying skills that are functional for the child and then teaching and evaluating those skills in the context of developmentally appropriate routines and activities (Wolery, 2000). This is a conditional statement. If the first condition is not met—if the identified skills are not *functional*—then teaching and evaluating those skills *in the context of developmentally appropriate routines and activities* is extremely difficult, if not impossible. This is why formulating appropriate goals and objectives is so important. When the first condition is violated—when goals and objectives target isolated nonfunctional skills—teachers have to separate children from their peers for instruction, sometimes taking them to another location or a corner. This is drill (massed trials) instruction. It isolates children from their peers and from the routines and activities that are both the context and the curriculum of early childhood education. Activities in a developmentally appropriate classroom are not planned with one skill in mind (e.g., identifying colors), they are designed to provide opportunities for a variety of learning outcomes.

Indicators of High-Quality Goals and Objectives

Notari-Syverson & Shuster (1995) identified five indicators of high-quality goals and objectives: functionality, generality, ease of integration, hierarchical relationship between the goals and objectives, and measurability. Table 3.6 includes questions that address the five indicators. Introducing and discussing these questions at the IEP meeting provides an opportunity for the service providers and parents to clarify the reasons for intervention and instruction. Goals and/or objectives that do not measure up in the five areas can be reformulated and/or rephrased.

Functionality refers to the usefulness of the skill(s) for coping with the challenges of daily living and participating in routine activities. Interaction with peers and objects is also included under the heading of functionality. The question is: Will this skill increase the child's ability to engage with people, activities, and objects in the daily environment? Skills should be performed across environments (e.g., requesting help, replacing objects/materials after an activity) and are essential for completion of daily routines. Examples of the types of narrowly defined skills to be avoided are saying numbers 1 to 10 or

Table 3.6. Rating the quality of goals and objectives

Functionality
- Will the skill enhance the child's ability to participate independently in all or most of his or her natural environments?
- Will the skill increase the child's appropriate interactions with peers and objects in his or her natural environments?

Generality
- Can the skill be taught and thus generalized across a variety of people, activities, materials, and settings?

Integration
- Do the child's peers without disabilities demonstrate the skill within a variety of daily activities and routines?
- Are there naturally occurring antecedents and logical consequences for the skill in the child's daily activities and routines?
- Can the skill be elicited easily in a variety of activities and settings?

Hierarchical relationship
- Is the objective necessary for achieving the goal?

Measurability
- Can the skill be seen and/or heard so that it can be counted?
- Can the product(s) of the skill be recorded?

Source: Notari-Syverson & Shuster, 1995.

stacking blocks. These skills are clearly not as important or meaningful as skills needed to achieve independence and to get along with others.

Generality, the potential for carryover, is an extremely important consideration when selecting instructional targets. Skills that represent a general concept or class of responses and skills that can be practiced across people, activities, materials, and settings fit into this category. The skills cited above (requesting help, replacing objects/materials after an activity) meet the criteria of generality as well as functionality.

Integration refers to the ease of teaching the skill in the context of daily routines in natural environments. Serving children with disabilities in inclusive settings requires planning specialized instruction. This process is expedited when the child's IEP goals and objectives reflect the philosophy and practices of the program. Instruction can take advantage of naturally occurring antecedents and logical consequences that occur throughout the day. For example, requesting help and replacing objects/materials after an activity can be taught in numerous activities and across most daily environments (e.g., preschool, family child care setting, home) because they are needed in numerous activities and across many environments. Thus, they meet the criteria of integration as well as generality and functionality. IEP goals and objectives should help children be viewed as members of the classroom community, not as somehow very different from everyone else.

Hierarchical relationship refers to the association between the goals and the objectives that enable their attainment. It should be possible to state with assurance that when the child attains all the objectives that accompany a goal, that goal has been achieved. For example, under the goal "Jace will participate in the morning circle routine" are two objectives that focus on the specific behaviors that Jace will learn in order to participate in this particular activity with his peers. These objectives are: "In morning circle, Jace will indicate 'I am here' when his name is called on 3 consecutive days"; and "In morning circle, Jace will respond to at least one question about the story of the day on 3 consecutive days." Jace is already performing the other behaviors that the teacher expects during morning circle. When he has learned these two additional behaviors, it can be stated with assurance that the goal of "participation in the morning circle routine" has been achieved.

The indicator *measurability* refers to decisions about what data will be recorded and *how* they will be collected. In many cases it is possible to measure the products of the skill; for example, it is relatively simple to know whether a child is successful at cutting with scissors, pasting, molding with clay, painting, and/or marking on a paper in response to a question or a direction. Best examples of the behavior can be saved in a portfolio to document performance and progress. The alternative to permanent products is observation and recording of the child's behavior while the child is engaged in the target skill. The limited number of dimensions on which behavior may be observed and measured include

- *Frequency or number*—how often the behavior occurs relative to the number of opportunities or during a constant time period
- *Rate*—how frequently the behavior occurs relative to a unit of time
- *Duration*—how long the behavior lasts
- *Latency*—how long it takes the child to begin the behavior once the direction or cue has been given
- *Topography*—the shape of the child's response (*how* the child performs the behavior)
- *Magnitude*—the intensity of the child's response

The dimension to be observed and measured depends on the target behavior. Specifically, it depends on what aspect of the behavior will be taught or changed. Frequency or number is the most commonly used measure. Recording frequency or number is appropriate when the observation period is held constant from one session to another or when the child has the same number of opportunities to respond each session. If the student has three opportunities to respond every day in the morning circle routine, then the number of responses in 3 consecutive days (because it is held constant) could be used as a criterion (e.g., "Jace will respond to at least two directions/instructions in morning circle for 3 consecutive days"). In situations in which opportunities to respond are not directly controlled, frequency can be used *only* if the observation period is held constant each day. The objective for Joey, who always plays with the same toy for the entire 20 minute free-play period, is an example: "Joey will select and play with at least three *different* toys during free-play period."

Rate is a measure of both fluency and accuracy. It is especially useful when the length of observations vary. Rate is computed by dividing the number of behaviors by the unit of time. For example, the objective for Abby is to increase the number of spoonfuls of food eaten with her self-feeder. Rate would be the best measure because the length of snack time and lunch varies from one day to the next. The first measurement for Abby during baseline was eight bites in 20 minutes, or .4 per minute.

Duration is an appropriate criterion when how long a behavior lasts is of concern. The two types of duration are total duration and duration per occurrence. If, for example, the objective is to increase play with a peer during morning free play and at recess, then a decision needs to be made as to whether to record the time for each social play episode *or* the total duration of social play in one or both of the designated periods. When the duration of each play episode is recorded, the frequency of play episodes is also recorded. These data make it possible to calculate the frequency of play episodes, as well as mean, median, and mode duration of the behavior (if desired).

Topography refers to the precision or appropriateness of the performance. Measurement of topography assumes a description of both correct and acceptable and incorrect examples of the behavior. Topography may be reported as frequency, rate, percentage, or duration of the response. For example, topography might be rated on a 1–5 scale. Then the number of opportunities in which correct topography is observed (ratings of 4 or 5) may be compared with the total number of opportunities. Topography is not often a concern. An example of when it might be used is in judging the correctness of letter formation, in which case there is a permanent product, so measurement is straightforward.

Magnitude is the strength, force, or intensity of a response. Precise measurement of intensity requires some type of automated apparatus. However, in some cases the magnitude of a behavior can be determined, albeit subjectively, by evaluating the effect of the response on the environment. The force of a response may be determined to be acceptable or unacceptable depending on a criterion included in the operational definition of the behavior. For example, acceptable speech might be operationally defined as speech that is audible from a distance of 5 feet.

Some skills are easier to measure than others (e.g., the number of questions the child responds to about a story), but ultimately any *behavior* is measurable. The following are *not* behaviors and thus are not measurable: feelings (e.g., "improved self-concept"), sensory experiences (e.g., "hear his name"), and broad concepts (e.g., "increased receptive language skills"). If restated as behaviors, feelings, sensory experiences, and broad concepts *can* be measured. For example, Jace's improved self-concept may be evident in increased responses to and initiations of peer play requests during recess. These behaviors can be measured. Sensory experiences, "hearing," "seeing," "feeling," and "smelling," are not measurable in natural environments, but it is possible to record children's responses to these experiences. For example, we can note whether Jace turns toward the person who says his name or comes when called. Broad concepts should be stated as the specific skills that constitute evidence of the category. It is possible, for example, to state numerous observable behaviors that are evidence of receptive language (e.g., "follows one-step directions," "answers questions about the story").

Measurability Issues

Adding the following four questions to the measurability indicator of Notari-Syverson and Shuster's (1995) quality monitoring scheme helps to sort out objectives that can or cannot be taught *and measured* in the context of routine activities:

1. *Does the objective propose to measure an appropriate dimension of the target behavior?* Consider this example of an inappropriate criteria: "Jace will respond to three routine questions (roll call, weather, day of the week) in morning circle by pointing to the appropriate picture on his communication device (without a prompt) 80% of the time for a week." "Pointing" requires measurement of frequency. Saying "80% of the time" is ambiguous: "80%" suggests that the percentage of opportunities will be measured, and "of the time" suggests measurement of a temporal dimension of the behavior, which is duration. To be measurable, the objective should read: "Jace will respond to three routine questions every day for a week (roll call, weather, day of the week) in morning circle by pointing to the appropriate picture on his communication device (without a prompt)." Using percentage as the dimension of measurement (e.g., "80% of the time") is usually not appropriate and it always complicates data recording requirements. (See additional discussion of the use of percentages below.)

2. *Does the objective propose to measure a meaningful dimension of the behavior—performance that the adults in the child's environment consider worthwhile and valuable?* Consider this example: "Sarah will walk (with her walker) from the round table to the restroom door and from the round table to the outside door to get in line on four of five consecutive days." The problem here is that the parents and the teachers were not concerned with the target behavior of walking: Sara has already learned to use her walker. What they really wanted her to learn was to move faster and to do so consistently because it took her far too long to move from one place to another. Her parents and the teachers think she should be able to walk the distance in less than 4 minutes and that she should do it *every* day. This is the modified objective: "Sara will walk (with her walker) from the round table to the restroom door and from the round table to the outside door to get in line in 4 minutes or less, five consecutive opportunities."

3. *Is it clear how to elicit the desired performance?* Consider this objective: "When shown any two letters or small pictures and asked to say 'same' or 'different,' Jessie will respond correctly 9 of 10 trials." The stimulus con-

ditions are not clear. When the teacher was preparing to assess and then teach this behavior, he did not know how much disparity there should be between the letters or pictures and whether to present 10 pairs of letters and 10 pairs of pictures or one set of each for 10 trials. Restated, this objective reads: "When shown 10 pairs of two-inch letters or small pictures with minimal differences and asked to say 'same' or 'different,' Jessie will respond correctly 9 of 10 trials.

4. *Can performance of the behavior be measured in the context of daily routines and activities?* Even though the objective in the above example has been restated so that the stimulus conditions are clear, it is *not* a good objective. Jessie's performance cannot be measured in the context of daily routines and activities. The teacher will have to present 10 to 20 trials in a massed trial format in order to assess and teach this behavior. This is an example of an objective in which the way the objective is written actually limits the potential for embedding instruction and assessment into existing classroom activities and routines. Theoretically, ease of measurement should not be a factor in deciding whether a particular skill should be targeted for instruction. However, it must be a consideration in natural environments because there is not sufficient staff in preschools to assign one person to do nothing but observe and record behavior. Thus, it is highly desirable to target behaviors that can be measured while simultaneously carrying out daily activities and routines. Here is a way to rewrite the objective so that performance can be measured (and taught) in the context of daily routines and activities: "When shown small objects with minimal variation in color, shape, size, and function (three to five a day in the context of ongoing activities) and asked to say 'same' or 'different,' Jessie will respond correctly 9 out of 10 trials."

Bateman and Linden (1998) noted that problems related to measurability are among the five most common problems in IEP goals and objectives. Bateman and Linden were particularly concerned with the use of percentages, noting that "percentages seem to be worshiped unduly" (p. 70)—people seem to think that by simply attaching a number (usually a percentage) to an objective they make it measurable. Here is one of Bateman and Linden's examples of what they call a "not-so-wonderful goal": "Karen will improve her handwriting by 80%." The problem with this goal is readily apparent: If only 80% of the words in an essay were legible, then one of five words would *not* be legible. Performance of this behavior at the stated criterion level (80%) would not be acceptable.

The misuse of percentages where social behavior is concerned is even more worrisome (Bateman & Linden, 1998). Consider, for example, this goal: "Levi will have acceptable behavior 80% of the time." Imagine what it would be like to be around a child whose behavior was unacceptable 20% of the time. Acceptable social behavior has not been learned if it is exhibited on only eight of ten occasions. How could "80% of the time" be a *goal*? Again, performance of the behavior at the stated criterion level would not be acceptable.

Finally, this goal statement provides a third example of the misuse of percentages: "Given a short paragraph, James will be able to identify the main idea with 95% accuracy." This is an example of the third measurability question discussed above. It is not clear what constitutes acceptable performance of the behavior because the stimulus conditions are not clear. Should James be given 100 short paragraphs, from which he will need to identify the main idea in 95 of them? Or should he be given one paragraph in which he would be expected to *almost accurately* identify the main idea?

The examples of objectives provided by Bateman and Linden are obviously for school-age children. However, many goals and objectives developed for preschoolers are not-so-wonderful goals and they have other problems. Michnowicz, McConnell, Peterson, and Odom (1995) analyzed the goals and objectives in the IEPs of 163 preschoolers. Nearly 50% had no social goals or objectives whatsoever. When there were social goals and objectives, 68% of the social objectives lacked criteria and 45% were rated as unmeasurable *as written*.

When writing objectives, we need to remember that "percentage" refers to the number of times a behavior occurs per total number of opportunities, multiplied by 100. Saying "80% *of the time*" is meaningless because the total number of opportunities for the behavior to occur is not specified. Percent is a useful measure when accuracy is a primary concern and when a permanent product is generated, as is the case with a spelling test or a page of addition problems (not preschool activities). Percent data are also used to summarize the responses recorded in an interval recording system, which, as noted above, are not common in most classrooms because recording requires the observer's undivided attention. Teachers rarely have the time to collect this type of data. Moreover, percent should not be used when the total number of opportunities to respond is less than 20, in which case one change in the numerator will produce greater than a 50% change.

The purpose of the criterion component of the objective is to tell the teachers what measurement system to develop so that they can judge whether what they have taught has in fact been learned. As noted above, the criterion component should include or at least imply the measurement procedures (the *how*), the schedule (*when* and *how often* measurement will occur), and an indication of *how well* the student is expected to perform for the behavior to be considered satisfactory. Unless the criterion component includes or implies a feasible and appropriate measurement system, the teacher cannot assess whether the child can perform the behavior. This leads to instruction of behaviors that are already in the child's repertoire.

SUMMARY

IDEA provides precise guidelines for assessment and planning for infants and young children with disabilities and their families. Assessment has a number of distinct purposes—screening, diagnosis, eligibility determination, intervention planning, monitoring, and evaluation. The purpose of assessment must be considered to ensure that appropriate assessment strategies and/or instruments are selected. Assessment for the purpose of intervention planning (i.e., IFSP and IEP development) may be conducted using norm-referenced or criterion-referenced assessment (providing that the instruments address age-appropriate and functional skills and the child can demonstrate the necessary response requirements), or more contemporary assessment approaches (e.g., authentic assessment, child-centered planning) may be used. Contemporary methods tend to consider the child's performance in natural environments such as the home or child care center. Assessment results should inform the development of IFSP/IEP goals and objectives. Although failed items on assessments aren't necessarily appropriate outcome statements or objectives, they may suggest areas of need and they provide information on a child's present levels of performance. Parent priorities and needs related to participating in natural environments should also have a significant influence on the development of goals and objectives. And finally, in writing behavioral objectives, it is critical that they be functional and evaluated in the context of developmentally appropriate routines and activities.

•••••••••••••••••••••• **STUDY QUESTIONS** ••••••••••••••••••••••

1. Describe major changes to the IDEA in the 1997 and 2004 reauthorizations.

2. Describe the IDEA guidelines related to assessment.

3. Describe the major reasons/purposes for assessment and the key question that is addressed by each type of assessment.

4. Differentiate norm-referenced and criterion-referenced assessment and tell how they differ from more contemporary alternative assessment approaches.

5. Describe and give examples of authentic assessment.

6. Describe the procedures and goals of the child-centered planning process.

7. Indicate major differences between IDEA requirements for the IFSP and the IEP.

8. Describe development of an IFSP.

9. Describe the role of the service coordinator.

10. Describe development of an IEP for a preschooler.

11. Differentiate goals and objectives in terms of development, purposes, and form.

12. What are indicators of high-quality goals and objectives?

13. List and describe the dimensions on which behavior can be observed and measured.

14. How do you decide what dimension of a behavior to measure?

15. What questions should we ask to sort out objectives that can or cannot be measured in the context of routine activities?

16. What is the purpose of the criterion component of an objective and why is use of percentages problematic?

4

Naturalistic Curriculum Model

Mary Jo Noonan

· · · · · · · · · · · · · · · · · · · **FOCUS OF THIS CHAPTER** · · · · · · · · · · · · · · · · · ·

- Curriculum models in early intervention and preschool special education

- Naturalistic approaches in early intervention curricula

- Content, instructional approaches, and evaluation methods of the naturalistic curriculum model

- Age appropriateness and developmentally appropriate practice considerations

- Steps in implementing the naturalistic curriculum model

C urriculum is often defined as an organized and sequenced set of content to be taught: It is the "what to teach" (Bailey, Jens, & Johnson, 1983). Another, broader, definition includes instructional techniques, or "how to teach," so that curriculum is defined as content and teaching techniques ("what and how to teach"). And sometimes content is not specified; instead, curriculum is defined by a process for deriving content and planning instruction, rather than specific content and procedures. In this chapter, curriculum includes all three approaches: content, techniques, and a process for deriving content and planning instruction.

CURRICULUM MODELS

Three curriculum models have characterized early intervention for infants and young children with special needs: 1) the developmental model, 2) the developmental-cognitive model, and 3) the behavioral model (Bailey et al., 1983; Hanson & Lynch, 1989). These models are continually being modified so that they are more immediately relevant to the needs of young children and their families. The most recent modifications focus on the child interacting with the social and physical environment–naturalistic considerations. This chapter briefly reviews traditional curriculum models and their current naturalistic modifications. The naturalistic components of the models are then synthesized and presented as a naturalistic curriculum model for early intervention. Finally, this chapter provides a series of steps for implementing the naturalistic curriculum model.

Developmental Model

The developmental curriculum model was perhaps our initial approach to early intervention for infants and young children with disabilities. It was borrowed from the compensatory programs for children living in poverty in the 1960s (e.g., Head Start; see Chapter 1). It is sometimes referred to as an enrichment model because compensatory early childhood programs attempted to enhance or enrich the experiences of children living in poverty by providing them with experiences similar to their age peers living in more economically privileged circumstances.

The goal of the developmental model is to assist infants and young children to progress through the typical sequences (or milestones) of child development. It is primarily a content model. The content consists of the developmental sequences of physical development (gross motor and fine motor), adaptive development (self-help and daily living skills), social development, and communication development. Instructional strategies are to simulate activities engaged in by infants, toddlers, and preschoolers who do not have disabilities. The activities provide opportunities for demonstrating or encouraging the targeted milestones. Recent approaches to developmental curricula such as activity-based instruction recommend that developmental skills be embedded and taught during naturally occurring activities and routines (Pretti-Frontczak & Bricker, 2004; Horn, Lieber, Li, Sandall, & Schwartz, 2000).

More current applications of the developmental curriculum model include an emphasis on child and caregiver interaction. Both partners in the interaction are considered the appropriate unit of focus for assessment and instruction because interaction is a cyclical process: The behavior of each member of the dyad affects the behavior of the other members. The shift in the developmental model to include this more naturalistic perspective (child and caregiver interaction) is compatible with the philosophy of early intervention as "family centered." Early intervention involves all members of the family system, not only the infant or child who has a disability.

Developmental-Cognitive Model

The developmental-cognitive model is a theory-driven model based on the work of Jean Piaget (1952, 1954). Piaget theorized that cognitive development occurs as a result of physiological growth and the child's interaction with the environment. The curriculum model is considered a constructivist or interactionist approach defined by content and instructional techniques. The content is similar to the developmental model but emphasizes skill sequences of the sensorimotor period of intellectual development (birth through age 2). Cognitive skill sequences typically address five areas of early learning: object permanence (understanding that objects exist even when they are not in sight), means for obtaining environmental ends (using objects as tools to accomplish a goal), causality (using people or mechanical objects to make things happen), imitation (copying verbal and gestural behavior), and schemes (manipulating or interacting with objects appropriate to the nature of the objects). Some curricula also include skills from the preoperational period of intellectual development (ages 2–7 years).

Instructional techniques in the developmental-cognitive model reflect Piaget's interactionist theory: Tasks that are challenging are presented to the child to create a state of cognitive "disequilibrium." As the child attempts to solve the challenge of the task, he or she must intellectually organize the new information and adapt previously learned information in light of the new. The cognitive processes of organization and adaptation are referred to as "equilibration." In the 1970s, this model was applied to early intervention in the constructive interaction adaptation model (Bricker, Bricker, Iacino, & Dennison, 1976) and also in a compensatory education curriculum model (Weikart, Rogers, Adcock, & McClelland, 1971).

As the developmental-cognitive model was applied to early intervention, some researchers added a social development component. This naturalistic perspective is based largely on the work of Jerome Bruner, a psycholinguist (Bruner, 1975, 1977). Bruner described early social skills as social-cognitive behaviors that serve an early communication (or prelinguistic) purpose. Such skills include following an adult's visual line of regard (the infant's gaze shifts to look where the adult is looking), joint attention (adult and infant demonstrate concurrent and sustained attention to the same object/activity), and turn taking.

In addition, the developmental-cognitive model includes a naturalistic component of environmental control (Dunst et al., 1987; McCollum & Stayton, 1985). Infants and children learn environmental control when their behavior has a predictable effect on their social and physical environments. Environmental control is significant because it decreases children's dependence on adults to identify and/or meet their needs. Teaching environmental control skills involves attending to the child's subtle ways of responding to environmental stimuli and reinforcing behaviors that could potentially communicate needs or desires. For example, if an infant winces when a spoon of food is presented, the parent might withdraw the food saying, "Oh, you don't want any more of that right now," and give the child some milk instead. Responding to the infant's wince as a communication may eventually teach the child environmental control (in this case, how much or when he or she is fed) using specific facial expressions.

Behavioral Model

The behavioral curriculum model is an instructional techniques model based on the principles of behavioral psychology. Behaviorists such as B.F. Skinner, Sidney Bijou, and Donald Baer described human development and learning as resulting from environmental interactions in which individuals experience relationships among stimuli, actions, and the consequences of actions (reinforcement or punishment). As a curricular approach, interventionists or teachers may alter stimuli to be more noticeable or meaningful to a child (e.g., pointing to a stimulus), help a child make a correct response so the consequence can be experienced, or provide more individualized or powerful reinforcement to strengthen the consequence. These techniques are referred to as direct instruction and include strategies such as prompting, shaping, and reinforcing. Direct instruction is implemented in a precise and consistent fashion. Learning is monitored through frequent data collection, and instructional plans are modified based on evaluation of the data.

In the behavioral model, naturalistic components include goal selection and instructional techniques. Goal selection is referenced to environmental needs or expectations. One method to determine environmental needs is to ask parents, caregivers, and other family members to describe their routines, the child's participation in the routines, and what they would like the child to learn to be more fully included in the routines (Mullis, 2002; Wolery, 1996).

Instructional techniques in the behavioral model have shifted from teacher-focused direct instruction techniques to more naturalistic procedures. For example, instead of teaching a preschooler to use two-word phrases by looking at picture cards and describing them ("big truck"), two-word phrases are taught throughout the day in free play, snack time, circle time, and storytime when the child initiates speech. Naturalistic techniques include teaching skills in sequence with other skills as they would typically occur (Sailor & Guess, 1983), at the times when they are needed (Hart & Risley, 1968), using natural stimuli and consequences (Falvey, Brown, Lyon, Baumgart, & Schroeder, 1980), and with strategies that promote independent, child-initiated behaviors (Halle, 1982).

The naturalistic concern that newly acquired skills are generalized is addressed in the behavioral model by planning for generalization when skills are initially taught. Instructional procedures referred to as "general case" methods facilitate generalization by targeting a generalized skill (e.g., grasping small objects) rather than a discrete skill (e.g., grasping a raisin) as the objective and providing instruction in several situations in which the skill is needed (Horner & McDonald, 1982). For example, the toddler who has difficulty with finger feeding because of poor fine motor skills has the objective to improve grasping (not just finger feeding) and is taught to grasp many small objects of various weights and shapes throughout the day.

The developmental, developmental-cognitive, and behavioral models have each incorporated naturalistic strategies and perspectives (see Table 4.1 for a summary of the models and their naturalistic components). The boundaries that once differentiated these models are becoming blurred as each emphasizes naturalistic considerations. A monograph on recommended practices in early intervention/early childhood special education (Sandall, McLean, & Smith, 2000) promotes the following assessment and intervention practices that illustrate the growing emphasis on naturalistic curriculum procedures:

1. Professionals rely on [assessment] materials that capture the child's authentic behaviors in routine circumstances.

2. Professionals assess children in contexts that are familiar to the child.

3. Professionals assess not only immediate mastery of a skill, but also whether the child can demonstrate the skill consistently across other settings and with other people.

Table 4.1. Traditional curriculum models in early intervention and early childhood special education

Curriculum model	Curriculum type	Key features	Naturalistic components
Developmental	Content	Developmental skill sequences	Sequence of infant/child and caregiver interaction
Developmental-cognitive	Content and teaching techniques	Developmental skill sequences / Sequences of cognitive skill development	Sequences of social-cognitive development / Sequences of environmental control skills
Behavioral	Teaching techniques	Direct instruction	Skill sequencing / Incidental and milieu teaching techniques / Generalization strategies

4. A variety of appropriate settings and naturally occurring activities are used to facilitate children's learning and development.

5. Services are provided in natural learning environments as appropriate. These include places in which typical children participate, such as the home or community settings.

6. Environments are provided that foster positive relationships, including peer–peer, parent/caregiver–child, and parent–caregiver relationships.

7. Specialized procedures (e.g., naturalistic strategies and prompt/prompt fading strategies) are embedded and distributed within and across activities (pp. 24–25, 34–35, 37).

Assessment practices are considered part of the naturalistic curriculum model because they address the content of curriculum (intervention goals). In the naturalistic model, the child is assessed in natural environments engaged in activities that are typical of peers who do not have disabilities. This assessment strategy ensures that intervention goals represent skills that are relevant to the child and family and have an immediate usefulness. Furthermore, assessing under naturalistic conditions increases the likelihood that assessment results accurately reflect the child's abilities and needs. Similarly, intervention occurs in natural environments (as opposed to special settings serving only children with disabilities) in which the skills will actually be needed. Notice that natural environments address social situations as well as physical situations. The next section describes what might be termed a hybrid naturalistic model.

A NATURALISTIC MODEL

The major goal of the naturalistic curriculum model is to enhance the young child's environmental control, participation, and interaction in natural experiences consistent with the cultural values and expectations of the family. The naturalistic model is a process model of curriculum, with content derived through environmental assessment, and instruction using naturalistic behavioral techniques. Natural environments are the "sources and contexts" of intervention (Dunst, Hamby, Trivette, Raab, & Bruder, 2000, p. 151). This model is appropriate for all infants and children with disabilities, including those who have autism (Schwartz, Billingsley, & McBride, 1998; Strain, Wolery, & Izeman, 1998). The remainder of this chapter describes the major characteristics of the naturalistic curriculum model: content, context, methods, cultural relevance, and evaluation. Note that contextual and cultural considerations are embedded throughout the model.

Content of Instruction

In the naturalistic curriculum, goals for each child are developed on an individualized basis, reflecting the skill demands of natural, age-appropriate environments. The content "grows with the child" and is responsive to the requirements of the increasing number of environments that young children participate in as they get older. Chapter 5 describes the process of identifying these goals.

Age-Appropriate Skills Content that is age-appropriate features skills and activities typical of infants and children who do not have disabilities. The naturalistic model encourages participation and interaction across the full range of family routines and activities. Family routines and activities and age-related expectations for infants and young children will be influenced by the family's culture and values. For example, whether a caregiver immediately responds to an infant's crying is influenced by culture and child-rearing values. Similarly, expectations that toddlers "help out" during household chores (e.g., whether the child takes his or her dish to the sink) is heavily influenced by culture and family values. Therefore, the naturalistic curriculum model includes strategies to obtain family/caregiver information about family routines, activities, and expectations for their child's participation therein.

For neonates, the most important aspect of the environment is parent–infant interaction. Infants "control" their environment through behavior that affects the quality and quantity of incoming stimulation. This is one of the first ways infants learn to affect their environments.

The work of Brazelton has been particularly influential in understanding and designing interventions to promote infants' control of their environments (Als, Lester, & Brazelton, 1979; Brazelton, 1982). According to Brazelton, the newborn engages in a neurological and physiological system of interaction, disorganization, reorganization, and then a return to interaction. As infants attend to and interact with the environment, they eventually become overstimulated. This overstimulation causes neuromotor and physiological disorganization. When disorganization occurs, the infant may fuss and withdraw from the environment by looking away or falling asleep. Withdrawing from the environment allows the infant to reorganize neurologically and physiologically and reestablish homeostasis (internal stability) and energy/drive for subsequent environmental input when desired.

Parents usually learn to recognize their infant's signals and determine when their interactions are appropriate. They notice when the infant has received adequate stimulation and needs to rest. A successful parent–infant interaction is one in which there is mutual responsiveness, with the parent and infant each responding according to the signals of the other. For example, when the parent talks to the infant, the infant stops moving and stares at the parent. The parent pauses and talks again; the infant shows intent interest. The cycle is repeated several times. Finally the infant looks away. The parent recognizes this as a signal that the baby has tired and needs a rest from interaction, ceases the game, and rocks and cuddles the baby gently.

When an infant has a disability, however, his or her signals may not be easy to recognize or interpret. Infant specialists may observe the infant/caregiver dyad and provide feedback or reinforcement when the parent or caregiver shows sensitivity to the infant's behavior and effectively obtains, maintains, or terminates the infant's attention. In this way, parents learn to become responsive to their infant, and the infant learns age-appropriate social-interaction skills. The distinctive feature of Brazelton's (1982) approach to enhancing infant–caregiver interaction was to provide feedback and reinforcement when the caregiver demonstrates appropriate sensitivity or responsiveness to the infant's behavior. The interventionists never take the infant from the caregivers to demonstrate interaction skills. Instead, the interventionists promote parent competence and self-confidence by observing and reinforcing instances of appropriate responsiveness. Watching the caregiver's interaction style also allows interventionists to learn about cultural and interpersonal styles that are effective, although different from their own styles. Cripe and Venn (1997) extended this approach—building on effective strategies used by caregivers—to intervention with families who have toddler and preschool-age children.

As the infant gets older, there is increased interaction with the physical environment. The social environment expands beyond parents to include siblings, relatives, and family friends. The naturalistic curriculum will include a wider range of behaviors to accomplish environmental interaction and control, particularly social, cognitive, and communication skills. For example, the infant may demonstrate environmental control by crying when a sibling takes a toy away, which results in the parent retrieving the toy for the infant.

During the first year of life, the infant learns the turn-taking and signaling skills that form the basis of later social and communication interactions. Like sensorimotor behaviors in Piaget's model, social-cognitive skills develop in a progression leading to mental representation (thinking) and symbolic thought; that is, the ability to use words to represent thoughts and actions (Seibert, Hogan, & Mundy, 1982, 1987). When parents respond to an infant's vocalizations as a request to repeat a playful episode, they are teaching the infant that the vocalization is a communication signal: "Do it again." For example, the parent's pause after a playful episode, the infant's communicative signal, and the repetition of the play is a turn-taking routine, much like the turn taking involved in conversation.

During the toddler years, the child's play expands in sophistication, and he or she begins to show an interest in the play of other children. Toddlers participate increasingly in the routines of other family members, sometimes as play (e.g., sweeping with a toy broom as the father sweeps the kitchen floor), and sometimes as a contributing member of the family (e.g., carrying a dish to the table, taking a turn playing ball with a sibling). Much of a toddler's participation in routines and activities in the home involves daily living activities such as dressing or bathing. Initially, participation may be in the form of cooperation: lying still while having a diaper changed, or raising arms as a T-shirt is removed. Toddlers also begin to learn skills that will allow them to participate in preschool, many of which are group participation skills (following simple directions, sharing, attending to a task or speaker). And finally, during the preschool and kindergarten years, play, self-help, and school-related skills take on even greater importance. As in the case of social interaction routines, cultural and individual parent/caregiver preferences will influence family daily living routines and expectations for child participation.

The current emphasis in early childhood curriculum is a model referred to as *developmentally appropriate practices* (DAP) (Bredekamp & Copple, 1997). There are two components to DAP: age appropriateness and individualization. Early childhood programs that ascribe to developmentally appropriate practice emphasize a child-centered curriculum characterized by individual choice making and exploratory play, rather than a teacher-directed structured curriculum with a specific set of objectives identified for all children. The DAP model is based on the assumption that if children are allowed to explore their interests, their interests will guide them to choose and learn content that they are developmentally ready to learn.

Infants and children with severe disabilities, however, will not always be ready to learn the same activities as their age peers with mild or no disabilities. To support the integration of infants and young children with and without disabilities, however, curricular activities should be age appropriate, even when the activities do not correspond to readiness levels. The activities should serve as a context for instruction. Specific objectives, or the way in which children with disabilities participate in activities, are individualized to address unique needs. Allowing for different types and levels of participation in the early childhood curriculum is consistent with the basic tenets of DAP: curriculum should be age appropriate and individualized. For example, a preschool child with a disability selects a puzzle during morning free play and hands the pieces one at a time to a peer who puts the puzzle together. She has chosen an age-appropriate activity that is also of interest to her friend who does not have a disability. Although not able to assemble the puzzle, she is able to select puzzle pieces and to play cooperatively with a peer. Chapters 12 and 13 provide numerous strategies and examples for promoting peer interaction and independence in age-appropriate activities and integrated settings.

The age-appropriate content of the naturalistic curriculum model includes the skills needed by the young child to participate in natural social and physical environments. Each family's social and physical environments are unique and influenced by culture, individual preferences, and interpersonal styles. Environments expand as the infant grows and develops, and the content of the naturalistic curriculum model expands accordingly to address the increasing range of behaviors needed for control, participation, and interaction. When a discrepancy exists between age-appropriate and readiness levels, adapt the age-appropriate content to the child's abilities and needs.

Skills for Participating in Present and Future Environments   The naturalistic curriculum model selects curricular content by identifying and analyzing the routines and activities of natural environments. There are a number of ways to approach the identification and analysis of routines and activities. One method is to interview parents or caregivers, asking them to describe their daily routines and activities and the infant's or child's present participation in these routines and activities. Potential goals and objectives are formulated as each routine and activity is discussed (Cripe & Venn, 1997; McWilliam, 1992). The routines and activities identified in this ecological assessment will reflect the child's capabilities, interests, and temperament. For example, a child recovering from a hospital stay may play for short periods of time and only with one or two other children to avoid roughhousing. In contrast, another child may enjoy roughhousing and show the greatest amount of participation with large groups of children.

The uniqueness of each family is reflected in an ecological assessment of the home. Routines and activities will vary from one family to another depending on factors such as family members present in the home, work and/or school responsibilities, social/recreational interests and preferences, and interpersonal needs and strengths. Culture will be reflected in the family's lifestyle, and will likewise be reflected in the daily routines and activities from which curricular content is derived. For example, culture might influence family member roles (who does which chores), arrangements for mealtimes and sleeping, and the extent and nature of participation in social or religious activities.

Another ecological assessment strategy focused on skills needed in future environments is the survival skills model. Survival skills are behaviors that early childhood educators expect or require of children in child care, preschool, or kindergarten settings (McCormick & Kawate, 1982; Murphy & Vincent, 1989; Noonan et al., 1992; Vincent et al., 1980). These lists of essential skills were derived from surveys of preschool and kindergarten teachers. Survival skill assessments and instructional approaches are discussed in Chapter 14.

The naturalistic model may include early intervention goals derived from the developmental and developmental-cognitive models. In these models, intervention goals are identified by comparing the child's skills to sequences describing typical development: Instruction begins with the skill that the child fails to demonstrate in the sequence of a developmental assessment. Developmental assessment usually includes social, communication, daily living, fine motor, gross motor, feeding, and cognitive skill sequences.

Developmental goals are included in early childhood assessment and curriculum development if they serve as appropriate evaluation measures that result in meaningful, age-appropriate objectives. These conditions would conceivably be met in providing services to children who are at risk or who have mild delays/disabilities, the majority of children served in most early intervention programs. Developmental assessments may not be appropriate as evaluation measures or curriculum assessments for children with severe or multiple disabilities because changes in performance often will not involve the achievement of milestones, nor are developmental sequences necessarily the most efficient sequences for instruction (Baer, 1970). Instead, skill adaptations may be more practical goals for achieving age-appropriate and functional skills for these children.

Context for Instruction

Context is a characteristic of the naturalistic model that differentiates it from other early intervention curriculum models. The naturalistic model focuses on natural experiences (social and nonsocial learning opportunities) for determining the content of instruction, selecting and implementing the instructional methods, and evaluating child progress. Instruction is conducted as "situated learning" (Dunst et al., 2000), occurring in the context of family-guided routines (Cripe & Venn, 1997). As an example of the importance of typical experiences in the naturalistic curriculum model, consider a 2-year-old named Missy who attends a community playgroup once a week. The playgroup usually consists of five 2- to 3-year-olds who participate together in a song time, a physical development activity, and a snack. Missy plays with the other children and follows the simple rules of the activities, such as passing toys and taking turns. Observations in the home and reports from the family, however, indicate that Missy is usually on the sidelines watching as her two sisters (ages 4 and 5) play. Missy's parents would like her to play with her sisters. Note that home experiences provide very different information than the playgroup regarding Missy's social and play skills. An instructional plan is designed to reflect the characteristics of the home environment. Given that the home environment includes Missy's 4- and 5-year-old siblings, the instructional plan is directed at the play behavior of the siblings as well as Missy. Missy's sisters are taught to invite Missy to play with them and are shown various ways that Missy can join in, even when she doesn't know how to play their games, and Missy is taught to crawl close to her sisters when she wants to play with them. The success of instruction is evaluated in the home, during after-school hours, and on the weekends when the sisters typically play together. In all phases of this instruction—goal selection, instruction, and evaluation—the context has a significant influence.

For newborns, the most important environment is their home, the environment in which most of their social experiences occur. As the infant develops beyond the first few months of life, the social interaction context of the family expands and begins to include the extended family and friends. In addition, the infant increasingly attends to environmental stimuli, including objects. In the toddler and preschool years, the physical environment broadens to include settings outside the home, such as the neighborhood, playgrounds, parks, and shopping centers. Toddlers and preschoolers interact extensively with objects in their environment and are becoming more and more independent in their interactions. Their social spheres now include peers, as well as neighbors and family members.

At all ages, culture, individual lifestyles, and family preferences will influence the proportion and amount of time the child spends in various environments. For example, some families may have a large extended family that provides child care as needed. They may choose not to enroll their child in preschool. Weekend social activities may primarily be family gatherings and church activities. In contrast, other families may not live near their extended families, and thus may rely on community child care programs and in-home babysitting services. They may have smaller social networks comprised of a few friends and/or work colleagues. They may regularly participate in their community's weekend family events, such as children's activities at the museum and recreation center sports.

The context for instruction in the naturalistic curriculum model is natural experiences. Natural experiences are the source of curricular content, as well as the instructional environments. The number and variety of natural experiences expand as infants and young children grow and at all times include an array of experiences that are unique to each family.

Instructional Methods

The naturalistic model uses instructional methods that are minimally intrusive; that is, instruction that appears similar to naturally occurring events. In addition, there must be a "goodness of fit" between the instructional methods and the child's temperament. Temperament refers to a personal behavioral style that includes the dimensions of activity level, intensity, mood, persistence, and reaction to new experiences. Its greatest influence is not on what a child does, but how he or she does it (Pelco & Reed-Victor, 2003). A concern for temperament means that teachers must pay close attention to a child's response to instructional methods. For example, if a child "resists" the instructional prompt of physical guidance, the teacher should try other types of prompts (e.g., a model).

Instructional Procedures for Newborns and Infants   During the neonatal period, while curricular content focuses on parent–infant interaction, the primary instructional procedure is Brazelton's approach (described earlier in this chapter) to observe parent–infant interaction and provide positive and descriptive feedback when the parent is responsive to the infant's signals (Als et al., 1979; Brazelton, 1982). For infants beyond the first few months, a number of early interventionists suggest instructional techniques similar to Brazelton's, but focused on a larger repertoire of interactions, compatible with broadening social experiences (Dunst et al., 1987; McCollum & Stayton, 1985). For example, to assist the infant in gaining control over the environment and to teach parents to be more effective in promoting social interactions, Dunst and colleagues (1987) recommend the following interaction approaches:

1. Being sensitive to the child's behavior
2. Reading the child's behavior as intents to interact
3. Responding to the child's initiations
4. Encouraging ongoing initiations
5. Supporting and encouraging competence

These interaction approaches can be implemented through guided learning, violations of expectations, introduction to novelty (Dunst, 1981), and incidental tcaching (Hart & Risley, 1968). Note that families of some cultural backgrounds may not view parent–infant interaction as a priority (Chen & McCollum, 2001).

In *guided learning*, play or instructional situations are carefully arranged so that they attract the infant's attention, appear highly motivating, and are at a level of difficulty that is optimally challenging. An example of guided learning is to present a 10-month-old girl who explores objects by banging them with a variety of objects (e.g., wooden spoon, metal spoon, whisk broom) and a variety of surfaces for banging (e.g., an aluminum cookie sheet, wicker basket, or magazine). The situation is enticing to the infant because she enjoys banging objects, and the availability of several objects and surfaces is challenging. The environmental arrangement of the task guides learning. It also reflects sensitivity to the infant's present level of performance, encourages her to participate in the activity without adult instruction, and supports and encourages competence.

The procedure of *violating expectations* requires that a predictable and repetitive play sequence be established. The sequence is then altered without warning. Violations of expectations surprise the infant, often increasing the infant's attention and curiosity (motivation) and stimulating a communicative response (a quizzical look at the adult, a vocalization, or a laugh), as if to say, "What happened?" An adult who covers and uncovers her smiling face repeatedly with a cloth in a game of Peekaboo violates the infant's expectations if she uncovers her face and is suddenly not smiling or has her eyes closed. The infant will usually respond to such a violation with a communicative response, and the adult should respond to any communication by the infant as a request to reestablish the expected sequence.

Using novelty is a minimally intrusive technique that can motivate exploratory behavior. For example, rather than place all the infant's toys around her, give her only one or two toys a day. Change the toys from day to day and they will encourage play because they seem more interesting. This technique encourages infant-initiated behaviors.

Enhanced milieu teaching (EMT) refers to a group of instructional techniques in which a predetermined child behavior is used to identify occasions for instruction. For example, when an infant reaches for a toy that is out of reach (the predetermined behavior), instruction is conducted to encourage more developmentally sophisticated behavior (the desired response is modeled or prompted, "Tell me what you want"). EMT is a strategy that responds to the infant's behavior as an intent to interact, and thus may shape social interaction behaviors. EMT is discussed at length in Chapter 9.

Instructional Procedures for 2- Through 6-Year-Olds   EMT methods are important instructional procedures for 2- through 6-year-olds. They are highly effective for promoting independent and child-initiated behaviors. Systematic teaching procedures that involve more controlled and adult-directed instruction are also included in the naturalistic curriculum model but with specific techniques to facilitate generalization. For example, the general case instructional procedure (Horner & McDonald, 1982) is teacher-directed and more tightly structured than incidental teaching, but it is effective in promoting generalization.

General case instruction uses two strategies: objectives are described as generalized skills rather than discrete skills ("child will grasp raisins or small candies, T-shirt bottom, and cup" rather than "child will grasp raisins"), and generalized skills are taught across a variety of situations with a variety of materials (e.g., at breakfast, when getting dressed in the morning, after recess). In selecting situations or materials, choose those that represent the range of characteristics of situations or materials to which the skill is intended to generalize. Both of these techniques are a part of general case instruction.

Instructional procedures within the naturalistic model emphasize instruction that is as subtle as possible (while still being effective); promotes generalization; and fits into the natural settings, routines, and activities of the child and the family. The more naturalistic the instruction, the greater the likelihood that new skills learned will be generalized and used in the natural situations in which they are needed.

Cultural Relevance

Research has shown that culture influences learning, largely through its effect on learning styles and interpersonal communication (Tharp, 1989). In the naturalistic curriculum model, a number of psychocultural variables are embedded so that instruction is responsive to the child's learning and communication style. These variables include, but are not limited to

- Instructional arrangements (individual work, group work, oral presentation, and so forth)
- Teaching procedures (connection to children's experiences, pace of instruction, and so forth)
- Communication style (eye contact, direct prompting, questioning, calling on children, and so forth)
- Reinforcement strategies (public acknowledgement, type of reward, and so forth)
- Performance expectations (remaining seated, oral response, voluntary response, and so forth)

Although these variables may have a profound impact on learning, individuals are not usually cognizant of them. Thus, a child's parents or caregivers probably cannot inform you of their child's learning style and communication preferences. The teacher will need to observe family interactions with the child who has a disability, as well as with other members of the family, for evidence of learning style and communication preferences. Once identified, these may be included in the instructional plan. For example, parents may wait for what seems to be an extended period of time for children to respond to a direct question. Lengthy "wait time" has been found to be characteristic of many Native

Americans (Yamauchi & Tharp, 1995). Failure to incorporate long wait times in instructional plans may result in ineffective teaching. For young children, this may mean a slower pace for typical give-and-take games between parents and children. Chapter 7 describes strategies for addressing cultural relevance throughout instruction.

Evaluation Methods

The primary focus of evaluation in the naturalistic curriculum model is generalized outcomes in natural settings. Generalization is promoted through general case instruction (described in Chapter 6) and assessed in settings that are similar to the instructional settings but in which instruction has not occurred. For example, a 4-year-old is taught to ask for a turn at play rather than take objects from his sister and the children next door. Generalization is assessed in natural noninstructional settings, including the child care program and the park on Saturdays. The assessment is conducted under naturalistic conditions in which the skill is expected, rather than in clinical or contrived settings typical of traditional assessments. Chapters 5 and 6 review strategies for evaluating children's instructional progress.

IMPLEMENTING A NATURALISTIC CURRICULUM

The following seven steps provide a guide to implementing a naturalistic curriculum. The following steps include descriptions of how content and strategies from the traditional models and related services can be included with the naturalistic curriculum approach.

Step 1: *Conduct child-centered planning.* As described at length in Chapter 5, the first task in the naturalistic curriculum model is to get to know the child and the family. Child-centered planning (Mount, 1994; Vandercook et al., 1989) is an opportunity for the early intervention/early childhood special education team to discuss who the child is and a positive vision for the child's future. The purposes of child-centered planning are to:

- Identify the current and potential resources and natural supports in the child's home and school environments

- Ensure that key people in the child's life are fully aware of the child's strengths

- Develop a common vision for the child's participation in natural environments (McCormick, 2003b, p. 245)

Although it is important to learn about the child's needs and family concerns, person-centered planning emphasizes the positive: family and community resources and supports, the child's talents and strengths, and positive dreams and visions for the child's future. The intention is to direct intervention efforts at making these plans and dreams a reality, rather than try to "fix" the child's disability.

Step 2: *Conduct ecological assessment.* Referring to the vision and the child's ideal day discussed in Step 1, the team now lists the routines and activities that will comprise the child's day. Some routines and activities will already have been established in the home and/or classroom, and some will be new, having been generated from the person-centered planning discussion. The child's participation in these routines and activities will be assessed to determine his or her current skill levels and instructional needs. Detailed procedures on conducting ecological assessment are provided in Chapter 5.

Step 3: *Develop instructional objectives.* Information obtained from the ecological assessment is used to formulate instructional objectives. One or more objectives may be written for each routine or activity, dependent on the child's performance in the activity and the team's judgment of the relative importance of addressing the noted discrepancies. For example, the child may demonstrate a skill need (e.g., responding to a peer or adult's question) that has applicability across many activities throughout the day. Instructional objectives in the naturalistic model have the following characteristics:

- Instructional objectives support participation in naturally occurring routines and activities.
- The context(s) for instruction is specified.
- Instructional objectives address generalized skills.
- A functional criterion is included.

The following objective illustrates these four characteristics:

> Given a small spoon with a built-up handle at snack and lunch at preschool and dinner at home (naturally occurring routines, generalized across settings and adults), Juanita will grasp the spoon and scoop thick pureed or sticky foods such as mashed potatoes, pureed vegetables, or pudding (generalized across food types) and raise the spoon to her mouth with half or more of the food remaining on the spoon, maintaining a grasp until she has the food in her mouth (functional criteria) for five of six scoops, for five consecutive meals.

A comprehensive discussion of developing instructional objectives for IFSPs and IEPs is included in Chapter 3.

Step 4: *Develop instructional plans.* Individualized instructional plans are formulated for each objective. In addition to identifying information such as date, name of child, and objective, all instructional plans should include six components (see Figure 4.1):

- *Contexts or occasions for instruction:* When and in what situations will the instructional plan be implemented? Who will provide the instruction?

General Case Intervention Plan

Child: Fia Corrado   **Interventionist(s):** Lani Smith, Mom, Dad, & Kimo   **Date:** 2/04/05

Objective: When Fia wakes up in the morning or after a nap, she will vocalize any sound(s), such that the sounds are audible outside the room where she has been sleeping on 8 of 12 consecutive opportunities.

Contexts/occasions for intervention:	Child response:	Consequences for correct response:
When you notice that Fia is awake, in the morning, after a nap, at home, or preschool	Fia will vocalize any sounds, such that they are audible outside the room where she has been sleeping.	Pick Fia up immediately and say, "Oh you are ready to get up now!" and carry her out of the room.
Physical positioning and/or materials: On her right side, with one pillow between her knees and one under her head; with her left knee and hip flexed		
Intervention techniques: 1. Approach Fia and talk to her until she vocalizes, or for 3 minutes (do for 5 days). 2. Enter the room so Fia can see you, wait 6 seconds before talking to her. After 6 anticipated correct responses (within the 6-second delay), move to step 3. 3. Wait outside the room for 10 seconds.	**Task analysis (if applicable):** n/a	**Consequences for incorrect or no response:** Approach Fia and say: "Are you ready to get up?" Wait 6 seconds. If she vocalizes, respond as you would for a correct response. If she doesn't, leave the room for 6 seconds. If she vocalizes within that time, enter the room and respond as you would for a correct response. If she doesn't vocalize, pick her up and try again next time.

Figure 4.1. Instructional plan format.

- *Physical positioning or materials arrangement:* Does the child require any special positioning to demonstrate the skill objective? How or where are the materials presented? Are any specialized materials needed?
- *Instructional techniques:* What techniques will be used to teach the skill and increase the likelihood of the child demonstrating the skill correctly? What logical antecedents (Pretti-Frontczak & Bricker, 2004) will be provided to motivate and assist the child to make the correct response?
- *Child's response:* In operational terms, what is the specific response expected? Will any approximations or variations of the skill be accepted as correct?
- *Consequences for correct response:* How will the child be reinforced for a correct response? Is the natural reinforcer obvious, or can it be made more obvious? Will any additional instruction be provided if the child responds correctly?

- *Corrections for incorrect response:* What instructional techniques will be implemented if the child does not respond or makes an incorrect response? If the child makes a correct response following the correction procedure, is reinforcement provided?

Because most instruction will be implemented across more than one situation, and because objectives are developed as general case objectives, instructional plans are written as general case plans (Horner, Sprague, & Wilcox, 1982). Chapter 6 focuses on the development of instructional plans and provides detailed descriptions of each of these instructional components.

It is also necessary to develop data collection systems to monitor the effectiveness of instruction. As noted in Chapter 5, the type of data collected must correspond to the criterion level specified in the goal. For example, if the child must share materials at least three times during three consecutive play sessions, the number of times (or frequency) the child gives materials to a peer must be recorded. Data are graphed so that progress may be monitored. If progress does not occur, or occurs too slowly, the instructional plan should be modified. Chapter 5 provides a complete discussion of measurement, data collection, and evaluation methods.

Step 5: *Prepare an instructional schedule.* Once instructional objectives and plans have been developed, instructional opportunities must be identified and scheduled. A scheduling matrix (see Figure 4.2) is useful for creating an individualized schedule. The first step in filling out the matrix is to complete the left column by listing a daily schedule of activities. If the child is enrolled in a center-based or home-based infant program that meets one or two hours per week, two matrices may be developed—one for the infant program and one for days when the infant does not receive services from the infant program. If the child attends child care or preschool, the daily program schedule is listed as it occurs during the child's daily schedule.

The second step is to list the child's instructional objectives across the top of the matrix. In the third step, the box under each instructional objective corresponding to its associated activity is checked to indicate that the objective will be taught during that time. The team reviews the entire daily schedule to determine if other activities might also be appropriate times for instruction. If so, the corresponding box is also checked. For example, if a toddler has a goal to share during playtime with neighborhood peers, the box under the *sharing* objective and next to the *playtime with neighborhood peers* activity is checked. The team also checks the box next to the *free-time* activity during morning preschool and *playtime with siblings* in the late afternoons.

If it is not possible to address all instructional objectives as often as desired, the team (including the family) should establish priorities and decide which objectives will receive the most attention. If there are not enough natural opportunities for addressing some of the instructional objectives, it may be necessary to create naturalistic occasions. For example, a preschool child

Scheduling Matrix

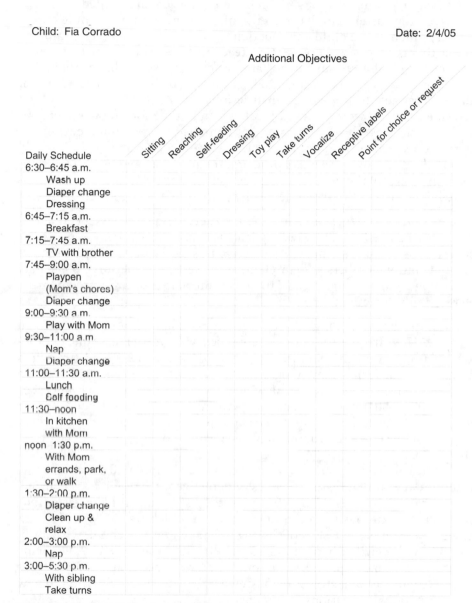

Child: Fia Corrado   Date: 2/4/05

Additional Objectives

Daily Schedule	Sitting	Reaching	Self-feeding	Dressing	Toy play	Take turns	Vocalize	Receptive labels	Point for choice or request
6:30–6:45 a.m.									
Wash up									
Diaper change									
Dressing									
6:45–7:15 a.m.									
Breakfast									
7:15–7:45 a.m.									
TV with brother									
7:45–9:00 a.m.									
Playpen									
(Mom's chores)									
Diaper change									
9:00–9:30 a.m.									
Play with Mom									
9:30–11:00 a.m.									
Nap									
Diaper change									
11:00–11:30 a.m.									
Lunch									
Self feeding									
11:30–noon									
In kitchen									
with Mom									
noon 1:30 p.m.									
With Mom									
errands, park,									
or walk									
1:30–2:00 p.m.									
Diaper change									
Clean up &									
relax									
2:00–3:00 p.m.									
Nap									
3:00–5:30 p.m.									
With sibling									
Take turns									

Figure 4.2. An example of a scheduling matrix.

may receive instruction on changing her T-shirt after naptime if more instructional opportunities to work on her dressing goal are needed.

Given the current emphasis on teaching during natural learning opportunities, much of the child's instruction may occur at home. The implication of this is that early intervention teachers must shift their focus from
teaching the children to supporting families/caregivers to enhance their children's learning (Jung, 2003; Mullis, 2002). Family/caregivers must decide when
they are best able to implement instructional plans. A family may feel too
pressed for time to work on a self-feeding plan in the morning while preparing for work and school, but may feel comfortable in implementing the
instruction at the evening meal and at lunchtime on weekends. If the child
attends child care or a preschool program, the instructional needs (and individual matrices) of the other children, as well as staffing ratios, must be considered in finalizing the schedule for the entire group of children.

Step 6: *Implement instruction.* After the instructional plans have been developed and scheduled, teaching begins. Instructional plans are implemented as
accurately as possible so that their effectiveness can be determined. Program
staff and family members who implement the same instructional plans may
observe one another periodically to be certain that they are implementing
the plans in the same manner.

Step 7: *Monitor progress.* Progress on instructional plans should be monitored
regularly. How frequently data are collected will vary. For some instructional plans, very precise data will be collected by the infant specialist when
the baby attends the infant program once a week. The family may keep
simple data (a checklist) indicating which days they were able to implement
the instruction and whether the child performed the skill independently or
with help. If the child attends a preschool program, data may be collected
daily on high-priority instructional plans; lower priority goals may be monitored less frequently.

Because most instructional objectives will be formulated as general case
objectives, it is also necessary to assess whether generalization has occurred.
Generalization is assessed by observing the infant or child in situations
in which the skill has not been taught, but in which its use would be expected. For example, the skill of sharing was taught at preschool, with a sibling, and with neighborhood peers. Generalization is assessed by observing
the child at a family picnic with cousins or with peers at a baby sitter's
home. Generalized objectives are mastered only when generalization to new
(noninstructional) situations is demonstrated.

The more frequently data are collected, the more accurately progress
can be monitored. When enough data have been collected and graphed to
create a fairly clear picture of performance (usually five or six data points),
the data are reviewed and a decision is made whether to continue the plan
as is or to change it. If progress is not as expected, only one part of the instructional plan is modified so that the effectiveness of the change can be

evaluated (again, after five or six data points are collected). Frequent progress monitoring will result in a dynamic instructional plan that is responsive to individual differences and changing needs.

These seven steps yield an individualized curriculum that is based on the unique ecology of an infant or child and family beginning with the assessment process and continuing through the development, implementation, and ongoing evaluation of instructional plans. As noted previously, Chapter 5 describes the development and monitoring of instructional plans in detail.

The naturalistic curriculum model draws on the naturalistic trends of the developmental, developmental cognitive, and behavioral curriculum models. It respects the unique culture, preferences, and lifestyle of each family by promoting increased participation and interaction in natural environments, including the home, neighborhood, child care, and school environments. Goals are derived through ecological assessment procedures and address skill needs associated with age-appropriate activities as well as social interaction with parents, siblings, and other significant individuals. Once goals are established, instructional plans are developed using systematic teaching procedures. The child's progress is then monitored through frequent data collection to ensure program effectiveness. When progress is not as expected, instructional plans are modified accordingly.

SUMMARY

This chapter has described the naturalistic curriculum model for infants and young children. The intent of the model is to develop individualized intervention plans that address the unique needs of children in their home, school, and community environments. Subsequent chapters provide more detail on conducting assessment and intervention procedures in naturalistic settings (Chapters 5 and 6, respectively) and specialized intervention procedures that address particular instructional needs such as adaptations for physical disabilities, strategies for behavioral challenges, and approaches to promote independence and social interaction (Chapters 7 through 14).

••••••••••••••••••••• STUDY QUESTIONS •••••••••••••••••••••

1. Identify and describe the three traditional curriculum models associated with early intervention and early childhood special education.

2. Discuss the naturalistic trends associated with each traditional curriculum model.

3. What is the goal of the naturalistic curriculum model?

4. What is the content of the naturalistic curriculum model? Describe at least two strategies for developing goals in the naturalistic curriculum model.

5. Explain the following statement: *In the naturalistic curriculum model, age appropriate activities are the context for instruction.*

6. Describe *naturalistic environments* that a 1-year-old, 2-year-old, 3-year-old, and 5-year-old might experience. How might the experiences and needs of a child in naturalistic environments vary from age 1 to age 5?

7. Discuss what it means to use *minimally intrusive* teaching procedures.

8. Discuss the focus of a naturalistic curriculum for an infant from 1 month to 5 months of age?

9. Identify and briefly define two instructional approaches in the naturalistic curriculum model that are appropriate for 2- through 5-year-olds.

10. Discuss how teaching in natural settings promotes generalization.

11. List and briefly describe the seven steps in implementing the naturalistic curriculum model.

5

Planning and Evaluation/Monitoring

Linda McCormick

•••••••••••••••••••••• **FOCUS OF THIS CHAPTER** ••••••••••••••••••••

- Structure for assessment, planning, and evaluation/monitoring
- Child-centered planning procedures
- Ecological theory
- Ecological assessment procedures
- Portfolio assessment procedures

To benefit from experiences in an inclusive setting, the young child with disabilities needs direct, systematic, and individualized instruction. This instruction should be embedded in the child's daily schedule. Broadly speaking, it should focus on teaching the child 1) to participate in the range of age-appropriate activities and routines in the setting (e.g., moving about the room, making choices about activities and materials, playing alone and with peers, responding to peer and adult initiations, participating in conversations) and 2) to accomplish the developmental skills identified in the child's individualized education program (IEP) (e.g., requesting desired objects, using plurals, producing three-word phrases, asking and answering questions, recognizing and naming shapes and colors).

Careful planning is essential and should address the following questions:

1. *What does this child need to learn to be as independent as possible and participate with peers in daily routines and activities in the setting?* Goals and objectives will depend on the child *and* the expectations of adults in the environment. The focus is on identifying behaviors that will have immediate usefulness and benefits for the child in the present setting and in future environments (e.g., kindergarten).

2. *How should we teach this child?* The most commonly used specialized instructional procedures are naturalistic approaches such as milieu teaching, activity-based intervention, embedded and distributed trials, and high-probability procedures. These procedures incorporate environmental arrangement, adaptations, and prompts and prompt-fading procedures. Specialized instruction may also involve assistive equipment or technology, peer-mediated strategies, and systematic instruction.

3. *Who should teach this child and when and where should the child be taught?* Naturalistic instructional approaches intersperse brief instructional trials throughout the day in age-appropriate activities and routines. Decisions need to be made as to who will be responsible for implementing the special instruction at the specified points throughout the day.

4. *How do we know what (or if) the child has learned?* The only way to ensure that teaching has been effective is to collect data on the child's behavior during and after instruction.

The procedures described in this chapter—child-centered planning, ecological assessment/planning, and portfolio assessment—address the first question (how to decide *what* to teach), the third question (*who* should teach and *where* and *when*), and the fourth question (has the teaching been effective). Specialized instructional procedures and strategies to address the second question (*how* to teach) are described in detail in subsequent chapters.

To place these procedures into the bigger picture, recall from Chapter 3 that there are four purposes of assessment: screening, diagnosis and eligibility determination, intervention planning, and monitoring and evaluation. Child-centered planning and ecological assessment/planning are intervention-planning procedures. Portfolio assessment is a monitoring/evaluation procedure. Chapter 3 also emphasizes the importance of considering *functionality* and *age appropriateness* in planning for young children with severe disabilities. Functionality and age appropriateness are inherent in all three of the planning and evaluation procedures described in this chapter.

Child-centered planning is a procedure for gathering information from the family and others who have an interest in the child. It can be incorporated into any assessment approach. The goals and ideas that are generated by this procedure expand and supplement information collected through objective measures of behavior (e.g., standardized and criterion-referenced tests). *Ecological assessment* is a process for generating goals and objectives, identifying instructional strategies, and devising methods for data collection. As noted in Chapter 3, it is an example of an embedded assessment model, one of three categories of alternative assessment approaches (Losardo & Notari-Syverson, 2001). Assessments in this category are referred to as *embedded approaches* because they include observations of children's behavior in natural contexts (with different persons, using different materials, and in multiple environments). *Matrix planning,* sometimes called activity-based planning or routine-based planning, is closely linked to ecological assessment. Using a matrix-planning format ensures that objectives are taught in the context of daily routines and activities. Finally, *portfolio assessment* is a process for documenting and evaluating children's progress relative to the skills targeted by the ecological assessment process or by IEP goals and objectives. Specifically, portfolios provide evidence of whether and why instruction is working (or not working). Portfolio assessment is an example of authentic assessment, another one of the three categories of alternative assessment approaches.

CHILD-CENTERED PLANNING

Child-centered planning is a way for people close to the child to share their understanding and visions for the child. It can be incorporated as part of the ecological assessment process or any other assessment procedure. Reasons for incorporating child-centered planning as part of assessment are 1) to learn the things about the child that only those who love him or her and have an investment in the child's future can articulate (the immediate and extended family, peers of the child with disabilities [when appropriate], friends and neighbors of the family, related services providers, community preschool staff, early intervention staff, and special education personnel) and 2) to generate a *social validity* assessment that can be used to evaluate the outcomes of the assessment and planning processes.

Social Validity

Ideas about social validity originally grew from concerns about the appropriate selection of intervention targets in applied behavior analysis. As defined in the applied behavior analysis literature, social validity is the degree to which the impacts and/or effects of behavior-change efforts are what the "consumer" values (Kazdin, 1977; Schwartz & Baer, 1991; Wolf, 1978). In early intervention, of course, the family is the consumer of services, so it is the degree to which the goals and objectives and intervention are desired and valued by the family and other significant persons in the child's world that are the first consideration.

Child-centered planning provides an opportunity for the family and others who have a deep commitment to the child to contribute to the assessment and planning processes, *in addition to* their participation in the more formal assessment process that uses traditional testing instruments. The social validity question is: *Are the outcomes of the assessment and planning processes (goals and objectives, intervention procedures) what the family and other significant adults in the child's life want for the child?* The outcome of the child-centered planning process is a vision that serves as a social validity standard for all goals and objectives, intervention plans, and evaluation for the child.

Planning Session

The first step in child-centered planning is to bring together as many people in the child's life as possible to formulate a picture of the child's strengths and gifts and the people's dreams for his or her future. This planning session may last anywhere from one to three hours. (Sometimes, an additional session is necessary.) The facilitator (usually the teacher or another service provider) asks the following questions to draw out the participants' thoughts and feelings:

- What is *child's name* history?
- What are *child's name* strengths and gifts?
- What are *child's name* needs?
- What is your fondest dream for *child's name* future?
- In your opinion, what would an ideal day be like for *child's name*?
- What is your worst nightmare where *child's name* is concerned?

Following are directions for a child-centered planning session. Have a flip chart on an easel, a chalkboard, or large sheets of chart paper mounted on a wall for recording responses to the different questions. Designate a separate paper or section of the chalkboard for each question. The facilitator continues to record responses until all the participants have had a chance to express their thoughts. Sometime after the meeting, transfer the information from the chart paper or the chalkboard to regular-size paper and distribute it to the participants for their comments and additions. Finally, condense all of the input into a vision that will become part of the child's file (and his or her portfolio, if the teacher uses portfolio assessment). Table 5.1 shows the shared vision for a 3-year-old with severe disabilities that was developed through the child-centered planning process. This is exactly as the statements were recorded in the planning session.

The shared vision for the child's future that comes out of the child-centered planning process provides a standard against which to judge the outcomes (social

Table 5.1. Child-centered planning vision for Kaitlin

Kaitlin will
- Continue to be happy and healthy
- Move on her own
- Play with toys and enjoy games with her brother
- Enjoy being read to
- Feed herself
- Express her wants and needs so that anyone can understand
- Walk with a walker
- Sit up without assistance
- Have friends
- Always be in class with peers who do not have disabilities

validity) of the ecological assessment and planning processes. The goals and objectives and the intervention are socially valid if they are in line with what the family and others who participated in the planning process view as important.

ECOLOGICAL ASSESSMENT

Ecological theory has roots in anthropology. When noted anthropologist Ruth Benedict published her ideas about the relationship between humans and their social-cultural environment in 1934, she used the term *cultural relativity* to describe the notion that human behavior cannot be properly understood unless it is interpreted within a larger cultural context. Simply stated, a behavior that is appropriate in one cultural context (e.g., separate sleeping arrangements for infants and young children) may be regarded as inappropriate in another. Ecology, now a branch of biology, studies the relationship between living organisms and their physical environment.

Many decades after Benedict's work, psychologists introduced ecological principles into the domain of psychology with studies of the effects of the physical environment on people's social behavior, and, vice versa, the effects of social behavior on the physical environment (Barker, 1968; Barker & Gump, 1964; Bronfenbrenner, 1977, 1979; Wicker, 1979). These ecological psychologists insisted that the only way to get a valid picture of a child's functioning is by observing the child's behavior in the context of normally occurring routines in familiar settings.

Bronfenbrenner, probably the best known of the ecological psychologists, described the child as embedded in a series of interrelated systems that interact with one another *and with the child* to influence development. These nested systems both affect *and* are affected by the developing child. He labels the system closest to the child in the immediate environment as the *microsystem* (the family, child care settings, school). The microsystem is embedded within three more distal systems: the *mesosystem*, the *exosystem*, and the *macrosystem*. The child does not participate directly in these distal systems, but events that occur in them can indirectly influence the child (e.g., the parent's worksite).

The macrosystem, the furthest removed and most inclusive of the systems, is the social-cultural context (cultural beliefs, social structures).

Assessment based on ecological theory was first applied to developing goals and objectives for adolescents with severe and multiple disabilities by Brown and colleagues (1979) in the late 1970s. It is now widely used with children of all ages and types of disabilities and in many environments, including inclusive preschools and family child care settings (Edmiaston, Dolezal, Doolittle, Erickson, & Merritt, 2000; Grisham-Brown & Hemmeter, 1998; Haney & Cavallaro, 1996; McCormick & Noonan, 1996, 2002).

Ecological assessment is used to 1) identify IFSP or IEP goals and objectives and/or 2) to determine and plan for adaptations and supports and how goals and objectives will be embedded into daily activities and routines (if IFSP or IEP goals and objectives have already been developed from another source). The ecological assessment process is basically the same, regardless of the setting. It may be implemented in a classroom setting, a home, a child care setting, or a community setting (e.g., playground stores) before or immediately after the child with disabilities is placed in the setting.

This chapter describes implementation of ecological assessment in an inclusive early childhood program—ideally a program based on the developmentally appropriate practices (DAP) model advocated by the National Association for the Education of Young Children (NAEYC). With this model, daily activities and routines are chosen to reflect what children are interested in and enjoy, and the curriculum is sensitive to children's cultural values, beliefs, and styles and the range of developmental levels represented in the class. In programs based on the DAP model, the teachers mediate the understandings that children construct from their interactions with the environment in a way that advances their learning and development. The broad goals for *all* children are 1) to actively initiate and engage in interactions with their social and the physical environments; 2) to learn to make choices; 3) to develop social relationships; and 4) to feel independent, safe, secure, competent, and accepted.

Assessment Process

Figure 5.1 shows a completed ecological assessment form for Jace, a 3-year-old with Down syndrome. Jace is in his first week in a community preschool program. (This example includes only the first two pages of a four-page completed form.) The following are the steps that the team followed in the assessment process (McCormick & Noonan, 2002):

Step 1: *List the daily activities and routines.* In the first column of the form (where it says "Activity/Routine"), list daily classroom activities and routines in the order in which they occur on a typical school day. Because there are many teaching opportunities in every transition, some teachers like to list transitions as separate activities. For example, *transition from Arrival to Circle* would be considered a separate routine and listed after "Arrival." *Transition from Circle to Art* is listed as a separate routine after "Circle," and *transition from Art to Snacks* is listed as a routine after "Art" in the first column.

Step 2: *List major behavioral expectations.* Completing this step requires reflection and discussion. The objective is to list broad expectations *for the whole class* in the first column under the name of the activity or routine. Include those general expectations that differentiate the activity or routine from other activities and routines throughout the day. While every child in the class will not demonstrate every one of the behaviors every day, all of the children are expected to demonstrate these skills at some point.

Team members should avoid being too specific about expected behaviors (e.g., answer three questions about the story), as performance will depend on the story (it may not be long enough for each child to have three questions) and on the individual child. It is better simply to say "Answer questions about the story." Expectations should be *positive* and involve *active* engagement with the environment. "Sit quietly and don't bother peers" is an example of an expectation that violates this admonition. Keep in mind that children learn nothing that has functional or developmental value from "waiting in line" or "sitting quietly." For the brain and the body to grow, there must be active and positive engagement with the environment (Bredekamp & Copple, 1997).

Developing the list of expectations for all activities in a typical day takes some time. However, once completed, this list can be used for all children as long as the curriculum (activities and routines) remains the same. The one factor that affects expectations is the time of year. Expectations for children new to preschool in August will be less advanced developmentally than expectations later in the school year. Some teachers who use ecological assessment regularly have three or four different "expectations lists" that they use, depending on the time of year.

Step 3: *Score "Can do" or "Needs to learn."* The team discussion now shifts from activities, routines, and expectations for the class as a whole to the strengths and instructional needs of the child with disabilities. The task is to rate whether the child can (and does) perform the expected behavior or needs to learn it. There are two possible ways to approach this rating. If team members feel that they know the child well enough, they can complete the rating without observations. They can go down the list one by one, reach consensus, and check whether the child can perform the behavior or not. Then they write comments as to what the child actually does when called upon to perform the identified behavior. If the team cannot reach consensus as to whether the child can perform the behavior, there will be a need to observe the child for a day or two to determine the child's strengths and instructional needs as they relate to the expectations.

Step 4: *Formulate goals and objectives.* Recall from Chapter 3 that goals are short statements identifying the desired outcome of intervention or instruc-

Ecological Assessment

Team Members: Dayana, Melissa, Brandi, Yusong, Andreia

Child: Jace   Date: 2-2-03

Activities/Routines and Expectations	Can do	Needs to learn	Comments	Objectives
Activity/Routine: Arrival/free play				
• Say "Hi" and respond to "How are you?"		√	No response—does not look at teacher, just goes inside.	Greet teacher (eye contact + verbalization) at the door.
• Put belongings in cubby.	√		Looks for his photo and pushes his backpack into his cubby.	
• Select toy and play table or a center.		√	Just wanders around the room.	Select a toy or activity center.
• Play/share toys with peers.		√	When led to a chair or center, he plays alone.	Play cooperatively with peers.
• Put toys away when the signal sounds.		√	Doesn't want to stop playing—refuses to help with cleanup.	Return toys to the shelf.
Activity/Routine: Circle				
• Move to carpet area/sit in circle when music begins.	√		Follows the other children and sits—needs help crossing his legs.	
• Raise hand/say, " I am here" when photo is held up.		√	Raises hand (when prompted) but does not vocalize.	Respond to roll call photo without prompting and vocalize.
• Sing/do hand motions or rhythm instruments.		√	Sometimes imitates motions but doesn't sing.	
• Answer when asked questions about the story.		√	No response.	Respond to questions about a story (by pointing to pictures or verbalizing).
Activity/Routine: Art				
• Put on a smock.		√	Needs physical assistance.	Independently put on a smock and close the Velcro tabs.
• Get materials from the supply table as directed.		√	Needs physical/verbal prompts.	Independently retrieve art materials from the supply table.

Figure 5.1.   Completed ecological assessment for Jace.

Activities/Routines and Expectations	Can do	Needs to learn	Comments	Objectives
Activity/Routine: Art				
• Use materials properly.		✓	Cannot cut or squeeze glue—does fine with crayons.	Demonstrate cutting and gluing skills.
• Follow verbal/visual activity directions.		✓	Does not watch peers, so check the visual directions.	Follow verbal/visual directions for art activities.
• Clean up/remove smock.		✓	Doesn't want to stop—ignores the cleanup signal.	Put materials away when an activity is over.
Activity/Routine: Snacks				
• Wash & dry hands—throw away the paper towel.	✓		Can do, but wants to play in the water.	
• Find a chair and sit.	✓		Follows peers.	
• Pass plates and napkins.	✓		Manages with peer assistance.	
• Eat and drink independently.	✓		Does fine with a cutout cup. Eats most of the food he is given.	
• Throw trash in container.	✓		Imitates peers.	

Source: McCormick & Noonan, 2002.

tion. They describe behaviors that the child can reasonably be expected to accomplish in a 12-month period. In this assessment process, participation in the activity or routine is stated as the goal. Expectations that the child cannot yet perform in each activity or routine are stated as objectives. Note that objectives for Jace are stated in the fifth column of the Ecological Assessment form (Figure 5.1). Goals and objectives for Jace for the first three activities of the day are restated as a list on Table 5.2. These objectives (instructional targets) meet the criteria for meaningfulness and functionality; that is, they promote the child's full participation in activities and routines that define the class environment.

Embedding, described below, means providing teaching trials in the context of naturally occurring activities and routines. An important advan-

Table 5.2. Goals and objectives for Jace

Goal: Jace will participate in the morning arrival and free play routines.

- Jace will use eye contact and a verbalization (a greeting or an approximation) to address the teacher every morning upon arrival.
- Jace will select a toy and take it to the play table or go to an activity center every morning upon entering the classroom.
- Jace will share toys and take turns with peers during free play every day.
- Jace will return his toys to the shelf when the signal sounds every day.

Goal: Jace will participate in morning circle.

- Jace will raise his hand (without prompting) and approximate "I'm here" or "here" when his photo is displayed at roll call every day.
- Jace will respond (by pointing and/or verbalizing) to at least one question about the story every day.

Goal: Jace will participate in art activities.

- Jace will put on his smock independently and close the Velcro tabs as directed for daily art activities.
- Jace will retrieve art materials from the supply table when the directions are given.
- Jace will cut paper (using adapted scissors) in daily art activities.
- Jace will squeeze the glue bottle and aim the glue as directed in daily art activities.
- Jace will follow the steps in the visual directions posted on the easel each day.
- Jace will participate in cleanup and return art materials to the supply table each day.

tage of using ecological assessment to identify instructional goals and objectives is that targeted behaviors are already *embedded* into the daily activities and routines. The procedures for embedding objectives *when they have come from another assessment procedure* are described below.

Step 5: *Plan instruction.* Figure 5.2, Instructional Planning Form, shows a planning form in preparation for developing a more detailed lesson plan. The objectives briefly stated in the first column are from the last column of the Ecological Assessment form. The other four columns detail required skills to perform the objective (What to Teach), instructional procedures (How to Teach), Adaptations and Supports, and Persons Responsible.

The What to Teach column lists the specific skills to teach to help Jace accomplish the objective (Jace needs to be taught to look at the teacher and to verbalize in response to the teacher's greeting). The third column, How to Teach, describes the specialized instructional procedures used to teach the identified skills.

In many ways, the planning that goes into the third column is most critical. Children with disabilities need specialized instruction—individualized instruction that is specially planned and provided to teach specific skills. Specialized instruction is basic to providing services for young children with disabilities. *Individualized instruction* in this context should not be defined to mean one-to-one instruction, although one-to-one instruction may occasionally occur in inclusive classrooms (with children without disabilities as well as those with disabilities). Specialized or individualized instruction provides environmental support, adult and peer assistance (encouragement, feedback, prompts), adaptations, and special equipment or technology to maximize the child's learning opportunities.

Table 5.3. Naturalistic instructional procedures

These naturalistic instructional approaches incorporate environmental arrangement, adaptations, and prompts and prompt fading procedures.

Enhanced milieu teaching	Incidental teaching expanded to include environmental arrangements and adult-initiated interactions (Hart & Rogers-Warren, 1978; Kaiser, 2000).
Activity-based intervention	Specific intervention approaches such as milieu teaching and incidental teaching incorporated into ongoing activities (ABI; Bricker & Cripe, 1992).
Embedded and distributed time delay trials	Short systematic instructional interactions provided within existing activities and routines (Wolery, 2001).
High-probability ("high-*p*") procedures	Strategies whereby an adult delivers a series of requests to which a child responds consistently immediately before delivering a request to which the child does not respond consistently (Santos, 2001).

The belief that specialized instruction should not interfere with children's interactions and participation in the classroom has led to the development of instructional approaches that resemble the methods used with typically developing children in early childhood programs based on the DAP model. These approaches, called naturalistic approaches, provide brief instructional trials interspersed throughout the day in age-appropriate activities and routines. They are as much about *when* instructional trials are provided as *how* they are provided. Planning is essential. Table 5.3 provides a brief overview of the naturalistic instructional procedures that are described in detail in Chapter 9.

Adaptations and supports are listed in the fourth column of Figure 5.2. They also require team collaboration and careful planning. The broad goal of independent functioning is foremost. Adaptations and supports are provided only when necessary and then just enough to facilitate participation. Table 5.4 describes task adaptations and ways to provide supports during instruction. Finally, the team should discuss and decide who will be responsible for

Table 5.4. Adaptations and supports

Provide scaffolding.	Provide support, assistance, and encouragement until the child performs a new skill independently or gives evidence of understanding a new concept.
Provide practice.	Give the child many opportunities and encouragement to repeat tasks and routines.
Change the task.	Modify the task as necessary for the child to be successful, or provide a different task that accomplishes the same function.
Change the materials.	Provide alternate materials (e.g., different size, texture) to accomplish the task.
Augment directions.	Provide visuals depicting the sequence of steps in activities and routines, and cue the child to use these devices.
Change the response requirements.	Require a less sophisticated response (e.g., a word approximation rather than a word) or a response in a different modality (pointing rather than verbalizing).
Assign a partner.	Ask a peer to act as a model and/or helper for the task.
Provide adaptive equipment.	Provide whatever devices (e.g., switches, environmental control units) are necessary for meaningful participation and task completion.

Child: _Jace_

Objectives (briefly)	What to Teach	How to Teach	Adaptations and Supports	Persons Responsible
Greet teacher. • Morning • Recess	Look at teacher. Verbalize in response to teacher greeting.	Position your face at Jace's eye level. When he attends, provide greeting. Use mand model (say "Hi") with progressive time delay.	Be sure to position your eyes at Jace's eye level.	Dayana, Brandi, or Yusong
Choose toy or activity.	Move independently to toy shelf. Select toy. Sit (at table or on floor) and manipulate toy. or Move to a center and engage in center activity.	Physically guide Jace to toy shelf or activity center. Display a preferred and nonpreferred toy. Say, "What do you want?" Prompt Jace to select the preferred toy (progressive time delay). Same procedure for center. Say, "Where to you want to play?" Guide Jace to the center (physical prompt—progressive time delay).	Arrange Jace's favorite toy and a nonpreferred toy on a shelf at eye level.	Dayana, Brandi, or Yusong

Figure 5.2. Instructional planning form.

providing the instruction and supports for each objective and list these names in the last column of the Instructional Planning Form.

Step 6: *Plan data collection.* The last step in the ecological assessment process is development of a comprehensive evaluation/monitoring plan. The team needs to collect sufficient data to determine whether instruction is accomplishing the desired outcomes. The data collection matrix for Jace is shown in Figure 5.3. This particular form was prepared for "Arrival/Free play." It is kept on a plastic clipboard on a hook near the door to the classroom. There is a similar form for each of his other activities. These are also on clipboards near where the activity takes place or on the corner of the teacher's desk.

Name: *Jace*   Activity: *Arrival/Free play*   Week: *4/11 to 4/15*

Objective	Type of data	Monday	Tuesday	Wednesday	Thursday	Friday
Greet teacher.	Frequency count Indicate type of prompt					
Select toy or activity **Take to table or activity center.**	Frequency count Indicate type of prompt					
Share and take turns.	Anecdotal notes Indicate peer(s)					
Return toys to shelf.	Frequency count Indicate type of prompt					

Figure 5.3. Data collection matrix.

The objectives for the activity are noted in the first column, and the type of data that will be collected in the second column. The type of data to record and the dimension of the behavior to be measured depend on the target behavior. As discussed in Chapter 3, the most common types of quantitative data are frequency/number, rate, duration, latency, topography, and magnitude.

Methodology

The selection of methodology to document behavior change depends on the nature of the evaluation questions. Most of the procedures described in this chapter and in other chapters in this text generate quantitative data. It is impossible to overemphasize their importance. However, they can only answer *specific* questions about the effect of intervention on *particular* behavioral outcomes. Efficacy questions about more broadly defined quality-of-life outcomes such as communication, social interactions, how children interact with others, and general comfort and well-being in the setting or activity require a different type of data collection procedure. The target behaviors are still observable, of course, but the questions are better suited to qualitative data collection procedures.

Qualitative data collection procedures are descriptive and interpretive: They are appropriate for answering questions about broader and more complex behaviors. A major difference in quantitative and qualitative data is that the latter does not require definition of the specific dimensions of the behavior prior to data collection. Examples of questions that can be answered with qualitative data are: "Which activity centers does Jace seem to prefer?" "Which peers is Abby most attracted to?" "When and with whom does Anisa attempt communication?" "What does Anisa communicate *about*?" "Who initiates play in the housekeeping center?"

Both quantitative and qualitative data collection procedures yield valuable and meaningful information, and both require a significant commitment of time and energy (Schwartz & Olswang, 1996). Whether the lens is finely focused to collect quantitative data or focused on a broad spectrum of the child's behavior and the context in which the behaviors are embedded to yield qualitative data, the actual recording and analysis of the data must be implemented in a systematic and rigorous fashion. The important points to remember are 1) to match the data collection procedure to the question and 2) to use multiple data sources to the extent possible.

At the end of the week, the data from all the activity matrices for Jace are graphed or otherwise summarized and analyzed by the team to determine whether progress is satisfactory or if there is a need to modify the program and continue instruction. Permanent product samples and anecdotal records are also reviewed weekly, and selections made for Jace's portfolio. Portfolio assessment is discussed below. The specifics of quantitative data collection, reporting, and analysis are discussed at length in Chapter 6.

PORTFOLIO ASSESSMENT

Portfolio assessment is formative assessment that relies on compilation of the child's work and other artifacts (purposefully collected and assembled in an organized fashion) to provide a picture of the child's progress toward achievement of his or her goals and objectives over a specified period of time (typically a school year). It is a response to the fourth question noted at the beginning of this chapter: *How do we know what (or if) the child has learned?*

Triangulation is a concept from qualitative research that refers to collecting material in as many different ways and from as many diverse sources as possible. Well-developed portfolios provide a representative sample of a broad spectrum of behavior, using triangulation to document significant and meaningful behavior change in developmental, academic, and social arenas. Triangulation is assured by providing repeated examples of the child's behavior in different situations, including descriptions of performance in formal test situations. The greater the variety of data provided, the better the overall picture. For example, a preschooler's portfolio might include audiotapes documenting the child's improving oral language skills, teacher observation notes, photos of the child engaged in play with peers, parent reports of improved behavior at home, and a checklist showing improvements in independent toileting skills.

Portfolios can answer questions that cannot be answered by traditional assessment and data collection procedures (Schwartz & Olswang, 1996); for example, they can answer such questions as "How well is Jace participating in art activities?" "How well is Jace learning the snack routine?" "How well is Jace communicating with peers throughout the school day?" Because they are not clear as to the types of data to collect, teachers and other practitioners sometimes avoid asking broad questions such as these where the child's behavior is related to specific contextual variables. They are very different from questions such as "Did providing a verbal prompt increase Jace's initiation of block play during the free-play period?" that ask for objective quantitative data. These questions require multidimensional information.

There is no intent to suggest the superiority of one type of question over another. Both are important and both have strengths as well as weaknesses. Both add meaningful and valuable information that contributes to the evaluation process. Specific questions that focus on highly discrete behaviors (the type of behaviors often defined on IEPs) generate objective quantitative data. However, intervention at the preschool level also seeks broadly defined outcomes such as friendships, success and comfort with peers, engagement in group activities, and participation in daily routines. Broad questions that focus on functional outcomes generate subjective qualitative data (Schwartz & Olswang, 1996). Answering both types of questions using the methodology that matches the question is the ideal. Systematically applying both qualitative and quantitative data collection procedures enables teachers to evaluate acquisition of new skills *and* functional use of new skills in natural environments.

Keep in mind that the purpose of the portfolio is to provide information for monitoring and evaluating a child's progress and making informed decisions about future programming. Qualitative data may be collected through interviews (with the child or the child's significant others), observations (both descriptive and interpretive), photographs, audio- and/or videotapes, anecdotal records, and reflective journals. These data are more useful for developing a picture of the child in context. Quantitative data provide information about specific behaviors that are the focus of intervention. Quantitative data collection depends on operationally defining and then measuring changes in the performance of the target behaviors. Quantitative data collection procedures are described in detail in Chapter 6.

Planning and Construction

Lynch and Struewing (2002) suggested that the following issues be considered in preparation for portfolio construction:

- *What do you intend to assess?* Have a clear reason for assessing the particular variables you have chosen. Are you concerned with collecting information on achievement of IEP goals or more general information about developmental progress? Will the information be used to evaluate the effectiveness of instruction or to plan future instruction?

- *How will the portfolio process be integrated with other assessment strategies?* Think about whatever assessment procedures you are already using. These procedures and the portfolio process should supplement one another. Decisions need to be made about the types of records and work samples that will be most useful to document children's development and accomplishments.

- *How will you gain the support and cooperation of everyone on the team?* All personnel (e.g., paraeducators, assistants, therapists, volunteers) need to be involved in the initial planning for the portfolio process *and* regularly scheduled meetings thereafter. Initial meetings may focus on reviewing samples of portfolios, developing a proposed "contents checklist," and deciding specific data collection procedures.

- *How will you inform the parents?* Lynch and Struewing (2002) suggested writing a letter to the parents explaining the purpose of the portfolio, the portfolio process, and how the portfolio will be organized. The letter should encourage parents to visit the classroom and look through the portfolio with the child. The parents can jot down comments made by their child when sharing his or her work. A date stamp and sticky notes are placed near the portfolio for this purpose.

Materials and data for inclusion in the portfolio should be carefully selected and organized, depending on the purpose of the assessment. Each entry should have a descriptive label that tells the date, the person who provided the entry, and a notation as to why it is important. Possible entries include observational data, summaries of work samples, pre- and post-checklists, calendars, summaries of accomplishments, summaries of anecdotal records, graphs, rating scales, language samples, notes from interviews with the child about his or her favorite activities, and videotapes and audiotapes (Lynch & Struewing, 2002). Children are active partners in the process; they are directly involved in the selection as well as the development of materials for their portfolios. There should be a specific purpose for including each entry. Samples of the child's writing, painting, cutting, collage construction, drawing, math, dictation, and quotations taken early in the school year and then near the end of the year are included to show progress in those areas. A list of favorite books read to (or by) the child may also be included. If regularly writing in a journal is part of the school routine, copies of pages of the child's journal that provide insight into developing writing skills and cognitive processes may be included.

Photographs of group projects (e.g., cooking experiences, special school events, field trips) document the participants "in action" as well as the outcome of their efforts. Photos should be mounted in such a way that there is adequate space for text describing the activity, whatever comments are dictated by the child, and notations as to how the relevant skills and concepts are evident in the picture. Photographs are particularly beneficial for documenting the performance and products of children with severe disabilities. For example, the portfolio might include photos of the child building block structures, riding a tricycle at recess, interacting with peers, pouring juice at Snacks, and stacking cups at the sand table. Photos are also a way to show growth in

Confidence:

> A photo of the child purposefully moving his wheelchair in the direction of the activity center for free play
> A photo of the child in a wheelchair confidently leading her class down the hall and then down the sidewalk to the waiting bus

Social and communicative interactions:

> A photo of the child adding paper to a collage he is making with a peer
> A photo of the child giving a picture communication card to her peer in exchange for a toy
> A photo of the child responding to the request of a peer to share a toy

Photos such as these also show parents that their child is an active member of the class.

Anecdotal records are brief, factual, and nonjudgmental notes that document the child's progress in classroom routines and activities. A special form specifically for anecdotal notes can be developed and made available for adults in the class, or anecdotes can simply be recorded on index cards. If an "Anecdotal Record Form" is provided, there should be a place to note the child's name, date and time, activity context, and the name of the recorder, in addition to the specific child behavior (e.g., a skill related to an IEP goal).

Organization

There are a number of ways to organize and store the information. The portfolio may be an expandable folder, a cardboard or plastic box, a large loose-leaf notebook, or some other container. The only requirement is a way to divide the content into sections with marker tabs for easy filing and retrieval. Portfolios may be organized by content areas, time periods (months, quarters, semesters), IEP goals, developmental domains, activities, or thematic units. The first page of each section describes the contents of that section.

The first section of the portfolio should include a list of the child's IEP goals and objectives (for children with disabilities), a description of the classroom with the general program philosophy and general classroom goals, a table of contents, and a copy of the letter to parents that is mentioned above. Parent comments on their child's progress and notes from parent conferences may also be included with this introductory material to document teacher–parent planning where there are specific concerns and follow-up (Lynch & Struewing, 2002).

Portfolios should be in a location that is easily accessible to both teachers and children so that they can be updated every day. Portfolio supplies (e.g., blank forms, a hole punch, plastic bags or clear envelopes for tapes and other three-dimensional objects, pencils and pens) and a camera may be kept nearby in a box or drawer. After the children leave each day, 10 to 15 minutes can be devoted to selecting the materials and placing them in the appropriate sections in the children's portfolios, photographing projects that are too large to fit in the portfolios, and printing photos (if a digital camera is used). Teachers typically include no more than two or three entries within each section of the portfolio each week.

Remember, the purpose of the portfolio is to help the team understand, document, and improve present practice and future programming. As everyone on the team should assist data collection, they should also be involved in regular portfolio review meetings to consider patterns of child behavior, whether the children are progressing at a desired rate, and areas of the program that need improvement. For children with disabilities, the team's focus will be on evaluating the portfolio information to make decisions about the children's behavior, knowledge, and accomplishments. Their growth over time and the quality of progress toward achievement of IEP goals help the team decide whether present arrangements need to be modified and expanded.

Perhaps the most challenging aspect of portfolio assessment is finding the necessary time to collect, select, review, and evaluate work samples. However, most teachers consider it worth the effort because, in addition to providing instructionally relevant information about their students' growth and development, portfolio assessment shows respect for children, and it is far more meaningful to parents and administrators than the scores generated by traditional assessment procedures. Parents gain an understanding of their children's interests as well as their development and accomplishments in the context of the daily routines and activities of the preschool program.

All children can benefit from portfolio assessment, but it is a particularly useful tool for children with severe disabilities and those with culturally and linguistically diverse backgrounds whose progress is difficult to measure with traditional assessment strategies. Portfolio assessment provides information about the learning *process* as well as the *products* of learning. By documenting functional behavior in natural contexts, it establishes the critical link between assessment and instruction. Teachers and team members can reflect on their instructional procedures and make sound instructional decisions in a timely manner.

SUMMARY

This chapter has described three planning and evaluation/monitoring processes: child-centered planning, ecological assessment, and portfolio assessment. Child-centered planning generates a vision for the child that can serve as a social validity standard for goals and objectives and intervention procedures. Ecological assessment identifies the behaviors which, when learned, will enable the child to fully participate in activities with typically developing peers in inclusive settings (preschool classroom, child care setting, after-school care) and natural environments (home, extended family settings). Portfolio assessment is a way to collect data for purposes of planning and modifying instruction and to monitor progress. These procedures differ from traditional assessment tools and procedures in that they are multidimensional: They use numerous methods and sources of information across contexts and across people to formulate a picture of children's abilities in actual activities in natural environments.

• STUDY QUESTIONS •

1. What are the four questions that teachers need to address when planning instruction?

2. Discuss the role of child-centered planning, ecological assessment/planning, and portfolio assessment in the context of the four basic purposes of assessment.

3. Describe the specific purpose of and procedures for the child-centered planning meeting(s).

4. Describe the desired outcome of the child-centered planning process.

5. Discuss the concept of social validity and its relevance to assessment and planning.

6. Describe the roots of ecological theory and ecological assessment.

7. How is the information generated by ecological assessment used?

8. Describe the ecological assessment process.

9. Describe procedures for planning program monitoring.

10. Describe the purposes of portfolio assessment.

11. Discuss the reason for and procedures associated with triangulation.

12. Describe the issues to consider when preparing a portfolio.

13. Describe the materials and data that are typically included in a portfolio.

6

Instructional Procedures

Mary Jo Noonan

• **FOCUS OF THIS CHAPTER** • • • • • • • • • • • • • • • • • • •

- Systematic instruction in natural settings
- Effective prompts and encouragement
- General case instruction
- Generalization procedures
- Writing instructional plans
- Monitoring systematic instruction

S ystematic instruction is consistent instruction conducted according to an individualized plan. The purpose is to assist and encourage infants and young children with disabilities to acquire skills needed for participation in natural experiences, now and in the future. Assistance and encouragement is individualized to address the child's learning, developmental, and temperamental characteristics. Types of assistance vary from arranging materials, to providing reminders, to giving physical guidance. All types of assistance have the effect of helping the child with a disability demonstrate a skill. Encouragement procedures refer to motivation and are included in instruction to arouse interest and to reinforce desired responses. Although assistance and encouragement procedures will be defined and described separately, it should be noted that they often overlap in their functions. For example, moving an infant's toy closer will make it easier for him to reach (assistance), and the movement attracts his attention (assistance) and interest (motivation). This chapter will describe systematic instructional procedures for the naturalistic curriculum model.

Naturalistic and *systematic* are not incompatible constructs. Although *systematic* emphasizes consistent instruction, it does not require unnatural and mechanistic instruction. Furthermore, it does not require instructional plans to be so rigid that the teacher or infant specialist responds without regard for the interests or spontaneity expressed by the child. Consistency is important to instructional effectiveness, but it must be balanced with sensitivity and responsiveness to the child.

A systematic instructional approach provides for program integrity and accountability. Strategies are precisely formulated and instruction is always conducted in a similar manner. Furthermore, when a teacher or infant specialist shares the plan with other members of the intervention team, the plan on paper is a true representation of what is being implemented. The extent to which a systematic instructional plan is teacher-directed and structured corresponds with the needs of the young children. When new skills pose difficult challenges, a great deal of teacher direction may be needed; whereas, when skills are nearly accomplished, less structure and teacher direction are required. Finally, consistent instruction allows for objective evaluation of program effectiveness. Evaluation of the plan is important so that it can be modified if progress is not as expected. It is also important to the field of early intervention that effective procedures be documented.

TEACHING IN CONTEXT

As previously noted, the instructional situation is a key feature that distinguishes the naturalistic curriculum model from other models. Specifically, instruction happens during naturally occurring routines and activities. The most fortuitous natural learning opportunities are those that promote development/ learning through four qualities: interest, engagement, competence, and mastery (Dunst, Bruder, Trivette, Raab, & McLean, 2001). Learning opportunities that attract a child's interest and result in high levels of engagement are ones that the child will likely attempt and continue to pursue. In addition, learning opportunities that increase a child's competence and feeling of mastery will be highly reinforcing.

Teaching during naturally occurring routines and activities is vital to the success of the naturalistic curriculum model because it affords the availability of naturally occurring prompts (assistance) and motivational variables that can maintain new skills in the absence of instruction. Naturally occurring prompts and motivational variables should be identified during assessment or while planning instruction so that they may be incorporated into the instructional plan, either by highlighting them (making them more noticeable) or pairing them with their instructional counterparts. These strategies are discussed in greater detail below.

Distributed Trial Format

Providing instruction throughout the course of the day during naturally occurring routines and activities employs a *distributed trial format* (Mulligan, Guess, Hovoet, & Brown, 1980; Wolery, 1994). In distributed trials, the child performs other behaviors between instructional trials. The instructional trials are often dispersed throughout the day. This teaching arrangement provides a variety of natural stimuli, prompts, and corrections during instruction. For many infants and young children, this will be effective instruction with the benefit of promoting generalization. For others, however, it may be ineffective because the variety of stimuli may lead to confusion and an apparent nonsystematic approach to instruction. It may also be difficult to include a sufficient amount of instruction during the day relying solely on distributed trials.

Discrete Trial Format

One approach to teaching children with autism relies almost exclusively on a *discrete trial* format (also known as *massed trial instruction*) (McEachin, Smith, & Lovaas, 1993). In the discrete trial format, a teaching trial (prompt, student's response, correction or reinforcement) is presented repeatedly for a number of trials (10 or 15). For example, if a child is being taught to point to a photo on a communication board, a teacher sits down with the child and spends 5 or 10 minutes repeatedly guiding her hand within 2 inches of the picture, reinforcing her if she then points to the picture by giving her the favorite toy represented by the photo, or if she doesn't point to the picture, guides her hand to touch the picture as a correction. In discrete trial training, as soon as this teaching sequence is completed, the toy (reinforcer) is taken back from the child, and the trial is repeated.

Although discrete trial instruction is artificial rather than naturalistic, Bambara and Warren (1993) have suggested four situations when it may be appropriate. First, some skills occur repeatedly in natural situations, such as infant games (Peekaboo) or self-feeding (scooping cereal). Second, if a child is having difficulty learning a particular step in a chain of skills, providing several warm-up practice trials of the difficult step may increase the child's success when practicing the chain. Third, warm-up sessions may help the child learn difficult or complex discriminations, such as the front and back of his clothing. Repeatedly asking the child to point to the discriminating features indicating the back of his shirt and pants could be practiced several times before changing his clothes. Similarly, functional academics (often involving complex discriminations) may be most efficiently taught in a massed trial format initially (e.g., telling time). And fourth, some children may have difficulty learning certain skills in natural settings, possibly because of distracting stimuli. Using a discrete trial format may help them learn the skill initially, before being taught to use the skill in natural situations. Bambara and Warren caution, however, that discrete trial training should only be used as an adjunct to naturalistic instruction: It should never be the sole means of instruction because it mitigates against generalization. Furthermore, it is extremely important to include specific strategies that promote generalization (see section on General Case Instruction below) within the discrete trial training sessions (Strain, Wolery, & Izeman, 1998). And finally, teachers must be sensitive to the child's interest and responsiveness during discrete trial training. If the child loses interest quickly or is not cooperative during discrete trial instruction, this may suggest that naturalistic instructional situations would be more effective.

PROVIDING ASSISTANCE

The assistance component of systematic instruction is implemented *before* the child is expected to demonstrate a response. Asking a child to respond without assistance is using a trial-and-error method. When learning new responses, trial-and-error learning results in repeated errors (Bereiter & Englemann, 1966) and confusion. This is why assistance is provided. Assistance strategies include prompting, cuing, shaping, and fading.

Assistance procedures can also be provided *after* the child attempts a target response. If the child does not respond, or does not respond as desired, the assistance is a correction procedure. The correction procedure should be different from the assistance initially provided because an ineffective procedure should not be repeated. Correction procedures should also have a high probability of resulting in the desired response so that a second error does not occur. Assistance can also be provided after the child demonstrates a correct response to highlight the desired response. For example, a child says, "Doll," and a parent says, "Doll—yes, that's your baby doll."

Prompts

Anything that helps a child make a desired response is a *prompt*. There are two kinds of prompts: natural and instructional. Natural prompts are environmental stimuli that "occasion a response" (Holland & Skinner, 1961). Prompts do not cause or elicit a response; instead, they signal a response. This happens because of reinforcement when an appropriate response occurs. A toddler, for example, quickly learns that when Dad says, "Let's watch cartoons!" (prompt), if she turns on the TV (response), Dad will watch cartoons and play with her (outcome). The predictability of the prompt-response-outcome relationship increases the likelihood that an appropriate response occurs when a natural prompt is present.

Instructional prompts are provided when natural prompts are inadequate or ineffective to teach a new skill. An instructional prompt can be as subtle as a glance, or as intrusive as physical guidance. The amount of assistance provided by a prompt depends not only on its intensity but also on the young child's ability to use it. If an infant does not understand speech, a verbal direction will not provide assistance. Likewise, if a child does not imitate, a model cannot serve as a prompt. For some infants and children, however, verbal directions and models are effective. Good prompts are ones that help a child make a response, rarely result in errors, and are as nonintrusive as possible while still being effective (Dunst et al., 1987).

Prompts can be identified by the type of assistance they provide. Common prompts include

Indirect verbal: Asking a question or making a statement that implies what is needed. For example, "What do we need to do now that we're home from our walk?" (meaning "Go to your room for a nap"), or "It's time for breakfast" (meaning "Raise your arms and I'll pick you up and take you into the kitchen").

Direct verbal: Making a specific statement to inform a child what needs to be done. "Say 'good morning'" or "Put your arm through the sleeve" are direct verbal prompts.

Gestural: Moving a hand or body part as a nonverbal prompt. It may be a conventional gesture that people are acquainted with such as pointing, or an unconventional gesture known only to the child and/or her family, such as a sibling stamping his foot to prompt his sister to run to him.

Model: Demonstrating a desired response. The demonstration can be verbal or gestural. Verbal models might encourage a child to name things. Gestural models often prompt a child to engage in a variety of actions with objects (e.g., demonstrating how to roll, bounce, or shake a small ball).

Tactile: Touching the child. The tactile prompt is used to get the child's attention, or as a reminder that a certain body part must be moved to make a response. Touching an infant's chin, for instance, may prompt the infant to open his mouth to eat.

Partial physical assistance: Guiding a child by touching or manipulating a body part. The prompt is partial because complete guidance is not provided; the child must do some of the response. Guiding a child's elbow, or supporting the weight of an object as an infant picks it up, are examples of partial physical assistance.

Full physical assistance: Providing complete guidance by touching or manipulating a body part. Guiding an infant's hand and helping her push a button with her finger is a full physical assistance prompt.

Spatial: Placing a stimulus in a location that increases the likelihood of a correct response. Placing a preschooler's toothbrush in front of others on the counter is a spatial prompt.

Movement: Altering the location of a stimulus to attract attention. A parent may hold up two shirts and ask her child if he'd like to wear the blue one or the red one, shaking each shirt as she mentions it. The movement prompt assists the child to look at both shirts before choosing.

Visual/pictorial: Providing assistance through pictures (drawings or photographs), colors, or graphics. Placing a red mark on the back of an inside neckline, waistband, or clothing tag is an example of a visual/pictorial prompt.

Auditory: Using sound (other than speech) to assist a child to make a desired response. Tapping an object is an auditory prompt.

When formulating systematic instruction, prompts are operationally defined, not simply identified by type. For example, in a plan to teach a toddler to point to and choose a toy, a partial physical assistance prompt is defined as "grasping her shoulders to maintain a forward and relaxed position." Clear definitions are necessary for consistent implementation.

Prompts can be used individually, in combination, or sequentially (Snell & Brown, 2006a). When an individual prompt is used, the prompt is given once. When a combination of prompts is used, two or more prompts are presented concurrently. Combining prompts increases the intensity of the prompt (Skinner, 1938) and may thereby increase instructional effectiveness. In assisting a young child to move into a standing position, for example, a combination of three prompts may be used: A sibling 1) holds the child's hands and nudges her up while a parent 2) provides support at her hips and 3) says, "Up, up, up."

Natural prompts may be paired with artificial ones as a strategy to teach the child to recognize natural ones. For instance, in teaching a preschooler to say "Please," the natural prompt of "Would you like some _____?" is paired with the instructional prompt of saying "Pl" (the first two letter sounds of "Please"). Pairing natural and instructional prompts is a particularly valuable strategy for teaching in natural situations because the natural prompt will always be present, even when the instruction is not.

A *prompt sequence* is a series of two or more prompts. For example, a three-step sequence consisting of verbal direction, modeling, and physical guidance may be used to teach a toddler the initial step of putting his T-shirt on. The sequence begins with the teacher saying "Hold your T-shirt at the bottom." A second prompt is provided by modeling how to hold the T-shirt. If the child does not imitate the model (demonstrating the desired response), a third prompt is given as a correction by guiding the child's hands to grasp the shirt. The verbal direction and model provided prior to the response are a two-step prompt sequence; the physical guidance in the correction procedure creates a three-step prompt sequence. The prompt sequence is always implemented in the same manner.

Prompt Hierarchies

A prompt hierarchy is a prompt sequence ordered according to the amount of assistance provided by each. The hierarchy can range from least to most assistance ("increasing assistance"), or from most to least ("decreasing assistance"). An example of a four-step hierarchy is

1. Verbal
2. Gestural
3. Partial physical assistance
4. Full physical assistance

If the above hierarchy begins with the verbal prompt, it is a least-to-most hierarchy; if it begins with full physical assistance, it is a most-to-least hierarchy.

In implementing a least-to-most assistance hierarchy, the first prompt or "level of assistance" is provided. If the child does not respond as desired within a specified time period (e.g., 5 seconds), the caregiver or teacher proceeds through the prompt hierarchy, providing the next prompt and waiting the specified length of time. When the desired response is demonstrated, the child is reinforced. The least-to-most hierarchy provides only as much assistance as the child needs. More intrusive prompts are automatically faded as the child responds to the less-intrusive prompts. Thus, the least-to-most assistance hierarchy is minimally intrusive.

Some young children, however, become "prompt dependent" when a least-to-most hierarchy is used. They wait for prompts that provide more assistance because they learn that eventually they will be given help (Glendenning, Adams, & Sternberg, 1983). Another problem with least-to-most hierarchies is that prompts that provide minimal assistance allow for errors (Csapo, 1981; Day, 1987).

A *most-to-least assistance hierarchy* may eliminate the problems of prompt dependency and high error rates associated with the least-to-most hierarchy. In a most-to-least hierarchy, the prompt that provides the most assistance is used first. When the child demonstrates the response at a criterion level (e.g., a specified number of times), instruction proceeds to the next level. When an error occurs, the previous prompt level is implemented as a correction. If the criterion for progressing through each level is more conservative than necessary, instruction is not efficient. Errors, however, are kept to a minimum.

As noted earlier, not all prompts are equally effective for all infants and young children; some children will not use particular prompts. Prompt hierarchies, therefore, are formulated on an individualized basis. For example, a young child who is irritated by touch does not respond well to physical guidance. Such prompts are not included in prompt hierarchies for her. Or, for some children, a verbal prompt provides a great deal of assistance, and a slight gestural prompt provides less assistance.

Graduated Guidance

A less structured prompting strategy, but one that is responsive to day-to-day performance, is graduated guidance. In graduated guidance, the teacher or parent/caregiver watches as the child attempts a skill and determines how much assistance is needed. Initially, much assistance is provided to ensure success. As the child acquires the skill, the amount of assistance is reduced. This procedure is similar to the most-to-least prompt hierarchy, because the amount of assistance is gradually reduced. The actual amount and type of assistance, however, differ from the most-to-least assistance prompt hierarchy because the amount is sometimes increased. Furthermore, the amount and type of assistance is determined *while* the child is attempting the response, rather than being predetermined (Snell & Brown, 2006a). In using graduated guidance to help an infant place toys in a container, the infant specialist sits close by and watches. The infant's hand is guided to the container when it appears that he will miss it. More assistance is provided when it appears that he might drop the toy. When graduated guidance is properly implemented, errors rarely occur and only the least amount of assistance necessary is provided.

Cues

A cue is a prompt that directs attention to a particular dimension of a stimulus or task. For example, pointing and saying "Pick up your spoon" is a cue because it directs the child to a specific object. The most effective cues are ones that direct attention to the most important features of a stimulus. Pointing to the handle rather than the bowl of the spoon is a more precise cue, and it is potentially more effective because it informs the child where to place his hand. Skilled teachers are keen observers of young children, noting when cues are needed to direct attention to important stimulus features. Like prompts, cues can be of various forms: verbal, tactile, physical, movement, or spatial, for instance.

Errorless Procedures

As previously mentioned, the most desirable assistance procedures minimize errors. Some instructional procedures are virtually error free. *Time delay* (Snell & Gast, 1981; Touchette, 1971) is an errorless procedure in which an instructional prompt is paired with a natural one. Over successive trials, the time interval between the natural prompt and the instructional prompt is gradually increased until the child responds to the natural prompt alone. A mother may use time delay, for example, to teach her child to raise his arms when he wants to be picked up. When he is fussing and appears to want her to pick him up, she says, "Do you want me to hold you?" (the natural prompt) and guides him to raise his arms (the instructional prompt). She repeats this 0-second delay procedure several times over the next 2 days whenever her son appears to want her to pick him up. On the fourth day, when he fusses, she asks if he wants to be held, and then pauses for 2 seconds. This pause gives her son a chance to raise his arms without assistance. If he does, she immediately lifts him up. If he does not, she guides him to raise his arms and lifts him up. She uses this 2-second delay procedure for 2 days. Every 2 days the interval increases by 2 seconds. Eventually, her son raises his arms before the prompt, responding independently to the natural prompt, "Do you want to be held?"

Several types of delay schedules have been shown to be effective (Snell & Brown, 2006a). *Progressive schedules* begin with a 0-second delay (the natural and instructional prompts are paired), and the delay increases a fixed amount each trial (0 sec, 1 sec, 2 sec, 3 sec, and so forth; or 0 sec, 2 sec, 4 sec, and so forth). In *blocked schedules,* the initial trial(s) is at 0 seconds, and all subsequent trials are at a fixed interval (0 sec, 0 sec, 0 sec, 0 sec, 4 sec, 4 sec, 4 sec, 4 sec, 4 sec, and so forth). This schedule is easier to implement accurately than the progressive schedule. A *blocked and progressive schedule,* the third alternative, begins with several trials at 0 seconds, and then progresses through a schedule of increasingly longer delays, with several trials at each level (0 sec, 0 sec, 0 sec, 2 sec, 2 sec, 2 sec, 4 sec, 4 sec, 4 sec, and so forth). The progressive delay schedule moves through the delay sequence very quickly and may result in errors for young children who have severe disabilities and don't "catch on" to the strategy. The blocked, or blocked and progressive, schedules provide a longer opportunity to learn to wait for prompts when the correct response is not known and thus minimizes errors.

In time delay, correct responses following the instructional prompt are *waited corrects,* and correct responses following the natural prompt are *anticipated corrects.* Both types of correct responses are reinforced. This decreases the likelihood of the child responding incorrectly during the delay. If the child doesn't know the correct response, she waits for the instructional prompt and responds correctly to receive reinforcement.

If an error occurs, a correction procedure is implemented. A typical correction procedure for time delay is to guide the correct response and return to the previous delay for a few trials. If several errors occur, the instructional plan is evaluated and modified. If the errors are occurring before the instructional prompt (*non-waited errors*), the reinforcer may not be effective and a different, more powerful one, is needed. Sometimes non-waited errors occur because the child doesn't realize that if she waits, a prompt will be provided to help. Waited errors suggest that the instructional prompt is not effective and a different prompt is needed.

Stimulus shaping and fading procedures are prompting strategies in which an easily recognized prompt is gradually altered (stimulus shaping) or reduced (stimulus fading) until its appearance matches that of the natural prompt. If

Stimulus fading to teach number concept

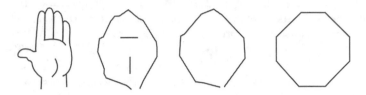

Stimulus shaping to teach the stop sign

Figure 6.1. Sample materials for stimulus fading and stimulus shaping.

materials such as pictures are used, a series of prompts are prepared prior to implementing this procedure, with slight modifications to each stimulus. Modifications from one stimulus to the next are subtle so that the child responds correctly as the prompts gradually approximate the natural one. Figure 6.1 illustrates materials for stimulus fading and shaping.

Guidelines for Effective Prompting

As noted above, systematic instruction must be implemented accurately and consistently, regardless of which prompting procedures are used. Too often prompts are repeated even though an instructional plan specifies that the prompt be given once. If the child does not respond or responds incorrectly, the correction procedure specified in the instructional plan is implemented—the prompt is *not* repeated (unless that is the correction procedure). Repeating prompts leads to prompt dependency, the situation in which the child learns not to attend or respond because more help will be given. Adhere to the following guidelines for prompting:

1. Implement prompting procedures as specified in the instructional plan. Do not repeat prompts unless indicated in the plan.
2. Be certain that the child is attending to you or to the relevant stimuli (e.g., task materials) *before* implementing the prompt.
3. Deliver prompts so that they are clear and easily recognized.
4. Select prompts that are the least intrusive, yet effective enough to minimize errors.
5. Change the prompt if the prompt is ineffective (the child makes several errors).

6. Use prompts and cues that help the child notice the naturally occurring ones. Natural and instructional prompts can be paired.

7. Use cues that focus attention on the most relevant characteristics of the stimuli.

Fading Prompts and Cues

Instructional prompts must be eliminated for the child to respond under natural conditions. A good instructional plan is one that provides the assistance necessary for correct responses and gradually eliminates assistance while maintaining correct responding. A plan for fading prompts is a part of systematic instruction.

Prompt fading procedures all have one thing in common: They result in the instructional prompt becoming less noticeable. One method of fading is to decrease intensity. The intensity of a verbal prompt can be faded by speaking more and more softly (as in "Take another bite"). Physical assistance is faded by gradually moving the assistance away (e.g., helping a child hold a crayon with hand-over-hand assistance can be faded by moving guidance from the hand to the wrist, the wrist to the forearm, to the elbow, and so on). Physical guidance is also faded by decreasing pressure (the touch associated with hand-over-hand assistance gets increasingly lighter until eliminated), or time (hand-over-hand assistance is first provided the entire time the child is coloring, then 90% of the time, 80% of the time, and so on).

Prompt fading strategies are related to the type of prompt: auditory prompts become quieter, spatial and movement prompts become smaller, visual prompts become lighter. The key is to make the prompt less noticeable in a subtle manner so that the child responds correctly as he did to the original prompt. Note that the most-to-least and least-to-most prompt hierarchies are complete prompt fading strategies when the least intrusive prompt of the hierarchy is a natural one.

Errorless prompting techniques (time delay, stimulus shaping, and stimulus fading) incorporate prompt fading as part of the strategy. In time delay, the instructional prompt is faded temporally; in stimulus shaping and fading, characteristics of the task materials/stimuli are gradually altered/reduced until only the natural ones remain.

PROVIDING ENCOURAGEMENT

Encouragement, the motivational component of systematic instruction, is provided through reinforcement procedures *after* the child demonstrates the desired response. Motivation is addressed *before* the response is expected using interesting or enticing materials, settings, or situational arrangements. Selecting objectives or skill steps that are challenging also provides motivation prior to response. *Well-formulated systematic instruction includes procedures that provide assistance and encouragement before and after the child's response.*

When encouragement is provided after the opportunity for demonstrating the response, it is usually *positive reinforcement.* Desired responses may also be encouraged by selectively reinforcing approximations of the response with shaping strategies or changing criterion designs. Motivational procedures implemented before a response are usually *environmental arrangements* that create a more interesting or challenging task, such as selecting attractive materials or teaching a basic skill in a play situation.

Positive Reinforcement

Positive reinforcement is a consequence that increases the likelihood of a response being repeated. It is defined by its *effect*. Something that is reinforcing for one child or one situation may not be reinforcing for another child or another situation. Most young children live in "reinforcement-rich" environments. Parents reinforce them with smiles, praise, frequent physical contact, and attention for almost everything they attempt or accomplish. Such naturally occurring encouragement, however, is not adequate for young children with disabilities. They may not notice the encouragement, or the encouragement may not be powerful enough relative to the skill difficulty. When encouragement is not effective, the child is not receiving positive reinforcement. (Remember, positive reinforcement is defined by its effect.)

Young children with special needs who have difficulty acquiring new skills or do not recognize naturally occurring encouragement should be provided with *instructional positive reinforcement*. Instructional positive reinforcement is "artificial" reinforcement that is not typical of a situation. It is provided as part of systematic instruction to address a specific skill need. Instructional positive reinforcement may include verbal praise ("Good, you got your toy!") or nonverbal praise such as hugs, smiles, pats on the back, or highly desired objects or actions (favorite toy or food, clapping). Ideally, instructional positive reinforcement is paired with naturally occurring reinforcement to help the child recognize naturally occurring reinforcement. For example, when an infant is learning to grasp objects, the natural reinforcement is obtaining the object and having it available for play. Instructional positive reinforcement might include verbal praise ("Hurray! You touched it!") and smiles, plus assistance to shake and play with the toy.

When a child is first learning a skill, instructional positive reinforcement should be provided every time the response occurs. This is a continuous schedule of reinforcement (CRF). As the child progresses in learning the skill, instructional positive reinforcement is provided less often (e.g., every second response or every third response [*a fixed ratio schedule*], or perhaps every 30 seconds, or every minute [a *fixed interval schedule*]. As the child approaches mastery of the skill, the instructional positive reinforcement is faded so that it is less recognizable. It is provided on a *variable interval schedule* (approximately every 2 minutes).

Effective instructional positive reinforcement in the motivational component of systematic instruction highlights naturally occurring reinforcement and is gradually faded. When instructional reinforcement is eliminated, natural reinforcers maintain the behavior. Reinforcement is gradually faded by changing the reinforcement schedule. Reinforcement may also be made less noticeable by decreasing its intensity or quantity, or by delaying when it is delivered.

Shaping and Selecting Reinforcement

Positive reinforcement provided contingent on an approximation of a desired response is called shaping. For example, any vocalization beginning with "b" is reinforced as an approximation to "bottle." As the toddler achieves success, an approximation of "buh" is required for reinforcement, and other vocalizations beginning with "b" are ignored. This encouragement strategy is *reinforcing successive approximations or selective reinforcement.*

Shaping, or reinforcing successive approximations, can be implemented systematically by using a *changing criterion design.* In a changing criterion design, a response is reinforced when it meets a particular standard (criterion). The standard gradually changes (increases or decreases) until the desired standard is achieved. For example, a preschooler is reinforced for playing independently for 30 seconds. When the preschooler demonstrates 30 seconds of independent play on three occasions, the criterion is raised to 45 seconds. Each time the preschooler meets the criterion three times, it is increased by 15 seconds, until the objective of 5 minutes of independent play is achieved. The changing criterion design is effective because the reinforcement schedule remains predictable, even though it is thinned. Furthermore, natural reinforcers assume a more powerful role as the child learns a functional behavior and instructional reinforcers are delayed (e.g., as the preschooler learns to play, the natural enjoyment of play is reinforcing).

When reinforcement is withheld from a previously reinforced behavior, the behavior is eventually eliminated. This is called *extinction.* If the criterion in the changing criterion design is altered too drastically or too quickly, extinction may inadvertently occur because the child does not anticipate reinforcement. Returning to the example of the preschooler learning to play, if the initial criterion of 30 seconds of play was doubled and raised to 1 minute (instead of 45 seconds), the child gives up after about 45 seconds, not realizing that there is still an opportunity for reinforcement. After several occasions of playing alone for brief periods of time and not being reinforced, the child's independent play is extinguished.

Environmental Arrangements

As previously noted, environmental arrangements can provide encouragement. Environmental arrangements that can be modified to encourage learning include the instructional situation, materials, and style of presentation. The *instructional situation* is the context of instruction—the where, when, why, and with whom. The place and time is the where and when of instruction. Natural places and times ensure a real need for the skill, and natural reinforcers are available. For example, teaching a preschooler dressing skills weekly at the public swimming pool is a very motivating time and place. The why of instruction refers to the activity used for teaching. A meaningful activity teaches the purpose of a skill and thus provides motivation. Functional skills, such as dressing, are taught when activities that require the skills typically occur. Referring to the dressing example, there is no need to contrive opportunities to teach dressing. Morning and evening routines, and activities such as swimming, provide natural and motivating times for instruction. Basic skills, such as vocalizing, sitting, and reaching, should also be taught within meaningful activities. The "with whom" of instruction involves the teacher or parents/ caregivers as well as other individuals. Including preferred people, such as parents, grandparents, siblings, or peers, in an instructional situation increases motivation. A toddler, for example, is highly motivated to "be like his big brother," and makes more of an effort to work on his sitting skills while playing with his brother.

Materials provide another opportunity for enhancing motivation. Attractive, age-appropriate, and interesting materials are more appealing than drab materials. New or different materials increase motivation because they are novel (Dunst, 1981). And materials that correspond to the physical and intellectual capabilities of the child hold the child's attention because they contribute to the "do-ability" of a task or activity.

Style of presentation involves the affective characteristics of instruction. Most of what infants and young children do should be fun, and that requires the instructional style to be enthusiastic, playful, and appropriate to the activities in which they occur. If instruction is enjoyable, the *level of task difficulty* must be appropriate to the child's current levels of performance. An appropriate level of task difficulty is one in which the task is slightly beyond the child's present ability so that it is challenging. The task is not so easy that it is boring, nor so difficult that it seems insurmountable.

When a task is too difficult, it may be broken down into component steps through *task analysis.* A task analysis is constructed by thinking through the steps of a task, doing the task yourself, or observing a competent adult/child doing the task. Table 6.1 illustrates a task analysis that was constructed by observing a competent 2-year-old demonstrate the task. Task analyses should be individualized to the child, and include more and smaller steps for difficult tasks or difficult portions of tasks and fewer and larger steps for easy tasks or easy portions of tasks (Gold, 1980).

Table 6.1. Example of a task analysis for putting on shorts (constructed by observing a competent 2-year-old perform the task)

1. Grasp shorts at the waistband with hands on either side.
2. Look for label on inside of waistband; if necessary, turn shorts so that label faces the back.
3. Squat and hold shorts close to floor.
4. Insert left foot into left leg of shorts.
5. Insert right foot into right leg of shorts.
6. Pull up shorts to hips, pulling up one side at a time until reaching the hips.
7. Grasp shorts at back of waistband and pull up over buttocks.
8. Grasp front of shorts and pull up to waist.

Response Generalization

Conditions: When she crawls to her toy box

Behavior: LiAn will request* a toy (by pointing to a toy in the toy box, by saying "toy," or by saying "please")

Criteria: On four consecutive opportunities

*(Instructional universe of requesting responses: reaching, pointing, vocalizing, naming, saying "please," saying "more")

Stimulus and Response Generalization

Conditions: When given finger foods* (crackers, raisins, sandwich pieces)

Behavior: Darryl will grasp** the food, pick it up, and feed himself

Criteria: At least five times per meal, four of five lunchtimes

*(Instructional universe of finger foods: cookies, crackers, cereal, banana slices, orange slices, raisins, sandwich pieces.) **(Instructional universe of grasping: light grasp, firm grasp, fine pincer, gross pincer, rake)

When general case objectives need to be simplified to correspond to the child's current level of performance, two or more short-term general case objectives can be formulated. It is important to include the multiple exemplars in each short-term objective, otherwise instruction will not be promoting generalization. Examples of three short-term general case objectives for the self-feeding objective are

Short-Term General Case Objective 1

> *Conditions:* When given finger foods (crackers, raisins, sandwich pieces)
> *Behavior:* Darryl will grasp the food
> *Criteria:* At least three times per meal, three consecutive lunchtimes

Short-Term General Case Objective 2

> *Conditions:* When given finger foods (crackers, raisins, sandwich pieces)
> *Behavior:* Darryl will pick up the food and raise it to his mouth
> *Criteria:* At least three times per meal, four of five lunchtimes

Short-Term General Case Objective 3

> *Conditions:* When given finger foods (crackers, raisins, sandwich pieces)
> *Behavior:* Darryl will pick up the food and feed himself
> *Criteria:* At least five times per meal, four of five lunchtimes

Note that the last short-term objective is identical to the long-term objective.

General Case Instruction

General case instruction adheres to the guidelines specified earlier in this chapter for systematic instruction. Assistance and encouragement procedures are stated in an instructional plan and implemented exactly as stated. When an instructional plan is developed for a general case objective, the stimulus and/or response exemplars are specified. The plan is designed so that exemplars are taught concurrently rather than separately. For example, for the short-term objective in which Darryl grasps raisins, crackers, and pieces of sandwich, the instructional plan includes daily opportunities for instruction with the three types of finger foods and the three types of grasp (this is in contrast to teaching Darryl to grasp raisins until the skill is mastered, then to grasp crackers until grasping crackers is mastered, and so on). Figure 6.3 is a general case instructional plan for this objective.

Other Generalization Procedures

A number of other methods have been demonstrated to facilitate generalization (Stokes & Baer, 1977). These methods can be incorporated into general case instructional plans to increase the likelihood of generalization. There are five generalization procedures in addition to the sufficient exemplar strategy:

1. Program common stimuli
2. Introduce to natural maintaining contingencies
3. Use indiscriminable contingencies
4. Mediate generalization
5. Train loosely

Program Common Stimuli In this technique, materials or stimuli from the generalization situations are used in the instructional situation. For example, if a preschooler must learn to drink with a straw from a milk carton for school, the family may assist their child to learn the skill at home. They implement the program common stimuli technique by using the same type of milk carton and straw at home that are used at the preschool. When the child learns to drink from the milk carton at home, he or she is likely to generalize and demonstrate the skill at school where the same stimuli are present. The program common stimuli technique is also a good generalization technique when instructional objectives address skills needed in subsequent environments (e.g., teaching cutting in preschool with the same types of scissors that will be used in kindergarten).

Introduce to Natural Maintaining Contingencies Natural maintaining contingencies refer to the reinforcers and schedules of reinforcement that occur in settings in which skills are needed. In this strategy, generalization is promoted by gradually shifting from instructional reinforcers and reinforcement schedules to natural ones. Natural and instructional reinforcers initially

	Date begun: 9/27/05	
Child: Darryl	Date completed:	
Objective: Finger feeding (grasping finger food)	Interventionist(s): Anna and Mom	
Conditions: When given finger foods (crackers, raisins, and sandwich pieces)		
Response: Darryl will grasp the food		
Criterion: At least 3 times per meal, 3 consecutive lunchtimes		

Intervention Context	Prompting/Facilitation Techniques	Consequences

Setting(s):
  Mondays: infant center
  Others days: home
 	
Routine(s)/Activity(ies):
  Lunch
 	
Skill Sequence(s):
  Makes choice
  Grasps food
  Asks for more
 	
Occasions for Incidental Intervention:
  n/a
	Positioning and Handling; Special Equipment/Materials:
	  Seated in adaptive high chair with tray
	  Crackers, raisins, sandwich pieces
	
	Environmental Modifications:
	  Place finger foods on plate with high lip.
	
	Prompting/Facilitation:
	  Guide Darryl's hand as needed toward food; wait 6 seconds.
	
	Additional Generalization Procedures:
	  Use same plate at home and infant center (program common stimuli).
		Reinforcement:
		  Verbally praise Darryl for picking up food
		  Provide physical assistance to help Darryl get food to his mouth.
		
		Corrections:
		  Place Darryl's hand on top of the food piece; wait 6 seconds. If he grasps the food, provide full physical assistance to help Darryl get his food to his mouth. If he still does not grasp the food, provide full physical assistance.

Figure 6.3.   Instructional plan incorporating generalization procedure (program common stimuli).

are paired, and then the instructional ones are faded. When assisting a toddler to pull her panties and shorts up, for example, a parent's verbal praise and hug are immediately followed by allowing the child to leave the bathroom and return to play. Verbal praise and the hug are gradually eliminated, and returning to play (the natural reinforcer) continues to reinforce pulling her pants up. This natural contingency is in effect at child care and at grandma's house, and thus generalization is likely.

Use Indiscriminable Contingencies   The term *indiscriminable* means "difficult to notice" or "not too obvious." Reinforcers that are instructional are often obvious and contrived. Very noticeable instructional reinforcers may be necessary in the early phases of learning, but they interfere with generalization to other settings in which the skill is needed and similar reinforcers are not available. Gradually decreasing the obtrusiveness of an instructional reinforcer increases the likelihood of generalization. As noted earlier in this chapter, reinforcement is faded by decreasing its intensity (making verbal reinforcement quieter) or frequency (shifting to leaner and less predictable schedules of reinforcement, such as a variable interval schedule). For example, in assisting a preschooler to learn turn taking in a game with a peer, the teacher initially sits close and briefly rubs the child's back as reinforcement. This is minimally intrusive because it does not interrupt play. As the child learns to take turns, the teacher rubs her back more briefly, and only every other time the child takes a turn. Eventually, she simply touches the child's back a couple of times during a play session when the child is taking turns. Finally, the teacher moves away and withdraws the instructional reinforcement completely, as playing operates as the natural reinforcer of turn taking.

Mediate Generalization   In this technique, a strategy is taught. Examples include naming the letters of the alphabet by singing a song, or saying a poem to remember which months of the year have 30 days and which have 31. These are cognitive strategies and are applicable to toddlers and preschoolers. Other types of strategies could be included as mediational techniques. For example, teaching a child to put on his shirt by first laying it out on a flat surface such as the bed is a strategy that he can use across environments. Or, teaching a child with cerebral palsy to hold a peg on her wheelchair tray to stabilize movements is a mediational strategy that she can use across tasks requiring controlled fine motor movements (e.g., self-feeding, art activities, communication board use).

Train Loosely   In the train loosely technique, generalization is facilitated by relaxing a systematic instruction that is typically implemented in a highly consistent manner. Instead of providing precisely the same prompt, reinforcement, and correction procedure each time instruction is conducted, the components of the instructional plan vary slightly from time to time. What constitutes an acceptable response may also vary, but the variation must not extend outside the response class. Minor variations in prompting, reinforcement, corrections, and acceptable responses increases the likelihood that when a similar, noninstructional situation is encountered, generalization will occur. There is a caution, however, that if the instructional plan is implemented *too* loosely, the child will fail to acquire the skill because the benefits of the systematic instructional plan are eliminated (i.e., a predictable prompt-response-consequence relationship is no longer apparent).

When incorporating the train loosely strategy in systematic instruction, the plan should specify which components may be loosened, and acceptable examples of the component should be provided. For instance, if the prompt is trained loosely, then the plan might state: Provide a simple verbal direction, such as "Please come with me," "Let's get into the car," or "Please sit in your car seat." In implementing the plan, any of the sample prompts may be used, or prompts that are similar to the examples may be used. Each component of the instructional plan that is trained loosely should be written in this manner.

One or more of the five generalization strategies described in this section (program common stimuli, introduce natural maintaining contingencies, use indiscriminable contingencies, mediate generalization, and train loosely) may be included in a systematic general case instructional plan to supplement the train-

Date begun: 10/15/05

Child: Anisa

Date completed:

Objective: Signals to continue play

Interventionist(s): Karen, Mom, & Dad

Conditions: Given a pause during a repetitious song or rhyme game (e.g., Pat-a-cake, Peekaboo, "Row, Row, Row Your Boat," and so forth)

Response: Anisa will signal to continue play (e.g., eye contact, vocalizing, reaching out for adult, attempting to begin song/game again, and so forth).

Criterion: 3 times in 2 consecutive play periods

Intervention Context	Prompting/Facilitation Techniques	Consequences
Setting(s): After nap When Mom or Dad arrives home from work Routine(s)/Activity(ies): Repetitious songs or rhyme games Skill Sequence(s): n/a Occasions for Incidental Intervention: n/a	Positioning and Handling; Special Equipment/Materials: Sit Anisa on your lap (legs apart) facing you; support her lower back. Environmental Modifications: n/a Prompting/Facilitation: Play several seconds, then stop. Look directly at Anisa and wait 10 seconds. Additional Generalization Procedures: Vary song and rhyme game. Vary verbal corrections: "What?" "Whose turn is it?" "Do it again," and so forth. Accept any signal that seems to be a request to continue (train loosely).	Reinforcement: Reinstate game more enthusiastically than before; smile and laugh enthusiastically. Corrections: Provide a verbal prompt, such as "Do it again," or "What?" or "Whose turn is it?" Wait 5 more seconds. If she responds—reinforce. If still incorrect, begin a different game and try again.

Figure 6.4. Instructional plan incorporating generalization procedures (train loosely).

sufficient-exemplar strategy that is the heart of general case instruction. Figures 6.4 and 6.5 demonstrate instructional plans incorporating these procedures.

IMPLEMENTATION CONSIDERATIONS

There are three key variables associated with the successful implementation of systematic instruction: *amount of engaged time, contingent arrangement of reinforcement,* and *errors kept to a minimum.*

Amount of Engaged Time

Engaged time refers to the time in which the child is actively participating in instruction. The more time spent actively engaged in instruction, the greater the amount of learning (Anderson, 1976; McWilliam, 1991; Walker & Hops, 1976).

Child: Jacob	**Date begun:** 10/16/05	
Objective: Toy play	**Date completed:**	
	Interventionist(s): Rob	
Conditions: When playing with brother, cousin, or neighbor		
Response: Jacob will shake or bang small toys (squeak ball, rattle, wooden spoon)		
Criterion: For 3 seconds or more, 6 times		

Intervention Context	Prompting/Facilitation Techniques	Consequences
Setting(s): Living room, brother's room, or lanai **Routine(s)/Activity(ies):** While brother waits for school bus When Mom babysits neighbor and/or cousin **Skill Sequence(s):** n/a **Occasions for Incidental Intervention:** Whenever Jacob laughs at peer's play	**Positioning and Handling; Special Equipment/Materials:** Side lying or prone over a pillow **Environmental Modifications:** Toys must be within easy reach. **Prompting/Facilitation:** Shake or bang the toy 3 times within Jacob's reach; wait 5 seconds. **Additional Generalization Procedures:** After 2 consecutive correct, change to FR2 reinforcement schedule; after 2 more correct, change to VR3 (use indiscriminable contingencies).	**Reinforcement:** Praise both children for playing nicely; assist peer to help Jacob bang or shake the toy 3 or 4 more times. **Corrections:** Tap Jacob's arm and say "Play with your toy"; if he does, reinforce as stated above. If he still doesn't shake or bang the toy, physically assist him through a correct response; do not reinforce.

Figure 6.5. Instructional plan incorporating generalization procedure (use indiscriminable contingencies).

Instruction is more likely to be effective if it is implemented frequently *and* requires active responding on the part of the child (rather than the child being a passive recipient of instruction).

Contingent Arrangement of Reinforcement

Contingent arrangement of reinforcement means that interesting stimuli are provided immediately and consistently after the child demonstrates an instructional target. It also means that we should only use stimulation contingently. In the past, noncontingent stimulation, such as auditory stimulation (ringing bells), was implemented in an effort to improve or heighten sensory functioning (auditory attending) and overall environmental awareness. Noncontingent sensory stimulation has been shown to be ineffective (Dunst, Cushing, & Vance, 1985). Instead, specific skills should be taught. For example, rather than have a father hold his 1-year-old daughter on his lap and talk to her for 5 minutes to teach her to attend (noncontingent stimulation), he might bounce his daughter on his knee each time she attends to his rhyme about a bouncing baby (bouncing is arranged contingently).

Errors Kept to a Minimum

Instruction is more effective and efficient when *errors are kept to a minimum* (Bereiter & Englemann, 1966). Successful instructional techniques are those that help a child make a response and then provide reinforcement. If errors occur frequently and the child has few opportunities to experience the correct response and its resulting reinforcement, the instructional plan should be revised. More assistance, a different type of facilitation, or a more powerful reinforcer may be necessary.

There are two concerns related to the exclusive use of errorless instruction. First is the importance of allowing young children to make errors and experience natural corrections. Children should have opportunities to experience naturally occurring corrections, particularly when the corrections include informative feedback. For example, if a toddler takes a toy from her brother without asking, her brother may take it back. The child's ability to use the natural corrections should also be monitored. If the child does not seem to understand them, it would be useful to pair instructional corrections with natural ones, and gradually fade the instructional corrections. In the example of the sister taking the toy from her brother, for instance, the sister might look confused when her brother takes it back for himself. An instructional correction prompting the sister to ask her brother for a toy could be paired with the natural correction (the brother taking the toy back). This might help the sister understand why her brother took the toy from her.

The second concern related to errorless instruction is the importance of providing opportunities for young children to self-correct when errors occur (the preschooler whines, but no one comes to help him, so he self-corrects by raising his hand). Corrections should only be provided when no attempt is made to self-correct. There should also be consideration given to teaching young children problem-solving skills that enable them to generate possible solutions (i.e., self-corrections) to minimize their dependence on adults and instructional corrections. Regardless of the specific type of instruction used, the three major variables associated with successful instruction—engaged time, contingent arrangement of reinforcement, and minimal errors—should be addressed.

MONITORING SYSTEMATIC INSTRUCTION

A hallmark of systematic instruction is data-based decision making. A data-based decision is a judgment of whether to change or continue implementing an instructional plan. Objective evaluation of instructional effectiveness is determined by collecting data on skill acquisition, graphing the data, and interpreting the graphs. Traditionally, systematic instruction was characterized by extensive data collection (i.e., data were collected continuously throughout all activities on a daily basis). In a naturalistic curriculum model, however, concerns for flexibility and unobtrusiveness must be balanced with concerns for objective evaluation. Recommendations to achieve this balance are discussed following the descriptions of how to develop and implement data collection procedures.

Measuring Instructional Progress

Recall that the dimensions on which behavior may be observed and measured were discussed in Chapter 3. There are four types of measurement systems commonly used for monitoring instructional progress: frequency, duration, interval, and time sampling. Frequency is a count of each time a behavior occurs. If the opportunities for demonstrating a skill vary from day to day, the data may be reported as percentage (9 correct responses out of 10 opportunities is 90%). Duration is the length of time a behavior occurs (one occurrence of a behavior or the total time of several occurrences of a behavior). Interval recording indicates whether the behavior occurs or does not occur during a period of time (e.g., 30-second intervals). In time sampling, the data indicate whether the behavior occurs at the moment following a specified time interval (at 30 seconds, at 1 minute, at 1 minute 30 seconds, at 2 minutes, and so forth).

Three other measurement systems are useful for data-based decision making: latency, rate, and permanent product. Latency is the time between a prompt (natural or instructional) and the response. For example, it is the time between a father taking a turn at Pat-a-cake and his child taking the next turn. Latency is a relevant measure when it affects the usefulness or functionality of a skill. If a child takes too long to respond to his father in the Pat-a-cake game, the father assumes that the child is not interested and quits the game. Latency is also relevant when a child's response times are slow due to the effects of a disability. A child with a developmental delay may be slow to initiate her response because it takes her several moments to recognize a prompt and several moments more to determine how to respond. A child may also demonstrate lengthy response latencies because of a physical impairment that interferes with movement. Families and others need to recognize a child's need for longer response latencies and adjust interaction patterns and expectations accordingly.

Rate is a measurement of how quickly or slowly responses occur (also known as fluency). For example, an infant may eat 23 spoonfuls of cereal in half an hour, that is, a rate of .76 spoonfuls per minute. Rate is calculated by dividing the number of responses by a unit of time: 23 spoonfuls divided by 30 minutes equals the number of spoonfuls per minute. Rate is typically reported as the number of responses per minute, per hour, per day, or per week. Similar to latency, rate is a relevant measure when the quickness of a response influences whether it is functional or not. For example, a child feeds himself without adult assistance, but eats only three spoonfuls within 20 minutes. His family may not allow him to feed himself at home because it is impractical to spend so much time to complete a meal. Increasing how quickly this child eats would be a meaningful objective, and rate would be the appropriate measurement system.

Permanent product measures provide lasting evidence of responses and do not require direct observation. In much of general education, written tests provide permanent product measures of school achievement. In early intervention, a physical therapist asks a child to reach as far as possible in different directions and mark on a paper with a magic marker. The marks remain as evidence of the child's range of motion. Videotapes and photographs also provide permanent product data. Permanent product measures are useful because the child's behavior (or the effect of the child's behavior) may be reviewed time and again. Skills measured by other systems of direct observation (such as frequency or duration) cannot be directly reviewed again.

Selecting a Measurement System

The primary consideration in selecting a measurement system is choosing one that provides a clear indication of how well a child is performing a target skill relative to the criterion stated in the instructional objective. Matching the measurement system to the criterion is necessary to determine when a child has met an instructional objective. If the criterion states, for example, that the child will vocalize the initial sounds of familiar words beginning with "b," "p," and "m" on three consecutive opportunities, then each time the child says a word beginning with a designated consonant sound, his or her response is recorded as correct or incorrect (+ and −). This is event recording. When three consecutive plusses are recorded, the objective has been met.

Identifying Where and When to Collect Data

The where and when of data collection is determined by three factors: 1) conditions stated in the instructional objective, 2) generalization concerns, and 3) practical and naturalistic considerations. The first factor, conditions stated in the instructional objective, often indicates what times of day, or in what situations, the skill is to be performed. For example, an objective may state conditions such as "at breakfast, lunch, and dinner." Data must be collected during all three mealtimes to know when the criterion has been met. The second factor that will influence where and when data are collected is generalization concerns. For example, the criterion of "three consecutive opportunities during free play and snack time" indicates that data must be collected at two times— free play and snack time.

Recall that a general case objective is considered mastered when generalization to one or more noninstructional exemplars from the instructional universe is demonstrated. The child's performance with untrained exemplars is measured with *generalization probes*. Generalization probes are conducted when skill acquisition has been demonstrated with the exemplars specified in the objective. To conduct a generalization probe, the child is presented with a noninstructional stimulus/situation from the instructional universe. The examples of general case instructional plans in Figures 6.3, 6.4, and 6.5 include generalization probe components. Note that generalization probes can also be conducted periodically (e.g., weekly) prior to demonstrating complete skill mastery.

The third factor that influences where and when data are collected is practical and naturalistic considerations. Practical and naturalistic considerations go hand in hand. For example, it is impractical and unnaturalistic to expect a family to collect data on how quickly their child eats at every meal. In fact, for many families, it is impractical (and inconsiderate) to ask them to collect data. Instead, infant program personnel and early childhood teachers should assume primary responsibility for data collection. Practical and naturalistic considerations suggest that a teacher should not have a clipboard and stopwatch in hand during every activity. This would certainly interfere with a teacher's full participation in an activity, and, more important, may interfere with a teacher's ability to provide instructional prompts and other physical assistance that some children may need.

The balance between the need to collect data and practical considerations is achieved by collecting data on a regular basis for the three to five objectives that are each family's highest priorities. When it is impractical to collect data every day on each instructional priority, data are collected every other day, or once a week. It should be noted, however, that the performance of infants and young children with disabilities varies considerably from day to day. Therefore, the more frequent the data collection, the more likely that the data will provide an accurate measure of child progress and instructional effectiveness. Data should be collected on lower-priority objectives every 2 to 4 weeks.

It may be impractical to record data throughout an entire activity. When it is possible to assess the criterion of an instructional objective with brief periods of measurement, it may be more practical to do so. For instance, data may be collected on a child's rate of self-feeding during the first 10 minutes of each meal rather than through an entire meal.

Figure 6.6 is a data sheet for the instructional program presented in Figure 6.5. Tally marks are used to record the frequency of play episodes that last 3 seconds or longer. Another option would have been to record the duration of toy play. Given that the duration criterion is brief (3 seconds), duration does not seem to be the most relevant feature to measure. Instead, the objective is concerned with building the frequency of brief play episodes.

Interpreting Instructional Data

To interpret child progress and instructional effectiveness from data, it is necessary to chart the data on a graph. Because child performance data tend to be variable, it is difficult to judge whether the child is progressing by simply looking at numbers on a data sheet (Holvoet, O'Neil, Chazdon, Carr, & Warner, 1983). There are numerous graphing methods, but the most common is a line graph. On a line graph, the horizontal axis (abscissa) usually represents sessions or days, and the vertical axis (ordinate) is labeled with the variable being meas-

Frequency of Shaking or Banging a Toy for 3 Seconds or More

Week of	Monday	Tuesday	Wednesday	Thursday	Friday
10/17/2005	/	//	//	/	/
10/24/2005	/	/	//	///	///
10/31/2005	//	///	///	//	///

Figure 6.6. Sample data sheet for event recording.

ured (e.g., frequency, percent, latency). Figure 6.7 is a line graph depicting child progress as indicated on the data sheet in Figure 6.6.

Once the data are graphed, the next step is to judge whether progress is adequate or not. If the child is not progressing, or is not progressing as rapidly as desired, the instructional program is changed. The modified program is then implemented and monitoring continues. Graphs should be reviewed every five or six data points. The following guidelines (based on Browder, Demchack, Heller, & King, 1989; and Haring, Liberty, & White, 1981) should be observed in making data-based instructional decisions:

1. If the graph suggests that the child is approaching criterion, no change should be made to the instructional program.

2. If the child's performance is highly variable and is not approaching criterion, change the instructional program to improve motivation.

3. If the child's performance is fairly steady and is not approaching criterion, change the instructional program to make it easier. For example, use a more detailed task analysis or use a different prompt that provides more help.

In reviewing the data presented in Figure 6.7, Hank's toy play is not improving, and the data are fairly steady. Therefore, recommendation 3 applies: change the instructional program to make it easier. The prompting procedure in the instructional program is "Shake or bang the toy three times within Hank's reach and wait 5 seconds" (see Figure 6.5). A prompt that provides more assistance is one way to make the program easier. For example, a new prompt-

Shaking or Banging a Toy for 3 Seconds or More

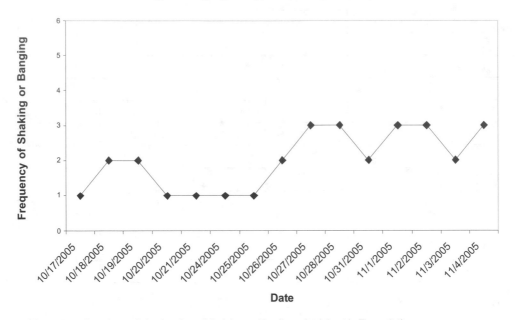

Figure 6.7. Sample graph for data-based decision making (from data sheet in Figure 6.6).

ing procedure is "Place the toy in Hank's hand and shake it or bang it several times. Stop in the middle of a banging or shaking motion and wait 5 seconds." This prompt provides more direct practice prior to expecting the response and requires Hank to continue the response when it is started for him.

SUMMARY

Systematic instruction is the consistent application of procedures designed to assist and encourage a child with disabilities to acquire or improve skills needed for participation in natural experiences. Assistance procedures include a wide variety of instructional prompting procedures, such as single prompts, multiple prompts, prompt hierarchies, and errorless procedures. Encouragement procedures are reinforcement techniques and environmental strategies that help motivate a child to demonstrate a desired response. Systematic instruction can be designed to promote generalized skill acquisition by stating instructional goals as general case objectives, applying general case instruction, and/or incorporating additional generalization procedures (program common stimuli, introduce to natural maintaining contingencies, use indiscriminable contingencies, mediate generalization, and train loosely) into the instructional plan. When systematic instruction is implemented, the effectiveness of the instructional program is monitored through frequent data collection. Based on the data, program modifications are made when skill acquisition is not as expected.

······················ STUDY QUESTIONS ······················

1. Discuss how it is possible for instruction to be both systematic *and* naturalistic.

2. Write a definition of systematic instruction.

3. Describe at least three situations when it might be beneficial to use discrete trial instruction.

4. Define and provide an example of the following types of instructional prompts: indirect verbal, direct verbal, gestural, model, tactile, partial physical assistance, full physical assistance, spatial, movement, visual/pictorial, and auditory.

5. Provide an example of operationalizing a partial physical assistance prompt for helping a child hold a paintbrush.

6. Describe the difference between most-to-least assistance and least-to-most assistance prompt hierarchies. When is it most appropriate to use a most-to-least assistance prompt hierarchy?

7. Describe the difference between a prompt and a cue. Provide an example of a prompt and a cue for assisting a child in recognizing her written name.

8. Provide examples of using time delay, stimulus shaping, and stimulus fading for teaching a young child to use a communication board with three line drawings on it.

9. Identify and define the various schedules of reinforcement. When is it most appropriate to use a continuous reinforcement schedule of reinforcement? When is it most appropriate to use a variable schedule of reinforcement?

10. Provide an example of how instructional reinforcement can be shifted from a fixed ratio schedule to a variable ratio schedule.

11. What is a changing criterion design? Describe an example of using the changing criterion strategy in teaching a preschool child a new skill.

12. Discuss how the instructional situation, materials, and style of presentation can be used to provide encouragement (motivation).

13. Write a definition of generalization.

14. Define and compare stimulus and response generalization.

15. Write a general case objective for the skill of taking turns.

16. Describe the major elements of a general case instructional plan.

17. Define and provide an example of the following generalization procedures: train sufficient exemplars, program common stimuli, introduce to natural maintaining contingencies, use indiscriminable contingencies, mediate generalization, and train loosely.

18. Discuss the following three considerations for implementing systematic instruction: amount of engaged time, contingent arrangement of reinforcement, and minimizing errors.

19. Develop a data collection strategy for teaching a child to play blocks with a sibling or peer. Draft a graph for charting the data.

7

Designing Culturally Relevant Instruction

Mary Jo Noonan

······················· **FOCUS OF THIS CHAPTER** ·····················

- *Instructional conversation* model of culturally compatible education

- Cultural variables that can be modified to promote participation and learning

- Stages in learning English as a second language

- Strategies to support young children who are learning English as a second language

Given the increasing cultural and linguistic diversity of the United States, it is critical that early childhood professionals be knowledgeable about procedures and strategies that are effective in meeting the needs of children from diverse backgrounds (Hains et al. 2000). Some children and their families of culturally and linguistically diverse backgrounds will be Americans from sociocultural minority backgrounds (e.g., African Americans, Chinese Americans, Appalachians, Navajos). Others will be relatively new to the United States and the American culture. Language experiences of children from culturally diverse families will vary from standard English to an English dialect or Creole; from bilingualism (or multilingualism) to little or no English. Proficiency in their home language, as well as English, may be severely limited.

Culture has been defined as the "shared implicit and explicit rules and traditions that express the beliefs, values, and goals of a group of people" (Kalyanpur & Harry, 1999, p. 3). From an instructional point of view, the purpose of recognizing culture and its dynamics is to provide a basis for designing effective educational arrangements and practices. Addressing cultural considerations does not imply stereotyping. Instead, knowing a child's culture may offer insight into the norms or standards that influence behavior and thinking (Goodenough, 1981). Part of this insight involves identifying learning styles and preferences that, if honored, will increase the effectiveness of instruction.

Cultural *and* linguistic variables must be addressed to provide an optimal educational experience; they are an inextricable part of learning, affecting all daily experiences and communications. Although it is nearly impossible to sort the effects of universally effective teaching practices from those of cultural accommodations, it is likely that both contribute to student learning (Goldenberg, 2004). This chapter, however, focuses on environmental arrangements and instructional approaches that have been shown to be effective for children whose home culture and/or language are different from that of school or early intervention services.

CULTURALLY COMPATIBLE EDUCATION

Children come to early childhood settings with social, communication, and behavioral competencies learned from experiences with their families and home communities. These experiences establish the expectation that behavior that was effective and acceptable for them in the past should be effective and acceptable in the present and future. A cultural mismatch occurs when the child's expectations are not realized in the early childhood setting. *Culturally compatible education* is an instructional approach characterized by modifications to the social, communication, and behavioral expectations of a learning environment to mirror the expectations of a child's home and community environment (Jordan & Tharp, 1979; Tharp, 1989; Tharp & Gallimore, 1988). The intent is to establish an educational environment that is familiar and consistent with children's competencies and expectations, thereby increasing participation and improving learning.

Instructional conversation (IC) is an empirically tested model of cultur-ally compatible education (Tharp, 1989; Tharp & Gallimore, 1988; Tharp & Ya-mauchi, 1994). In contrast to a western model of American schooling that is highly routinized (structured around recitation) and dominated by a teacher, IC builds on a dialogue between children and their teacher, with the teacher weav-ing prior knowledge and experiences with new material. The IC model modi-fies the learning environment to address four cultural factors: 1) sociolinguis-tics, 2) cognition, 3) motivation, and 4) social organization.

Sociolinguistics

Sociolinguistics refers to the conventions or rules of conversational style. Stud-ies have shown that when particular sociolinguistics of the classrooms are modi-fied to more closely match those of children's home environments, student parti-cipation and learning improve (Allen & Boykin, 1992; White & Tharp, 1988). The sociolinguistic variables that have been modified are wait time, discourse struc-tures, and speech volume and eye gaze.

Wait Time The time provided for individuals to speak and respond has been referred to as *wait time* (Rowe, 1974). For a number of Native American Indian cultures, student participation is greater if wait time is extended (Green-baum, 1983; Phillips, 1983; Winterton, 1976). In contrast, children who are Na-tive Hawaiians participate more in school when classroom discussions allow for negative wait times; that is, when children speak when someone else is speaking (*overlapping speech*) rather than wait for the speaker to finish (White & Tharp, 1988). To promote participation in an early childhood "circle time" with children of Hawaiian ancestry, for example, encourage them to speak out and overlap their responses with others as they would do in a conversation with family members in their home environment. This is in contrast to giving children turns or requiring them to raise their hands and wait to be called on.

Discourse Structures Verbal interaction during instruction, including presentation of materials, voice inflections, and body movements, occurs some-what rhythmically and may be established by the teacher or children (Tharp & Yamauchi, 1994). For example, a *call-and-response* rhythm characterizes the interactions of African American children and adults (Franklin, 1992; Hale-Benson, 1986). This tempo and participation structure, similar to a negative wait time, is a form of active listening in which the listener calls out and verbally responds to the speaker. Its pace has been likened to a *contest* or rhythmical back and forth *volley* between speaker and listener (Hale-Benson, 1990). Es-mailka and Barnhardt (1981) conducted a study of Athabascan Native Ameri-can teachers in Alaska and their Athabascan students in a school in which the students were performing at or above national norms on standard measures of school success. They observed that the students set the rhythm during in-struction and the teachers entered the activity later, following the tempo set by the students. These participation structures are in striking contrast to a *switch-board* structure that characterizes traditional Western classrooms in which the teacher regulates who speaks and when he or she speaks (Philips, 1976, 1983). In both examples described above, it appears that providing children with familiar participation structures seems to promote engagement. A number of varied participation structures have been identified across Native Americans (Erickson & Mohatt, 1982; Greenbaum, 1983; Philips, 1976, 1983), African Americans (Hale-Benson, 1986, 1990), Latinos (Goldenberg & Gallimore, 1991), and Hawaiians (Au, 1980; Au & Mason, 1981).

In an early childhood setting, for example, a teacher should first watch children interacting in small groups, taking note of the rhythm of the children's activity and interactions to support their participation through discourse structures. Do the children take turns or work concurrently? Do they watch one another or work more independently? Does one child seem to direct the group? Does the pace of the activity or conversation seem slow or fast? As a group, are they quiet or talkative? When does a child initiate or enter a conversation? For how long does a child speak? What seems to cue a child to stop speaking? After careful observation of the groups, the teacher may enter the group, carefully following the existing rhythm of participation, pacing herself to match the tempo of the group, adhering to apparent conversational rules (e.g., the group may allow children to speak for as long as they wish), and allowing the children to direct their activity as they were doing before she joined their group.

Speech Volume and Eye Gaze Voice level, ranging from soft to loud, is another sociolinquistic variable that differs across cultures and may affect children's participation in educational/intervention settings. Native Americans tend to speak at a soft volume (Darnell, 1979; Key, 1975). Because of their quiet tone, teachers who are not Native American may believe that the children are sullen or lack interest. And if non-Native American teachers speak in loud voices, the Native American children may judge their teachers to be mean. As a sign of politeness and respect, children from African American and many Native American cultures avoid or do not sustain eye contact with teachers; however, this may be perceived as rude or noncompliant by adults of other cultures (Darnell, 1979; Greenbaum, 1983; Johnson, 1971). To promote children's participation in early childhood settings, teachers should accept speech volume and eye-gaze patterns from children's home cultures. Teachers can identify family expectations for these behaviors by observing the children interact with their parents and other familiar adults, or discussing the expectations with individuals who are knowledgeable about the practices of the pertinent culture.

Cognition

The second component of the IC model, cognition, refers to the thinking, problem-solving, and learning processes. Cross-cultural research suggests that culture has a significant influence on individuals' preference for instructional approaches and the conditions under which instruction is most effective (Winzer

& Mazurek, 1998). This component is sometimes referred to as *learning style* (Hilliard, 1989). Providing children with instructional situations that match their learning styles will increase their comfort level and understanding and thereby facilitate their participation. Cognitive or learning style variables that appear frequently in the literature include verbal thinking versus visual thinking, field dependence versus field independence, cognitive tempo, and cooperation versus competition.

Verbal Thinking versus Visual Thinking The dominant educational model in North America relies heavily on a verbal learning style rather than a visual style (Tharp, 1989; Tharp & Gallimore, 1988). In a verbal learning style, children are expected to learn information presented sequentially through oral explanations and written assignments. In contrast, the visual style presents learners with a context (perhaps a story) for linking the new information with previously acquired knowledge and experience. The actual presentation of new content may also include visual examples and opportunities for observation and participation. Cultures that tend to be characterized by verbal thinking include Euro-Americans, Japanese Americans, and Chinese Americans, and cultures that tend to prefer a visual learning style include Native Americans and Native Hawaiians. Other *preferred learning modalities* may include the kinesthetic (movement), tactile (touch), and multiple modalities (Shade, 1994; Shade, Kelly, & Oberg, 1997). In early childhood settings, verbal *and* visual thinking styles can be supported by presenting instructions, cues, and materials in both formats. For example, use charts with simple pictures to accompany verbal instructions, use visual activity schedules (a series of simple line drawings depicting each of the day's activities) concurrent with teacher directions to transition to the next activity, and provide tape recorded instructional reminders to support paper and pencil or art activities.

Field Dependence versus Field Independence Closely associated with the verbal versus visual learning style is a cognitive style for processing information referred to as field dependent or field sensitive (Ramirez & Castenada, 1974) and field independent (Witkin, Moore, Goodenough, & Cox, 1977). According to Witkin and his colleagues, learners who are field dependent prefer a holistic style of instruction similar to the visual style presented above. They tend to be passive in receiving information, group-oriented, cooperative, and socially motivated. The field-dependent style is characteristic of collectivist cultures (the group is more valued than the individual) such as African Americans (Shade et al., 1997) and Mexican Americans (Ramirez & Castenada, 1974). Children who have a field-dependent learning style are sensitive to others' judgments and prefer close personal relationships (Correa & Tulbert, 1991). In contrast, children who have a field-independent style of learning are more likely to be from individualist cultures (the individual is more valued than the group), such as Euro-Americans and Asians (Shade et al., 1997). In general, these children prefer analytic, competitive, task-oriented, and experiential learning activities. They appear to be self motivated and prefer to work independently. They are not strongly affected by others' judgments and favor formal relationships with teachers (Correa & Tulbert, 1991). Their learning style is similar to the verbal learning style described above. In an early childhood setting, for example, a reading comprehension activity for field-dependent learners might be a cooperative learning group in which small groups of children create a scene with building blocks depicting an event of the story. This would be in contrast to a field-independent activity in which the teacher asks the group questions about the story, expecting the children to raise their hands and respond individually.

Cognitive Tempo Cognitive tempo refers to the tendency to be primarily impulsive or primarily reflective. The degree of impulsivity or reflectiveness is judged by the extent to which alternatives are considered when more than one solution is possible. When children are impulsive they tend to act quickly and without a course of action, make many errors, and have poor attention. On the other hand, reflective children respond more slowly, carefully, and systematically. They are persistent in their work, hold high standards for themselves, and make few errors. An impulsive learning style has been linked to reading and problem-solving difficulties (Epstein, Hallahan, & Kauffman, 1975). Some differences across ethnic groups have been reported for performance and cognitive tempo. Ayabe & Santos (1972) found that American second graders of Japanese and Chinese ancestry could perform at a fast tempo with significantly fewer errors than their Hawaiian, Filipino Americans, and Samoan American peers. Another study of young Asian Americans and Pacific Islander Americans indicated that cognitive tempo did relate to ethnicity (Kitano, 1983). Ordered according to the degree of reflectiveness, Chinese American children were the most reflective, followed by Hawaiian, Japanese Americans, Korean Americans, and Filipino American. Some gender differences were also noted: Chinese American boys were more reflective than the girls, and Japanese American and Hawaiian girls were more reflective than the boys in their respective ethnic groups.

In an early childhood setting, children with impulsive learning styles will be most successful working independently if tasks are simple. For more complex tasks, however, children with impulsive learning styles should be guided in strategies for analyzing and problem solving. For example, if 3-year-olds with an impulsive learning style are presented with a pouring task at a learning center, most will be able to participate independently following a single demonstration. For a learning center task of tanagrams (matching geometric blocks to a model pattern), however, the children will be more successful if they are guided through a specific strategy for fitting the blocks to the pattern. The guidance should be repeated many times until the children can demonstrate the strategy independently.

Cooperation versus Competition Competitive classroom structures tend to be the norm in American schools. Children are encouraged and rewarded for high achievement, particularly when it is accomplished independently

(Winzer & Mazurek, 1998). This style of schooling fits with capitalism and Euro-American values. Some cultures, however, value cooperation, sharing, and contribution to the group over competition, independence, and individual achievement. Children whose families place priority on cooperation and group efforts may be unwilling to compete, may look to peers for assistance, and may avoid excelling at tasks because they are reluctant to be singled out and commended for their work. If educators are unaware of how a cultural value of cooperation may be affecting children's performance, they may incorrectly assume that some children are lazy, unmotivated, or of low ability (Grossman, 1995; Winzer & Mazurek, 1998). And it is important to note that a competitive instructional setting does not optimize the educational achievement of children who are cooperatively oriented (Widaman & Kagan, 1987). Consistent with supporting children with a field-dependent learning style, cooperative learning groups are beneficial to children from cultures that place a high value on group contributions and collaboration. In the early childhood setting, a social skills lesson about *our neighborhood* could involve an outing exploring the community around the school. This is followed by a group activity in which children assemble a felt board picture representing what they learned about their neighborhood. The teacher facilitates conversation about the experience by commenting on what the children are including in their pictures and elaborating on statements they make. This would be in contrast to a more traditional approach in which the teacher stands in front of the group, describes the concept of *neighborhood*, and questions the children in a didactic format.

Motivation

A third component of the IC model is motivation. The general attitude of a child toward learning has been referred to as *trait motivation*, whereas, the child's desire to learn during a specific task is known as *state motivation* (Christophel, 1990). The distinction may be meaningful because culture can affect both differentially. For example, some children of a cultural minority group who feel particularly oppressed by the dominant Euro-American culture may approach their school experience with distrust and expectations for failure. Ogbu (1991) believes this is true for *involuntary minorities* (groups that did not become Americans by choice) such as Native Americans and African Americans. Tharp (1989) and Tharp & Gallimore (1988), however, have not found these characteristics in the Native American children they've studied. Nevertheless, being aware that some young children may come to school mistrusting the educational system or with an expectation for failure highlights the importance of developing positive personal relationships with students and providing curricular supports that ensure success.

Trait motivation has also been shown to have positive effects on educational outcomes for children of culturally diverse backgrounds, including some who have experienced high degrees of linguistic barriers, prejudice, and teasing. This has been the experience of recent Hmong, Vietnamese, and Korean immigrant children whose success has been attributed to trait motivation (Hirayama, 1985). These children approached schooling with strong parental, community, and cultural support for success.

State motivation, the drive to succeed at a specific task, has been shown to directly affect school participation and achievement of Hawaiian children and children from some Native American cultures (Tharp & Yamauchi, 1994). Classroom variables that seem to affect state motivation include relevance and interest level of materials, contingent reinforcement and punishment, and teacher–student relationships. For example, in one study, Native American children in first through third grades told stories to their teachers who transcribed them. The transcribed stories served as reading texts for the children. In a one-year, post-test, the children using their transcribed stories as texts made greater oral language gains than the children in a control group. Parents also reported that more language-related activities occurred in the home because of the culturally relevant materials (Butterfield, 1983). Studies of verbal praise and punishment indicate that Hawaiian children participate more when clearly articulated school-based incentives are used (D'Amato, 1981). In contrast, Navajo children participate more in school when overt reinforcement and punishment are omitted. They engage more in educational activities when adults give them autonomy in their learning and allow them to take responsibility for organizing and completing their assigned work (Jordan, Tharp, & Vogt, 1985).

Social Organization

The fourth and final element of ICs, social organization, refers to the ways in which schools, classrooms, and teaching are structured. The traditional American classroom is teacher-directed and relies primarily on whole class instruction and demonstration, followed by individual practice and testing. For some children of minority cultures, this social structure is associated with low attention to academic work and to the teacher, and greater attention to peers, often causing disruptions (Gallimore, Boggs, & Jordan, 1974). Instead, these children participate and learn more in classrooms organized around small-group instruction and cooperation that allow for peer interaction and support. The effectiveness of small-group social organization over the more traditional teacher-directed, individualized, and competitive classroom has been demonstrated for children who are Native Hawaiian (Tharp, 1989), Native American (Leith & Slentz, 1984; Lipka, 1990; Philips, 1976), African American (Slavin, DeVies, & Edwards, 1983), and Mexican American (Castenada, 1976).

The IC model for teaching children of diverse cultural backgrounds provides an engaging learning environment that maximizes children's participation. Table 7.1 summarizes the IC variables, components of each, and recommendations for inclusive early childhood settings. Instruction is built around instructional exchanges that are sensitive to *sociolinguistic* variables, such as wait time and participation structures. *Cognition* variables are addressed by allowing children to use their preferred learning styles. Many children of cultur-

Table 7.1. Instructional conversation model variables, components, and recommendations for culturally diverse and inclusive early childhood settings

Variable	Examples of components	Recommendations for promoting children's participation and learning
Sociolinguistics	Wait time	Observe groups of children and notice the wait time (time between conversational turns) during their interactions. Adhere to this observed wait time in classroom interactions (note that some wait times may be negative and characterized by overlapping speech).
	Discourse structures	Observe groups of children and notice the tempo and style of the interactions (highly active, calling out, reserved, slowly taking turns, and so forth). Enter the group, taking care to follow the preestablished tempo. In didactic instruction, mirror the tempo observed in the children's groups and/or allow the children to set the rhythm of instruction.
	Speech volume and eye gaze	Accept the children's speech volume and eye gaze. Recognize that if a child's speech volume or eye gaze differs from your expectations, it may be a cultural variable rather than a sign of disrespect.
Cognition (learning style)	Verbal versus visual thinking (and other learning modalities)	Use visual and tactile prompts/materials to support verbal instruction. Notice if the children are moving a great deal while engaged in learning activities. If so, allow the movement if they remain on task.
	Field dependent versus field independent	Provide complete demonstrations or samples of tasks and activities, as well as step-by-step instructions. Teach in meaningful contexts (e.g., teach games on a playground or in the home setting in which they are likely to occur naturally). Schedule group work as well as individual work and notice which tends to be the more effective instructional arrangement (when are children most successful?). Use the more effective instructional arrangement for most instruction.
	Cognitive tempo	Provide extra guidance and assistance for complex tasks to the children who appear to have an impulsive learning style. Teach the children methodical and systematic approaches (learning strategies) to use when confronted with complex tasks.
	Cooperation versus competition	Use group instruction and cooperative learning groups for children from cultures that are group-oriented rather than individualistic and competitive. Provide group incentives and group awards rather than individual ones. If calling on children to respond during an activity, allow peers to assist in a child's response.
Motivation	Trait motivation	Recognize that some children may not trust the educational system and may expect to fail. Provide a nurturing and accepting environment, rewarding the children for participating and attempting tasks. When instructional corrections are necessary, provide them privately and in a positive, constructive manner.
	State motivation	Become familiar with the cultures of the children you teach. Use materials and activities familiar to them (e.g., children's own stories, community settings and events) as the context for instruction. Show caring and concern to the children to build rapport and a personal relationship. Provide immediate feedback for correct responding.
Social organization	Small-group versus whole-group instruction	Use predominantly small-group instruction and cooperative learning groups for children from cultures that are group-oriented.
	Teacher-directed versus child-directed activities	During small-group instruction, allow the children to follow their interests and direct the group.
	Peer interaction versus peer–teacher interaction	For children from cultures that are group-oriented, allow for extensive peer interaction (children helping one another and working collaboratively).

ally diverse backgrounds learn better visually than verbally. Content taught in the IC model is culturally relevant to enhance *motivation*. Furthermore, teachers are sensitive to how children respond to direct and structured behavioral consequences, realizing that some children learn well this way, while others learn better with a fair degree of autonomy. And finally, the overall *social organization* of the learning situation is dominated by small-group instruction and peer interaction.

A SUPPORTIVE LANGUAGE-LEARNING ENVIRONMENT

Children of culturally diverse backgrounds may also be children who did not learn English as their first language. If they are not yet attending school, they may be totally immersed in their family's native language and have little exposure to English. Others who attend early intervention settings, child care, preschool, or school programs may be in the process of acquiring English as a second language (ESL). In either situation, these children, known as English language learners (ELLs), have unique needs associated with their cultural and linguistic diversity that must be addressed in providing effective education.

Salend (2001) proposed that school-age children progress through six stages in ESL learning:

1. *Preproduction or silent period.* Initially, children are quiet and focus on comprehension. They rely on contextual and other clues (e.g., peer modeling) to derive meaning and to express themselves nonverbally. Nonverbal response modes are an appropriate expectation during this phase.

2. *Telegraphic or early production period.* When children acquiring a second language begin speaking, they do so with short two- and three-word sentences. It is apparent that their comprehension is quite limited. Simple language activities, such as naming and responding to easy questions, may be helpful.

3. *Interlanguage and intermediate fluency period.* Longer phrases and complex sentences emerge during this period, sometimes mixing first and second languages. This is an appropriate time to focus on vocabulary development and encourage children to test their expanding abilities with their new language.

4. *Extension and expansion period.* Comprehension has clearly improved and children produce complex sentences during this period. Specific instruction in grammar and vocabulary is helpful.

5. *Enrichment period.* In this period, children can benefit from learning strategies to help them with specific language needs (e.g., a particular rule of grammar).

6. *Independent learning period.* Children can participate and learn effectively across a range of instructional activities and in heterogeneous peer groups.

Although the six stages of second language learning proposed by Salend were formulated with reference to school-age children, in all likelihood younger children follow the same progression once they are exposed to a second language for extended periods of time (e.g., when they enter a center-based or school-based program). Being familiar with these stages of second language learning will help professionals understand and set appropriate expectations for children learning English. A professional familiar with these stages, for instance, will not assume that a toddler—a recent immigrant to the United States and an ELL—who has never spoken in a playgroup conducted in English is delayed in language development without first observing the child in his home in which his native language is spoken. Instead, the professional will recognize that it is common for ELLs to go through the *preproduction or silent* stage. Second language learning expectations for young children and those with language delays/ differences need to reflect children's current level of language development in their native language. For example, if a child has not yet begun to use single words or point to pictures to label objects in her native language, labeling objects with English words would probably not be an appropriate expectation.

Recommendations to Support ELLs

Professionals should assume that all children, even those with communication delays and/or cognitive disabilities, can learn a second language to the same extent that they have acquired a first language; there is no evidence to the contrary (Barrera, 1993). Six approaches to instruction are helpful to young children in acquiring ESL (Barrera, 1993; Bunce, 2003; Laturnau, 2001; Salend & Salinas, 2003): 1) capitalize on *all* communication skills, 2) focus on content, 3) teach in context, 4) provide relaxed environments and comprehensible input, 5) use cooperative learning methods, and 6) teach coping strategies.

Capitalize on All Communication Skills In providing services to young children with special needs who do not have English as their first language, a primary concern is that they have an effective way to communicate. Effective communication allows children to understand their experiences and the expectations of others, to have their needs met, and to continue developing their communication skills. Remember that all communication is not verbal: Prelinguistic and nonverbal communication skills must also be supported. To support children's present communication skills and concurrently address their academic goals, instruction should continue in their native language (including the use of academic materials in the native language) if possible. As children acquire English, English may become their stronger language and the language of instruction. For infants and young children who are not in school, this may mean that a family member or friend who is fluent in the child's native language plays a central role in the delivery of early intervention services if the teacher does not speak the native language. When children who are ELLs begin school, they may receive bilingual instruction so that their communication, language arts, and other academic skills may be addressed concurrently. If instruction in a child's native language is not possible, verbal communication should be supplemented with visual cues, gestures, facial expressions, modeling, and other concrete prompts to assist the child in understanding.

Focus on Content   While teaching and interacting with children who are ELLs, teachers and others should respond to the *intent or meaning* of a child's communication rather than the form or grammar. In other words, children's grammar should not be corrected, but rather the adult should respond appropriately to the child's message (e.g., if the child requests "me wants up," pick her up rather than correct her grammar!). Responding to a child's communicative intent will foster a climate that welcomes and encourages communication; frequently correcting a child's communication or requiring more sophisticated use of grammar may inadvertently punish attempts to use the new language. Responding to meaning rather than form is based on observations of how parents *naturally* facilitate language acquisition with typically developing children and is the same strategy recommended for children who are delayed in learning language (but are not ELLs).

Teach in Context   Although a primary recommendation is to focus on the content of a child's communication, this does not imply that English is not taught. English is taught *in context*—that is, in the course of a child's typical schedule of activities—when the vocabulary and communication are needed. Teaching in context not only provides natural reinforcers for communication, it links communication to meaningful events. For example, in preparation for lunch during preschool, teachers can emphasize key vocabulary and sing self-help and mealtime songs ("This is the way we wash our hands, wash our hands, wash our hands. . . ."). Repeating words and phrases about hand-washing while actually doing it is more meaningful than taking a child aside and asking him to imitate the words or phrases associated with picture cards. Songs are an effective instructional approach because they generally include repetition: Repetition helps to teach children the rhythm, pitch, volume, and tone of their new language.

During the course of daily activities in the home, child care center, or school, the naturalistic language teaching strategies of *expansion* and *elaboration* should be implemented (see also Chapter 9). An adult *expands* on a child's utterance by repeating a slightly lengthier version of what the child says. For example, if the child is building with blocks and says, "Block fall," the adult can reply with an expansion, "The block fell down." An *elaboration* also expands on what the child says, but differs from an expansion because it adds more information: "The red blocks fell and made a loud noise!"

Other strategies for teaching language in context include 1) teaching literacy through whole language, 2) using focused contrasts to illustrate grammatical forms, and 3) recording instructions on audiotape. The first strategy, whole language, is *teaching in context.* Rather than (or in addition to) an instructional time designated for literacy activities, literacy instruction is embedded throughout the day in various subjects/activities. In a child care setting, familiarizing children with books may occur as part of creative movement and cooking activities (rather than *reading time*). And in a kindergarten class, learning phonetic sounds can be embedded in community walks that are a part of social studies (identifying initial sounds as objects are named during the walk), calendar time during morning circle (identifying initial sounds of the days of the week, the weather, and so forth), and art activities (identifying initial sounds of shapes and colors). Conducting prereading, reading, and other language arts in a variety of activities takes advantage of natural teaching opportunities and maintains an emphasis on language learning throughout the day. *Focused contrasts,* the second strategy for teaching in context, are comments made by an adult to illustrate two closely related grammatical forms. Bunce (2003) provided the following focused contrast example of what an adult might say as a child is playing with dolls: "The mommy *is* walk*ing* to the house. Look! She walk*ed* in" (p. 393). Frequent experience with the two closely related grammatical forms will help the child understand the differences in meaning. And, *recording instructions on audiotape,* the third strategy for teaching in context, may help a child improve receptive language skills by giving her the opportunity to review instructions for an activity as many times as she feels is necessary to understand them.

Provide Relaxed Environments and Comprehensible Input   Comprehensible input means that the child is provided with communication that is understandable given his present language abilities (Krashen, 1982; Krashen & Terrell, 1983). A relaxed environment is usually one with comprehensible input and a situation in which the child feels free to use his developing language skills (adults accept all communication attempts and respond to meaning). In the early stages of second language learning, the goal is to help the child learn the new language; later the goal will be for the child to use the new language to obtain new knowledge or skills.

The distinction between learning a new language and using a language to learn refers to two kinds of language proficiency: basic interpersonal communicative skills (BICS) and cognitive/academic language proficiency (CALP) (Cummins, 1984). Daily conversation is associated with BICS. It takes place in context-embedded situations that are rich in paralinguistic and situational cues. In contrast, CALP is associated with more decontextualized academic situations. One cannot assume that a child's BICS and CALP are equivalent. In other words, for a child who is learning ESL, it cannot be assumed that because she uses English well in oral conversation that she has adequate proficiency for learning academics in English (Bunce, 2003). While focused on decoding and learning a language, a child cannot also be expected to learn *through* that language—the processes are too different (Westby, 1985).

For many young children who are ELLs and receiving early childhood special education, the emphasis on second language learning will be focused on BICS. As these children acquire the basic communication skills in English, it is critical that they be provided with a relaxed environment and comprehensible (meaningful) input. The following are recommendations for providing comprehensible input:

1. *Adjust speech.* Speak in simple, short sentences using vocabulary in the child's repertoire. Simple sentences are those with a straightforward gram-

matical structure, such as subject-verb ("Anisa eats."), verb-object ("Bring cup."), and subject-verb-object ("Dog has your shoe!"). In simplifying sentences, avoid using idioms, slang words or phrases, and pronouns.

2. *Provide descriptions.* Talk about what the child is doing or observing while the activity is in progress. ("You found the teddy bear card. You matched the cards. You have another turn.") Providing descriptions of ongoing events links language to context. Because the intent is to provide meaningful input in a relaxed situation rather than to elicit conversation, use comments rather than questions.

3. *Use concrete and contextual cues.* Concrete cues are prompts that are clear and obvious, rather than subtle or abstract. Examples include visuals (pictures, charts), modeling, gestures, facial expressions, voice changes, and pantomimes. Contextual cues are prompts provided in a specific place or time to take advantage of additional information in the environment. Placing a picture on a classroom cubby of a child holding her lunch bag and sweater is an example of a concrete cue indicating where the child should place her sweater and lunch bag. It is also a contextual cue because the picture is placed on the cubby, providing additional information about the place where her belongings are to be stored. Placing the cubbies close to the classroom door would be an additional contextual clue because the children would be likely to see them the moment they walked into the classroom.

4. *Use familiar and holistic experiences.* Familiar experiences may assist a child in comprehending language because the materials, setting, and expectations are already understood by the child. For example, providing rules for using playground equipment, such as a slide ("Climb up the ladder, not up the slide."), will be easier for a child to understand if she has experience with slide. A child who has experience with a slide may know that she may fall if she attempts to climb up the slide (rather than the ladder), or that another child may bump into her or knock her down if she is climbing up the slide when the other child is coming down. The child's experience provides a context that aids in understanding the language. Using familiar adults in providing intervention may also add to the familiarity of the experience. Holistic experiences provide a more meaningful context for understanding language compared with discrete or isolated ones. For example, providing step-by-step directions for a task (such as an art activity) may be helpful, but the directions will be more understandable if the child can see the finished product concurrent with the step-by-step guidance.

5. *Teach new vocabulary.* In preparation for an activity, review a few new vocabulary words that are central to talking about the activity. If visiting an animal shelter, for example, reviewing the names of the animals ("cat," "dog," "rabbit," "guinea pig") and relevant verbs ("pet," "hold," "carry," "lock") might help the child in understanding language during the visit. Key words may be highlighted through repetition, increased volume, or exaggeration.

Use Cooperative Learning Methods Cooperative learning methods are described in detail in Chapter 11. They are advantageous to children who are ELLs for a number of reasons. First, they may minimize stress by allowing for observing and nonresponding. Lowering stress may help the child attend to the activity and may provide *safe* opportunities for speaking. More linguistically capable peers serve as models, providing descriptions, directions, and questions in a meaningful context. The relaxed group setting is an opportunity for building peer support networks This can be done informally (some children initiate assisting others) or formally (through strategies such as a buddy system—assigning a peer to provide assistance), or by peer tutoring (peer assigned to teach a specific task).

Teach Coping Strategies Some children who are ELLs may be shy or hesitant to ask for help or clarification. Others may be from cultures in which it is inappropriate to ask for help directly. When adults observe that a child needs help or clarification, they can model "Help, please" with a calm expression and a smile to teach that asking for assistance is permissible. For a child who is not yet using speech, the child may be guided to take another's hand as a request for assistance. The child can be taught that it is permissible to ask peers for assistance. Providing children who are learning English with coping strategies may alleviate stress and frustration when they do not understand what to do or what is expected. Similarly, other learning strategies may be beneficial for ELLs, particularly in early childhood education settings. For example, a child may be taught to ask "Say it differently, please" if he doesn't understand a direction, or he may be taught to "look and follow" what a peer is doing if he doesn't understand what is expected.

PUTTING IT ALL TOGETHER: CULTURALLY AND LINGUISTICALLY RESPONSIVE INTERVENTION

In many cases, the cultural and linguistic considerations discussed above will need to be interwoven to create an appropriate and responsive intervention program for a young child with disabilities, whether the child is receiving services at home, at a community child care setting, or in school. Which strategies are used will be individualized to each child, family, and setting. Table 7.2 summarizes strategies to support ELLs. The following are examples for an infant, toddler, and kindergarten student:

Mei Mei: An Infant Receiving Home-Based Services

Mei Mei is 13 months old. She and her parents and 5-year-old brother are recent immigrants from Hong Kong. Mei Mei has low muscle tone and is learning to sit during playtime, eat snacks and meals, get dressed, and take a bath. She communicates mostly with gestures (pointing to what she wants) and facial expressions (pouting or crying when she is unhappy). She is very attached to her mother. One of Mei Mei's goals is to request *more* of an activity. This will be taught in the context of a repeti-

Table 7.2.   Recommendations and strategies for a supportive language-learning environment in inclusive early childhood settings

Recommendation	Strategies
Capitalize on all communication skills	Respond to nonverbal communication (facial expressions, gestures, and so forth) as well as verbal communication. Provide instruction in child's strongest language. Use visual cues, gestures, facial expressions, and other concrete cues when teaching in English.
Focus on content	Respond to meaning (the intent of the child's communication). Do not correct grammar.
Teach in context	Teach during ongoing activities (e.g., label objects during activity). Use expansion and elaboration. Teach literacy through the whole language method. Use focused contrasts to illustrate grammatical forms. Provide audiotaped instructions.
Provide a relaxed environment and comprehensible input	Recognize that a child's conversational skills (basic interpersonal communicative skills—BICS) are probably not equivalent to the child's ability to learn through the language (cognitive/academic language proficiency—CALP). Adjust speech (simplify). Provide descriptions. Use concrete and contextual cues. Use familiar and holistic experiences. Teach new vocabulary.
Use cooperative learning methods	Use small-group activities. Assign children to assist one another. Assign peer tutors.
Teach coping strategies	Model requests for assistance from adults or peers. Teach child to ask for clarification. Teach child to observe and imitate peers.

tious turn-taking game while seated on her mother's lap. Examples of cultural and linguistic accommodations to this activity are as follows:

Cultural accommodations. Mei Mei's mother and brother will first model the game (holding hands, facing each other, singing, and rocking back and forth, and stopping; brother says, "more" and the game begins again). Modeling the complete activity may assist Mei Mei in understanding the expectation if she is a *field-dependent* learner. While the brother and mother model, the interventionist will note if the *wait time* for turn taking appears to be very short (or overlapping) or long. When it is Mei Mei's turn with mother, the interventionist will prompt Mei Mei's mother (if necessary) to match the wait time observed when the brother modeled the activity. The interventionist will also encourage Mei Mei's brother to play the game with her. Although he is only 5 years old, he regularly helps care for Mei Mei (a *social organizational* variable).

Linguistic accommodations. Mei Mei's brother and mother will sing to her in Cantonese—the language they use in their home—during the turn-taking game as a strategy to *provide a relaxed environment and comprehensible input*. When the repetitious game stops, any gesture or verbalization will be accepted to indicate "more." Accepting any communication form *capitalizes on all communication skills*. Mei Mei's mother or brother will respond by restarting the game (*responding to meaning*) and saying something similar to "Play again!" alternately in Cantonese and English. Saying "Play again!" *expands* on Mei Mei's response, *teaches during an ongoing activity*, and provides comprehensible input by using both languages (*using simple speech, a familiar experience*, and *contextual cues*).

Toa: A Toddler in Early Head Start

Toa and his family are originally from American Samoa. They moved to the United States 4 years ago when Toa was 12 months old to have greater access to family health care. Toa is now 3 years old and attends Early Head Start five mornings a week. He speaks softly in English, using single words or two-word sentences, and often avoids eye contact with adults. Toa has spina bifida and is unable to move around the classroom independently. One of his goals is to request assistance as needed to do an activity (imitate movements, retrieve an object that is out of reach).

Cultural accommodations. Two of Toa's aunties are classroom volunteers. His aunties will be asked to assist in conducting free-play activities similar to those that their children play at home (*addressing state motivation by using familiar activities*). An example is a body part song ("Where is your_____") that Samoan adults frequently play with children ("O fea o iai lou _____ ?" [ulu, isu, gutu, taliga, mata, lima]). Classroom staff will pay close attention to Toa and will model "Help, please" when he appears to need assistance in imitating the song motions or obtaining a material or toy that is out of reach. Staff will respond and provide assistance immediately to any verbalization or gesture, *accepting low speech volume and eye gaze* (even if Toa doesn't make eye contact). If Toa does not say "Help, please," staff will model the request a second time while providing assistance.

Linguistic accommodations. Responding to any verbalization that Toa makes as a request for assistance will *capitalize on all communication skills* and is a response to *meaning rather than grammar*. Repeating the model when Toa does not imitate, it provides *expansion*. And finally, teaching Toa to request assistance is a *coping strategy* that Toa may be able to use in situations when he lacks comprehension.

Maile: A Kindergarten Student

Maile is a 5-year-old of Hawaiian descent who lives with her grandparents and three siblings in a rural coastal area. She attends a developmentally appropriate, fully inclusive kindergarten. Maile has developmental delays and is working on preacademic skills similar to those of her classmates.

Cultural accommodations. Use small-group activities for practicing preacademic skills, allowing children to help one another, model for one another, and converse while they work (the Hawaiian culture tends to be *group-oriented and values peer interaction*). Ask the class as a whole to talk about their activity to summarize the lesson. Allow more than one child to talk at a time (*negative wait time*) and to call out answers (Hawaiian *discourse structure*).

Linguistic accommodations. Accept *pidgin* (Hawaiian *creole* English) grammar when Maile responds (*capitalize on all communication skills; focus on content*). In addition to accommodating her group-oriented cultural style, using the *small-group activities* also will provide a linguistic accommodation that will promote more language use. Use *peer tutors* within the small-group situation when Maile needs assistance with assigned tasks.

SUMMARY

Supporting children of diverse backgrounds to participate and learn in early intervention/early childhood special education requires that cultural and linguistic variables be addressed. The *instructional conversation (IC)* model describes modifications to sociolinguistic, cognition, motivation, and social organization variables that have been shown to improve children's participation and learning in educational situations. The modifications are designed to align a child's experiences and expectations in educational environments with those of home environments. Children of diverse cultures may also benefit from linguistic accommodations: some children will have languages other than English as their first language, and others may have learned a cultural variation of standard English. Six approaches can assist children in acquiring English) capitalize on *all* communication skills, 2) focus on content, 3) teach in context, 4) provide relaxed environments and comprehensible input, 5) use cooperative learning methods, and 6) teach coping strategies. Instructional strategies for diverse learners should include cultural *and* linguistic accommodations and be designed on an individualized basis.

•••••••••••••••••••••• **STUDY QUESTIONS** ••••••••••••••••••••••

1. Referencing the definition of culture, discuss several ways in which culture may influence a child's educational experiences.

2. Identify and describe the three components of culturally compatible education.

3. Define the four cultural factors associated with the Instructional Conversation (IC) model: sociolinguistics, cognition, motivation, and social organization.

4. Choose one sociolinguistic variable associated with the IC model and provide an example of how it may be modified to support a child's learning in a home-based early intervention setting and in an inclusive preschool setting.

5. Discuss various ways that cooperative learning groups can be modified to create culturally compatible education.

6. List and describe Salend's six stages that school-aged children progress through when learning English as a second language (ESL).

7. Describe a rationale for bilingual instruction for children who are ELLs.

8. What does it mean to "teach in context" for children who are ELLs? Provide an example for a preschool setting.

9. Define and contrast the terms *basic interpersonal communication skills (BICS)* and *cognitive/academic language proficiency (CALP)*. What is the implication of the concepts for addressing the needs of young children who are ELLs?

10. Identify and describe three strategies for providing children who are ELLs with *comprehensible input*.

8

Teaching Children with Autism

Mary Jo Noonan

Children with autism, or *autism spectrum disorder* (ASD), include children who vary widely in their abilities and educational needs. Autism was first defined as a disorder in 1943 by the psychologist Leo Kanner. He had encountered a number of children who had behavioral characteristics and needs that were strikingly different from children with mental retardation and developmental delay. In particular, the children with autism had typical physical growth and development, but they also had social relationship difficulties, speech–language delays and differences, an obsession with environmental sameness and/or stereotypy (repetitive movements such as finger flicking), and self-stimulation. Since that time, definitions and diagnostic criteria have been promulgated by a number of organizations/policies (e.g., Individuals with Disabilities Education Act, Autism Society of America, Diagnostic and Statistical Manual of the American Psychological Association [DSM IV-TR]), but the central defining characteristics of the disorder have not changed. Current diagnostic criteria distinguish among individuals with few or mild characteristics (Asperger syndrome) and those with more or pronounced characteristics (pervasive developmental disorder [PDD], including autistic disorder). In this chapter, the term *autism* will be used to refer to all labels/disorders on the autism spectrum, but keep in mind that the characteristics and needs will vary in number and degree (from mild to severe).

CHARACTERISTICS OF AUTISM

Many of the distinguishing characteristics of autism have important implications for instruction. Specifically, they suggest that certain content, instructional approaches, and environmental arrangements will be more effective than others. The following characteristics of children with autism should be considered in designing specialized instruction.

Communication and Social Needs

One of the most noticeable concerns of children with autism is that they have significant communication and social delays or differences. For example, a mother may be worried when her 18-month-old child is not attempting to communicate or socialize (e.g., not pointing or otherwise indicating that she wants desired objects, not gesturing or vocalizing to be picked up or to get attention, not playing typical baby games such as Peekaboo, crying when tired or frustrated but not looking to an adult for comfort). Frequently children with autism make little or no eye contact. They appear isolated and unaware of people and events in their environment. Some have socialization and communication behaviors that are markedly different from their age peers. For example, a child with autism may talk using only phrases and sentences imitated from cartoons. Or the child may play with toys in a repetitive and/or ritualistic manner (e.g., sorting and lining up plastic dishes) rather than in more object-specific or socially influenced ways (e.g., playing "tea party" with the cups and dishes) as age peers would do.

Generalization Needs

The behavior of children with autism is often characterized as *rigid.* The children tend not to transfer skills learned in one situation to another, and they have difficulty in adapting or modifying skills to fit new situations. For example, a child with autism may learn to pop open the toothpaste lid but not generalize the skill to the pop-up top on the shampoo bottle; or she may learn to say "please" when she wants something to drink, but she may not transfer the use of the word to dinnertime when she wants something to eat or to play activities to request a particular toy.

Preoccupation with Sameness

Many children with autism are most content and capable when expectations, materials, and other environmental variables remain constant or unchanged. For example, the child who sorts and lines up plastic dishes may be content while organizing the materials, but if asked to stop and put the materials away, he may become upset, even to the point of having a tantrum. Similarly, if he completes the task and someone disturbs the orderliness of his work (moves the toys aside, or puts them away), he may react very strongly. When children with autism have a strong preference for consistency or order, it is not uncommon for families to be extremely cautious to avoid disturbing the materials or environmental arrangements on which the children focus.

Challenging Behavior

Children with autism frequently have numerous behavioral challenges. They may isolate themselves (hide under furniture), act aggressively toward others (hit, kick, push), injure themselves (bite, pinch, head-bang), and/or demonstrate other socially inappropriate behaviors. As discussed in detail in Chapter 10 (Procedures for Challenging Behavior), challenging behavior usually serves a communication purpose. Because children with autism have significant communication needs, it is not surprising that challenging behaviors are present.

Dawson and Osterling (1997) have suggested that effective programs for children with autism, given the children's unique characteristics and concerns, should include the following:

1. *Curriculum content emphasizing attending skills, imitation (gestural and verbal), language comprehension and use, appropriate toy play (functional and symbolic), and social interaction (with adults and with peers).* Attending and imitative skills are emphasized because they are *tool skills* that facilitate subsequent learning (and are often lacking in children with autism). Language comprehension and use and social interaction skills are included because they are high-need areas for children with autism. Appropriate toy play is a cognitive skill area that is included because children with autism often have difficulty understanding the social purpose of objects and the use of symbols (language learning relies on the use of symbols).

2. *A highly supportive teaching environment and generalization strategies.* The term *highly supportive* implies that instruction is carefully planned and executed based on the unique needs and strengths of the child. Supportive teaching often includes instructional objectives that are just slightly beyond the child's current performance level, direct instruction methods (see Chapter 6), and a consistent schedule (see Chapter 13). Because generalization difficulties are prevalent among children with autism, generalization strategies should be included in all instructional plans (see Chapter 6).

3. *Learning environments that are predictable and routine.* As discussed fully in Chapter 13, predictability and routines teach children what to expect. In turn, knowing what to expect supports children in demonstrating appropriate behavior and promotes independence. Importantly, predictability and routines add *order* to what would otherwise seem a chaotic world. Children with autism commonly show a high preference for orderliness. Establishing predictable and routine learning environments capitalizes on a preferred learning style, creates a familiar and comfortable situation, and thereby facilitates learning.

4. *A functional, positive approach to problem behaviors.* A functional approach to problem behaviors focuses on teaching socially appropriate alternative responses to replace the problem behavior. In other words, children are taught socially acceptable ways (usually a communication skill) to get what they want (reinforcement), thereby eliminating the need for problem behavior. In addition, a number of positive strategies should be employed to prevent problem behavior, and the use of punishment should be avoided. Chapter 10 describes functional and positive assessment and intervention procedures for challenging behavior.

5. *Carefully planned transitions to next settings.* Transitions are often difficult times for children with autism because changing from one activity to the next has the effect of ending an ongoing routine. As already discussed, children with autism prefer sameness and orderliness; ending a routine is viewed as disruptive. Therefore, transitions need to be planned and related skills (identifying next activities, putting away materials) should be taught.

6. *Family involvement.* As emphasized throughout this text, family support is a critical component of early childhood special education. Because the extensive communication, social, and behavioral needs of children with autism may affect all aspects of family life, supports might include involving family members in planning and implementing interventions. For example, family members can participate in developing and conducting an intervention to teach a child to make eye contact and to point to a desired object (a social-communication objective).

The above six items describe components of effective *programs* for children with autism. The remainder of this chapter focuses on *instructional procedures:* Those described elsewhere in this text that have proven to be effective with young children who have autism, and those designed specifically for children with autism. The chapter concludes with a description of five model programs for children with autism.

GENERAL INSTRUCTIONAL PROCEDURES

The following eight instructional approaches have been shown to be effective for children with autism, presumably because they fit with the children's learning styles and address critical developmental needs: 1) direct instruction, 2) naturalistic instruction, 3) general case instruction, 4) cues (versus general prompts), 5) fading prompts and cues, 6) group instruction, 7) augmentative communication, and 8) positive behavior support. Although these procedures are discussed in detail elsewhere in this text, this discussion focuses on special considerations in applying the procedures with children who have autism.

Direct Instruction

Chapter 6 fully described direct instruction, which is defined as the consistent use of one or more prompts, a correction procedure, and a reinforcement strategy to teach an operationally defined behavior. For example, a child may be taught to ask her sibling to play with her by handing the sibling a toy. There may be a three-step prompting and correction procedure: 1) the adult points to the toy and waits 4 seconds; if no response or an incorrect response 2) the adult hands the child the toy, points to the sibling, and waits 4 seconds, and if no response 3) the adult guides the child to the sibling, guides the child to hand the sibling the toy, and says, "Jamie, please play with me." When the child hands the sibling the toy, the adult plays the child's favorite music softly as the reinforcer. Using a precise and consistent direct instruction procedure fits with the preferences for sameness and predictability that characterize the learning styles of many children with autism. And, indeed, research indicates that children with autism learn relatively quickly with systematic instruction (Dawson & Osterling, 1997; Lovaas, 1987).

As with any application of direct instruction, it is important to individualize the prompts and correction procedures for each child. Children with autism *tend* to respond better to visual prompts compared with auditory prompts; however, teachers must be responsive to each child's performance data for each instructional plan. In other words, view each instructional plan as a "worksheet" to be modified based on its effectiveness. If the data for an instructional plan indicate that a child doesn't use a prompt (i.e., rarely or never responds correctly to a prompt), eliminate that prompt from the plan and use ones that *are* effective in eliciting correct responses.

Attentional Issues In addition to ensuring that prompts are individualized, it may be necessary to include an attentional prompt in the direct instruction plan. Many children with autism attend predominantly to objects and the physical world and seem to ignore the social world. For some children, a prompt eliciting attention to the teacher (or adult) prior to the prompt associated with the instructional objective will improve instructional effectiveness. Returning to the example above of teaching a child to ask a sibling to play, the teacher might call the child by name and make eye-to-eye contact prior to delivering each prompt.

Although eye contact is a typical way that children demonstrate attention, there may be other valid indicators of attention for children who rarely make eye contact. Some children may stop their play and become still. Others may turn their attention from one set of materials to another. And still others may orient their body and/or face toward the speaker even though they don't make direct eye contact. If direct eye-to-eye contact is difficult to achieve, look for other indicators (such as the three presented here) that the child is attending, implement the direct instruction, and monitor learning. If the child shows progress, direct eye contact may not be a requisite to effective instruction. Attentional prompts may still be included in instruction; however, attention may be operationalized as a behavior other than eye contact.

Reinforcement Issues   Because of significant social delays/needs, children with autism may not be reinforced by verbal praise or affection—reinforcers commonly used with young children with special needs. It may seem difficult to identify potential reinforcers for children with autism because they do not show the same interests as their peers without disabilities. The following are three examples of approaches that may be used to identify instructional reinforcers: 1) test the effectiveness of verbal praise and social reinforcement, 2) conduct a reinforcer survey, and 3) assess the use of high-probability (high-p) activities, including stereotyped behaviors.

The first approach, *testing the effectiveness of verbal praise and social reinforcement,* is suggested for pragmatic reasons: Before assuming that verbal praise or social reinforcement will not be effective (even when a child has significant social needs and/or does not make eye contact), test it as part of a direct instruction plan. If the instructional plan is effective, then a very natural and highly generalizable reinforcement strategy has been identified and is available for instruction.

Reinforcer assessment, the second approach, includes two procedures that may be used to identify a set of highly preferred items (could include food) that are likely to function effectively as reinforcers. One procedure is to conduct a *reinforcer survey,* either by asking a child to name favorite items or presenting numerous items to a child (often two at a time) and noting the child's most frequent choices. Observing a child's choices is often used for children who do not speak or cannot name their preferences. Studies have indicated that choice assessments evaluating a number of potential reinforcers is a valid method of identifying items that will be effective reinforcers (Pace, Ivancic, Edwards, Iwata, & Page, 1985; Piazza, Fisher, Hagopian, Bowman, & Toole, 1996). Research on children's self-report of potential reinforcers, however, suggests that self-report is not always an accurate method for identifying effective reinforcers (Northup, 2000; Northup, George, Jones, Broussard, & Vollmer, 1996).

Another procedure for assessing potentially effective reinforcers is to measure the time a child spends engaged (interacting) with items that appear to be highly preferred. Items are presented to the child one at a time, and then are rank-ordered according to duration of engagement. The longer a child interacts with an object, the more likely it is that the object will be an effective reinforcer. This procedure has been shown to be valid and easy to administer (Hagopian, Rush, Lewin, & Long, 2001; Pace et al., 1985).

Applying the Premack principle, using high-probability (high-p) activities as reinforcers, is a third approach that may be used for assessing reinforcer effectiveness. High-p activities are identified by noting which activities a child most frequently chooses in free-play situations with access to a variety of materials. The child is then given access to a high-p activity as a reinforcer for a correct response. Instructional progress can be used to confirm or disconfirm whether the activity is an effective reinforcer. Although children may enjoy engaging in some activities for extended periods of time, access to an activity reinforcer can be brief (10 or 15 seconds). Some teachers prompt the child by saying "My turn!"—signaling that the child should hand the teacher the play item (or turn away fro the activity) and return to the instructional activity. Stereotypy (repetitive movements with or without objects) can also be used as a high-p activity reinforcer and may be especially effective if its availability is restricted to when it is provided as a reinforcer (Hanley, Iwata, Thompson, & Lindberg, 2000).

Direct instruction is an effective and valuable approach to teaching skills to children with autism. For direct instruction to be maximally effective, instructional prompts should be individualized, attentional prompts may need to be added, and reinforcement assessments may be used to improve reinforcer effectiveness.

Naturalistic Instruction

As described in Chapter 9, the hallmark of naturalistic instruction (or *milieu teaching*) is providing instruction at times determined by the child's interest (e.g., when the child points to something out of reach, when the child attempts to gain a peer's attention). A premise is that child-determined occasions for instruction will be highly motivating because the child is actively engaged and goal oriented. If the child is highly motivated, naturally occurring reinforcement should be effective. Given that many children with autism are socially isolated and favor consistency, naturalistic instruction is a good fit. Rather than attempting to draw the child's focus to the adult's interest and searching for effective artificial reinforcers, attend to the child's focus and conduct instruction when the child indicates a high level of motivation.

Another advantage of naturalistic instruction for children with autism is that it promotes generalization. As noted in the introduction to this chapter, children with autism tend to be rigid in their learning and have difficulty with generalization. Naturalistic instruction promotes generalization because teaching situations vary considerably: Incidental teaching occasions throughout the day will involve different people (children and adults), different activities, different materials, different responses, and different reinforcers. The variety of stimulus conditions promotes generalization (Stokes & Baer, 1977). In addition, reinforcers associated with naturalistic instruction are likely to be naturally occurring, and thus promote generalization because they are available in noninstructional situations.

Instructional plans for incidental teaching are identical in format to other direct instruction plans, except that the *child-determined occasions for instruction* are specified. To implement the plans, teachers or family members follow their typical routines and maintain a watchful eye for the *occasions for instruction* (e.g., when the child expresses frustration [bangs the toy or whines] after a wind-up toy stops moving). When an occasion for instruction is observed, the adult approaches the child and follows the prompting procedure specified in the instructional plan. The prompt may be to make eye contact with the child and wait 5 seconds (a time delay to encourage communication), it may be to model the expected response ("Help, please"), or it may be another type of prompt (e.g., verbal direction, physical guidance). Correction and reinforcement procedures are also implemented as stated in the instructional plan.

General Case Instruction

As previously discussed, direct instruction is effective with children who have autism because of its consistency and predictability. Although consistency of instruction promotes learning new skills, it may impede generalization, particularly among children who like sameness and orderliness. As noted in Chapter 6, it is critical to develop direct instruction plans that include strategies to promote generalization. Incidental or *milieu* teaching is one way to promote generalization (discussed above). Another strategy is general case instruction (discussed in Chapter 6). Recall that in general case instruction, the behavioral objective is stated as a generalized skill; instead of an objective to *request a drink of water*, for example, the objective is to *request a desired item (drink, food, toy, clothing)*. The skill variations are carefully selected to represent the range of items represented by the general case objective (*request a desired item*) and are taught concurrently rather than sequentially. Other generalization strategies (e.g., teaching across people, places, materials, times; using mediational strategies) may also be included to increase the likelihood of generalization.

Cues

Chapter 6 defined prompting strategies, including cues. *Cues are prompts (anything that helps a child make a correct response) that direct a child's attention to salient characteristics of a stimulus.* For example, an identifying characteristic of an alphabet letter is its shape rather than its color. And for a child learning to discriminate a lowercase *b* from a *p*, *d*, and *q*, salient characteristics include the direction and location of the straight line relative to the circle. A cue that would direct a child's attention to the location and direction of the straight line may be to make the line portion of the *b* bold and to draw it as an arrow pointing up (↑). Cues are a particularly effective type of prompt for children with autism because some children with autism have difficulty attending to multiple and relevant stimulus characteristics. This is known as *stimulus overselectivity* (Lovaas, Koegel, & Schreibman, 1979; Lovaas & Schreibman, 1971). Providing cues rather than other types of prompts highlight the discriminative characteristics of stimuli that children with autism might otherwise not notice.

Fading Prompts and Cues

Because children with autism prefer consistency, they may become *prompt dependent.* In other words, they may rely on instructional prompts or cues (and the adults who provide the prompts and cues), even after they have acquired a new skill. Prompt dependency limits independence and generalization. To counteract this tendency, a direct instruction plan should specify steps for fading instructional prompts so that children respond to naturally occurring prompts. Fading is the gradual removal of a prompt by decreasing its saliency (a verbal prompt gradually gets quieter; a pictorial or visual prompt gradually gets smaller or lighter), physical proximity (a prompt is gradually moved away from the stimulus), or temporal proximity (the time between a natural prompt and an instructional one is gradually lengthened). If fading is conducted too quickly, errors result, or the child does not respond. Therefore it is important that fading be conducted gradually with careful monitoring for errors. If errors occur, the saliency of a prompt should be increased to reestablish correct responding, and a more gradual fading procedure should be used.

Group Instruction

Early intervention and early childhood special education services provided to young children with autism tend to emphasize individualized instruction. Often the children are assisted by *skills trainers* who provide extensive one-to-one instruction for several hours per day in a child's home and sometimes in a child's classroom. Although research supports that intense (predominantly one-to-one instruction) intervention is associated with greater developmental gains for many children with autism compared with programs that are less intense (Lovaas, 1987; McClannahan & Krantz, 1993), it is important that the level of intensity (amount of instructional time and proportion of time spent receiving one-to-one instruction) be individualized to match each child's needs (Strain, Wolery, & Izeman, 1998). Strain and his colleagues also note that there is no empirical evidence that one-to-one instruction is superior in quality to larger child-to-staff ratios. Instead, they suggest that the quality of instruction and the competence of the teachers may be the more important variables.

In addition to one-to-one instruction, all children with autism should receive group instruction. Group instruction is important for children with autism

because the diagnosis of autism is based on extensive communication and social needs. The group arrangement provides the necessary context for teaching
communication and social skills with peers—a context that is otherwise not
available. Chapter 11 describes in detail several additional benefits of group instruction (e.g., opportunity for observational learning, peer modeling, turn taking) as well as group instructional procedures.

It is important that group instructional arrangements be age appropriate:
Infants and toddlers may be in groups for child care and recreation programs
(especially parent-toddler programs), and their groups tend to be small (two to
six children or parent–child dyads). Children age 3 and older are frequently in
large groups of 20 or more children for child care, preschool, kindergarten, and
recreational programs. They may also receive instruction in small groups (three
to six children) within the large-group setting.

As noted in Chapter 11, children may need to be taught how to participate
in groups and eased into group situations (Collins, Gast, Ault, & Wolery, 1991;
Koegel & Rincover, 1974). A child may begin group instruction with just one
other child. When she demonstrates progress on her instructional goals and
learns basic group-participation skills such as responding to a peer and sitting
quietly while the other child takes a turn, a third child may be added to the
group. Additional children may be added to the group, in turn, as the child with
autism demonstrates success in the small-group arrangement.

Augmentative Communication

Although augmentative communication is not an instructional procedure per
se, it is a support/adaptation that may facilitate language acquisition and reduce
problem behaviors. As noted in the introduction to this chapter, significant
communication needs is a defining characteristic of children with autism.
Many young children with autism have little or no spoken language, and therefore may have a difficult time communicating their desires and needs. Chapter
10 noted that most challenging behavior serves a communicative function.
This implies that problem behavior is occurring because appropriate communication skills are lacking.

Augmentative communication provides an alternative means for children
who do not speak to express their wants and needs. As reviewed in Chapter 13,
there are a number of augmentative communication systems and modes from
which to select, including gestures, sign language, and visual systems (symbols, pictures, and/or photographs) that may be arranged in books, on boards,
or on key rings. Electronic devices, including ones that "speak," are also available. Although visual systems in books or on key rings are popular because
they are portable and can be understood by a wide audience, one system is not
inherently better than another. Indeed, some children will use a combination
of systems. The important thing is that all children have an effective means to
express themselves. If children are not talking by age 2, they should be taught
some form of augmentative communication. Research indicates that augmen-

tative systems do not interfere with the development of speech and may actually facilitate speech (Beukelman & Mirenda, 1992; Daniels, 1994; Romski & Sevcik, 1993; Van Tatenhove, 1987).

Speech pathologists are important members of the intervention team for children with autism, and may be instrumental in developing and teaching a child to use an augmentative communication system. Once a communication mode and system has been selected, instructional considerations mentioned previously in this chapter (direct instruction, naturalistic instruction, general case instruction, cues, and fading prompts and cues) should be incorporated into the instructional plan to teach the child to use the augmentative system. The Picture Exchange Communication System (PECS) is a pictorial augmentative communication system developed specifically for children with autism. It is described in detail later in this chapter.

Positive Behavior Support

As previously mentioned, children with autism frequently have severe behavior challenges associated with their communication needs. Chapter 10 describes the positive behavior support model designed to identify the function of problem behavior, prevent the need for problem behavior, teach alternative replacement behaviors (usually communication skills), and eliminate the reinforcement that maintains the challenging behavior. Because it is a *communication-based* approach (Carr, Levin, McConnachie, Carlson, Kemp, & Smith, 1994), it is particularly well-suited to children with autism who often have significant communication needs. Positive behavior support strategies should be incorporated throughout a child's day and across the adults and settings the child frequents.

Summary of Instructional Procedures

The eight instructional approaches addressed in this chapter (direct instruction, naturalistic instruction, general case instruction, cues, fading prompts and cues, group instruction, augmentative communication, and positive behavior support) are addressed in detail in other chapters in this text. They are highlighted here because they address one or more of the unique learning characteristics and needs of children with autism. Direct instruction is an effective teaching strategy because children with autism have a learning style that appreciates consistency. On the other hand, the strong preference for sameness that children with autism may have mitigates against generalization. Naturalistic instruction and general case instruction are proven approaches that facilitate generalization during the initial acquisition stage of learning. A preference for sameness also means that prompt fading must be planned and implemented very carefully to ensure independent responding and prevent prompt dependence. Group instruction addresses the social needs of children with autism to develop peer relationships and associated communication skills. And finally, augmentative communication and positive behavior support address the considerable needs that most children with autism have relative to communication and social skills.

SPECIAL PROCEDURES FOCUSED ON CHILDREN WITH AUTISM

In addition to the instructional procedures described above and in other chapters in this text, instructional procedures have been developed specifically for children with autism. Some are variations of the procedures described in the first part of this chapter; others are unique. The special procedures described in this section are not exhaustive, but they are ones used extensively with children who have autism. There are three special procedures: 1) discrete trial training, 2) floor time, and 3) Picture Exchange Communication System (PECS).

Discrete Trial Training

Also known as DTT, discrete trial training is a direct instruction method. It is typically conducted in a one-to-one teaching arrangement in which an interventionist implements a direct instructional plan repeatedly. The repeated trials format (also referred to as *massed trials*) is contrary to the earlier recommendations in this chapter that direct instruction be implemented throughout the day at times when a skill is needed, often using naturalistic (milieu) teaching strategies. Although the repeated trials format is associated with generalization concerns, DTT is the foundation of the *Young Autism Project* developed and directed by Ivar Lovaas, a leading researcher in the field of autism. The name Lovaas has come to be almost synonymous with DTT. Lovaas has held firm to his belief that DTT should be central to intervention for young children with autism and points to program evaluation data as support for his position (Lovaas, 1987; McEachin, Smith, & Lovaas, 1993).

As indicated above, DTT is a massed trials arrangement of direct instruction. Skills are taught with a consistent delivery of a prompt, correction(s), and reinforcement. When one trial is completed, the next trial begins. It is common to present 10 to 20 trials of DTT per skill. If a child is being taught to recognize his printed name, for example, two cards are placed on a table in front of him, one with his printed name and one with another name. The child is prompted, "Timmy, point to your name." When Timmy points to his name (with or without additional prompts), he is reinforced as indicated in the instructional plan. The two cards are then rearranged in front of Timmy and the instructional plan is implemented again. This process is repeated until the specified number of trials has been conducted.

Although *recommended practices* for children with severe disabilities have advocated for more naturalistic trial arrangements with instruction occurring (*distributed*) throughout the day and embedded in meaningful activities (Snell & Brown, 2006b; Westling & Fox, 2004), there may be situations when the repeated trials format of DTT would be more effective than the distributed trial arrangement. Bambara and Warren (1993) suggested that repeated trials are well-suited to shaping new behaviors. Over successive repeated trials, the adult or teacher can gradually modify and reduce prompts, requiring that the child perform the skill with increasing independence. It is also easier to ensure that a sufficient number of trials are conducted each day and that instruction is implemented consistently when a repeated trials format is used. Another advantage of repeated trials for children with autism is that they fit with learning styles that are characterized by orderliness and consistency.

DTT may be a primary method of instruction for some children with autism; however, it is essential that strategies for generalization be implemented for all instructional objectives. The highly systematized and consistent nature of DTT may facilitate initial skill acquisition, but it will also hinder generalization. Strategies such as naturalistic instruction (milieu teaching), general case instruction, and other generalization techniques (e.g., *mediate generalization, use naturally occurring reinforcers*; see Chapter 6) must be implemented concurrently with DTT.

Floor Time

Floor time is the cornerstone of the *Developmental, Individual-Difference, Relationship-Based (DIR)* intervention model for young children with autism (Greenspan & Wieder, 1997, 1999). The DIR model and floor time procedures emphasize following a child's lead to establish communicative interactions, building social relationships, supporting affective development, and facilitating sensory development. This approach is in clear contrast to the DTT model, which is highly directive and controlled by the teacher. In floor time, the parent or teacher attempts to *enter the child's world* by joining the play or activity initiated by the child. In contrast, the objective of DTT is to shift the child's focus from her own world to the world beyond herself by attending to the adult/teacher, following directions, and participating in activities initiated by the adult or teacher.

Parents are often the primary interventionists in conducting floor time because the strategy is designed to build or strengthen a child–adult relationship—a relationship that is often weak or severely lacking when the child has autism. Floor time sessions are typically conducted for 20 to 30 minutes, 8 to 10 times per day (Greenspan & Wieder, 1999); with the overall amount of intervention varying from 10 to 25 hours per week (Schertz & Odom, 2004). Floor time is conducted by first observing the child and deciding how to approach and enter the play. In observing the play, the child's emotions and temperament are noted. Next, the adult approaches by acknowledging the child's emotional states and interests ("You are excited about collecting your dinosaurs and putting them all in the same place"). The adult may then enter the child's play by assisting with the activity, being careful to let the child direct the course of events and set the emotional tone. The adult can also extend and expand the child's play, making supportive comments and being careful not to be intrusive. Supportive comments may be descriptive of the activity ("I think you've found all the dinosaurs") or tone ("You are so happy to have the dinosaurs all together!") and may include statements or questions that clarify and support creativity ("The dinosaurs seem happy to be together. Can other animals join them? Which ones? Now that they are all together, what are the dinosaurs going to do next?"). When the child responds by building on the adult's comments, he "closes the circle of communication." The child's responses may be verbal ("The dinosaurs are family. They live together") or nonverbal (the child picks up a dinosaur, looks at its face, smiles, and makes the dinosaur dance). It is up to the adult to follow the child's lead, enter the play again, and open a new circle of communication. The floor time strategy can be used with functional and/or socially influenced play, as well as perseverative, stereotypic play. In addition, floor time can be conducted even if a child says "no" by commenting and building on the child's mood and response ("You don't want anyone else to touch your dinosaur." "Should I put it back?" "Where should I put it?").

In addition to following a child's lead and expanding on her play, floor time can include adult responses that 1) obstruct the child's play and create problems to be solved; 2) introduce symbolism (pretend play with objects; dress-up; puppetry); 3) develop abstract thinking by talking about feelings, alternative outcomes to problem situations, and a wide range of real and pretend topics, and asking questions ("why" questions, opinions); and 4) develop motor planning skills by helping children learn to "undo" situations (uncover a hidden toy, fix a mistake with a puzzle) and engage in multiple-step activities (Greenspan, Wieder, & Simons, 1998). Typically, the adult challenges the child gently with attempts to open communication circles, and responds empathically and supportively to the child's mood and reactions.

Picture Exchange Communication System (PECS)

For many children with autism, understanding the *meaning* and *use* of language is a primary communication concern. Language meaning, or *semantics*, requires a cognitive understanding of objects, actions, and how the environment "works." Language use (or *pragmatics*) involves social knowledge and includes skills such as conversational turn taking and using words and a voice tone appropriate for the social rules of the situation. Pragmatics also includes an understanding that language is a communication *tool* used to accomplish objectives. For example, if we are thirsty we use language to ask for a drink of water, or if we don't understand something, we ask for clarification. Some children with autism have speech that is limited to echolalia, repeating what others say to them apparently without understanding the communication. In other situations, children with autism memorize phrases and sentences from observation of others or videos/DVDs and television. Some of these children use the memorized phrases and sentences appropriately to comment while playing or to respond to others' comments and questions. Sometimes only the adults most familiar with the child (parent or skills trainer) recognize the origins of the language. Although these children have difficulty generating novel communications (and this ultimately restricts their communication abilities), they demonstrate functional levels of semantic and pragmatic skills because they can use the phrases and sentences effectively.

PECS is an augmentative communication approach designed to address the semantic and pragmatic communication needs of children with autism (Frost & Bondy, 1994). PECS uses photographs or simple line drawings to create communication books and schedules. Children use the pictures/symbols to communicate by removing them from the book or schedule and handing them to an adult. For example, a child may take a "breakfast" picture (line drawing showing bowl and cup) off the daily schedule and hand it to her mother as they walk to the table for breakfast. When breakfast is finished and the child needs to wash up for school, she returns to the schedule, places the breakfast picture on it, removes the bathroom picture, and hands it to her parent. By using the communication pictures/symbols in a schedule, a child learns that symbols have meaning. Concurrently, the PECS schedule helps the child learn daily routines and expectations. This creates meaning and expectations in the child's life and establishes a context for communication. Although the child may not initially comprehend the word "breakfast" following repeated use of the PECS breakfast symbol, she may come to understand that the symbol means it's time for the morning meal ("breakfast").

The PECS program is detailed in a training manual and uses basic behavioral intervention techniques, such as shaping and reinforcement, for instruction (Frost & Bondy, 1994). Children are first taught to use individual pictures to initiate a request. Verbal prompts are not used to avoid prompt dependency and promote initiations. The program then builds vocabulary and sentence structure, beginning with the simple grammatical form "I want ____." Children are also taught to comment and respond to questions. PECS is used widely and regarded as an effective and worthwhile program (Siegel, 2000; Yamall, 2000). Although there are a number of published reports describing its effectiveness (Bondy & Frost, 1993, 1994; Peterson, Bondy, Vincent, & Finnegan, 1995; Schwartz, Garfinkle, & Bauer, 1998), experimental data supporting its use are just beginning to emerge in the literature (Charlop-Christy, Carpenter, Le, LeBlanc, & Kellet, 2002).

MODEL PROGRAMS

Numerous intervention models have been developed to address the unique and significant needs of children with autism. Five exemplary programs for children with autism are described here. These programs were selected because they are well-established, are supported with program evaluation data and/or experimental data, and represent comprehensive approaches to addressing the needs of children with autism. The five programs that will be described are

1. Young Autism Project
2. Pivotal Response Training

3. Developmental, Individual-Difference, Relationship-Based (DIR)
4. Project TEACCH
5. Project DATA

There is consensus that intervention for children with autism needs to start early (often before a child is 2 years old) and must be fairly intense (sometimes 30 to 40 hours per week) (Strain et al., 1998). A key difference in the five programs is the extent to which the intervention approach is intrusive or nonintrusive. An intrusive program is one requiring that the child attend and follow the instructions of the adult or teacher. Nonintrusive approaches attempt to enter the child's world and capture his attention without interference or upset. Two behavioral models, the Young Autism Project and Pivotal Response Training, are fairly intrusive models. Project TEACCH is less intrusive, and the DIR model is perhaps the least intrusive approach. Project DATA is a hybrid of approaches and is halfway between intrusive and nonintrusive. The remainder of the chapter describes each of these exemplary model programs for children with autism.

Young Autism Project

Developed by Ivar Lovaas in the 1960s at the University of California–Los Angeles, the *Young Autism Project* is the most established program of those described here. Without question, it is the program with the largest database. As noted earlier, DTT is the central feature of the program. DTT procedures, data collection strategies, scheduling and implementation recommendations, and programs (i.e., lessons) are fully described in a recently published manual (Lovaas, 2002). Instruction covers 15 areas, all of which are addressed within a year's time. Program areas focus on self-help, early academics, and communication skills and include the following: establishing cooperation with simple requests; matching and sorting; early receptive language; nonverbal imitation; play skills; verbal imitation; receptive labels; arts and crafts; self-help skills; expressive labels; reading and writing; color, shape, and size; *I want, I see, I have*; prepositions; and emotions. Most of the intervention is conducted in a one-to-one situation with the child and the interventionist seated across from each other. Following 6 to 12 months of intensive one-to-one intervention, Lovaas recommends that children gradually be moved into nursery/preschool programs with an individual assistant.

Lovaas reported that nearly half of the children with autism who participated in the Young Autism Project have *recovered* (Lovaas, 1987; McEachin, Smith, & Lovaas, 1993). He defined recovery as having an adequate IQ and the ability to participate in mainstream education. There has been much controversy in response to the Lovaas data and the claims of recovery (Mesibov, 1993; Schopler, Short, & Mesibov, 1989), with most of the criticisms and questions focused on the manner in which participants were selected (i.e., were they representative of most children with autism, or were they primarily children with mild autistic characteristics?) and the outcome measures (i.e., do the assessment tools adequately measure the most important behavioral concerns of children with autism?). Despite the controversy, there is widespread agreement that children who participate in the program frequently make substantial skill gains. The Young Autism Project remains one of the most well-respected model programs for children with autism.

Pivotal Response Treatment

The *pivotal response treatment* model developed by Lynn and Robert Koegel and their colleagues at the University of California–Santa Barbara is an outgrowth of the Young Autism Project. The Koegels worked with Lovaas in the 1970s and developed their model to address what they believed were some of the shortcomings of the Young Autism Project, primarily the artificial nature of the intervention situation, the appearance that children were unhappy during DTT, and issues with generalization. The Koegels believed that children with autism could be self-motivated. Their model uses behavioral procedures (direct instruction) and provides intervention in the context of play and functional activities. Child choice is incorporated throughout the model. They have also built a theoretical framework that defines and provides a rationale for identifying *pivotal responses*, key skill areas that can greatly enhance the overall development of children with autism. Pivotal response areas are the core of their approach.

Pivotal responses refer to skill areas that, when acquired, produce "large, collateral improvements in other areas" (Koegel, Koegel, Harrower, & Carter, 1999). The model is described as an *efficient* intervention approach because it targets skills that affect wide areas of functioning and does not simply teach a series of isolated skills. Pivotal response areas were identified as key areas for intervention because they are typically high-need areas for children with autism. There are four major pivotal response areas: 1) responsivity to multiple cues, 2) motivation, 3) self-management, and 4) self-initiations.

Responsivity to multiple cues, the first pivotal response area, addresses *stimulus overselectivity*, a characteristic of many children with autism. Stimulus overselectivity means that a child has difficulty attending to multiple cues, and instead attends to a limited number of stimulus features, often irrelevant ones. Stimulus overselectivity results in serious difficulties acquiring social and language skills and a failure to generalize. Direct instruction is used to highlight relevant stimulus characteristics and requires that a child respond to multiple cues. Motivation, the second pivotal response area, is evident when a child responds often and quickly to instruction and shows indications of positive affect, such as interest, enthusiasm, and happiness. Increases in motivation have been associated with decreases in disruptive behaviors. Motivational strategies include providing choices throughout the day, using natural and functional reinforcers (rather than artificial ones), interspersing maintenance trials (practice with previously acquired skills) with acquisition trials, and reinforcing attempts. The third pivotal response area is self-management. It is considered a critical skill for success in inclusive environments. Self-management includes the child setting goals and selecting reinforcers, self-monitoring progress, and requesting reinforcement when appropriate. The self-monitoring strategy used to teach children to be aware of their own behavior is gradually faded, and the generalization of self-monitoring to natural environments is assessed. The fourth pivotal response area is the communication skill of self-initiation. Self-initiation refers to spontaneously asking questions, seeking information, and initiating conversations. Such skills are often lacking in children with autism, but are critical for learning in natural environments without adult intervention.

Developmental, Individual-Difference, Relationship-Based (DIR)

The floor time procedures reviewed earlier in this chapter were developed through the DIR model, a model designed by Stanley Greenspan at the George Washington University Medical School in the District of Columbia (Greenspan & Wieder, 1999). The DIR model focuses on broad developmental areas of need—such as emotional development—rather than on specific skill needs or skill areas, as in the Young Autism Project and Pivotal Response Training. Greenspan views autism as a multisystem, regulatory disorder affecting sensory processing, reactions to stimuli, and forming relationships.

The focus of DIR is on nurturing the child's development of *self* and self-expression. Individualized intervention plans are designed based on an assessment that produces a functional developmental profile. The profile indicates a child's strengths and needs related to emotional development; sensory, modulation, processing, and motor planning; and relationships and interactions. An individualized plan for a child is comprehensive and includes floor time (following the child's lead; problem-solving activities; special, motor, and sensory activities); speech therapy; sensory integration therapy (occupational and/or physical therapy); a daily educational program (inclusive program when possible); perhaps biomedical intervention (e.g., medications that might help a child's attending); and a consideration of nutrition, diet, and other programs designed to improve sensory motor skills.

Project TEACCH

TEACCH (Treatment and Education of Autistic and Related Communication Handicapped Children) was developed in the early 1970s by Eric Schopler at the University of North Carolina at Chapel Hill (Mesibov, 2005). TEACCH is a statewide program serving infants through adults with autism and their families in North Carolina. The model utilizes a combination of approaches to design an individualized program based on a child's skills, interests, and needs. Intervention approaches are selected to fit with the *culture of autism* or the learning styles of many individuals with autism; for example, a preference for sameness and consistency or a preference for visual prompts rather than verbal ones. Individual programs designed through Project TEACCH emphasize altering the environment to accommodate the characteristics of a child (e.g., allowing a child to maintain orderly arrangements of items), using visual organizers (e.g., picture schedules), implementing work systems (e.g., daily work organized in baskets), and providing direct instruction. More so than the model programs discussed thus far, TEACCH includes a family support component and considers aspects of an individual's life beyond independent work skills (e.g., communication, social, leisure areas).

Project DATA

Developed by Ilene Schwartz and her colleagues at the University of Washington, Project DATA (Developmentally Appropriate Treatment for Autism) is a model program designed to merge recommended practices in early childhood education with those in early childhood special education and autism (Schwartz, Sandall, McBride, & Boulware, 2004). Unlike the other model programs, the central feature of Project DATA is a high-quality inclusive early childhood program designed in accordance with developmentally appropriate practice (see Chapter 1). Children with autism attend the early childhood program for approximately 12½ hours per week. Individualized instruction is provided by embedding the instruction in the ongoing classroom activities and routines. Strategies that promote generalization and maintenance are also implemented in regular classroom activities. The other components of Project DATA were developed to support the success of each child with autism in the inclusive early childhood program. These support components include 1) extended instructional time, 2) technical and social support for families, 3) collaboration and coordination across services, and 4) transition support. Extended instructional time provides approximately 8 additional hours per week of individualized intensive services focused on each child's individual needs. Intensive services may include a range of effective approaches such as DTT, naturalistic instruction (milieu teaching), and embedded instruction. Technical and social support for families consists of monthly home visits, resource coordination (e.g., child care, parent support groups, community services), parent support and networking get-togethers, and a father's evening. Collaboration and coordination across services is a support to facilitate communication among professionals who provide services to the family and/or child but are not a part of Project DATA (e.g., a family may hire a speech therapist for their child). And finally, transition support involves strategies to assist the family and child as the child exits Project DATA and enters a new school (often a public school).

SUMMARY

Autism, or ASD, is a diagnosis based on social and communication difficulties, an obsession with sameness and/or stereotypy, and self-stimulation. These unique characteristics have implications for instruction. This chapter reviewed several instructional approaches described elsewhere in this text that have been shown to be effective with children who have autism. These strategies include 1) direct instruction, 2) naturalistic instruction, 3) general case instruction, 4) cues (versus general prompts), 5) fading prompts and cues, 6) group instruction, 7) augmentative communication, and 8) positive behavior support. They are highlighted here because they address the unique educational needs of children with autism and are well-suited to the learning styles of most children with autism. In addition, DTT, floor time, and PECS were described— three instructional approaches developed specifically for children with autism. The chapter concluded with descriptions of five model programs: the Young Autism Project, Pivotal Response Treatment, DIR, Project TEACCH, and Project DATA.

1. Describe the learning characteristics of children with autism. For each characteristic you identify, discuss the ways (positive and negative) that it might affect learning.

2. Briefly describe the eight general instructional procedures (direct instruction, naturalistic instruction, general case instruction, cues, fading prompts and cues, group instruction, augmentative communication, positive behavior support). Describe why each of these procedures may be important to providing effective instruction for children with autism.

3. Define discrete trial training (DTT). Discuss the pros and cons of using this procedure.

4. What is *floor time*? Compare and contrast it to DTT.

5. Describe how you might use PECS to help a 4-year-old with autism who doesn't speak to participate in an inclusive preschool classroom.

6. Define and describe the four pivotal response areas of the pivotal response treatment program. Propose an intervention strategy to teach a skill in each of the four areas.

7. Discuss several ways that Project DATA merges recommended practices for children with autism.

8. Drawing from previous chapters that have discussed culture and learning, discuss cultural issues that might affect parents' receptivity to each of the model programs for children with autism.

9

Interventions in
Natural Environments

Linda McCormick

• **FOCUS OF THIS CHAPTER** • • • • • • • • • • • • • • • •

- Enhanced milieu teaching procedures

- Activity-based interventions

- Embedded and distributed time delay trials

- High-probability procedures

- Arranging the physical and social environments

- Adapting instructional methods and materials for children
  with sensory impairment

- Adapting instructional methods and materials for children
  with limited motor abilities and/or health impairments

E ffective instruction of functional and developmentally appropriate skills in inclusive settings depends on how well the adults are able to implement naturalistic instruction procedures, structure the environment, and adapt methods and activities. This chapter describes environmental structuring to promote engagement, communication, interaction, and play, as well as methods for adapting common classroom procedures and activities to increase participation of children with disabilities. These instructional procedures, called naturalistic intervention or naturalistic instruction, were initially implemented and researched in the context of language intervention. Over the past several decades they have been shown to be effective across a range of behaviors and multiple settings. They are now well established as preferred practices in early childhood special education (ECSE).

NATURALISTIC INSTRUCTION PROCEDURES

Procedures that come under the umbrella of naturalistic intervention share the following common characteristics (Rule, Losardo, Dinnebeil, Kaiser, & Rowland, 1998):

- The context for instruction is routine events and activities in natural environments (e.g., homes, preschools, child care settings)
- Instruction addresses functional skills that have immediate application
- The instructors are individuals (teachers, parents, siblings, paraeducators, peers) who have interactions with the child by virtue of their presence in the child's environments
- Instructional interactions are initiated by the child or by an adult capitalizing on the child's focus of attention and interests
- Instructional interactions take advantage of the child's motivation in order to evoke a target behavior
- Desired materials or events are provided as the natural consequence of the child's responses

Naturalistic instruction procedures can be applied in a range of natural or least restrictive environments to address a variety of skills that promote children's development and participation. This chapter describes four naturalistic instructional procedures: enhanced milieu teaching (Kaiser, 1993b; Kaiser, 2000), activity-based intervention (Pretti-Frontczak & Bricker, 2004; Losardo & Bricker, 1994), embedded and distributed trials (Wolery, 2001), and high-probability ("high-*p*") procedures (Santos, 2001).

Enhanced Milieu Teaching Procedures

A series of classic studies in the 1960s and 1970s documented the effectiveness of a set of procedures for facilitating children's language and communication skills (Hart & Risley, 1968, 1975). These procedures were first called *incidental teaching* and somewhat later *milieu teaching*. The initial research grew from observations of caregivers interacting with their typically developing infants and young children.

The initial research was expanded in the 1990s to include teaching of pre-linguistic, cognitive, social, motor, and adaptive skills (Brown, McEvoy, & Bishop, 1991; McCathren & Watson, 2001; Nordquist, Twardosz, & McEvoy, 1991; Warren, Yoder, Gazdag, Kim, & Jones, 1993). With the addition of environmental arrangement strategies and responsive interaction strategies, the procedures now comprise a hybrid program called *enhanced milieu teaching* (EMT). They are the most thoroughly researched of the naturalistic instruction procedures. Our description of EMT in this chapter draws heavily from the work of Ann Kaiser and colleagues (Kaiser, Hendrickson, & Alpert, 1991; Kaiser, 1993b; Kaiser, Ostrosky, & Alpert, 1993; Kaiser, 2000).

EMT includes responsive interaction strategies, environmental arrangement strategies, and four *teaching* procedures (modeling procedure, the mand-model procedure, the time delay procedure, and the incidental teaching procedure [Kaiser, 2000]).

Responsive Interaction Strategies   The broad goal of responsive interaction strategies is to promote balanced communication between the child and an adult(s) in a conversational context. Responsive interaction seeks to facilitate engagement between the child and adults in his or her environments. The focus is on turn taking, sustained interactions, comprehension of spoken language, and spontaneous interactions. The adult seeks to follow the child's lead (his or her attention focus), balance turns, maintain the child's topic, talk about what the child is doing and/or joint activities being shared by the child, match the level of complexity of the child's language, expand and repeat the child's utterances, and respond communicatively to all of the child's verbal and nonverbal communication.

Environmental Arrangement Strategies   The six environmental arrangement strategies are to 1) provide interesting materials and activities, 2) place desired materials in sight but out of reach, 3) offer small portions of needed or desired materials, 4) provide many choice-making opportunities, 5) set up situations in which children need assistance, and 6) create unexpected situations.

The primary goal of the environmental arrangement strategies is to prompt communication. The interests and preferences of the child with disabilities are the natural stimuli for communication *and* the natural reinforcement for communication. Reaching for an object or otherwise expressing an interest in a particular material is tantamount to designating a reinforcer. The teacher simply uses one or another of the teaching procedures described below to prompt language and then immediately provides the material or activity in response to the child's communicative attempts.

The motive for providing a wealth of *interesting age-appropriate materials and activities* is to increase the likelihood that there will be many reasons for the child to communicate. Whenever the child wants something, there is an opportunity for teaching language. Placing materials that the child desires in *sight but out of reach* is a particularly effective way to prompt requesting. Preferred toys may be placed in clear bins (with tight lids), on high shelves, or simply on the far side of a table.

When a child has limited motor control, it is important for the material to be a distance apart from other objects so that it is obvious what the child is reaching for or looking at. Providing *small or inadequate portions of materials* such as snacks, blocks, or dress-up clothes virtually guarantees that the child will either protest or request more. If, for example, children are provided with an incomplete set of materials (e.g., the toothpaste is missing from the tray with the other toothbrushing materials) there is typically either a protest or a request for the missing object(s). An added advantage is that peers often get involved. When inadequate materials are provided, the children often prompt one another to communicate (e.g., seeing that Jace has finished pasting the one circle he was given on his clown face, Amelia says, "Tell Ms. Lee that you need more circles to paste"). The adult waits until the children notice that something is missing. When the child says "more" or simply points or extends an empty container, the adult models and/or prompts more elaborate requesting (e.g., "Want more juice," "Want more circles to paste").

Providing two or more possible materials or activities encourages a child to use language *to choose the item or activity he or she wants.* This works best when one of the choices is an item or an activity that is definitely disliked. There are many ways to create *a situation in which the child needs and thus will request assistance.* The child might need assistance activating a battery-operated toy, getting on a swing, or putting a straw in a juice container. Most important is to remember not to rush in with assistance and thus preempt the child's request. A *situation that violates the child's expectations* is very likely to elicit communication. Children are quick to comment on or protest absurdities and inappropriate actions such as holding a book upside down. Events or activities that are out of order, unexpected, or clearly absurd provide an opportunity to prompt communication. Calculated "silliness" has the additional advantage of helping children develop a sense of humor.

Each of the four teaching procedures has different goals and specific steps for implementation, and they also have commonalities. For example, they all use one or another of the six environmental arrangement strategies (described above) to set the scene for the instructional interaction; they all begin by establishing joint attention (the adult and the child attend to each other or simultaneously attend to the same material or activity); they all follow incomplete or incorrect child responses by providing an additional prompt; and they all end every teaching episode with a positive consequence (acknowledgement and expansion of the child's response) and provision of the material, assistance, or activity that the child desires.

Modeling Procedure   The goals of the modeling procedure are to teach turn-taking skills, generalized imitation skills, conversational skills, and basic vocabulary. The following are six steps to implement the procedure. In providing the actual verbal model (Step 3), be certain to say only what you want the child to imitate. In other words, "turtle," not "Jace, say 'turtle.'" Note also that the procedure begins with identifying an appropriate teaching opportunity and entering the situation by establishing joint attention.

1. *Note the child's interest (as indicated by his attention).*
   Jace is looking at the new addition to the aquarium—a turtle.
2. *Establish joint attention.*
   The teacher kneels beside Jace and also focuses attention on the turtle.
3. *Present a verbal model that labels or describes the focus of interest.*
   The teacher says "turtle."
4. *When the child imitates the model, acknowledge and expand his or her response and provide access to the material or activity.*
   "Yes, that is a *turtle.* Here, take the turtle food and sprinkle it on the water."
5. *If child does not imitate the model or responds with an unintelligible, partial, incorrect, or unrelated response, present the model a second time (called a corrective model).*
   The teacher says "turtle" again.
6. *If the child does not respond or responds incorrectly to the corrective model, then provide corrective feedback and access to the material or activity.*
   "That's a *turtle.* Here, take the *turtle* food and feed the *turtle.*"

Because the model procedure tells the child exactly what he or she is expected to say, it is especially appropriate for skills that a child is just beginning to learn. Once the child demonstrates progress using the model procedure, one of the other EMT procedures (described next) may be used.

Mand-Model Procedure The goal of the mand-model procedure is to prompt the child to use emerging forms across environments. Note that the mand is an indirect prompt ("Tell me what you want.") and thus requires that the child has previously demonstrated the form of the expected response. The mand-model procedure is implemented as follows.

1. Note the child's interest (as indicated by his or her attention).
2. Establish joint attention.
3. Present a verbal mand.
   The teacher says, "Tell me what you want," depending on the focus of attention.
4. If the child responds correctly, acknowledge and expand his or her response and provide access to the material or activity.
   "Oh, you want to feed the turtle. Here's the turtle food."
5. If the child does not provide a correct response or responds with an unintelligible, partial, incorrect, or unrelated response, present a second mand or present a model if the child's interest is waning or a response is not forthcoming.
   "Tell me what you want."

6. When the child responds correctly to the mand or model, acknowledge and expand his or her response and provide access to the material or activity.

"Oh, you want to feed the turtle. Here's the turtle food."

7. If the child does not respond or responds incorrectly, provide corrective feedback and access to the material or activity.

"You want to feed the turtle. Here's the turtle food."

Time Delay Procedure The goal of the time delay procedure is to establish environmental stimuli as the occasion for communication. The child is prompted to initiate communication rather than simply respond to another person's initiations (as in the modeling and mand-model procedures). Think of time delay as "wait time." It is the time allowed for the child to respond before a mand or model is given. Be sure to provide the time delay without verbal or gestural prompts: Simply look at the child and wait. Take the following steps to use the time delay procedure:

1. *Identify or create occasions when the child needs or want materials, assistance, or access to an activity.*

2. *Establish joint attention.*

Jace is looking at his favorite music box, which is on a shelf he cannot reach. The teacher kneels beside Jace and also focuses attention on the music box.

3. *Introduce time delay.*

The teacher looks at Jace and waits expectantly.

4. *If the child responds correctly, provide material, assistance, or access to an activity.*

"You want your music box. Here it is."

5. *If the child does not provide a correct response, present a mand or model.*

"Tell me what you want" and/or "music box."

6. *When the child responds correctly to the mand or model, acknowledge and expand the child's response, and provide access to the material or activity.*

"You want your music box. Here it is."

Incidental Teaching Procedure The goal of the incidental teaching procedure is to teach more elaborate language and improve conversational skills. It differs from the other procedures in that it is used *after* the child has produced a verbal, vocal, or gestural request. The child's request may be followed by a model, mand-model, or time delay to encourage use of more advanced linguistic forms and continuing conversation. Begin the incidental teaching procedure in the same manner as the other EMT procedures (create a situation to promote communication or identify the occasion for instruction and establish joint attention). Once the child verbalizes a request, implement either the modeling, mand-model, or time delay procedure. The incidental teaching procedure steps are

1. Identify or create occasions when the child needs or wants materials, assistance, or access to an activity.

2. Establish joint attention.

3. When the child initiates a request, teach more intelligible, complex, or elaborate language by

    Modeling a new or more difficult form of the request.

    Using the mand-model procedure to encourage conversation.

    Using time delay to encourage the child to produce more advanced language.

Application of EMT requires planning, preparation, and practice, but there is virtually no limit to the number and variety of skills that can be taught. The natural environment is altered to engage the child's attention and thus teach desired behaviors. The procedures can be as readily applied and effective with children who use alternative and augmentative communication as with those who use the verbal modality as their primary means of communication.

Also, peers can play an important role in EMT. As in the example above with Amelia and Jace, they may inadvertently prompt a communicative response. Or teachers may prompt one peer to cue another. For example, the teacher might say to Anisa, "Tell Jace that he needs to say 'My turn' to let you know what he wants."

Activity-Based Intervention

There is a substantial body of research supporting the use of activity-based intervention (ABI) with young children with disabilities (Pretti-Frontczak et al., 2003; Pretti-Frontczak & Bricker, 2004). Other terms used to refer to ABI procedures are *embedded intervention/instruction*, *routines-based intervention/instruction*, and *integrated therapy*. As these terms imply, training trials are dispersed and occur within the context of ongoing activities (Bricker, 1998). Teaching the skills "eating independently," "pouring juice," and "requesting more" at snack time would be an example of ABI.

The following are the basic premises underlying ABI (Bricker, 1998):

• Child-initiated activities and actions are most likely to hold the child's attention.

• Daily routines and planned or child-initiated activities are opportunities for instruction of IFSP and IEP goals and objectives.

• Instruction should use naturally occurring antecedents (materials, prompts) and consequences (logical outcomes).

- Instruction should develop skills that will enable the child to become more independent in current and future environments and skills that will generalize to a variety of settings.

The first step in ABI is to arrange the physical environment and decide the activities within which the teaching episodes will be embedded. Bricker (1989) defines an activity as a sequence of events that has a beginning and a logical outcome, and requires a variety of both initiated and reciprocal actions by the child. Table 9.1 provides suggestions for selecting activities to provide opportunities for a child to learn and practice specified objectives. The majority of activities in preschool and child care programs that adopt developmentally appropriate practices would easily meet these criteria. Bricker (1989) recommends arranging the physical space in the classroom (or home) to enhance efficiency, accessibility, and independence. In a 1994 study, to elicit target behaviors, Losardo and Bricker arranged the classroom to resemble a grocery store. Shelves were stocked with food items and empty food containers. Table 9.1 offers suggestions for selecting activities for ABI.

ABI uses a variety of materials to assist the child to acquire targeted behaviors. The four general criteria for selecting materials are that they should be relevant to the child and the activity, multidimensional, developmentally appropriate, and appropriate to promote generalization (Pretti-Frontczak & Bricker, 2004).

After selecting appropriate activities and arranging the environment, decide *how* the targeted skills will be taught. In ABI, as in EMT, the teaching episode is generally child-initiated. However, it is the adult's responsibility to ensure that antecedents (e.g., models, mands, comments) for producing desired responses occur frequently during the day so that the child has adequate occa-

Table 9.1. Suggestions for selecting activities for ABI

1. Select activities that group similar objects for different children. For example, telling stories with puppets is an activity for circle time that lends itself to teaching "identifying objects by their function."
2. Select activities that group different goals/objectives for the same child. For example, Jace has three objectives that can be taught in the context of snack preparation: a language objective ("naming objects"), a cognitive objective ("matching colors and shapes"), and a fine motor/self-care objective ("pouring").
3. Select activities that can be adapted for varying ages and skill levels. For example, an activity such as "Yes, you can," which teaches children to help with simple tasks, can easily be adapted to different ages and skill levels: Jace is assigned tasks that are equally important but less physically demanding.
4. Select activities that require minimal adult direction and assistance. For example, most free-play activities and some clean-up routines require minimal direct assistance from adults once they begin.
5. Select activities that provide many opportunities for child initiations. For example, the activity "Up, up, and away" requires children to name a peer and then pass a balloon to that peer. Each game provides numerous opportunities for children to initiate to peers.
6. Select activities that are motivating and interesting. Routines and activities that are fun and inherently reinforcing are more likely to keep children engaged and therefore learning.

Source: Bricker & Norstad,1990.

sions to initiate the desired teaching opportunities. The adult then responds in a reciprocal manner to the child's initiation and joins the child in the activity. Teaching episodes may also be initiated by adults or peers, using a variety of antecedents to evoke the target behaviors if the child does not initiate an interaction. The consequences are inherent in the activity. They are the logical outcomes of the interaction.

Embedded and Distributed Time Delay Trials

There is considerable overlap among the naturalistic instructional procedures. Both EMT and ABI provide trials within daily routines and activities; the difference is that they do not *necessarily* plan for and use *time delay trials.* Time delay procedures are an efficient and effective way to help children learn to perform new behaviors independently. The terms *embedded* and *distributed* refer to *when* in the naturally occurring routines and activities the trials are provided (Mulligan, Guess, Holvoet, & Brown, 1980; Wolery, 1994). *Embedded* means that the trials are inserted into the naturally occurring activities and routines. *Distributed* means that there are opportunities for the child to perform other behaviors between the instructional trials.

Wolery (2001) provided a clear description of specifically how to embed and distribute time delay procedures in classroom activities. The delineation of the procedural steps that follows is taken directly from Wolery's narrative, including the example he uses of application of the procedures with a child named Isaiah.

Step 1: *Identify the specific skills to be taught.* Time delay can be used to teach any type of skills. The three skills that have been identified for Isaiah are using words to request, using action words to describe his play, and pushing down and pulling up his pants during toileting routines.

Step 2: *Identify activities and routines when the skills will be taught.* The procedures may be implemented during only one activity, during multiple activities, or during transitions between activities. Decisions about when to embed time delay depend on what is being taught, how many teaching opportunities are possible, and teacher responsibilities. Isaiah's teachers decide to teach the first skill (requesting) during snacks and meals and free play. The second skill (using actions words) will be taught during free play and outdoor play, and the third skill (getting pants up and down) will be taught during toileting routines.

Step 3: *Decide how many trials will be given and how often.* Wolery suggests aiming for approximately five trials per day for each skill. Set a minimum and a maximum time between trials. For example, you might decide on at least 2 minutes and no more than 10 minutes between trials. It was decided that Isaiah's first skill (requesting) would be taught in two circumstances: each time he made a nonverbal request and whenever he was given a choice. If Isaiah did not make a verbal request in 3 minutes, the teacher asked him if he wanted something. For action words, the teacher used the rule "at least 2 minutes but no more than 10." The skill "pushing down and pulling up pants" was taught each time Isaiah was taken to the bathroom.

Step 4: *Select a time delay procedure.* Decide whether to use constant time delay or progressive time delay (Ault, Gast, & Wolery, 1988). Both begin with 0-second trials. Then, with constant time delay (which is somewhat easier to use), the response intervals of delay trials are all the same length. With progressive time delay, the response intervals gradually increase over trials or days. Whether to use constant time delay or progressive time delay depends on the child. If the child waits for help and is attentive, then the constant time delay procedure is the best choice. With children who have difficulty waiting, use the progressive time delay procedure. With Isaiah, the decision was to use constant time delay for requesting (because he attends and waits for what he wants), progressive time delay for using action words, and constant time delay for pushing down and pulling up his pants.

Step 5: *Identify a task cue and a controlling prompt.* A task cue is a question, a command, or a naturally occurring situation that signals the child to perform the target behavior. This response signal at the beginning of the trial is called the *discriminative stimulus.* For the first skill, Isaiah's obvious interest in a material or activity (a naturally occurring situation) was the task cue for him to use words to request. For the second skill, using action words, the task cue was an adult asking, "What are you doing?" For the third skill, pushing down and pulling up his pants during toileting, standing in front of the toilet (a naturally occurring situation) was the task cue. It is also important to identify controlling prompts. Because Isaiah is a good imitator, it was decided to use a verbal model (e.g., "Want milk") as the prompt for requesting. The prompt for action words (e.g., "running," "throwing") was also a verbal model. Physical prompts were used for the toileting routines.

Step 6: *Select a reinforcer.* The range of potential reinforcers for preschoolers is virtually unlimited. Possibilities include activities, brief play or just "hanging out" time with favorite adults, or toys. As noted above, one of the strengths of naturalistic instruction is that activities and materials in the environment that the child finds interesting and fun serve as both the antecedents and the reinforcers for targeted skills. Where Isaiah is concerned, seeing a food, drink, or toy he wants is the antecedent for requesting, and receiving the desired food, drink, or toy is the reinforcer for requesting. Allowing him to continue with his play and acknowledgement are the reinforcers for using action words. Adult interaction is the reinforcer for pushing down and pulling up his pants during toileting routines.

Step 7: *Determine the number of 0-second trials to use.* The purpose of the initial 0-second trials is to establish the all-important relationship between the task cue and the response. In order to accomplish this, it is important to offer the prompt immediately after the task cue and then provide reinforcement immediately after the response. It can take as long as 5 days at the 0-second delay level, but usually 2 or 3 days are enough time for the child to learn the relationship. Isaiah's teachers will provide 2 days of 0-second trials at snacks and lunch for requesting, 4 days of 0-second trials for action words, and 3 days of 0-second trials for managing his pants.

Step 8: *Determine the length of the response intervals.* The length of the response interval is now increased by 1 or 2 seconds every 2 or 3 days. A child who is slow to respond will need a longer interval. There is no need for a stopwatch: Simply counting "1001, 1002, and so forth" (silently) is accurate enough. The decision for Isaiah is to provide a 4-second interval for requesting and for managing his pants. The interval for using action words will be increased by 1 second every 2 days.

Step 9: *Select a monitoring system.* Data collection is critical to determine whether the program is working as intended. There are three possible responses with 0-second trials: correct, incorrect, or no response. An incorrect response on 25% or more of the trials for 2 or more days suggests the need for a more controlling prompt. A "no response" on 25% or more of the trials suggests the need for a better reinforcer.

There are five possible responses with the delay trials: 1) correct *before* the prompt, 2) wrong *before* the prompt, 3) correct *after* the prompt, 4) wrong *after* the prompt, and 5) no response. A wrong response before the prompt on 25% or more trials for 2 or more days indicates a need to teach the child to wait (Wolery, Ault, & Doyle, 1992). Waiting is taught as follows:

* Assemble a set of small cards with abstract symbols on them
* Show the child a symbol card and ask "What's this?"
* Wait about half a second and give the child a name for the symbol (e.g., "a flob").
* Immediately reinforce the child for imitating the name.
* Gradually lengthen the time before naming the symbol (the child must wait for the symbol to be named before he can imitate and claim the reinforcer).
* If necessary, gently place fingers to the child's lips as an additional cue to wait.

If the child is wrong *after* the prompt on 25% or more trials for 2 or more days, a more controlling prompt is needed. A "no response" on 25% or more trials for 2 or more days indicates the need for a better reinforcer. Similarly, the reinforcers should be modified when the child is correct only *after* the prompt on 90% or more trials for 3 consecutive days. Begin to provide a more desirable reinforcer for correct responses *before* the prompt than for those *after* the prompt.

Step 10: *Implement the plan and monitor its use and effects.* The importance of planning and rigorous application of the procedures cannot be overemphasized. Wolery (2001) recommended frequent review of the steps to be sure that the procedures are implemented precisely as planned, careful attention to the child's behavior after an embedded trial to be sure that he or she continues to participate in the activity, and careful monitoring of the number of trials each day to be sure that enough teaching is occurring.

High-Probability Procedures

Behavioral momentum procedures rely on delivering a set of simple requests (usually three to five) to which there is a high probability that the child will respond, followed immediately by a request to which the child is *not* likely to respond. The high-probability requests are referred to as "high-*p*" requests: the low-probability requests are called "low-*p*" requests. These procedures were initially used to reduce noncompliance in classrooms and other settings (Davis & Brady, 1993), but over time they have been extended to a broad range of behavioral outcomes. Examples include teaching social skills, responding to indirect questions and comments, and increased use of augmentative communication devices (Davis, Brady, Hamilton, McEvoy, & Williams, 1994; Davis & Reichle, 1996; Santos & Lignugaris/Kraft, 1999; Santos, 2001).

Why is presenting a sequence of requests for performance of skills that are already in the child's repertoire (that the child easily and consistently performs) followed by a request for performance of a new skill that the child does not (or cannot) perform on a consistent basis effective? The answer is the increased reinforcement. The initial sequence of requests (the high-*p* requests) generate an increased rate of positive responses and thus a high rate of reinforcement. Together, the increased response rate and the increased reinforcement rate create a behavioral momentum that increases the probability that the child will respond to a low-*p* request.

Santos (2001) provided a detailed description of the three major steps in the high-probability procedure and examples of application of the procedure in the classroom and at home.

Step 1: *Identify high-*p *and low-*p *requests.* Identify a series of requests that the child is likely to respond to consistently and fluently (the high-*p* requests) and a low-*p* request that the child either does not respond to or responds to inconsistently. The high-*p* and low-*p* requests may require either motor or language responses. Requests during transition times may require motor response (e.g., "Please return the crayon and scissor boxes to the shelf," "Please get your backpack," "Please put on your jacket"). Requests during other activities may require verbal or augmentative communication responses. These requests may ask the child to name or label an object, person, or activity (e.g., "What are you making with those beautiful colors?" "Who is your partner on this project?"), select from an array of items (e.g., "Would you like _____ or _____ today?"), or describe objects or events/activities (e.g., "What color is _____?" "How do you _____?"). Santos (2001) used the example of Adrian. His mother says that he responds to requests to identify/name objects (e.g., "What is this?") 80% of the time. However, he has difficulty responding to his mother's specific request to put away his toys when he is finished with them. His mother decides to use labeling objects as her high-*p* request to encourage Adrian to begin responding to the low-*p* request "Let's put your toys in the toy box."

Step 2: *Use routines, activities, and materials in the environment.* Observe the child to identify favorite toys and materials and preferred routines and activities. These high interest stimuli, routines, and activities are the ones to incorporate into high-probability procedures. Adrian's favorite toys are those that he can pull apart and put together such as Mr. Potato Head. His favorite activities are art activities. He especially likes enjoys using markers, paint, glue, construction paper, and crayons to create pictures that he can take home. Adrian's teacher and his mother plan to use these preferred toys and materials and activities as the context for high-probability procedures.

Step 3: *Deliver three high-*p *requests and one low-*p *request.* Actual implementation of the high-probability procedures in a classroom routine or activity takes only 1 to 2 minutes. It is comparable to the game Simon Says. The teacher delivers the sequence of high-*p* requests (e.g., "Pat your tummy," "Raise one knee," "Put your hands on your head"), followed by the low-*p* request ("Sit on your carpet square"). High-probability procedures can be used with the other naturalistic instructional procedures described in this chapter. See Table 9.2 for an example provided by Santos (2001) of high-probability procedures used with Adrian during tabletop activities. The goal is for Adrian to respond consistently to the teacher's comments. The teacher uses a silly comment (calculated silliness as in EMT) in the first low-*p* request. Adrian's picture has a *red* bird.

Timing of the delivery of the requests and the reinforcement is crucial: The goal is to build momentum. The high-*p* requests must be delivered in rapid succession, followed *immediately* by appropriate reinforcement. Santos (2001) contended that high probability procedures are best used as a short term intervention. If the game goes on too long, it could become predictable and tiresome for the child, resulting in challenging behaviors to escape or avoid having to respond to the adult.

Table 9.2. Example of high-*p* procedures used with Adrian

	High-*p* Request	High-*p* Request	High-*p* Request	Low-*p* Request
Teacher *requests*	"Adrian, what are you making?"	"Who's that?"	"What's that on top of the house?"	"That looks like a *yellow* bird."
Adrian *responds*	"My house!"	"Adrian and Mommy."	"A birdie."	"No, it's a red bird!"
Teacher *praises*	"Oh, that's a beautiful house."	"That's really nice."	"You drew a pretty bird on the house."	"Oh, that's right, it is a *red* bird."

ENVIRONMENTAL STRUCTURING

The six environmental arrangement strategies that form one component of EMT were described earlier in this chapter. This section describes more general environmental structuring procedures. Carefully arranging pertinent elements of the physical and social environments is a relatively easy way to influence child learning and behavior.

Arranging the Physical and Social Environments

The physical environment should be arranged to encourage learning, independence, social interactions, and communication. The layout of the room, the materials, and the equipment are all variables in the physical environment, as are noise level, lighting, visual and auditory input, physical accessibility of materials, and technology. The social environment includes group size and scheduling.

Layout   Most early childhood classrooms include, in addition to a children's bathroom and a storage area, a block center, a writing center, an art center (with sink and storage), a housekeeping center, a discovery learning area, and a quiet reading area. Placement of these areas, their number and size, the way the materials are arranged, and the rules of access to each area all need to be considered when there are children with disabilities in the program (Sainato & Carta, 1992). This is not to say that they will necessarily need to be modified. The rule is to modify *only* if it is clear that the child cannot participate in the activity center even partially or at a less sophisticated level unless the space is rearranged or modified (McCormick & Feeney, 1995). In most cases, no modifications will be needed for children with disabilities.

When space modifications are necessary for a child who uses a wheelchair, a walker, or some other method of mobility, they generally involve widening the routes to activity centers, the bathroom, the cafeteria, and the playground. Also, arrival and departure areas need to be cleared of furniture, equipment, and carpet and should be wide enough for wheelchair mobility and access.

Materials   The available materials in a setting will depend to some extent on the range of ability levels of the children in that setting. The typical preschool setting includes

- "Low-tech" tools (e.g., crayons, chalk, chalkboards, magic markers, bulletin boards, poster paper)
- Natural materials (e.g., sand, clay, water, live specimens, magnets)
- Active play materials (e.g., tires, seesaws, tricycle)
- Construction toys (e.g., blocks, Legos, Lincoln Logs, Tinker Toys) and manipulatives (e.g., puzzles, beads, pegboards, games)
- Creative materials (e.g., playdough, scissors, paint, crayons, glue, clay)
- Literacy materials (e.g., books, tapes, flannel board, CDs, interactive software)

- Dramatic play materials (e.g., dolls, puppets, dress-up clothes, child-size kitchen furnishings, kitchenware) and furnishings and materials for themes such as store, bus, or restaurant

Engagement is an important consideration when selecting materials. To benefit from an activity, children must be engaged in developmentally and contextually appropriate ways with the materials and objects that are part of the activity. Materials are selected to be interesting and appealing because young children are more likely to attend to and manipulate complex and colorful materials and objects. Because children tend to initiate communication when they are engaged with preferred materials, increasing opportunities for interactions with these materials enhances use of language.

Research suggests that engagement can be increased by providing a supply of preferred materials and rotating them in and out of play areas (McWilliam, Wolery, & Odom, 2001). Toy rotation ensures that toys continue to be novel and appealing. The benefits of toy rotation are increased engagement, more varied play skills, and increased sharing (McGee, Daly, Izeman, Mann, & Risley, 1991). To implement a toy rotation plan, first code toys and materials according to the dimensions of size, complexity, developmental level, category, and sensory quality. Next, divide toys/materials into sets. There should be at least one item in each set reflecting the different dimensions. For example, each set should have at least one item from each of these categories: manipulatives, building materials, dramatic play objects, visual motor toys. Each set should also have toys addressing the different sensory modalities. Number and store the sets. Finally, initiate toy rotation by beginning with two sets. At the end of the week, replace set 1 with set 3. At the end of the second week, replace set 2 with set 4. Thus, half of the toys are "new" each week.

Toy rotation does not include all toys and materials. Some items, such as dolls, dress-up clothes, books, and blocks, are always available. Engagement with the permanent toys and items increases with the toy rotation play because there is a potential to use them in new ways as the sets are rotated.

Equipment   *Equipment* refers to furniture (shelves, tables, chairs, desks, easels) and what might be considered "high tech" items such as laser disc players and tape recorders, VCRs, slide projectors, overhead projectors, and computers (with interactive software). The first consideration when purchasing equipment is safety; then, design and attractiveness. Well-designed equipment helps children develop large and small muscle coordination, concepts about the physical world, creativity, social skills, and self-awareness. Like materials, equipment should have sensory appeal (color, design, texture, sound) and be an appropriate size. All areas (e.g., toy shelves, bookcases, coat hangers, sensory tables, activity centers) should be accessible to all children. There should be at least some tables (including a computer table) and easels in the classroom that are high enough for a wheelchair to fit underneath. Materials should be at children's eye level and shelved at a height that allows them to be retrieved and replaced by any child in the class.

In early childhood special education, technology is a tool for learning, communicating, and participating in daily routines and activities. Augmentative communication is discussed at length in Chapter 12. Computers and adaptive devices (e.g., switches, alternative keyboards, touch tablets) encourage autonomous behavior and increase possibilities for children with disabilities to interact with the environment. Most classrooms now include a computer center in which children can work individually or with a partner or a small group.

Group Size   Social density refers to the number of children present in an activity area, and spatial density refers to the amount of space available to those children. They are interrelated aspects of group size. Modifications of either factor can affect the degree of crowding in an area or a classroom, which, in turn, affects classroom dynamics (specifically, the social interactions) (Zirpoli, 1995). Reducing the size of activity areas has been shown to increase social interactions among preschoolers (Rubin & Howe, 1985), but they should not be so small that there is crowding. During storytime, children will be more attentive if they are spaced equidistant from one another (in chairs or on the floor) rather than allowed to arrange themselves (Krantz & Risley, 1977).

Scheduling   Preschool programs typically have routines associated with arrival, self-care, mealtimes and snacks, rest time, and departure. There are several fairly large blocks of time (indoors and outdoors) when children choose their own activities and other blocks of time designated for teacher-guided large-group activities. Hart (1982) noted that the best schedules list approximate time periods. Rosegrant and Bredekamp (1992) agreed, suggesting a general time schedule that can easily be adapted when children become thoroughly engrossed or when they show evidence of losing interest. Children with disabilities should follow the same consistent schedule and daily routines as their peers without disabilities.

Activity time blocks are linked by transitions—movement to another activity or routine. There is a high probability for disruptive behavior before, during, and after a transition. Three sets of circumstances increase the probability for disruptive behavior during transitions: 1) if children are not sure what to do next, 2) if children do not have adequate time to end one activity and clean up before preparing for the next activity, and 3) if there is not ample warning before a bell or buzzer (or other warning) announces that it's time to move to another activity. Table 9.3 provides suggestions for smooth transitions.

Transitions between activities and other routines require careful structuring to teach new skills during these times (Sainato, Strain, Lefebvre, & Rapp, 1987; Wolery, Anthony, & Heckathorn, 1998). Assigning teachers to areas and activities (called zones) rather than to children increases engagement and decreases waiting times (LeLaurin & Risley, 1972). For example, a teacher is assigned to the housekeeping area during indoor free play or to the wheel toy area during outdoor play in the same way that a teacher would be assigned to provide music or read a story. The teacher is responsible for teaching and supervising children in the assigned area.

Table 9.3. Suggestions for smooth transitions

- Give several notices that the activity will end shortly and reiterate what the next activity will be.
- Point to the next activity on a large visual schedule that is posted where everyone can see it.
- Allocate sufficient time to end an activity and cleanup before beginning preparation for the next activity.
- Have self-directed activities available and allow children to move to those activities independently if they finish early.
- Use the time productively when waiting for the children to assemble for a large-group activity (e.g., sit and look at pictures in a book or talk with children already assembled).
- Provide specific instructions and practice with transition behaviors; for example, where and how to line up, where and how to put away materials, acceptable quiet activities to do while waiting, and so forth.

Zone assignment significantly reduces waiting time (waiting has no positive benefits for children). There are no learning or engagement opportunities and a high probability for disruptive behavior when children are standing or sitting in line. To maximize engagement and minimize disruptions, every child should proceed independently, when ready, from one program activity to the next (Hart, 1982). As soon as children finish their art projects, for example, each one cleans up, proceeds to the sink to wash hands, and then moves to the story circle area and sits down. A teacher is sitting in the story circle area talking about and showing pictures in the book they will read when everyone assembles.

ADAPTING INSTRUCTIONAL METHODS AND ACTIVITIES

The guidelines for developmentally appropriate practice (Bredekamp & Copple, 1997) clearly recognize the importance of individual differences and the need to adapt curriculum procedures and activities to accommodate these differences. In addition, both general educators and special educators acknowledge that there is no one instructional method that can be effective with all children (with or without disabilities) *or* with all skills. All children require prompts, repetitions, and some systematic instruction at one time or another to learn a new skill or follow through with a routine. The only difference in which children with disabilities are concerned is that to learn a new skill or routine, they are likely to need more prompts, more repetitions, and more systematic instruction.

There are numerous ways to adapt instructional and play materials to facilitate the participation of children with disabilities in routines and activities. In most cases the focus is on adapting one or another of these aspects of the materials: accessibility, stability, and ease of handling. An object or a material can be stabilized on a surface by using Velcro, Dycem, or some other nonslip product. Adding handles or attaching a string to some items makes them more easily retrievable. Also, simply increasing or decreasing the size of items can make them easier to handle. Toys and other objects can be made more accessible by arranging them on low shelves. Providing a variety of toys and materials that require two or more partners and specific props and roles to structure play activities during dramatic play increases interactive play (DeKlyen & Odom, 1989).

Physical and occupational therapists (and parents) support teachers by demonstrating techniques for positioning, lifting, carrying, and transferring. They also help with ideas for adapting equipment and modifying materials for young children with physical impairments. For example, materials such as adapted scissors, adapted puzzles, and adapted eating utensils and cups need not be specially purchased. They are easily made from standard materials using Velcro, glue, and tape. Building up a spoon or fork handle with layers of tape may facilitate grasping so that a child can feed himself. Velcro straps added to a musical instrument allows a child with an unsteady grasp to shake the tambourine as well as her peers without disabilities.

Table 9.4 provides some general suggestions for methods and procedures that can help *all* children (including those with disabilities) learn to attend, follow directions, and generally succeed in classroom routines and activities. There may be a need for further modification and adaptation of activities and procedures to make them developmentally appropriate for children with sensory impairments and children with limited motor abilities and health impairments.

Table 9.4. Suggestions for adapting methods and activities for all children

To Help Children Learn to Attend:
- Position the children in a circle for group activities so that they can see one another.
- Teach the children to look at the speaker when being spoken to.
- Recognize that some children with disabilities will not be able to block out background sounds, so pair auditory communication with visual communication (gestures, symbols, and pictures).

To Help Children Learn to Follow Directions:
- Show the children that following directions is appreciated by saying "Thank you for (and repeat the direction)" when they comply.
- Ask the children to listen while you describe the steps in the task, and then provide the directions one step at a time.
- Provide easily recognizable visuals showing the steps in the activity.
- Provide examples and demonstrations; e.g., an example of a possible product so that the children understand the goal of the activity.
- Be sure that instructions are relevant and specific and use terms that you are sure the children understand.

To Teach Children to Succeed:
- Point out cause/effect relationships ("Yes, it will start if you hold down the switch") to help the children feel confident that they will be successful.
- Provide specific feedback so that the children do not have to guess whether they are doing what is requested.
- Be sure that your verbal and nonverbal behaviors are consistent—that confirmation and appreciation are delivered in an enthusiastic tone. Children respond to tone and facial expressions.
- Be sensitive to fatigue—even the simplest tasks often require exceptional effort for children with disabilities.
- Provide specific practice on expected behaviors: Learning is less likely to occur incidentally for children with disabilities.
- "Talk the child through" the activity.
- Post easy to understand visual schedules showing the sequence of daily routines and activities in line drawings or photographs.

Children with Sensory Impairments

Hearing and vision impairments are common among children with severe disabilities. Sobsey and Wolf-Schein (1991) estimated that two of every five students with severe disabilities have sensory impairments. Although the majority of children identified as deafblind or having dual sensory impairments have some vision or hearing, the combined effects of the impairments severely impede development of communication and social skills. They can make use of some information presented through the visual and auditory modalities, but the stimuli need to be enhanced and supplemented with tactile teaching methods. Early development of meaningful communication and appropriate social skills are primary goals for toddlers and preschoolers with sensory impairment (as for their peers).

Deaf or Hard of Hearing Hearing impairment can range in severity from mild to profound and can be bilateral or unilateral. Children with losses in the mild to moderate range are usually called hard of hearing; those with hearing loss in the severe and profound range are considered deaf. Children who are deaf are unable to process spoken language without amplification (e.g., a hearing aid). Children who are hard of hearing may or may not need a hearing aid to process spoken language. They may have a prelingual hearing loss, meaning that the hearing loss occurred prior to spoken language acquisition, or a postlingual loss—a hearing loss that occurred after language acquisition. Specialists who work closely with the family and teachers to ensure understanding of the child's hearing impairment and to maximize language development and communication opportunities throughout the day include an early intervention specialist, an audiologist, a speech pathologist trained to work with children with hearing impairment, a teacher of the deaf or a deaf mentor.

Be the time they reach preschool age, most children with hearing loss have been fitted with a hearing aid if they need one. Amplification devices are provided as soon as possible in infancy to maximize the use of residual hearing. The audiologist, family, and teachers work as a team to support optimal use of the device. The audiologist and the parents will familiarize the teachers with the specifics of the child's hearing device, which may be a hearing aid or a cochlear implant. Then it is the teacher's responsibility to 1) ensure that the child wears the aid consistently, 2) inspect the cords regularly for wear, 3) keep the earmolds clean, 4) ensure that the receiver does not get wet, 5) check the batteries daily, and 6) replace batteries as needed. (Teachers should always have extra batteries on hand.)

When the deaf child is in preschool, the family has made the important decision about how their child will communicate—whether with signs or speech. Approaches that emphasize speech (sometimes called "oral approaches") stress the importance of teaching the child to produce intelligible speech and to be able to understand spoken language (with amplification and lipreading). Those who advocate approaches that emphasize signing, or "manual communication," believe that manual communication is a more fully accessible and naturally acquired language for children with significant hearing losses. The ECSE teacher's role is to understand and support whichever approach the family has decided on.

Keep in mind that the child with limited hearing has developed a different view of the world—it is a purely visual world. Sound has little or no meaning; sight, movement, touch, and smell are the experiences through which learning occurs. Although children with hearing impairment represent as diverse a group as children in any other disability category, there are some considerations that are common to most children with hearing impairment. With some specific adaptations, children with hearing impairment can participate in and benefit from an inclusive setting as long as communication is free of barriers and early language acquisition is emphasized. Most of the following methods recommended for children with mild-to-moderate hearing impairment are equally beneficial for children with language/communication disorders and attention deficits, and for those who are learning English as a second language:

1. *Seat the child in front of the speaker in circle activities.* Placement near the speaker maximizes hearing and enables the child to read speech and see facial expressions.

2. *Speak in a normal teaching voice.* There is no need to enunciate or speak loudly. Use natural gestures and visuals (e.g., photos, pictures, symbols, objects) to supplement oral presentations.

3. *Speak the child's name when addressing her.* Wait until she is looking at you before speaking.

4. *Indicate the referent.* When referring to someone or something in the immediate environment, touch, point, or nod in the direction of the referent.

5. *Do not stand in front of a strong light source when speaking to the child.* The child is deprived of important visual cues when your face is in the dark.

6. *Teach peers attention-getting techniques and remind them to speak one at a time and to look at the child when addressing him.* Even preschoolers learn very quickly to touch the student lightly on the shoulder and look him in the face while talking to him.

7. *Learn and use as many signs as possible.* If the child signs, learn and use functional signs (e.g., "all finished," "sit," "toilet") and encourage peers without disabilities to use them also.

For children who are profoundly deaf, additional accommodations may be necessary for full participation and continued exposure to a language rich environment. Inclusive settings may have co-teachers—one with signing skills or experience working with deaf students. The educational assistant may have special training in working with deaf students, or an educational interpreter may be present in the class part- or full-time to facilitate communication during storytime or other instructional interactions. These professionals will be able to assist teachers with necessary accommodations.

Because they typically have communication difficulties, young deaf children may be less likely to participate in cooperative play activities that are language- or sound-based, and when they do participate with peers, they tend to prefer groups of two rather than larger groups. Development of cooperative play can be facilitated by modeling and encouraging use of social play materials (e.g., dolls, blocks, balls) and by coaching peers to include their classmate with hearing impairment in their play routines.

Visual Impairment A child with visual impairment may be identified as partially sighted or blind. The impact of the impairment depends on the age of onset, the amount of functional vision, the etiology (whether it is progressive or nonprogressive), and other disabling conditions. Children with severe visual impairment do not have sufficient visual acuity to easily participate in everyday activities. They experience difficulties with locomotion (crawling, walking), fine motor skills, social interaction, and communication.

Specialists in visual disabilities work closely with the family and with teachers to facilitate optimal adaptations or accommodations for the child with visual impairment. In addition, the team will include an orientation and mobility (O & M) specialist who will work with the child directly and provide consultation to other team members.

Specifically, the O & M specialist teaches the child to use his or her compensatory senses to move around safely and efficiently in the school environment. This professional, together with the specialist in visual disabilities, also works with the teachers and other team members to help them adapt and modify methods and equipment to achieve the child's communication, motor, and sensory instruction goals. Facilitating communication skills is especially important for children with visual impairments. The following are suggestions for working with children with visual impairments:

1. *Provide verbal cues for the child as to what is going to happen next.* For example, "Do you smell the orange juice? I'm going to put the juice cup in your hand now. It is half full of orange juice."

2. *Provide physical cues about how to carry out a task or activity.* For example, gently guide the child to the housekeeping center: place one hand on a bowl and put a spoon in the other hand.

3. *Label actions and objects as they are occurring.* For example, "We are putting the art materials away so that we can get ready to go outside."

4. *Ensure exploration and manipulation of all parts of an object.* It is important for the child to understand the relationship of the parts of the object to the whole.

5. *Let the child know where you are.* Keep the child informed as to your physical location in the classroom. For example, "I'm leaving the block area now to go and begin preparing for snacks. Peter and Taylor are still here to build blocks with you."

6. *Help the child make connections between events.* For example, "When that bell rings, it's almost time to go home—you hear everyone hurrying to put away their materials and get their coats. Then we all stand in line by the door."

7. *Provide detailed verbal directions and explanations.* For example, "After you locate your cubby and put away your backpack, walk over to the nearest table and sit down. Ms. Rice will have some of your favorite toys there and you can choose what you want to play with."

8. *Show peers how to be friends and helpers.* Teach peers to identify themselves: "It's me, Timmy. I will pull out the chair for you if you want to sit here."

Children with Limited Motor Abilities and/or Health Impairments

Included under the heading of health impairments are asthma, allergies, diabetes, rheumatic fever, leukemia, tuberculosis, sickle cell anemia, epilepsy, lead poisoning, and cystic fibrosis. Whether the impairment is chronic (persisting over a long period of time) or acute (having a short but severe course), these children require medical consultation and dietary supervision. Very often, the medications prescribed for these conditions have an effect on classroom behavior. For example, a commonly prescribed asthma medication is correlated with inattentiveness, hyperactivity, drowsiness, and withdrawn behavior.

Physical impairments include those resulting from congenital anomalies (e.g., absence of a limb) and other causes (e.g., spina bifida, cerebral palsy, muscular dystrophy, spinal cord injury). Physical disabilities affect overall developmental progress as well as participation in the classroom program. There may be many interruptions of home, preschool, and peer group experiences because of repeated and prolonged hospitalizations, surgeries, and illnesses.

The physical and occupational therapists and the parents work closely with the teacher to ensure proper seating and positioning for the child with physical impairment. Proper seating and positioning counteract poor circulation, muscle tightness, and pressure sores. It helps the young child to feel physically safe and secure while at the same time aids respiration and digestion and reduces the possibility that the child will develop additional deformities (Rainforth & York, 1991).

There is a wealth of creative ideas for adapting typical preschool activities for children with *limited motor ability* (Sheldon, 1996). Some special adaptations are described in Table 9.5. Keep the following considerations in mind for children with physical and health impairments:

1. *Material and equipment modifications and adaptations should be kept as simple as possible.* The point is to change and modify *only* to the extent absolutely necessary to accomplish the desired purpose.

2. *Procedures and planned experiences should be as similar as possible to those of peers without disabilities.* The rule is that the less intrusive the

Table 9.5. Activity adaptations for children with limited motor abilities

Circle Time
- Have the group sit in chairs rather than on the floor so that everyone is at eye level with the child in a wheelchair.
- If a child has communication difficulties, provide picture boards from which the children choose a song or story or respond to calendar questions.
- Read stories that include children with disabilities.
- Increase peer interactions by modifying the words of songs to call for interaction: "If you're happy and you know it, hug a friend, or give five" and so forth.

Art Activities
- Provide a variety of surfaces for painting; consider attaching paper to the wall, the refrigerator door, or the floor as alternatives to a table or easel.
- Cut off the legs of an easel; a child may find it easier to kneel or sit on a short stool.
- Use Velcro or yarn to fasten a paintbrush to the child's hand or wrist.
- Encourage the children to paint with their fingers, feet, and other body parts.
- Use edible paint (Jell-O and water, pudding, marshmallow whip) so that hand mouthing is not a problem.

Sensory Play
- Provide a subset of sensory items on a tray on the floor or on a table that is wheelchair accessible.
- Place sensory items in a Ziploc bag and tape it to the table or wheelchair tray so that the items are easy to handle.
- Provide sponges, honey, peanut butter, marshmallow, fluff, mashed bananas, cotton candy, snow, whipped gelatin, and so forth for the children to experience the different textures.
- Blow bubbles, play with bubble wands, or use automatic blowers for children who may have difficulty blowing.

Books
- Be sure that bookshelves are at different levels so that the books are accessible to everyone.
- Provide headphones and tapes so that the children can listen to the stories.
- Provide a bookstand for children who are unable to hold a book.
- Include a variety of textured books (homemade or commercial).

Fine Motor
- Adapt wood puzzles by adding large knobs on the pieces.
- Provide puzzles with auditory stimulation (music plays when a puzzle piece is fitted in the correct place).
- Provide large fine motor items—smaller items can be substituted as children with fine motor limitations become more proficient.
- Use Velcro to prevent materials from sliding on the table or tray.

Dramatic Play
- Incorporate items that are large and easy to grasp and manipulate.
- Label shelves with pictures as well as words to facilitate easy cleanup.

Snacks
- Use bowls with suction to avoid sliding and "sippy" cups to avoid spills.
- Identify and assign (on a job board) suitable jobs to the child with limited motor abilities.
- Assemble all the children at the snack table, even if they are not all eating.

Gym and Playground
- Provide a scooter board for the child with limited motor abilities: He can push himself around or be pulled by a peer.

(continued)

Table 9.5. *(continued)*

- Provide a wading pool full of balls for the children to sit in and explore.
- Encourage wagon, blanket, and sheet pulls—a peer can pull the child.
- Ensure that sand tables and swings are accessible.

Computer Center
- Encourage cooperative interactions with the battery-operated toys, switches, and computer games.
- Provide speech output devices that peers can program for a child with no speech.
- Provide alternative keyboards, touch-sensitive screens, and other appropriate peripherals.
- Place stickers on special keys for a particular program to help the children locate them more easily.
- Set a template or overlay over a keyboard so that only certain keys show.

Source: Sheldon, 1996.

strategy, the higher preference it should be given. Avoid experiences that differ from those provided to peers without disabilities, interfere with daily routines, call undue attention to the child, or promote dependence (McCormick & Feeney, 1995). When alternative activity arrangements are necessary, the modifications should be as rich and varied as activities provided to peers without disabilities.

3. *Optimal positioning for all activities is the goal.* Optimal positioning allows the child to relax, focus attention on the activity, and have sufficient controlled movement for independent functioning.

SUMMARY

This chapter described four naturalistic instruction procedures—enhanced milieu teaching, activity-based intervention, embedded and distributed trials, and high-probability ("high-*p*") procedures—that are intended to be implemented in the context of daily routines and activities (including play) in the natural environment. These procedures can promote children's development and participation in a range of natural or least restrictive environments. This includes home and community settings as well as preschool and other center-based settings. Moreover, they are as effective with toddlers as they are with preschoolers, and parents and other family members, therapists, paraeducators, and peers can implement these procedures as effectively as teachers. In addition to naturalistic instruction procedures, this chapter described ways to 1) structure physical and social environments to influence behavior and learning and 2) adapt instructional methods and activities to accommodate individual differences.

••••••••••••••••••••• STUDY QUESTIONS •••••••••••••••••••••

1. List the characteristics common to all naturalistic intervention procedures.

2. Describe and give examples of the six environmental arrangement strategies included in enhanced milieu teaching.

3. Describe and contrast the four enhanced milieu teaching procedures, noting both their commonalities and their differences.

4. Describe activity-based intervention, including the basic premises underlying the procedures.

5. Describe procedures for embedded and distributed time delay trials.

6. Describe the rationale and procedures for high-probability procedures.

7. Contrast the four naturalistic instructional procedures— enhanced milieu teaching, activity-based intervention, embedded and distributed time delay trials, and high-probability procedures.

8. Discuss how room layout and space variables affect learning, independence, social interactions, and communication.

9. Describe a toy rotation plan and discuss the role of toy rotation in increasing engagement.

10. Describe desired characteristics of equipment for an inclusive preschool classroom.

11. Discuss how group size and scheduling affect learning, independence, social interactions, and communication.

12. Discuss and give examples of ways to adapt instructional and play materials to facilitate participation of all children with disabilities in routines and activities.

13. Discuss and give examples of ways to adapt instructional and play materials to facilitate participation of children with sensory impairment in routines and activities.

14. Discuss and give examples of ways to adapt instructional and play materials to facilitate participation of children with limited motor abilities and/or health impairments in routines and activities.

10

Procedures for Challenging Behavior

Mary Jo Noonan

Most challenging behavior of young children is within the bounds of developmental expectations and is resolved through maturation, general parenting, and developmentally appropriate practices in early childhood education. For example, a toddler may cry when corrected or frustrated, a preschooler may hit a peer to obtain a toy, and a kindergarten child may talk back to a parent. Without specialized assessments and intervention, the toddler who screams will probably learn to use words to express her feelings, the preschooler will develop patience and learn the rules about sharing and turn taking, and the kindergarten child will come to understand that he must listen and be polite when corrected for misbehavior. Although these behaviors can be frustrating to professionals and parents, they are typical behaviors of the early childhood years and not cause for alarm. Professionals who work with young children must remember that on a daily basis children are confronted with the complex task of learning socially appropriate behavior. Rather than focusing attention on *managing* misbehavior, a proactive approach to helping children learn appropriate behavior should be emphasized.

For some young children, however, challenging behaviors may be serious and require a specialized approach. These challenging behaviors may be prioritized according to levels of severity: 1) destructive, 2) disruptive, and 3) distracting (Janney & Snell, 2000). Destructive behaviors are high priority challenging behaviors because they are health- or life-threatening (e.g., eye poking, biting, kicking, scratching). These behaviors may be self-directed or directed at others. Disruptive behaviors are second priority because they are not harmful and therefore are of lesser concern. They do, however, interfere with teaching and learning, and may limit a child's participation in a variety of environments and activities. "Acting out" behaviors (e.g., destroying materials, yelling, throwing things), and frequent social withdrawal (e.g., turning away or hiding from others) are examples of disruptive challenging behaviors. Distracting behaviors such as noises, repetitive hand movements, and echolalia are third priority because they are annoying or bothersome but not harmful.

Destructive behaviors require specialized intervention. Disruptive behaviors, because they interfere with learning, should also be addressed. Distracting behavior, however, should not be addressed through the specialized strategies addressed in the remainder of this chapter unless there is evidence that it is likely to develop into destructive or disruptive behavior, or if its elimination is a high priority for the family (Division for Early Childhood, 1998). Instead, distracting behaviors should be dealt with through more informal procedures such as stating rules before each activity, providing reminders for appropriate behavior, or suggesting that the child return to task or begin a new task.

This chapter is concerned with serious challenging behaviors that require specialized interventions. A *positive behavior support (PBS) model* is advocated because it emphasizes techniques that *prevent* challenging behavior and *teach* appropriate replacement behavior. It is a respectful, typical, and individualized approach (Dunlap & Conroy, 2003; Janney & Snell, 2000).

A POSITIVE BEHAVIOR SUPPORT (PBS) MODEL

PBS is a multicomponent intervention model that 1) includes families as team members in assessment, planning, intervention, and monitoring; 2) assesses when, where, with whom, and *why* challenging behavior occurs; 3) restructures environments, lifestyles, and activities to prevent further occurrences of challenging behavior; and 4) teaches appropriate social-communication behaviors that serve the same purpose as challenging behavior. The PBS model emphasizes the use of proactive, educational, and reinforcement-based methods (Carr, Robinson, & Palumbo, 1990; Horner, Albin, Todd, & Sprague, 2006; Lucyshyn, Horner, Dunlap, Albin, & Ben, 2002). A basic premise of PBS is that challenging behavior is a method of communication for the child. Thus, it is important to identify what the child is communicating with the challenging behavior so that a socially appropriate replacement behavior may be identified and taught.

   PBS differs from more traditional behavioral approaches in several important ways (see Table 10.1); for example:

1. Traditional behavioral approaches are narrowly focused on the child and on reducing or eliminating the child's challenging behavior. In contrast, PBS emphasizes that *behavior occurs in context*. It focuses not only on the child and the challenging behavior, but also on understanding and modifying broad and specific environmental variables, including the physical setting, overall lifestyle, activities, schedules, persons present, nature of social interactions, and events preceding and following the challenging behavior (Luiselli & Cameron, 1998).

2. Traditional behavioral assessment focuses on the topography (physical characteristics and appearance) and quantification of the challenging behavior. In contrast, PBS emphasizes *functional assessment* to identify the purpose (usually a communication function) of the challenging behavior and situational variables that predict the occurrence/nonoccurrence of the challenging behavior and alternative appropriate behavior. PBS recognizes

Table 10.1.   Comparison of traditional behavioral approaches and PBS

Elements of approach	Traditional behavioral approach	Positive behavior support
Focus	Challenging behavior	Environment, child, challenging behavior, communication need (replacement behavior)
Assessment	Description and quantification of challenging behavior (what, when, where, with whom, frequency, rate, duration, intensity)	Function (purpose) of challenging behavior and conditions associated with occurrence/nonoccurrence of challenging behavior, and alternative appropriate behavior
Intervention	Punishment or other aversive techniques	Environmental preventative arrangements and reinforcement-based instruction

that challenging behavior exists because it has been reinforced: It has been an effective response for the child (Neilsen & McEvoy, 2004).

3. Traditional behavior modification approaches rely on punishment or other aversive interventions to decrease or stop the challenging behavior. In contrast, PBS uses *positive interventions* that address the function of the challenging behavior. These interventions include arranging the environment to prevent or eliminate the need for challenging behaviors and teaching socially appropriate replacement behaviors (behaviors that serve the same purpose as challenging behaviors).

The PBS model evolved to address efficacy and ethical issues associated with traditional behavioral approaches that relied on punishment and aversive techniques (Horner et al., 1990). First, behavioral reductions obtained through punishment and aversive interventions were frequently not maintained and were often accompanied by increases in new challenging behaviors. PBS addresses these concerns by teaching new socially appropriate behaviors that serve the same purpose as the challenging behaviors. Such new behaviors receive the same reinforcers and thus are maintained (e.g., if crying and calling for a parent both serve the same purpose of getting parental attention, parental attention is the reinforcer for both behaviors). Furthermore, new challenging behavior will not emerge as replacement behavior when challenging behavior is eliminated because the child is obtaining the desired reinforcement with the new socially appropriate behavior. Second, many professionals are uncomfortable with the use of punishment or aversive interventions for ethical reasons: Physical punishments (e.g., water mist, forced exercise, electric shock) and restraints that would not be considered appropriate for individuals without disabilities should not be used with children who have disabilities. An additional ethical concern is that undesirable side effects, such as aggression or withdrawal, frequently occur with punishment. PBS addresses these concerns because it avoids punishment and relies on preventive and reinforcement-based methods. A final issue is that punishment or aversive procedures are insufficient interventions because they do not result in the child learning appropriate behavior. PBS addresses this issue because it is an educational approach that always includes an instructional component to teach a socially acceptable replacement behavior.

Major Components of the PBS Model

The PBS model has three major components: a crisis plan, functional assessment, and a support plan. The crisis plan is an emergency plan focused on stopping the behavior and maintaining safety should the challenging behavior occur prior to developing and implementing the support plan, or when the challenging behavior occurs despite having the support plan in place. It is *not* an intervention (Carr et al., 1994). Functional assessment includes various evaluation methods directed at determining the purpose (i.e., *function*—and there may be more than one) of the challenging behavior, as well as identifying

Table 10.2. The positive behavior support model

PBS model components
Functional assessment
• Purpose/function of challenging behavior
• Contextual antecedent variables and triggers
Support plan
• Crisis management procedures
• Supports to prevent challenging behavior
• Supports to encourage appropriate behavior
• Supports to teach effective replacement behaviors
• Supports to maintain and generalize behavior changes
• Data-based monitoring

environmental and antecedent situations associated with the occurrence and nonoccurrence of the challenging behavior (Neilsen & McEvoy, 2004). A hypothesis of the function of the challenging behavior provides direction for selecting a socially appropriate replacement behavior. Understanding situations and variables associated with the occurrence and nonoccurrence of challenging behavior is important for designing environmental arrangements that prevent challenging behavior and that support socially appropriate replacement behaviors. The support plan is a multicomponent strategy built on the information obtained in the functional assessment. A support plan includes preventive strategies and supports for appropriate behavior, replacement behaviors, and maintenance and generalization (Carr et al., 1994, Janney & Snell, 2000). Table 10.2 summarizes the components of the PBS Model. Each of these components will be discussed in detail in the remainder of the chapter.

Influences on Appropriate and Challenging Behavior

Before turning our attention to the details of implementing the PBS model, it is important to consider the variables that influence whether challenging behavior occurs or not. Four influences are social judgment, maintaining variables, variables that trigger challenging behaviors, and contextual influences.

Social Judgment Whether a behavior is considered a problem or not is a matter of opinion, or *social judgment*. Behavior is essentially "neutral" and is considered a problem only when someone *decides* that it is inappropriate. In early intervention/early childhood special education (EI/ECSE), that *someone* might be a parent, a close family friend, or a professional who is involved with the child. Because it is a subjective decision, it is possible that all members of a child's team might not agree that the behavior is a problem. Furthermore, each individual's judgment of whether the behavior is a problem has a number of influences, including culture, education, experiences, relationships and history with the child, child development philosophies and perspectives, expectations for children, and so forth. For example, if a toddler yells out after she eats each bite of food, her mother may find this very upsetting and even embarrassing because she is concerned that it means her child is not well-behaved or dislikes mealtime. In contrast, a speech–language pathologist might be delighted, assuming that the child is attempting to communicate a request for more food. Or, a teacher may judge a child's hand-biting to be a serious problem because she fears he will injure himself. The child's parents may not be particularly concerned because the skin is not broken and their son doesn't cry when he bites himself. Who is correct about whether or not challenging behavior exists in these situations? This is a question that can only be answered by the entire team. However, as noted earlier in the text, family concerns should always be viewed as important and valid, and should usually carry more weight than professional opinion in decision making (Division for Early Childhood, 1998).

Variables that Maintain Behavior   A basic principle of behavior is that if it is maintaining or increasing, it is being reinforced. A corollary is that if the behavior is being reinforced, it is serving a *purpose* or *function* for the child. Thus, to effectively decrease or eliminate challenging behavior, it is necessary to conduct assessments that will identify the reinforcer. This tells us *why* a child is engaging in the behavior; it answers the question "What does the child *get* for the behavior?" With a hypothesis of what the reinforcer is, supports can be designed to eliminate reinforcement of the challenging behavior, thus rendering it ineffective (O'Neill, Horner, Albin, Sprague, Storey, & Newton, 1997), and to provide reinforcement for socially acceptable replacement behavior.

The reasons or purposes for challenging behavior are referred to as *functions*. There are four possible functions for challenging behavior: gaining attention; obtaining something tangible; escaping, terminating, or avoiding something; or self-regulation (self- or sensory-reinforcement) (Carr et al., 1994; Janney & Snell, 2000, Neilsen & McEvoy, 2004). If someone consistently and immediately approaches a child or talks to her when she engages in challenging behavior, *gaining attention* is a plausible hypothesis. The response may appear to be positive, such as redirecting the child to do something else or complimenting an appropriate behavior that occurred just prior to the challenging behavior. Or, the response may be sympathetic, such as holding the child and preventing the challenging behavior, or it may be a reprimand ("Stop that! Throwing things is not okay."). Regardless of the nature or tone of the response, if another individual usually responds to a behavior, attention may be the purpose. The second function of challenging behavior is to *obtain something tangible* such as a toy or food. It might be that the child requests something and is initially denied. When the request is not granted, challenging behavior occurs (e.g., a tantrum) and continues until finally the adult gives in and provides the desired item. In some situations, challenging behavior will serve to *stop, escape, or avoid an undesirable situation* or activity. This is the third function. For example, a child may repeatedly and forcibly kick the crib when placed in it for bedtime. If the typical result is removal from the crib, the child may be escaping the undesirable situation of having to go to bed. And finally, performing challenging behavior may be reinforcing to the child in that it provides sensory stimulation. For example, head banging may mask the pain of an ear infection, eye poking may provide interesting visual stimulation for a child who is blind, and continuous rocking may be very soothing to a child. Challenging behaviors that function as self-reinforcement are particularly difficult to decrease or eliminate because the variables that maintain the behavior reside within the child (internal stimulation) rather than as part of the social context that is amenable to change. Fortunately, most challenging behavior is not maintained by self-reinforcement (Carr et al., 1994).

Variables that Trigger Behavior   Although reinforcers are a powerful variable in maintaining and increasing behavior, specific events that precede a behavior can significantly affect whether or not it occurs. These *triggers* are called discriminative stimuli, or S^Ds (Carr, Carlson, Langdon, Magito-McLaughlin, & Yarbrough, 1998). They are specific events that prompt or cue behavior. For example, saying "No. That's not the way to do that!" may trigger a tantrum. Although knowing the trigger for a behavior does not tell us the purpose or function of the behavior, this information is important for assessment and planning because triggers can be highly predictive of appropriate and inappropriate behavior. If we can identify the trigger for a particular challenging behavior, we can eliminate or avoid that trigger and instead include triggers associated with appropriate behavior.

Contextual Influences   The context of challenging behavior refers to the physical, temporal, social, and physiological situation associated with the challenging behavior (Carr, Reeve, & Magito-McLaughlin, 1996). All elements of the context have the potential to increase or decrease the likelihood that challenging behavior will occur (Neilsen & McEvoy, 2004). For example, a child might be more likely to refuse to do schoolwork if it is a warm day (physical context), if it is late in the day (temporal context), if the classroom is crowded and bustling with activity (social context), or if she slept poorly the night before (physiological context). Contextual influences can account for variations in the observations of the behavior from situation to situation and time to time (Carr et al., 1994). These variations may result in different opinions among team members regarding the seriousness of the challenging behavior. It is important for team members to be aware of contextual influences so that they do not mistakenly assume that others' observations are inaccurate if they differ from their own. Furthermore, contextual influences are critical assessment data needed when planning interventions for challenging behavior.

These four major influences on behavior—social judgment, maintaining variables, variables that trigger challenging behavior, and contextual influences—are addressed throughout the remainder of this chapter. These influences determine whether professionals and parents judge that challenging behavior exists and are critical assessment data for constructing effective PBS plans.

FUNCTIONAL ASSESSMENT

As discussed in Chapter 3, assessment includes a broad array of approaches to evaluate a child's strengths and needs in the home and other environments in which the child frequently participates. Assessment for the purpose of developing a PBS plan examines the physical and social context in which challenging behavior occurs. Examining the context of challenging behavior produces information about why it occurs (function), with whom it occurs (social context), and when it occurs (physical and/or social context). It may also illuminate similar contexts in which challenging behavior does not occur. Information about the function and context of challenging behavior is best obtained using multiple assessment strategies, such as interviews and observational assessment (Neilsen & McEvoy, 2004).

Interviews

Interviews provide assessment data by asking questions of persons who are well-acquainted with the young child exhibiting the challenging behavior. It is common to interview one or both parents; sometimes other family members, baby sitters, early intervention personnel, early childhood educators, and/or others who see the child regularly are interviewed. The interview questions are preestablished and designed to elicit specific information about the behavior, the child's current communication and social skills, and the context in which the behavior occurs (Neilsen & McEvoy, 2004; O'Neill et al., 1997). Observational assessment is also conducted to cross-validate the interview data, provide quantifiable data, and examine data in situations not covered by the interview. Sample questions included in a functional assessment interview are listed in Table 10.3.

Cultural Considerations   When the professional conducting a functional assessment interview is of a culture different from the child's family, the interviewer must use effective cross-cultural communication skills. The interviewer must be aware of how culture affects values, judgments, and attitudes concerning challenging behavior, assessment, and intervention. In their model of cross-cultural competence, Kalyanpur and Harry (1999) suggested that the professional must first be aware of the influences of culture on personal beliefs and values concerning disabilities, families, and the issues being addressed. These are one's own cultural biases. If a professional is aware of personal biases, he or she can recognize that such beliefs and values are subjective and neither right nor wrong. Next, Kalyanpur and Harry recommend that the professional adopt a stance of *cultural reciprocity*, sharing personal values and beliefs with families. Personal disclosure invites families to respond likewise by sharing their own values and beliefs. As professionals and parents get to know one another through cultural reciprocity, they may gradually develop a relationship built on mutual understanding and trust.

As mentioned above, cultural differences among professionals and families may account for disparities in judgments as to the extent to which a beha-

Table 10.3. Questions frequently included in a functional assessment interview

Challenging Behavior
1. What are the behaviors that concern you?
2. What do they look like?
3. How often do they occur? (per hour, day, or week)
4. How intense are they? How do you judge how intense they are?

Communication and Social Skills
1. How does the child communicate basic needs such as hunger, thirst, or discomfort (wet diaper, not feeling well)?
2. How does the child communicate a desire for attention or to be held?
3. How does the child reject something, indicate "no," and express a preference?
4. For which adults or children does the child show a clear preference?
5. Does the child play simple turn-taking games (e.g., Peekaboo)? Please describe.
6. How does the child respond to new social situations (e.g., going to a playground for the first time, having visitors)?
7. How does the child interact when other children are present?

Physiological Context
1. Are there concerns related to eating?
2. Are there concerns related to sleeping?
3. What is the child's typical sleep schedule?
4. Does the child have allergies?
5. Does the child have frequent ear infections or other respiratory illnesses?
6. Does the child have any chronic health concerns?
7. Does there seem to be any relationship between challenging behavior(s) and eating, sleeping, and/or other health concerns?

Social Context
1. Is there a particular person who is usually present when challenging behavior(s) occurs?
2. Are there particular social situations that seem to be associated with challenging behavior(s)?

Environmental and Activity Context
1. What is the child's typical daily schedule?
2. Is there a particular place or activity that seems to be associated with challenging behavior(s)?
3. Is there a particular place or activity that is likely to be free of challenging behavior(s)?
4. What are the child's favorite places and activities?

vior is or is not considered a challenge or problem. Culture may affect a family's participation in assessment and intervention as well as their comfort level associated with recommendations from professionals. Throughout the assessment and intervention process, it is critical that professionals respect and honor family perspectives while continuing to build cultural reciprocity in their relationship.

Observational Assessment

Information from the functional assessment interview will indicate times and situations associated with the challenging behavior. It may also suggest probable hypotheses about the purpose that the challenging behavior is serving. This preliminary information is useful for planning times to conduct observational assessment. The purposes of observational assessment are to 1) confirm that the challenging behavior does indeed exist, 2) document occurrences of the challenging behavior, 3) provide further information on the contexts of the challenging behavior and variables associated with it, and 4) formulate hypotheses about the function (purpose) of the challenging behavior. Recognizing that challenging behavior usually serves a communicative purpose ("I want attention," "I don't want to do this," "I want that _____"), each observation of the challenging behavior may be recorded by filling in a notecard describing it in its social context. Carr et al. (1994) suggested that the notecard include the following contextual information: interpersonal situation (who is present), behavior, and social consequence (what someone says or does when the challenging behavior occurs). Figure 10.1 is a sample of an observation recorded in this manner.

Another format for recording observations of challenging behavior is an A-B-C record (Bijou, Peterson, & Ault, 1968). *A* represents the *antecedents* (conditions or events) that precede the challenging behavior, *B* represents the *behavior* (the challenging behavior and any other child behaviors), and *C* is the *consequence.* An A-B-C record is typically written on a piece of paper divided into three columns labeled A, B, and C. As in the example of the Observation of Challenging Behavior notecard shown in Figure 10.1, it is important that the *social* situation (interpersonal context and social consequence) be recorded, given the assumption that challenging behavior usually serves a communicative function. In addition, the observer may write a continuous description of the situation(s) and child behaviors. This provides a rich description of the context of the child's behavior. It may also provide information about several events preceding the challenging behavior and may uncover behavior chains associated with challenging behavior. For example, Figure 10.2 is an A-B-C record of the same events noted on the observation card in Figure 10.1. The A-B-C record reveals that Chelsea asked for the shovel twice before she took it from the toddler. Knowing that taking the toy was not Chelsea's first attempt to obtain it suggests that it might be possible to intervene before Chelsea's behavior escalates to challenging behavior.

Observational assessment should be conducted across several activities, settings, and days to obtain adequate information about the contexts and vari-

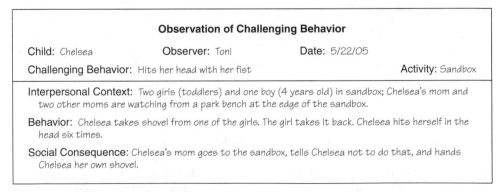

Figure 10.1. Sample notecard for describing the social context of observations of challenging behavior.

A-B-C ASSESSMENT

Child: *Chelsea*   Observer: *Toni*   Date: *5/22/05*

Challenging Behavior: *Hits her head with her fist*   Activity: *Sandbox play*

A	B	C
Two toddlers (girls) and one 4-year old boy are playing in the sandbox when Chelsea arrives. Chelsea's mom sits down on a park bench at the edge of the sandbox; two mothers are sitting on another nearby bench.	Chelsea stands by her mom and watches the children play.	The children remain focused on their play. None of the children look at Chelsea.
Chelsea's mom: "It's o.k., Chelsea. You can play, too."	Chelsea looks at her mom and says "Pail, Mom."	Chelsea's mother hands her a pail and some other sand toys.
	Chelsea slowly enters the sandbox, and squats off to the side. She watches the other children.	The other children continue with their play and do not look at Chelsea.
	Chelsea moves close to the girls and watches them dig in the sand with their shovels.	One of the girls looks at Chelsea and then moves, turning her back to Chelsea.
	Chelsea reaches toward a shovel and says, "Please . . . .. Me play."	One girl looks at Chelsea. Both girls move away from Chelsea a bit.
	Chelsea reaches again and says, "Please."	One girl turns to her and shouts, "No!"
	Chelsea takes the shovel from the girl who shouted at her.	The girl takes the shovel back and says, "Mine."
	Chelsea backs away, hits herself on the head six times, and begins crying.	Chelsea's mom goes to the sandbox, tells her not to do that, and hands Chelsea her own shovel.
	Chelsea cries softly and begins digging in the sand with her shovel	Chelsea's mom rubs her back and softly repeats, "It's o.k. It's o.k."

Figure 10.2. Example of an A-B-C record of challenging behavior (same situation as Figure 10.1).

ables associated with challenging behavior. In reviewing A-B-C records or behavioral observation cards, the consequences suggest the purpose or function of the behavior. In the example illustrated in Figures 10.1 and 10.2, the consequences are attention from the child's mother and receipt of the requested item. The A-B-C record also reveals a behavioral chain of two ineffective (but socially appropriate) verbal requests preceding the challenging behavior. And in this instance, the challenging behavior occurred only *after* the peer took the shovel back from Chelsea. This suggests that Chelsea's challenging behavior was triggered by the physical action of the toddler taking the toy rather than the verbal refusals that preceded the physical action. The antecedent situation of young children at play may also be associated with challenging behavior. It is plausible that Chelsea's challenging behavior occurs mostly with younger children who have not yet learned sharing or turn taking. Additional observations and A-B-C recordings will indicate whether these are plausible interpretations and predictable variables. Observations should be conducted until the information obtained indicates consistent patterns of consequences, behavioral chains, antecedent situations, and triggers. Sometimes observational assessment may be completed in a few hours; at others times, a few days.

Hypothesis Development

Once the interview and observational assessment information yield a clear picture of the child's challenging behavior and associated variables, hypotheses about the function (purpose) of the behavior and when it is likely to occur (context and triggers) must be developed. These hypotheses will be used to guide the development of the PBS plan.

Hypotheses About Function   Knowing why a behavior occurs (its purpose) is essential information for identifying a socially appropriate communication behavior that will be taught as an alternative response to the challenging behavior. Hypotheses about function will indicate why a challenging behavior occurs. *The effect produced by a behavior indicates its function. In other words, the consequence of a behavior reveals its purpose.* Referring again to the scenario described in Figures 10.1 and 10.2: Why did Chelsea hit herself in the head? To develop a hypothesis to this question, look to the effect or consequence of the behavior: Chelsea hit herself to obtain adult attention and a desired object (her mother went to her and gave her a shovel). Observing and recording many observations of the challenging behaviors across a number of situations and times will help to determine if both functions (attention and obtaining a desired object) are typical, or if one function occurs more frequently than the other.

As noted earlier in this chapter, there are four possible functions of challenging behavior: gaining attention, obtaining something, escaping/terminating something, or providing self-reinforcement. Escaping/terminating something would be the hypothesis when the child does not have to do an activity or is removed from a situation as a result of challenging behavior. For example, if Chelsea's mother removed Chelsea from the sandbox when she hit herself on the head, the hypothesis would be: Chelsea hit herself to escape/terminate playtime in the sandbox. Escape is a fairly common function of challenging behaviors and is often accomplished through tantrums and aggression.

Self-reinforcement is the hypothesis when challenging behavior is not consistently associated with one of the other three functions (gaining attention, obtaining something, escaping/terminating something), all of which are *socially mediated*; that is, requiring another person to accomplish their purpose (Carr et al., 1994). When challenging behavior serves the function of self-reinforcement, the child is being reinforced by the behavior itself. Self-reinforcement is sometimes referred to as *self-regulation*. The function of self-regulation is to adjust the child's sensory experiences and internal state of stimulation; that is, feeling calm or being alert (Janney & Snell, 2000). For example, eye poking may produce sensations of light that the child finds very appealing; children who hit or bite themselves may experience a reduction or masking of another pain (like an earache or headache) or may feel a "high" sensation as chemical endorphins are released by the central nervous system to sooth their pain. Behaviors such as hand flapping may be self-stimulating and serving as entertainment or play. Numerous studies have shown that providing alternative sensory stimulation (headphones with music, decorative lights, handheld electronic games, and so forth) may result in a reduction in self-reinforcing challenging behavior (Kennedy & Souza, 1995).

Hypotheses About Context and Triggers   Although the effect or consequence of challenging behavior indicates *why* it occurs, the social situation and other antecedents suggest *when* it is likely to occur. Contextual variables may be physical, temporal, social, or physiological. Continuing to analyze the situation of Chelsea in the sandbox, contextual variables that might increase the likelihood of her engaging in challenging behavior include the physical variable of being in the sandbox (perhaps the texture of sand is unpleasant and makes her irritable), the temporal variable of having been away from home for 2 hours while her mother ran errands, the social variable of toddlers (who don't share!) or crowding (four children in a small sandbox), or the physiological variables of hunger (lunchtime is approaching) and fatigue (nap follows lunchtime). As in developing hypotheses about the function of challenging behavior, it is necessary to look at many instances of challenging behavior to determine which are reasonable hypotheses. Reviewing many observational records of challenging behavior may yield this example of a hypothesis about the context of a challenging behavior: Chelsea is most likely to engage in challenging behavior when she is playing near several other young children in a crowded area.

As stated earlier in the chapter, *triggers* to challenging behavior are specific events or S^{D}s (discriminative stimuli) that significantly affect whether a behavior occurs or not. In the example of Chelsea's self-injury, Chelsea hit her head immediately after the toddler took the shovel from her. Additional observational records should be reviewed to determine whether there are similar discrete events that immediately precede Chelsea's self-injury. A hypothesis about a trigger for her challenging behavior may be that Chelsea is likely to hit herself when an object is taken away from her.

It is tempting to look to the antecedents to hypothesize *why* a challenging behavior occurs (e.g., Chelsea wants the shovel back), but the context, conditions, or triggers *do not* reinforce (i.e., maintain or increase) challenging behavior. Similarly, the toddler taking the shovel from Chelsea isn't *why* Chelsea hit herself. The toddler taking the shovel from Chelsea was the *trigger* for Chelsea's self-injury. Parental attention or actually obtaining the desired object was the reinforcing consequence (the effect/purpose) of Chelsea's challenging behavior.

As evident in the above examples, it is possible to develop hypotheses about the function, antecedents, and triggers of challenging behavior for each observation, but more valid hypotheses are likely if numerous observations are reviewed. In many cases, challenging behavior will serve more than one function and have multiple antecedent conditions and triggers associated with it. A list of hypotheses should be developed following a thorough review of all interviews and observational records. The family should be an integral part of this assessment and interpretation process.

Functional Analysis

The only valid way to verify hypotheses about challenging behavior is to test each one through a brief experiment called *functional analysis* (Carr, 1977; Iwata, Dorsey, Slifer, Bauman, & Richman, 1982). This often requires the support of a behavior specialist who has expertise in functional analysis and is not a part of the social situations associated with challenging behavior. If a behavior specialist is available, it is advantageous to conduct the functional analyses before developing the PBS plan. The results of the functional analyses will increase the likelihood that the PBS plan addresses the true antecedents, triggers, and functions of challenging behavior. Often, however, the precision and rigor of functional analyses are not necessary when adequate functional assessment information has been acquired through other sources, such as interviews and behavioral observations (Horner et al., 2006). For this reason, full details of how to conduct functional analyses are not presented here. Instead, it is recommended that functional analyses be conducted only when a behavior specialist is available to provide the necessary assistance.

DESIGNING POSITIVE BEHAVIOR SUPPORT (PBS) PLANS

PBS plans are designed assuming that the hypotheses are correct. They also informally test the hypotheses. Hypotheses about antecedent conditions and triggers are used to develop strategies to prevent challenging behavior from occurring and to promote appropriate behavior. Hypotheses about the function(s) of challenging behavior are used to select socially appropriate behaviors that will be taught to the child as alternatives or replacement behaviors so that the challenging behavior is not necessary. Components of a comprehensive PBS plan are

1. A Crisis Management Plan
2. Supports to Prevent Challenging Behavior
   - Modify or eliminate contextual variables
   - Modify or eliminate triggers
   - Interrupt escalating chain of behavior
3. Supports to Encourage Appropriate Behavior
   - Provide choice and high-preference situations
   - Embed cues

- Present positive social comments
- Create meaningful, interesting, and predictable routines and activities
- Use supported routines, task simplification, and preteaching

4. Supports to Teach Effective Replacement Behaviors

- Teach functionally equivalent communication responses
- Teach behaviors that are more effective than challenging behavior
- Teach proactively

5. Supports to Maintain and Generalize Behavior Changes

- Teach *effective* replacement behaviors
- Introduce delayed and intermittent reinforcement
- Teach across people, places, and activities
- Address all functions of challenging behavior concurrently
- Teach in controlled situations first; then in less controlled situations

6. Data-Based Monitoring

- Monitor challenging behavior
- Monitor replacement behavior

The appendix to this chapter includes a sample PBS plan. The remainder of the chapter describes how to construct each component of a comprehensive PBS plan.

Cultural Considerations

As described earlier in this chapter, culture will affect judgment concerning whether challenging behavior exists, interpretation of assessment information, and acceptability of intervention procedures. Professionals can facilitate family participation in designing intervention procedures by discussing the interpretation of assessment information and resultant hypotheses. Reviewing each instance of challenging behavior recorded during the observational assessment process can do this. First, discuss whether or not there is agreement that challenging behavior occurred during the observation. This will contribute to a continuing process of clarifying what is and is not challenging behavior (an issue that is highly influenced by culture). If there is agreement that challenging behavior occurred, come to consensus on the antecedents and consequences to the challenging behavior during that specific observation. Or if the family was not present for that observation, describe the observed antecedents and consequences to the family. And finally, referring to the consequences, discuss a hypothesis about *why* the challenging behavior occurred (function); and referring to the antecedents, note if a contextual variable or trigger that might increase the likelihood of the challenging behavior is present. The hypotheses are probably the most subjective and culturally influenced part of this process, but with continuous reference to the antecedents and consequences, it should be possible to reach consensus. Coming to a shared understanding of the contexts, functions, and hypotheses concerning the challenging behavior establishes a basis for working together to identify preventive and instructional strategies for eliminating the challenging behavior and promoting appropriate social and communication skills.

Crisis Management Procedures

During the assessment and intervention phases of PBS, challenging behavior may sometimes occur. It is necessary to have a plan for responding when this happens. Sometimes the occurrence of challenging behavior will seem minor and not very significant. At other times, it will be serious and will create a crisis situation in which the behavior is very intense or extreme, or the child or others are in danger of harm. Whenever challenging behavior occurs—whether it is minor or severe—the family and professionals who support the child should respond following a preestablished crisis management plan. Note that this is not an *intervention*; it is simply strategies for minimizing the immediate effects of challenging behavior and keeping the child and others safe until the PBS plan begins to take effect.

Carr and his colleagues (1994) provided five recommendations for a crisis management plan. First, occurrences of challenging behavior may be ignored. The parent or professional who observes the occurrence can casually turn away and *pretend* that the behavior did not occur. Second, if it's not believable to pretend that the challenging behavior did not occur, calmly redirect the child's attention by introducing a cue for appropriate behavior. For example, if the child is angry and throws a toy, a parent might approach the child with a favorite book and say, "Let's read a story together." Third, if the behavior is intense or severe, furniture or other objects may have to be moved to prevent the child from becoming injured. Fourth, it may be prudent to request children who are nearby to move to another location. And fifth, it may be necessary to momentarily restrain the child. In reviewing these five suggestions, it should be apparent that they don't teach appropriate behavior, but only serve to stop the challenging behavior and protect the child and others. Remember, a crisis management plan is a short-term plan only and is not likely to eliminate challenging behavior or the need for a multicomponent PBS plan.

Supports to Prevent Challenging Behavior

The hypotheses developed from the assessment information may include one or more contextual variables (antecedent conditions or situations) or triggers that seem to predict when challenging behavior is likely to occur. The PBS plan modifies or eliminates these variables whenever it is reasonable to do so (Neilsen & McEvoy, 2004). For example, if Chelsea is most likely to engage in self-injury at the playground when she is in a small area crowded with other children, that situation can be eliminated. There are activity areas at the playground other than the sandbox. If the sandbox is crowded, her parent can take her to a less crowded area for play. When the entire playground is crowded, her parents can make note of such times and change their schedule for visiting the playground. Similarly, if taking an object from Chelsea is a trigger for self-injury, her play environments can be arranged to include more than one of each type of toy so that others will be less likely to take a toy from Chelsea. Play in proximity to very young children (1- through 3-year-olds) might also be avoided in favor of 4- and 5-year-olds because the younger children are the ones who are most likely to take toys from others.

It is important to consider whether contextual variables and triggers associated with challenging behavior are necessary elements of a child's routines and activities. If, for example, Chelsea was going to start preschool in a few months, the PBS plan might initially include avoiding areas crowded with young children. In addition, the plan might also include a strategy to help Chelsea become accustomed to playing appropriately with an increasing number of young children in close proximity. If Chelsea has a younger sibling and/or is frequently with younger cousins, then it might not be feasible to remove the trigger of a child taking a toy from her. Other strategies that encourage appropriate behavior and teach socially appropriate replacement behaviors will have to be implemented, especially when the trigger is likely to be present.

In some situations, assessment information will have indicated that challenging behavior is associated with an escalating chain of behavior. For example, Chelsea made two verbal requests for the shovel that were unsuccessful (she was not given the shovel). Only then did she engage in self-injury. Additional assessment information might confirm whether Chelsea's challenging behavior typically follows repeated and failed communication attempts. If this is confirmed as a behavior chain leading to self-injury, one preventive strategy to include in a PBS plan is to interrupt the escalating behavior chain (Kazdin, 2001). When Chelsea's communicative requests are unsuccessful, the parent or professional can interrupt the behavior chain by restating the request and encouraging the other child or adult to fulfill the request, or the parent or professional can interrupt the chain by fulfilling the request. And if it's not appropriate or possible to satisfy Chelsea's request, she can be removed from the situation and redirected to another task that she enjoys.

Supports to Encourage Appropriate Behavior

In addition to strategies that prevent challenging behavior, a PBS plan should include contextual variables and triggers associated with *appropriate* behavior. Generally, high preference, child selected, and predictable situations, routines, and activities are associated with little or no challenging behavior (Janney & Snell, 2000). These antecedent/contextual variables provide the child with a sense of control.

Choice and High Preference Situations, Routines, and Activities Adults tend to spend much of their time doing things they enjoy. It makes sense that when people choose their own activities, they choose pleasurable ones. Exercising choice also extends to home living chores. Adults do their chores at times, in ways, and with materials they prefer. In contrast, many children—and particularly those with disabilities—are given very little choice in their daily lives. Instead, adults orchestrate their routines and activities, generally so that the daily schedule is convenient for the adults. This doesn't mean the adults don't give any consideration to the children's preferences and interests, but the daily schedule is often far from what the children would choose if they had the opportunity to create their own schedules. Honoring a child's preferences not only gives the child some control over his daily life, but it communicates respect for the child (Cameron, Maguire, & Maguire, 1998).

For most children, the adult-constructed schedule is not a problem and includes many things that children enjoy. However, when children have severe challenging behavior, they are often communicating a desire to control at least some of their world. As noted earlier, the purpose of most challenging behavior is to communicate "I want something" (attention, an object, or something to end/stop). Therefore, one way to decrease challenging behavior is to create a schedule reflecting child-choice (Dunlap et al., 1994; Dyer, Dunlap, & Winterling, 1990). Such a schedule would include situations, routines, and activities that are highly preferred by the child. For an infant or young child with limited communication, this means that parents and professionals must carefully observe to determine what preferences and choices the child is expressing. For example, an infant may be extremely fussy and demonstrate challenging behavior in the early morning because she wants to get out of her crib immediately on wakening and eat, in contrast to staying in the crib until both parents finish showering and dressing. Parents might be willing to adjust their morning schedules and alternate one getting up and feeding the infant while the other showers. Allowing the child to choose her wake-up and feeding time may be all that is necessary to eliminate challenging behavior in the early mornings.

Embedded Routines and Cues for Appropriate Behaviors Another strategy for encouraging appropriate behavior in situations in which challenging behavior frequently occurs is to introduce or *embed* routines and/or cues that prompt appropriate behavior (Carr et al., 1998). For example, Chelsea and her father may have an established and favorite affection routine in which Dad sings "Itsy Bitsy Spider" while walking his fingers up her leg, arm, neck, and face to the top of her head. Chelsea giggles with anticipation of the ticklish feeling whenever he does this. The song and the walking motion of Chelsea's father's fingers are routines and cues for appropriate behavior. The PBS plan can use this routine by embedding it at times they know Chelsea is likely to engage in self-injury. For example, when Chelsea is waiting her turn in a game with neighborhood children, her dad might unobtrusively sit behind her and sing softly in her ear and occasionally walk his fingers along her back or shoulders.

Because this routine is associated with appropriate behavior, it may serve as a prompt for Chelsea to continue demonstrating appropriate behavior. Similarly, if Chelsea has learned to take turns when prompted by a timer while playing with certain toys with her siblings at home, the cues of turning the timer to 5 minutes and stating, "O.K. Let's share this toy by taking turns every 5 minutes," could be introduced in the preschool setting as cues for appropriate behavior.

Two strategies to encourage appropriate behavior related to embedding are *interspersed requests* (Horner, Day, Sprague, O'Brien, & Heathfield, 1991) also known as *high probability requests* (Davis, Brady, Williams, & Hamilton, 1992)—and *positive social comments* (Kennedy, Itkonen, & Lindquist, 1995). The interspersed requests strategy can encourage appropriate behavior for children who demonstrate challenging behavior when asked to follow directions. The procedure is to make a few short requests that tend to be followed easily and are not associated with challenging behavior. Once the child has responded appropriately to easy requests, a more difficult request is made (*difficult* meaning that the request typically results in challenging behavior). Research has suggested that responding correctly to a few easy requests in quick succession establishes a momentum that promotes continued correct responding when a difficult request is made. An example would be asking a kindergarten child to take out his favorite pencil, point to a word that begins with the letter "b" (two easy requests), and copy the letter "b" (difficult request).

The interspersed request strategy may be considered when a child has demonstrated the ability to respond to a request (i.e., the response has already been acquired) yet engages in challenging behavior when the request is presented. As discussed earlier in this chapter, it is essential to consider whether demands being placed on a child are necessary and appropriate. This is especially true for the situation presented here—one suggesting that the request is not meaningful or important from the child's point of view.

The *positive social comments* strategy is similar to interspersed requests, but rather than make requests, the adult makes several comments that are likely to put the child in a good mood before she makes the difficult request. For example, a parent can say to a child, "Oh, you are holding your favorite Teddy. Teddy loves you!" (The parent makes the teddy bear hug the child.) "Teddy is happy to be with you. Here, take this medicine." (The parent gives the child a measured dose of an antibiotic the child doesn't like.)

Meaningful, Interesting, and Predictable Routines and Activities Just as the above strategy of positive social comments can put a child in a good mood and thereby decrease challenging behavior, constructing a child's experiences so that they are filled with meaningful, interesting, and predictable routines and activities can also promote a good mood and appropriate behavior (Cameron et al., 1998; Hemmeter & Ostrosky, 2003). For an infant, toddler, or young child, meaningful and interesting routines and activities might include many and varied play situations (home, early childhood programs, parks, playgroups, infant/

toddler exercise groups), brief outings to varied places as parents do their errands, and typical activities of daily living. Although daily living activities such
as mealtimes, bathing, and dressing may not seem inherently interesting or
meaningful from an infant or young child's perspective, these activities can be
done in ways that are sociable and enjoyable. Furthermore, when they are done
in preparation for play or an outing, they may come to be associated with
meaningful and interesting activities, and thus they become motivating.

Predictable routines and activities are associated with appropriate behavior because they provide order to the infant/young child's world. If the world
is predictable, there is a feeling of control; the world is not full of unanticipated
events and surprises (Noonan & Siegel, 2003). For example, if a child's morning routine is always the same—Mom or Dad wakes her up and cuddles her,
changes her diaper and plays a little, gives her a morning bottle, and dresses
her—the child will learn from the daily repetition that her bottle will be coming just after a little play. The child may not be aware that she knows this, but
if the routine were not in place, she would feel uncertain as to when and if
she'd be fed each morning. Predictable routines are also an important foundation for language comprehension (the child is more likely to learn the meaning
of "Time for breakfast!" if the phrase is said in the same context each day and
is immediately followed by her bottle and some cereal). Improving language
comprehension contributes to creating predictable routines and activities. It
has also been shown to be associated with decreases in challenging behavior
(Carr et al., 1994).

As children reach the age of 1, they usually begin to learn simple rules,
such as where they may and may not play, things they may and may not touch,
and so on. Simple rules teach children the expectations for appropriate behavior.
Most children are highly reinforced by positive attention from their family members and other adults, and thus are motivated to *be good*; that is, to comply
with expectations for appropriate behavior. Consistent enforcement of simple
rules results in predictable responses from adults, and thus promotes appropriate behavior (Alberto & Troutman, 2003). Having rules for young children does
not imply that punishment or harsh consequences must be imposed for in-
fringements. It does imply, however, that the child's behavior should be corrected (e.g., a firm "No") and redirected to appropriate behavior.

Supported Routines, Task Simplification, and Preteaching
Whether at
home or in an early childhood education setting, if young children are being
asked to perform tasks that are new and difficult, appropriate behavior during
the tasks can be encouraged by providing assistance. Assistance can include
supported routines, task simplification, or *preteaching.* Each of these strategies eases the demands being placed on the child. In *supported routines,* children are assisted in doing the most difficult parts of tasks that they are learning (Cameron et al., 1998). Teaching is focused on the easiest portions of the
task to minimize frustration and encourage participation. In *task simplification,* teaching an alternative, easier way to do a difficult task minimizes frus-

tration (Kern & Dunlap, 1998). *Preteaching* (also known as *priming*) is practicing or rehearsing a task before it is required in a more demanding or independent situation (Koegel, Carter, & Koegel, 1998).

Supports to Teach Effective Replacement Behaviors

Antecedent approaches for the PBS plan have been described: supports to prevent challenging behavior and supports to encourage appropriate behavior. Although these approaches are essential elements of a comprehensive PBS plan, they do not address the purpose or function of challenging behavior. This section of the PBS plan focuses on teaching appropriate behaviors that serve the same function as challenging behavior. If the child accomplishes the desired effect with the new replacement behavior, challenging behavior is not needed. Replacement behaviors that serve the same function/purpose as challenging behaviors recruit the same reinforcement that maintained the challenging behaviors (Carr, 1977). A very powerful PBS plan can be created by implementing antecedent strategies (supports to prevent challenging behavior and supports to encourage appropriate behavior) in conjunction with teaching *functionally equivalent* replacement behaviors.

   Proactive Instruction As noted throughout this chapter, the three major functions (purposes) of challenging behavior are to gain attention, to obtain something, and to escape/terminate something. Replacement behaviors for these functions must communicate "I want attention," "I want something," or "I don't want (to do) something." Teaching one or more of these replacement behaviors is *functional communication training* (Carr & Durand, 1985). To be effective, the function of the replacement behavior must match the function of the challenging behavior. In addition, effective replacement behaviors have the following characteristics:

1. They are relatively simple responses for the child to make.
2. They result in immediate reinforcement.
3. The resulting reinforcement is more powerful than that for the challenging behavior (Horner & Day, 1991; Horner, Sprague, O'Brien, & Heathfield, 1990).

Replacement behaviors must be simple responses because the child is already skilled at responding with challenging behavior. If the new acceptable response is more difficult than the challenging behavior, the child's perspective may be that it is not worth the effort to use the new response—the same reinforcement can be obtained by using the easier challenging behavior. Challenging behavior, because of its intensity and seriousness, usually produces an immediate and powerful result. Immediacy of reinforcement affects the strength of reinforcement. Therefore, if a socially appropriate behavior is going to be an effective replacement for challenging behavior, it must also produce an immediate effect. And finally, the reinforcement for the replacement behavior must be more powerful than that for the challenging behavior; otherwise the child will opt for using challenging behavior. Imagine the immediacy and strength of a parent's response when Chelsea hits herself in the head and begins to cry: Chelsea's mom calls from the park bench, "No, Chelsea!" as she runs to her. If Chelsea is taught to say "Please" as a replacement for self-injury when she wants something, her mother must respond as quickly and strongly as she would had Chelsea hit herself in the head: "Yes, Chelsea! You may play with the shovel." In this way Chelsea will learn that the replacement behavior can be more effective than the challenging behavior.

Socially appropriate replacement behavior must be *taught* proactively. The most effective instructional times will be situations in which the challenging behavior is likely (Carr et al., 1994). In our example of Chelsea playing in the sandbox, the PBS plan could include teaching the replacement behavior of saying "Please" in close proximity to toddlers playing with toys on the playground. The plan might state that Chelsea's mother would bring a bag with a number of high-preference- and playground-type toys (sand toys, balls, sidewalk chalk, and so forth) and situate Chelsea near a group of toddlers each time they visit the playground. When Chelsea shows interest in the toddlers' toys (stares at the toys or the toddlers, moves closer to the toys or the toddlers, or reaches in their direction), her mother whispers "Please" in her ear. If Chelsea imitates "Please" or approximates it, her mother observes the toddlers' response. If the toddlers don't immediately pass Chelsea a toy, Chelsea's mother quickly offers her an appropriate toy and says, "Yes, Chelsea, you may play too." At any time, if Chelsea reaches for a toy that the toddlers are playing with, her mother immediately guides Chelsea's hand away from the toddlers and their toys, whispers "Please," hands Chelsea an appropriate toy, and says, "Yes, Chelsea, you may play too."

Responding immediately and with *equal power* reinforcement to new replacement behavior will initially place significant demands on the adults involved in a child's PBS plan. This is a necessary first step in teaching the child that his or her new responses are very effective. For the obvious reasons of making PBS a practical approach, it is also necessary to teach children to wait a short time for reinforcement and to use socially acceptable behavior even when every response is not reinforced (Carr et al., 1994). These concerns are addressed by supports to maintain and generalize behavior changes (discussed below).

Redirection Although a PBS plan will include a number of strategies to prevent challenging behavior and render it ineffective and unnecessary, the behavior may still occur on occasion. As indicated in the discussion of crisis management procedures, there must be a plan for responding to it. Janney and Snell (2000) suggested that the response to challenging behavior should be neutral (i.e., the content of the behavior is not responded to) and the child should be redirected to appropriate behavior. Redirection is modeling or prompting the child to engage in appropriate behavior that serves the same function as the challenging behavior. Ignoring without redirection may be ineffective because the child is not being taught the appropriate response for the situation.

Supports to Maintain and Generalize Behavior Changes

The final components of a comprehensive PBS plan are strategies that support the absence of challenging behavior and the use of new replacement behaviors over time (maintenance) and in new situations (generalization). If the new functional communication skills (replacement behaviors) are more effective and result in stronger reinforcement, they will maintain and replace challenging behavior. Maintenance can be further enhanced by gradually introducing intermittent and delayed reinforcement as is more common to natural situations (Carr et al., 1994). Naturalistic schedules of intermittent and delayed reinforcement will be more practical than the immediate and continuous schedule of reinforcement that is necessary when first teaching a replacement behavior. Furthermore, intermittent and unpredictable schedules of reinforcement are more powerful schedules of reinforcement and result in responses that are more difficult to extinguish.

Maintenance   There are two strategies that are useful in helping a child accept delayed and less frequent reinforcement. The first strategy is to acknowledge the child's request, ask her to wait a few moments, and suggest that she do a simple, known task or activity while waiting (Carr et al., 1994). For example, if Chelsea says, "Please" while playing with her cousins, her mother may say, "Yes, Chelsea. I'll be right there with some toys for you. While you wait, please look through the book next to you." Using an activity to mark the duration of the delay in reinforcement provides the child with a concrete measure of time as well as a clear indication that reinforcement is imminent. It is imperative, of course, that Chelsea's mom follows through and gives Chelsea the requested toys as soon as Chelsea completes the book activity.

A second strategy for reducing the immediacy and consistency of reinforcement is behavioral chaining. This strategy is relevant when challenging behavior serves the purpose of escaping or ending an activity that the parents and professionals have decided is important and cannot be eliminated. In behavioral chaining, the required number of activity steps is gradually increased before providing reinforcement (Lalli, Casey, & Kates, 1995). For example, if a child engages in challenging behavior to avoid toothbrushing (and dental health problems have been ruled out as the reason he dislikes this activity), he may initially be required to brush just his front teeth. Once he has been doing this successfully and requesting "No more brushing" by shaking his head side to side, a second step of brushing his teeth on one side may be added. Thus, he is now required to brush his front teeth and his teeth on one side before he may request, "No more brushing." In this fashion, additional steps may slowly be added so that the child learns to complete the entire toothbrushing task before requesting a break.

Generalization   A true measure of learning is when a child demonstrates a skill in an appropriate situation other than where it was taught. Generalization of replacement behaviors is critical to eliminating challenging behavior. But generalization of new skills cannot be assumed. Instead, planning and implementing specific strategies are required to ensure that generalization occurs.

Generalization may be facilitated from the onset when teaching functional communication skills (some approaches to generalization assume that new skills must first be acquired before generalization can be addressed). A well-proven strategy is to teach the new skill across naturalistic conditions and a range of people, places, and activities, rather than first teaching under isolated conditions (Kazdin, 2001). Teaching situations should be chosen carefully to represent the range of naturalistic situations that the child is likely to encounter. This means that when teaching Chelsea to say "Please" when she wants a toy, the instruction should be conducted by her mother, father, grandparent, and early intervention professional. A range of play situations with young peers should also be selected: at the park, at home with her siblings, at her grandparents with her cousins, and during her weekly neighborhood playgroup. And, similarly, a range of play activities and materials should be represented (e.g., sand toys, books, crayons, small figurines, blocks).

The likelihood of generalization will also be enhanced if instruction addresses *all* functions of the challenging behavior concurrently (Carr et al., 1994). If the complete assessment of Chelsea's challenging behavior indicated that her self-injury served the purposes of requesting adult attention and obtaining something, instruction should address both concurrently. In situations in which Chelsea seems to be requesting a toy, her use of "Please" should be responded to with a toy and very positive and enthusiastic attention. And in situations when she doesn't seem to be requesting a toy, her use of "Please" should be followed with positive and enthusiastic adult attention.

If challenging behavior is particularly difficult to prevent in one or more situations, it is helpful to start with the easiest, most "controlled" situations (Carr et al., 1994). Controlled situations are those that have relatively few triggers for challenging behavior. For example, Chelsea's home and small neighborhood playgroup may be initial teaching situations with less distractions and triggers for challenging behavior than Chelsea's grandparents' home or the park. Once Chelsea is regularly using her new replacement communication skills at home and the neighborhood playgroup, instruction can be extended to her grandparents' home and the park.

Data-Based Monitoring

The final element of a comprehensive PBS plan is monitoring the results of implementation. Data collection procedures (as described in Chapter 6) should be conducted to monitor the elimination or decrease in challenging behavior and the acquisition or increase in functionally equivalent replacement behaviors. If the family chooses, they may participate in data collection; otherwise, the professional can collect data as feasible. The data should be reviewed regularly (every 1 to 2 weeks) and intervention plans modified if progress is not judged to be sufficient.

SUMMARY

Because of efficacy and ethical concerns, the traditional behavioral approach to challenging behavior has been replaced by a positive behavior support (PBS) model. The PBS model is superior to the traditional behavior model because it is more likely to have durable effects and it relies on positive and preventive methods rather than on methods that are reactive and punitive. At the heart of the PBS model is using functional assessment to identify the purpose (or function) of challenging behavior. Generally, challenging behavior serves a communication function (gaining attention; obtaining something tangible; escaping, terminating, or avoiding something). Knowing the purpose of challenging behavior provides direction for developing a PBS plan. All PBS plans include strategies to prevent the occurrence of problem behavior, to increase the likelihood of appropriate behavior, to teach socially appropriate behaviors that replace the challenging behaviors, and to promote maintenance and generalization of newly acquired skills.

•••••••••••••••••••• STUDY QUESTIONS ••••••••••••••••••••••

1. Identify and describe the levels of severity associated with challenging behavior.

2. Compare and contrast the traditional behavioral approach and the PBS approach to assessment and intervention for challenging behavior.

3. Discuss the efficacy and ethical issues associated with traditional behavioral approaches.

4. Discuss how *social judgment* influences whether challenging behavior exists.

5. Define *function* as it applies to understanding challenging behavior.

6. Identify and provide an example of the four functions of challenging behavior.

7. Define and provide an example of a *trigger* for challenging behavior.

8. Discuss how contextual influences affect challenging behavior.

9. Define and describe the crisis plan component of PBS.

10. What is the purpose of conducting a functional assessment?

11. Discuss and compare what is learned through interviews and direct observation methods of functional assessment.

12. Identify and describe the components of the notecard format for recording direct observations of challenging behavior.

13. How and why are hypotheses of challenging behavior developed?

14. List the components of a PBS plan.

15. Discuss how culture can affect judgment concerning whether a behavior problem exists, interpretation of assessment information, and acceptability of intervention procedures.

16. Identify and describe at least three strategies for preventing challenging behavior.

17. Describe the characteristics of effective replacement behaviors for challenging behavior.

18. Discuss two approaches for promoting generalization of behavior changes.

Appendix

Positive Behavior Support Plan for Chelsea

Positive Behavior Support Plan

Child: Chelsea C.   **Start Date:** 5/22/05

PBS team: Toni (early intervention program), Mom, Dad, Grandpa, Kelli (baby sitter)

Behavior of concern: Chelsea hits her forehead with her fist.

Hypotheses

Functions:

1) Chelsea hits her forehead to obtain adult attention.
2) Chelsea hits her forehead to obtain a desired object.

Contexts and Triggers:

3) Chelsea is most likely to hit her forehead when playing with younger children.
4) Chelsea is most likely to hit her forehead when she's in a crowded situation.
5) Taking something from Chelsea is a trigger for her to hit her forehead.

Crisis Management Plan

If Chelsea hits her forehead, follow the steps listed below:

1) Pretend you didn't see it or hear her. If it occurs a second time, proceed to step 2.
2) Approach Chelsea slowly, and calmly redirect her to move to a less crowded area and to play with a favorite toy. If she continues to hit herself, proceed to step 3.
3) Firmly hold Chelsea's hands down and away from her head. Talk quietly and calmly to her about the new toy you've placed in front of her. As she seems to relax her arms, ease your hold on her hands and guide her hands to the toy. As she shows interest in the toy, release your hold on her hands. If she shows interest in another toy or other kind of play during this time, ease your hold on her and follow her lead for play. If Chelsea doesn't calm easily, quietly sing some of her favorite songs ("Itsy Bitsy Spider," "You Are My Sunshine") and slowly rock her.

Positive Behavior Support

Behavior support strategies	Prevent problem behavior			Encourage appropriate behavior					Teach replacement behaviors			Maintain and generalize behavior changes			
	Modify/eliminate contextual variables	Modify/eliminate triggers	Interrupt escalating behavior chains	Provide choice and preferred situations	Embed cues	Present positive social comments	Create positive routines and activities	Use supported routines, task-simplification, and preteaching	Teach functionally equivalent communication responses	Teach more effective behaviors	Teach proactively	Use delayed and intermittent reinforcement	Teach across people, places, and activities	Address functions of problem behavior concurrently	Move from controlled to less controlled situations
• AVOID CROWDS, especially if a number of toddlers are present; seek out areas that are not crowded and/or areas with older children (ages 4+).	✓			✓			✓								
• BRING TOYS that are the same or similar to those that other children are likely to have at play areas (playground and park: balls, sand toys, small bike; pool: beach ball, swim ring, goggles, and so forth)		✓													
• STAY CLOSE and observe if Chelsea asks to play with toys that her peers have. If she makes a request that is unsuccessful (peer ignores her or says "no"), approach Chelsea, acknowledge her request ("Oh, you want to play with a ball"), and give her the type of toy she requested.			✓				✓		✓						
• STAY CLOSE in crowded situations. Quietly sing her favorite songs and rub her back.					✓		✓								
• INVITE OLDER PEERS (age 4+) for play.	✓	✓			✓		✓								

(continued)

Positive Behavior Support *(continued)*

Behavior support strategies	Prevent problem behavior			Encourage appropriate behavior					Teach replacement behaviors			Maintain and generalize behavior changes			
	Modify/eliminate contextual variables	Modify/eliminate triggers	Interrupt escalating behavior chains	Provide choice and preferred situations	Embed cues	Present positive social comments	Create positive routines and activities	Use supported routines, task-simplification, and preteaching	Teach functionally equivalent communication responses	Teach more effective behaviors	Teach proactively	Use delayed and intermittent reinforcement	Teach across people, places, and activities	Address functions of problem behavior concurrently	Move from controlled to less controlled situations
• GRADUALLY INTRODUCE YOUNG PEERS to Chelsea. First have her play close to one toddler and same-age peer. Provide requested toy if she is unsuccessful in requesting it, and redirect if she hits her forehead. As she is successful in this situation, add another peer to the group. Repeat until she is able to play with three or four young peers in close proximity.	✓							✓			✓				
• LET CHELSEA CHOOSE where and with what she wants to play on arrival at a play area. Have her choose among peers and toys.				✓											
• TEACH CHELSEA TO SAY "PLEASE" audibly and point to a desired toy. Sit close when she plays near peers with toys. If Chelsea looks at a toy intently (more than 5 seconds), whisper "Please" in her ear. If she doesn't imitate, model it and guide her to point to the desired toy. If the peer doesn't share, redirect Chelsea to play with a similar toy.					✓				✓	✓					

Behavior support strategies	Prevent problem behavior			Encourage appropriate behavior					Teach replacement behaviors			Maintain and generalize behavior changes			
	Modify/eliminate contextual variables	Modify/eliminate triggers	Interrupt escalating behavior chains	Provide choice and preferred situations	Embed cues	Present positive social comments	Create positive routines and activities	Use supported routines, task-simplification, and preteaching	Teach functionally equivalent communication responses	Teach more effective behaviors	Teach proactively	Use delayed and intermittent reinforcement	Teach across people, places, and activities	Address functions of problem behavior concurrently	Move from controlled to less controlled situations
• PROVIDE ENTHUSIASTIC ATTENTION whenever Chelsea makes a request by saying "Please."										✓	✓		✓	✓	
• TEACH CHELSEA TO WAIT. Once Chelsea has been making requests by saying "Please" (for at least 2 weeks), begin asking her to do something else before her request is honored (Yes, Chelsea, you may have a ball. Please drink this juice while I get the ball.).							✓					✓	✓	✓	✓

11

Group Instruction

Mary Jo Noonan

Children are often among peers, particularly if they spend time in child care, preschool, or kindergarten settings. Peer groups may also be present at home (if there are two or more siblings who are close in age), at family gatherings, with neighborhood children, and in public recreational environments such as the beach or playground. These situations provide opportunities for children with disabilities to learn to play and socialize with their age-mates (Elgas & Lynch, 1998). Skills associated with group play and socialization are important instructional objectives for children with disabilities, especially for children with autism and those who have significant social needs (Heflin & Alberto, 2001; Rotholz, 1987).

Instruction with two or more children simultaneously is *group instruction.* Successful participation in educational and social groups requires a wide range of skills, such as following group directions, responding to group-directed teaching techniques, following rules and routines, working/playing independently in close proximity to others, working/playing cooperatively with peers, turn taking, sharing, and waiting. These skills can *only* be taught in group situations. Group instruction has been shown to be an effective instructional arrangement for children of all ability levels, including those with severe disabilities (Bambara, Warren, & Komisar, 1988; Brown & Holvoet, 1982) and autism (Hoyson, Jamieson, & Strain, 1984; Kamps, Walker, Maher, & Rotholz, 1992; Taubman et al., 2001).

One reason that group instruction is effective is that it provides opportunities for observational learning, particularly when children of differing ability levels are grouped together (Brown & Holvoet, 1982; Singleton, Schuster, & Ault, 1995; Whalen, Schuster, & Hemmeter, 1996). In a toddler group, for example, Tommy, who does not say words, learns to vocalize for adult attention when he observes Kimi gaining attention by speaking. One study found that observational learning is enhanced when peer models verbalize each step of a task they are modeling (Werts, Caldwell, & Wolery, 1996). Another benefit of group instruction is that it can increase the total amount of time in which children are actively engaged in instruction. Rather than divide 30 minutes into three 10-minute individual instructional sessions for three children, all three children receive group instruction for the entire 30 minutes. The more time spent actively participating in instruction ("engagement"), the greater the gains (McWilliam, Wolery, & Odom, 2001).

Group instruction also benefits families and interventionists. In infant and toddler programs, it creates opportunities for families to meet one another and form relationships and support networks. Families might otherwise meet only program staff. Group instruction is a more efficient use of professionals' time (Collins et al., 1991; Rothholz, 1987). A one-to-one staff–child instructional arrangement is costly and time-intensive in terms of staff resources.

THE NATURE OF GROUPS

Participation in group instruction should be considered for all children with disabilities. The task is to match the child with the group. Groups can be characterized by their composition, interaction, and content.

Group Composition

The number and types of children included in a group are group composition considerations. Instructional groups have a minimum of two children. The largest groups can occur in child care and preschool programs serving a majority of children who do not have disabilities: Group size in these settings may approach 25 to 30. For a particular child, the decision on the size of the group is based on the following questions:

1. What size group is needed for the child to participate in the activities associated with the instructional objectives?
2. What size group is typical of the targeted activities and age peers?
3. For what size group does the child possess group skills?
4. What size group can the professional effectively manage?

Most groups in early intervention settings are small, composed of three to five children. Expectations for group skills should consider each child's current abilities related to group participation, instructional objectives, and developmental norms. Current abilities provide information for individualizing expectations. For example, a 3-year-old child who becomes upset in noisy situations may initially participate in a group with only two other children. When the child becomes comfortable in the small-group situation, participation in slightly larger groups may be considered. If a 4-year-old child has instructional objectives for participating in a community preschool program, she may receive instruction in a variety of small and large group situations typical of the preschool classroom. If her current ability levels suggest that large groups may be challenging for her, extra supports (e.g., sitting with a special friend) may be provided, or a special schedule for gradually increasing her time spent in the group may be implemented. Developmental norms must also be considered. Young children from 6 to 24 months of age typically engage in simple social interactions (e.g., smiling, turn taking in games such as Peekaboo); from 24 to 30 months of age they tend to play alone with toys; from 30 to 42 months they continue to play alone but near other children; and from 42 months of age and on, children play with their peers cooperatively (Wolery, McWilliam, & Bailey, 2005).

Group composition may be homogeneous or heterogeneous (Collins et al., 1991). *Homogeneous groups* include children who have similar skill levels and concerns or are close in age (within 6 to 12 months of one another). *Heterogeneous groups* include children with varied skill levels and concerns or children who are not close in age. Other child characteristics such as gender, temperament, and cultural/linguistic backgrounds also contribute to a group's homogeneity or heterogeneity.

Homogeneous groups are easier for instruction because the children are likely to have similar goals. Likewise, an activity that is of interest to one child in a homogeneous group is likely to be of interest to the others. Homogeneous groups have a major disadvantage: they do not include children who could serve as more competent models for others in the group. In addition, if all children in the group have significant concerns, severe physical disabilities, or limited expressive communication skills, active group participation may be difficult to accomplish. Planning and implementing instruction for heterogeneous groups may be more challenging for the professional, but the availability of competent peer models and varied group participation abilities are important advantages.

Group Interaction

A major rationale for group instruction is teaching social interaction skills. Social interaction skills are easily embedded and taught in the group. For example, Joseph can be taught to turn toward a named peer. And if the children already possess simple social interaction skills, the skills can be included within the group activity, as when older children hand materials to one another, or peers reinforce one another (Brown, Holvoet, Guess, & Mulligan, 1980; Zanolli, Daggett, & Adams, 1996). Some form of group interaction should be considered for all group instruction because it is a form of engagement that promotes attention to the group activity and peers.

Instructional Content

Most groups have a theme or purpose. Whatever the topic or purpose of the group, it should always be age appropriate. Organizing and planning instructional content around themes can be constructed as a *thematic curriculum approach* (Miller, 1996). A theme is selected for a specified period of time (e.g., 1 week, 2 weeks, 1 month) and carried out in activities, materials, and songs. For example, "weather" may be the theme in March. Bulletin boards depicting a variety of weather conditions are designed; numbers for the calendar are written on sun and cloud cut-outs; songs about sunshine, rain, and wind are sung during morning circle; stories about rainbows, summer fun, and snowy day adventures are placed in the book corner; and science and art activities addressing the weather theme are conducted. In addition to nature, common unit themes for early childhood settings include seasons, holidays, animals, birds, transportation, family, neighborhood, occupations, and so on. Many inexpensive books with ideas for implementing a unit approach are commercially available (Charner, 1993; Herr & Larson, 2003; Mindes, 2000; Schiller & Hastings, 1998; Schiller & Phipps, 2002).

Group instruction is conducted in the context of an activity, with individual objectives addressed for each group member. In a toddler group, for example, an activity with apples and oranges involves naming, identifying color, feeling texture, and tasting. One toddler practices his objective of *reaching* and *touching* when the apple and orange are presented; another toddler is encouraged to *imitate the names of the fruit,* and *point to her peer when her turn is finished.*

It is possible to organize children into groups even though each child may be participating in a different activity. This occurs in child care and preschool when children are allowed to select activities for independent activity times. Although the children are working independently, they are physically in a group (either at a table or on the floor). Learning to work independently and behaving appropriately while in close proximity to peers is an expectation of preschool and kindergarten classrooms.

Group Participation Skills/Objectives

Among the social and communication skills acquired during the early childhood years are a number that are relevant to participation in groups. Children learn skills for at least three types of group situations: 1) social/play, 2) independent activities/play, and 3) instructional/recreational. The following are examples of the types of skills required for each type of group situation:

- Social/play groups

  - Sharing
  - Turn taking
  - Helping
  - Cooperating

- Independent activities/play groups

  - Attending to task
  - Working/playing without assistance
  - Not bothering peers

- Instructional/recreational groups

  - Following group directions
  - Following rules and routines
  - Asking questions at appropriate times
  - Speaking at appropriate times
  - Staying with the group
  - Waiting/walking in lines

Many of the group skills listed here are learned in the toddler years (Murphy & Vincent, 1989); the others are learned later with increasing competence into the school years and through adulthood. Table 11.1 lists the group skills

Table 11.1. Group skills included on survival skills lists

Preschool Group Skills[1]	Kindergarten Group Skills[2]
Makes transitions from one activity to another	Initiates interactions with adults and peers
Complies with directions	Interacts with adults and peers when not the initiator
Follows rules and routines	Listens and attends to speaker in large group
Focuses on task	Demonstrates turn taking in a small group
Focuses attention on speaker	Attends to task for minimum of 15 minutes
Socializes with others	Adapts to transitions between activities throughout the day
Communicates with peers	Communicates with peers and adults
Communicates with adults	Asks questions of others
Takes turns	Lines up and stays in line
Shares materials/toys with peers	Raises hand and/or gets teacher's attention when necessary
Cooperates with/helps others	Waits to take turns and shares
Does not disturb others	Controls voice in classroom
Uses voice appropriate to activity	Stays in "own space" for activity

[1]*Source:* Noonan, Ratokalau, Lauth-Torres, McCormick, Esaki, & Claybaugh, 1992.
[2]*Source:* Vincent, Salisbury, Walters, Brown, Gruenewald, & Powers, 1980.

identified by teachers as important for success ("survival skills") in preschool (Noonan et al., 1992) and kindergarten (Vincent et al., 1980).

Note that the preschool group skills were validated as in the repertoire of 3-year-olds who did not have disabilities (Noonan et al., 1992). If a child does not demonstrate the group skills in Table 11.1, the skills may be appropriate instructional objectives. Also, group participation objectives may be identified through the person-centered planning and ecological assessment process described in Chapters 3 and 4.

PLANNING GROUP INSTRUCTION

There are many considerations when planning group instruction. Decisions about when and how objectives will be included must be made, and instructional techniques that facilitate group participation and take advantage of learning opportunities must be selected. Each of these important elements of groups—teaching group skills, organizing groups, facilitating group participation, and using group situations to support the instructional process—will be discussed.

Teaching Group Skills

Children as young as age 2 can be taught group participation skills, such as those listed above, using the direct instruction and naturalistic teaching strategies explained in Chapters 6 and 9. Begin with an objective that explicitly defines a group participation skill. For example, "Allana will join in and play with two peers in a 15-minute small-group play session (e.g., take a turn adding blocks to a tower, play a role in a game of 'house,' join in working on a puzzle) at least three times per week for 4 consecutive weeks." Then define the strategies that will be used to assist and encourage the desired behavior. For example, an adult may prompt Allana during the first 5 minutes of each playgroup by whispering a brief direction for participating in the activity ("Choose a puzzle piece"). Each time Allana demonstrates a correct response, prompted or unprompted, the adult could make a positive comment to the group about how nice they are playing. As Allana makes progress, the prompt might be faded by initially whispering her name, and then providing only the remainder of the prompt ("Choose a puzzle piece") if Allana does not respond within 5 seconds. This example includes the instructional strategies of a verbal prompt, time delay, and verbal reinforcement. As in all instruction, the child's progress should be monitored by frequent data collection.

When children have difficulty staying with a group or participating in a group, begin by rewarding the child for interacting and participating with only one other child. When the child learns to participate in this smallest group arrangement, add other children one at a time (Collins et al., 1991; Koegel & Rincover, 1974). If the child participates appropriately in a group situation but is not making progress with individual goals, it may be necessary to also conduct individual teaching sessions (Collins et al., 1991). This is an alternative to discontinuing the child's participation in the group when he or she is not progressing. It may provide enough extra help to allow the child to benefit from group instruction. The individual teaching sessions are discontinued when the child demonstrates adequate progress.

Organizing Group Instruction

Ideally, *all* children with disabilities receive instruction on at least one goal during a group activity. As noted above, children may have the same goals or they may have different goals. There are two approaches to incorporating instruction of specific goals/objectives into groups: skill embedding (Harris & Delmolino, 2002) and skill sequencing (Brown & Holvoet, 1982).

Skill Embedding   Skill embedding is much like the activity-based approach to instruction described in Chapter 9. The first step is to select an age-appropriate group activity. The activity may be a self-care or play activity (e.g., brushing teeth, playing "house") or a daily routine (e.g., circle time). The activity may also be a child's instructional goal. After selecting an age-appropriate group activity, review the child's objectives and select one or more objectives that fit logically into the activity. If there is more than one child with a disability in the group, select only two to four objectives per child. Imagine, for example, how Kimi's objectives of "grasping," "asking for more," and "manipulating objects" could be embedded in the activity of "playing with the kitchen bowls and utensils." All three skills can be taught during the activity: Kimi grasps the bowls and utensils when passing or receiving them from another child in the group, and she grasps the utensil while "stirring" in the bowl. Kimi asks for "more" when the bowl is out of reach and she manipulates objects by examining the utensils and bowls when they are given to her.

After selecting the activity and each child's objective(s), the next task is to write out the group activity as you would a script and indicate when each child's instructional trials will be presented. Figure 11.1 is an example of a group instruction plan that includes Kimi and the kitchen play activity. For each skill in italics, systematic instruction is implemented. Skill embedding may be used with traditional group instruction or with cooperative learning groups, described later in this chapter.

Skill Sequencing   Skill sequencing (Bambara et al., 1988; Guess et al., 1978) is similar to skill embedding. The difference is that objectives are chained and taught consecutively rather than distributed throughout the activity. Group skill sequences are constructed by first listing the objectives of the children who will be in the group. An age-appropriate activity or theme is then selected. Next, one to three objectives for each child are identified on the basis of their logical relationship to one another. The final step is to write the sequence as a script, indicating the order in which instruction will be conducted for each ob-

---

Group Lesson: Kitchen Play

Group: Kimi (12 months), Darron (14 months), and Kawika (11 months)

Lesson time: Mondays, 9:00-9:30

Interventionist: Allen

Start date: 5/20/05   End date: _____

Give each child two metal mixing bowls and two wooden spoons. Call each child by name and talk about the bowls and utensils as they are distributed.

Darron:	*Visually tracks* the utensils and bowl when they are given to him.
Kawika:	*Looks at the person calling his name* (when bowls and utensils are distributed).

Encourage the children to look at and pick up the bowls and utensils, assisting as necessary.

Demonstrate different ways to play with the bowls and utensils, turning them over, banging them on the floor, banging a utensil outside and inside a bowl, "stirring" with a spoon, and so forth.

Kimi:	*Grasps* the spoon and *manipulates* it.
Kimi:	As she repeatedly bangs on the bowl, move the bowl out of reach and look at her expectantly. Kimi will *ask for more*.
Darron:	*Visually tracks* the bowl and spoon as the interventionist bangs them together and moves them slowly in an arc, from right to left, and then left to right.
Kawika:	*Points to named objects* when the interventionist holds up the bowl and spoon.

Continue to encourage the children to play with the bowls and spoons. Repeat the above sequence (Kimi grasping and manipulating, Kimi asking for more, Darron tracking, and Kawika pointing to named objects) at least two more times.

Figure 11.1.   Sample group instructional plan with embedded objectives.

jective. If the kitchen play group in Figure 11.1 was reconstructed as a skill sequence, the plan might be as follows:

1. Kawika: Looks at the adult calling his name
2. Kawika: Points to named objects
3. Darron: Visually tracks the spoon and bowl (when given to Kawika)
4. Darron: Visually tracks the spoon and bowl (when given to Darron)
5. Darron: Visually tracks the spoon and bowl (when given to Kimi)
6. Kimi: Grasps the spoon
7. Kimi: Manipulates the spoon
8. Kimi: Asks for more (e.g., "More play" when the bowl is removed)

In this skill sequence, after Kawika looks at the adult calling his name, he is asked to point to something. There is a logical progression from the skill of looking to a skill that requires participation in the group (point to something). Darron visually tracks the spoon and bowl as they are given to Kawika. It is meaningful for him to do this after Kawika has pointed to the objects and is receiving them. The relationship between the skills enhances motivation to perform the skills. In skill sequencing, children have opportunities to learn the logical relationships between skills they are learning—relationships that are likely to be present under natural conditions.

The group activity may not always occur exactly as scripted in the instructional plan. The behavior and concerns of children may vary considerably from day to day. Instead, the script is to be used as a guide.

Facilitating Group Participation

Effective instruction requires frequent and appropriate participation by all children in the group. Participation is evidence that the child is actively engaged. Techniques to enhance group participation include quick pacing, selective attention, partial/adapted participation, group interaction, group responding, and group contingencies.

Quick Pacing   Pace refers to the speed with which instruction is directed from one child to the next in the group. Quick pacing has three advantages: it results in frequent instruction for all children, it helps children attend to the activity, and it decreases the likelihood of boredom and problem behaviors. To implement quick pacing, focus attention on each child for several moments, one at a time, to instruct specific skills. With practice, a teacher can become skilled at quick pacing.

Periodic attention is a technique associated with pacing. Occasionally, call the children by name in no particular order, or use some other attention strategy such as eye contact, pointing, or smiling to maintain or regain the children's attention. In addition to assisting the children to focus on the group activity, periodic attention rewards children for attending.

Selective Attention   Selective attention is another way to promote group participation. Praise children specifically for attending and participating. Social reinforcement should be delivered quickly and individually. In addition to praise, eye contact, smiling, gentle touching, or other social reinforcers may be used. Ideally, children who are not attending or participating will notice that they have been bypassed for reinforcement and attempt to imitate peers who were successful in obtaining reinforcement.

Partial Participation and Adaptations   Some children are not able to independently participate in typical group activities. Requirements for participation may be modified through *partial participation* or *adaptations.* Partial participation and adaptation are slightly different from each other. When a response requirement is limited to a portion of the response, it is partial participation (Baumgart et al., 1982). An adaptation is when response requirements are changed and an alternative response that serves the same purpose is substituted (Janney & Snell, 2005). For example, when children are expected to select their materials from a tray and one child is unable to grasp, partial participation may require that the child reach for the materials and open her hand. An adult or peer then assists her to grasp the materials and set them on a table. An adaptation is another option for this child. She could wear a strap on her hand fitted with Velcro, and the materials she reaches for could also have a Velcro strip. After reaching and aligning the Velcro on her hand with that on the materials, she completes the task independently. Partial participation and adaptations are discussed in greater detail in Chapter 13.

Group Interaction   To take full advantage of opportunities provided in group instruction, social interaction among the group members should be promoted. As noted in the rationale for instruction, group activities are the only context in which it is possible to teach social interaction with peers. The most direct way to promote interaction is to identify and target one or more social interaction skills for children in the group. These skills may or may not be IFSP/IEP objectives. Socialization skills are then taught by embedding them in the group activity or through skill sequencing.

Figure 11.2 shows a group activity in which preschoolers are passing materials one at a time (IFSP/IEP objectives are designated with an asterisk in the figure). In this example, passing materials is not an IFSP/IEP objective; it is included to encourage social interaction and to teach turn taking. Specific social interaction objectives are also included in the group sequence for three of the four preschoolers (indicated in bold print in the sequence). The fourth child, Daria, practices attending to the activity four times each time the sequence is conducted.

Group instruction can also be planned to include *interdependence* among group members. Interdependence occurs when each child's participation in the activity is dependent on another group member's participation (Brown et al., 1980). Each child has a clear and necessary role. Group members must attend to what their peers are doing to know when it is their turn. In the example in Figure 11.2, the requirement that children pass the materials so that their peers can take turns sets up an interdependent situation. Usually, however, inter-

---

Group Skill Sequence: Sand or Water Play

Group: Tomiko (36 months), Sean (32 months), Matthew (40 months), and Daria (36 months)

Lesson time: Tuesdays, 10:00-10:20

Interventionist: Anisa

Start date: 7/07/05   End date:

Tomiko	Sean	Matthew	Daria
*Pours from one container into another (uses both hands in fine motor activity)			***Attends to activity (watches peer)**
Passes containers to Sean	***Says "Thank you"**		***Attends to activity** (watches peer)
	*Imitates Tomiko		
	Passes containers to Matthew	Pours from one container into another	***Attends to activity** (watches peer)
		*Identifies named peer	
		Passes containers to Daria	***Attends to activity (receives containers)**
			Pours from one container into another
			Passes containers to Tomiko

Repeat sequence four more times using different actions requiring Tomiko to use both hands with objects in the sand or water play.

*Instructional Objectives

Figure 11.2. Sample group skill sequence with social interaction (social skill objectives are in bold print).

dependence involves a more complex activity. For example, if preschoolers are setting a table, one may have the task of wiping the table clean, another may be required to count out the appropriate number of dishes, cups, and napkins, and the third may be assigned to set the table. The group is interdependent because dishes, cups, and napkins cannot be placed on the table until the table has been cleaned by the first group member and the second group member has given the materials to the third.

Group Responding In the examples of group instructional plans presented thus far, most participation has been one child at a time. Group members may respond together. Group responding, also known as choral responding, increases each child's opportunities for active participation (Heward, Courson, & Narayan, 1989). Group responding can be verbal, with children answering questions,

singing songs, or rote reciting (e.g., counting), or nonverbal, with children performing motor responses. Making hand motions to a song, imitating the teacher
(e.g., demonstrating folding a paper in four), or playing with the activity materials (e.g., musical instruments) are examples of nonverbal group responding.

During group responding, the teacher should shift eye contact and attention
quickly among the children to let them know that their participation is appropriate. This requires that the group members be in close proximity to one another. Whether the response is verbal, nonverbal, or both, group responding has
two important advantages: 1) it assists group members to attend and participate
in the activity and 2) it minimizes the time that children must wait for a turn.

Group responding is more difficult to plan when group membership is heterogeneous, but it may still be feasible. For example, all children may be asked
to point at pictures as they are named in a story. Then there may be individualized response requirements: one child is required to vocalize and another to
say a word during the group response. Individualized response requirements
may include partial participation or adaptive participation. Chapter 13 discusses
partial participation and adaptive participation in detail. Partial participation
refers to performing one or more components of a skill or task, but not the skill
or task in its entirety. It is important that the child's participation in the task
include meaningful and important components. For example, if a child needs
adult assistance to drink from a cup, he may nod his head toward the cup to indicate that he wants a drink, and he may nod his head to indicate when he is finished drinking. Partial participation in this manner meets the criteria of being
meaningful and important because it provides the child with control over when
he takes a drink and how much he drinks. In contrast to partial participation,
adaptive participation involves changing how the skill or task is performed and
may involve the use of alternative or special equipment or devices. Instead of
having an adult assist a child with drinking from a cup, the child may drink
from a straw as a form of adaptive participation. Furthermore, the cup may be
in a weighted cup holder to hold the cup steady (another adapted component).

Group Contingencies   A group contingency is an instructional arrangement whereby reinforcement is provided when all group members demonstrate
a required response (Alberto & Troutman, 2002). Most of us are familiar with
group contingencies from elementary school experiences in which we lost or
gained privileges depending on the behavior of the entire class. If the entire
class did their spelling homework, for example, the class could earn 10 minutes
of free time after reading. If one or more members of the class did not do the
homework, however, the class did not earn the free time or was otherwise pe-
nalized. Because group contingencies rely on peer pressure (anticipated peer
acceptance or rejection) for their effectiveness, they may not be effective for infants or young children who have not yet acquired that level of social understanding. Group contingencies, however, have been demonstrated to be as effective as individual contingencies when teaching social skills to preschoolers
with disabilities (Kohler, Strain, Maretsky, & DeCesare, 1990).

Using Groups to Support the Instructional Process

Group instruction offers unique teaching opportunities. In addition to providing opportunities to teach social interaction skills, group situations are well suited for assistance, encouragement, and generalization strategies.

Assistance Procedures   Possibly the most important advantage of group instruction is the opportunity for *observational learning.* Observational learning, however, should not be left to chance. Instead, praise children who watch or imitate their peers ("I see you are doing it just like Carmen, that's good!"). Observational learning can also be facilitated by encouraging children to reinforce one another. Have children clap for one another, or have a child give stickers to peers for correct responses. Delivering reinforcement to peers enhances attention to them and facilitates observational learning (Brown & Holvoet, 1982).

Peer modeling can be used to prompt desired behavior. For example, Jason is asked to demonstrate how to spread paste with his finger. Brendyn observes Jason spreading the paste on his artwork. He also sees that Jason gets praised for doing that, so Brendyn spreads paste in the same way. Children imitate peers they identify with, more competent peers, and those they observe receiving reinforcement. Peer modeling is a good technique to teach social and communicative interactions—skills that cannot be modeled by an adult.

Group instruction also provides opportunities for *peer tutoring/prompting.* Peer tutoring/prompting uses other children in the group (usually more competent children) to provide assistance and encouragement. This is discussed at length in Chapter 12. Research has demonstrated that young children can deliver prompts effectively if they are directly taught to do so (Kohler & Strain, 1997). Prompting is maintained through group reinforcement: All children are reinforced if the children learning the new skills are successful. A kindergarten teacher might use peer tutoring and a group contingency to teach children to walk to the cafeteria quietly and in a line. Peer tutors are assigned and told to remind their partners periodically to "use a quiet voice" and to "walk slowly and stay in line." The entire class earns an extra story during storytime if they all walk quietly in a line to the cafeteria.

In homogeneous groups in which more than one child has the same objective, the effectiveness of instruction is enhanced by repetition of the same (or similar) instructional procedures. This is in conjunction with observational learning. A child may observe instruction implemented one or more times before being required to respond. Repetition has the effect of providing additional instruction. Similarly, repetition of the prompt highlights it and increases its saliency and effectiveness (Skinner, 1938). And if a peer is working on the same objective, but receiving a less intrusive prompt, a child may learn to respond to the less intrusive prompt (Brown & Holvoet, 1982). For example, Jimmy, a toddler who needs hand-over-hand assistance to put on his sweater, observes his peer putting on his sweater after a demonstration. Jimmy attempts to imitate, thus responding to a less intrusive prompt.

Encouragement Procedures   Children's attention is critical for effective instruction. Use selective reinforcement to reward attention to prompts: If a child attends, give her a turn (Snell & Brown, 2006b). Group instruction also provides opportunities for children to observe the consequences for not attending (losing a turn).

As noted earlier in the discussion on facilitating group participation, peers may be taught to provide reinforcement. There are several advantages for teaching peers to praise and encourage one another. First, in many cases, peer attention and reinforcement are more powerful than adult attention. Second, when peers provide reinforcement, friendships develop (we tend to like individuals who reinforce us). Third, children often generalize the use of peer reinforcement beyond the group instruction setting. Fourth, children may imitate reinforcing behaviors because such behaviors, in turn, earn reinforcement for them (reinforcement begets reinforcement). Do not teach peers to correct or otherwise punish one another for incorrect responding. This may be counterproductive to promoting friendships among the children.

Generalization Procedures   Group instruction can be used to enhance skill generalization. If group members are working on the same (or similar) objectives, use different materials and instructional stimuli for different children. This allows children to observe a range of stimuli associated with the target response and thus facilitates stimulus generalization (Stokes & Baer, 1977; Stokes & Osnes, 1988). When different materials and stimuli are used to teach the same response, slightly different responses may be appropriate to accommodate the differences in the materials and/or stimuli. Observing different appropriate responses assists children to learn the response class.

Most important, through group participation children *learn how to learn* in a group. Much of the instruction provided to children without disabilities is large-group instruction. Thus it is valuable to include children in more than one group and in groups of various sizes (including groups of 10 or more children, if possible). Variation across groups increases the likelihood that the children will generalize their group participation skills.

Snell and Brown offered the following guidelines for maximizing the benefits of group instruction:

1. Involve all members by using individualized instruction, teaching the same concept at multiple levels of complexity, and allowing for different response modes and modified materials.

2. Keep the group instruction interesting by keeping turns short, giving everyone turns, making turns dependent on attending, giving demonstrations, and using a variety of materials that can be handled.

3. Encourage students to listen and watch other group members as they take their turns. Praise them when they do.

4. Actively involve students in the process of praising and prompting others.

5. Allow students to participate in demonstrations and handle materials related to the skill or concept being taught.

6. Keep waiting time to a minimum by controlling group size, teacher talk, and the number of student responses made in a single turn.

7. Prompt cooperation among group members and discourage competition among them (2006b, p. 131).

While this chapter has focused primarily on group instruction delivered by a teacher, it is also possible to arrange groups to function somewhat independently with an adult preparing the activity and then monitoring rather than instructing the lesson. Cooperative learning groups are one such model.

COOPERATIVE LEARNING GROUPS

Described first by Johnson and Johnson (1975, 1983, 1986) and Johnson and Johnson (1981), the cooperative learning model has been shown to improve children's social interaction behaviors and promote positive peer interactions (Putnam, Rynders, Johnson, & Johnson, 1989). The model structures activities to teach children to encourage one another, celebrate one another's successes, and work toward common goals. It is well suited for use with heterogeneous groups in inclusive settings (McMaster & Fuchs, 2002).

Cooperative Learning Elements

Cooperative learning groups are instructional situations in which children perceive that they can reach their learning goals if and only if peers in their group also reach their goals. The teacher's role is to teach the necessary cooperative skills so that groups function effectively. Cooperative learning groups have four basic elements: 1) positive interdependence, 2) face-to-face communication, 3) individual accountability, and 4) group process.

The first element, positive interdependence, requires group members to work together to accomplish common goals. Methods for promoting positive interdependence are mutual goals; divisions of labor; dividing materials, resources, or information among group members; assigning students different roles; and giving joint rewards. The second element, face-to-face communication, requires group members to interact with one another to accomplish a task and goal. In the third element, individual accountability, students are each responsible for mastering the assigned material and for contributing to the group's efforts. Finally, in the fourth element, group process, students are expected to use appropriate interpersonal and small-group skills.

Cooperative Learning Strategies

Although cooperative learning groups are most commonly used with school-age children, they are also applicable to children in preschool and kindergarten.

The following is an adaptation of the major cooperative learning strategies (Johnson, D. & Johnson, R., 1986) for preschool and kindergarten children:

1. *Select or develop a unit with clear cognitive/preacademic objectives and list the cooperative skills to be taught.* Interpersonal and small-group skills, such as taking turns or assisting one another are examples of possible target skills.

2. *Plan a series of lessons or activities.* The objective is to teach cooperative skills in the context of cognitive/preacademic lessons and activities.

3. *Assign children to dyads or three-member groups.* Do not include more than one child with disabilities in each group. Maintain the same groups for all the lessons/activities in the unit.

4. *Encourage cooperative effort by the way materials are distributed.* There are many ways to do this to encourage group effort. For example, consider providing each group member with only part of the materials needed to complete the activity, or providing the group with only one set of materials.

5. *Introduce the lessons/activities by providing a clear and specific description (and demonstration if necessary) of what it means to be cooperative.* Define cooperation operationally by specifying the behaviors that are appropriate and desirable within the groups. Beginning behavior might include "staying near one another," "using quiet voices," and "taking turns." Contrast "working with a friend" and "working alone" by showing pictures of each and asking the children to discuss the pictures. Consider making a bulletin board with a "friends help each other" theme. It may require more than one session for the children to understand what it means to work with a partner to produce a single product. Stress that everybody is to have fun and that they will be successful if they work together and help one another.

6. *Assist and monitor.* Monitor groups carefully to see where assistance is needed, either related to the activity or to cooperation. Publicly praise children when they share and help one another and prompt collaboration and cooperation as needed. Say, for example, "What does taking turns mean? It means doing something one at a time." Intervene as necessary to clarify instructions or answer questions.

7. *Evaluate and provide feedback.* Take time at the end of each cooperative learning group activity to provide positive feedback on each group's product. It is particularly important to talk about cooperation efforts. Ask for examples of cooperation and comment on how well group members worked together.

The basic premise of the cooperative learning model is that accomplishing a goal together leads children to invest in one another's learning. In turn, this helps children build more realistic and multifaceted views of one another and encourages acceptance and positive feelings. The cooperative learning model uses group dynamics as a means of encouraging social interactions and friendships (Johnson & Johnson, 1981).

SUMMARY

Group instruction is an important component of early intervention and early childhood special education. It is particularly important for 2- through 6-year-olds who need group participation skills in inclusive early childhood settings. This chapter described strategies for facilitating participation in groups: quick pacing, selective attention, partial/adaptive participation, group interaction, and group responding. Techniques for using group arrangements to support the instructional process (assistance, encouragement, and generalization strategies) were also described.

STUDY QUESTIONS

1. Write a list of benefits associated with group instruction for children with disabilities.

2. Identify and describe a range of group activities that 1-, 3-, and 5-year-olds typically experience. What types of skills support their participation in each activity?

3. Discuss the pros and cons of homogeneous and heterogeneous instructional groups.

4. Identify three preschool children with special concerns. Make a list of the skills targeted on their IEPs. Discuss how you might *embed* two skills for each child in a group lesson about "our community."

5. Referring to the children and skills identified in Question 4, develop a skill sequence for a lesson about "our community" using at least two skills for each of the three children. Include children without disabilities in your plan and describe how they will participate in the group lesson.

6. Referring to a group lesson discussed in Question 4 or 5, describe how you might apply each of the following strategies to facilitate group participation: quick pacing, periodic attention, selective attention, partial participation, adaptations, group interaction, group responding, and group contingencies.

7. Develop a group lesson about insects that includes one of the children from Question 4. The group is a heterogeneous group in a mixed-age preschool class (3-, 4-, and 5-year-olds), and the child from Question 4 is the only child with a disability in the group. Discuss how you might use the group situation to enhance instruction with each of the following procedures: assistance procedures, peer modeling, peer tutoring/prompting, encouragement procedures, and generalization procedures. Discuss how you might structure this lesson for cooperative learning groups.

12

Interventions to
Promote Peer Interactions

Linda McCormick

•••••••••••••••••••••••••• **FOCUS OF THIS CHAPTER** ••••••••••••••••••••

- Rationale for social skills interventions
- Classroom-wide or large-group-based interventions for social skills
- Social skills interventions focused on individual children
- Social integration activities and direct instruction of social skills
- Facilitating and supporting communication with peers

The importance of peer-related social competence during early childhood is widely acknowledged. There is evidence that positive peer interactions are an important contributor to developmental progress and, conversely, that peer interaction problems are a primary predictor of children's future social competence difficulties (Brown, Odom, & Conroy, 2001; McWilliam et al., 2001).

Inclusive preschool environments have a decided advantage in promoting peer-related social and communicative competence, (Bricker, 1995; Lipsky & Gartner, 1997; Peck, 1995; Strain, 1990, 1995, 1999). However, this advantage does not occur automatically by simply placing children with disabilities in inclusive settings. One study found that about one third of the children with disabilities in the inclusive setting were socially rejected by their peers without disabilities (Odom, Zercher, Li, Marquart, & Sandall, 1998).

Many children with disabilities lack the basic social skills requisite to positive peer interactions (Brown, Odom, Li, & Zercher, 1999). Many are withdrawn and hesitant to interact with peers. They appear socially aloof and unaware of the initiations or needs of peers, and do not seem to know how to get the attention of a peer, share, ask for assistance, or communicate positive feelings. Promoting friendships between these young children and their typically developing peers is a major goal of inclusive preschools. It is also the major challenge.

There is no agreed-on definition of what is entailed in friendship for young children but there are a few agreed-on markers (Danko & Buysse, 2002). The most important is *reciprocity*. Friendships are special relationships in which children have a strong desire to be near or play with one another. Interactions are voluntary, based on mutual affection or liking, and involve common interests and shared activities.

This chapter draws heavily from research describing intervention procedures to enhance the peer-related social competence and friendships of young children with disabilities in inclusive settings and social communication with peers (Brown et al., 2001; Hancock & Kaiser, 2002). The common focus of these procedures is on

- Helping children become members of groups
- Helping children become socially competent
- Facilitating and supporting children's communication with peers

HELPING CHILDREN BECOME MEMBERS OF GROUPS

Brown et al. (2001) described three classroom-wide or large-group-based interventions: 1) developmentally appropriate practices (DAP), 2) affective interventions, and 3) group friendship activities.

Developmentally Appropriate Practices (DAP)

Recall from Chapter 1 that DAP guidelines as set forth by the National Association for the Education of Young Children (NAEYC) are guiding principles for quality early childhood programs (Bredekamp & Copple, 1997). They are recognized as the standard for services for *all* young children.

The DAP guidelines place a strong emphasis on the importance of environmental arrangements and procedures to facilitate and support social-communicative exchanges among children with and without disabilities. Routine activities and the way that space is arranged encourage active engagement and exploration with peers, and there are abundant opportunities for children with disabilities to interact with more competent peers. There also are well-planned learning/activity centers (e.g., manipulatives, pretend play, literacy, art, science), appropriate classroom materials, responsive adults, and socially responsive peers. Implementation of DAP is basic to planning for and implementing interventions to promote peer-related social competence.

In line with DAP guidelines, Chandler (1998) suggested the addition of a peer interaction play center called a PALS Center. This center can be one of the options (in addition to the other learning/activity centers) in an inclusive classroom. Limit the space set aside for this center to about 10 x 10 so that the children are close to one another. Include a child-size table and chairs and (optionally) a sign or poster with a picture of children playing in the center. Limit materials and toys to promote sharing. For example, there should be only one bottle of glue and a small box of pieces of paper and crayons that the children will need to share to make a collage. Possible games to promote peer interaction include Go Fish, Lotto, Bear Bingo, and Candyland.

Initially, the children may need to be prompted to play in the PALS Center. Activities should be brief (5 to 15 minutes), depending on the activity and the interest level of the children. Pair children who lack play skills and/or have social interaction difficulties with more competent peers, rotating peer partners so that all children have a chance to play with one another in the PALS Center. When the children are seated in the PALS Center, the teacher should introduce the activity, describe and/or demonstrate how to use the materials, describe the social activity goal, and then ask the children to play. If the children do not interact with one another spontaneously and frequently, the teacher should prompt and model play skills and assist with alternative forms of communication if needed. Table 12.1 shows the variables that have been found to promote peer social interactions in PALS Centers (Chandler, 1998). The PALS Center provides children with fun, nonthreatening play activities that promote peer interaction with minimal adult time and effort.

Affective Interventions

The second type of classroom-wide or large-group intervention is called *affective interventions* (or antibias activities). The purpose of affective interventions is to nurture children's positive attitudes about and perceptions of individuals

Table 12.1. Variables that promote peer social interactions in a PALS Center

Adult Variables
- Adult absence
- Simple instructions
- Minimal interactions with the children
- Prompts for peer interaction
- Discussion/feedback after the activity

Peer Variables
- Familiar peers
- Socially competent peers
- Integrated play groups
- Small play groups
- Same age and same gender peers

Materials
- Limited number
- Limited variety
- Only part of the materials provided to each child
- Developmentally appropriate materials
- Preferred/familiar materials and activities
- Social materials and activities

Activity Structure
- Single activity theme/goal
- Child-directed
- Cooperative goal
- Defined/familiar theme
- Roles and rules clear and specified

Source: Chandler, 1998.

with disabilities. They promote awareness of disabilities through photographs, books, and other printed materials. This can result in children without disabilities exploring and experiencing adaptive equipment, people with disabilities talking about their lives, the *careful* challenging of children's misconceptions and stereotyping, and teaching others about specific disabilities through a variety of experiences.

The affective interventions described by Favazza and Odom (1997) were originally implemented with kindergarten children. However, these strategies to teach and nurture young children's positive attitudes toward peers with disabilities are easily adapted for preschoolers. The components of this intervention are

- Storytime/discussion about children with disabilities
- Structured free-play with children with disabilities
- Guided discussions at home

The first component, *storytime/discussion*, is for children without disabilities. Books about disabilities are read and equipment related to the stories (e.g., a wheelchair, scooter board) is made available for the children to explore. After reading the stories, the major focus of the guided discussions is to highlight the similarities between children with and without disabilities. There are questions on five topics: story content, disabilities, highlighting similarities, equipment related to story content, and playtime experiences. The questions on story content relate to factual information about the story (e.g., "Who was the girl in the story?"). The questions about disabilities focus on the cause of the disability and the reasons why the equipment is necessary (e.g., "If a person has to use a wheelchair because he has been in an accident, can he still do many things well?"). The next set of questions focuses on how the character in the story is similar to the participating children (e.g., "What are some things that Jason in the story likes to do that you also like to do?"). If the story introduced a special piece of equipment, the children are encouraged to explore it and then asked questions such as "What are the different parts of a wheelchair?" "How does someone make a wheelchair turn corners?" The last set of questions relates characters in the story to the children's peers with disabilities. The children are encouraged to talk about their positive play experiences with their peers and any issues or concerns such as communication difficulties or difficulties related to motor limitations (e.g., stacking blocks, moving from one learning/activity center or activity to another). All questions are answered in a factual manner.

The 15-minute *structured free-play* sessions use environmental arrangement strategies to increase positive interactions. These strategies are limiting space, selecting materials and activities that promote social interaction, and rotating and limiting materials. Some materials and play activities have a greater potential for promoting social interactions than others (e.g., eating/cooking materials, farm animals and blocks, cookie cutters with playdough, wagons, games that require two players). The emphasis is on ensuring that children with and without disabilities have fun playing with one another in small groups. No prompts or instructions are provided.

Finally, there are weekly *guided discussions at home.* A copy of a story discussed in class depicting a child with a disability is sent home for the parents to read with their child. The parents are given the same questions used in class to assist them in discussing the story with their child.

Research has shown that few early childhood classrooms have materials that depict children with diverse abilities (Favazza, La Roe, Phillipsen, & Kumar, 2000). This intervention is especially timely in that it is a way to integrate emergent literacy activities into the curriculum and at the same time promote acceptance of children with diverse abilities. Another benefit of including activities and materials that depict children with diverse abilities is the increased self-esteem of *all* the children. Incorporating materials that celebrate and value all children into the classroom environment and curriculum challenges stereotypes. It is a positive and visible way to send the message that everyone belongs.

Group Friendship Activities

Group friendship activities are another classroom-wide or large-group strategy to build affection and prosocial behaviors (Brown, Ragland & Bishop, 1989; Brown, Ragland, & Fox, 1988; Frea, Craig-Unkefer, Odom, & Williams, 1999). Friendship activities capitalize on the observation that preschool-age children typically respond positively to physical affection. The frequency of children's social interactions is increased by embedding prosocial responses into common preschool games, songs, and other routine activities such as Simon Says, "The Farmer in the Dell," and "If You're Happy and You Know It." Prosocial responses include friendly statements, compliments, smiles, and other forms of encouragement as well as physical affection (e.g., high five, hugs, shaking hands).

Implementation of this procedure is straightforward. Children are taught a new song or game or they participate in one that is familiar. After the song, game, or activity has been performed in the usual manner, they are told, "Now we are going to play/sing this a little differently." They are instructed and prompted how to exchange physical and other forms of affection (e.g., hug, pat on the back, high five, handshake, smile, taking turns with or sharing an object). For example, the teacher would say to the children, "After singing 'The Farmer in the Dell,' instead of singing 'the farmer takes a wife' or 'the wife takes a child,' we will sing 'the farmer hugs a wife' or 'the wife hugs a child' and then everyone will do it. We will all hug the friend standing next to us."

Adapting the children's game Musical Chairs is another example of a friendship activity (Brown et al., 1989). Musical Chairs provides multiple opportunities for children to socially interact with peers and to observe others socially interacting with peers. As a friendship activity, each interruption of the music (the points at which children try to find a chair but chairs are inevitably one short) provides an opportunity for the children to positively interact with one another by making friendly statements, complimenting one another, or interacting affectionately. The prosocial behavior of all the children is encouraged with special attention to children with disabilities. To be maximally effective, friendship activities should be conducted daily for about 10 to 15 minutes.

One advantage of group friendship activities is that they provide opportunities for children with disabilities to observe peer modeling of positive social behavior and then actually practice the behavior with positive feedback (Brown et al., 1988, 2001; Twardosz, Nordquist, Simon, & Botkin, 1983). Another advantage is that these teaching opportunities are embedded within routine activities, thus they use naturally occurring antecedents and consequences.

HELPING CHILDREN BECOME SOCIALLY COMPETENT

Three approaches to intervention that focus on specific children are *enhanced milieu teaching* (EMT), *social integration activities*, and *direct instruction* (Brown et al., 2001). These procedures constitute an intervention hierarchy with the least intrusive and most normal—EMT—at one end and the most structured, explicit teaching of social skills at the other. Which procedure to use depends on the child and the circumstances, but the general rule is to begin with procedures that require minimal changes in classroom routines and few additional resources (the least intrusive and most normal type of peer interaction intervention), and then move to procedures that are more intense and involve more planning and preparation.

As noted above, classroom-wide or large-group interventions—DAP, affective interventions, and group friendship activities—are the least intrusive and most normal type of peer interaction interventions because they require minimal changes in classroom routines and few additional resources. However, if levels of peer interactions continue to be low, it is necessary to plan and implement one or some combination of the more intense individualized peer interaction interventions described in this section (Brown & Odom, 1995). These are discussed in order of level of intrusiveness.

Enhanced Milieu Teaching of Social Behavior

Recall from Chapter 9 that enhanced milieu teaching (EMT) is a naturalistic instructional procedure that entails structuring the environment to increase opportunities for social and communicative behavior, and matching instructional strategies to children's ongoing actions and interests. The adult follows the child's leads rather than expects the child to respond to prompts and directions.

EMT is a hybrid approach to naturalistic intervention in that it incorporates aspects of both behavioral and social interactionist approaches for promoting social and communicative interactions. It incorporates environmental arrangement to promote child engagement with activities and communication partners; responsive interaction techniques to promote social and conversational interactions and to model desired behaviors; and milieu teaching procedures to prompt, model, and appropriately acknowledge the use of new social and communication behaviors in functional contexts.

The following are the steps for implementing EMT to facilitate social behavior (Brown, McEvoy, & Bishop, 1991):

- *Identify unstructured activities that engage the child with disabilities and include one or more peers without disabilities.* Routine activities involving learning centers, outdoor play, meals and snacks, free play, and transitions are contexts that offer particularly good conditions for teaching social behavior.

- *Plan the prompting procedures (modeling, mand model, time delay, or incidental teaching) to encourage social interactions during the identified activities or whenever the potential for peer interactions arises.* Also consider whether adults or peers will provide the prompts for appropriate social responses. For example, at snack give Taylor a double quantity of fruit or crackers and prompt him to share with a "friend." The way to find out if a situation is a good context in which to prompt social interactions is to observe the child and note whether he or she is interested in the materials and/or peers that are involved in the activity. If Taylor frequently watches Corey play with a particular set of cars and animals during manipulatives, he is probably interested in Corey, the toys, or both. But if a child grabs a toy or other object from another child, it is safe to say that he is interested only in that toy or object. These are both excellent times to prompt social interactions.

- *Implement the teaching procedures.* The objective is to teach new social responses and provide opportunities for the child to practice and elaborate previously acquired social behaviors. For example, Jessie obviously enjoys the housekeeping center, but she never initiates interactions with peers. The teacher says to Jessie, "Remember how we ask our friends to play? I think Kaitlin would like to help you set the table. Say to Kaitlin, 'Want to help?'" Jessie imitates the teacher's model. She says to Kaitlin, "Want to help?" and Kaitlin responds, "I'll put the cups out." Jessie and Kaitlin carefully set out the plastic dishes on the small table. Then they each sit in a chair and pretend to drink from the cups. Whenever Jessie is playing alone, her teacher prompts her to ask a peer to play. Over time the teacher notes that Jessie is beginning to ask peers to play without the teacher's suggestion. Also, Jessie's peers are seeking her out and asking her to play with them during unstructured activities. These teaching procedures are described in Chapter 9. Table 12.2 provides additional examples of the use of enhanced milieu teaching procedures to promote social behaviors.

- *Acknowledge the peer (or peers) who reciprocally interacts with the child with disabilities.* In the example above, Jessie's teacher commented to

Table 12.2. Examples of use of enhanced milieu teaching procedures to promote social behaviors

Context	Teacher prompt	Child response	Peer response
Play: Susie is standing and watching LiAn playing with the dolls.	"Susie, ask LiAn 'May I play too?'" "LiAn, could you let Susie dress the smaller doll?"	Susie sits down next to LiAn and says, "Me play too?"	LiAn gives Susie the smaller doll and says, "This is her dress."
Snack: Jace needs help opening his milk carton.	"Jace, ask Angelica to help you. Say, 'Please help with my milk.'"	"Help please."	Angelica says, "I'll help you" as she twists the top of the milk carton.
Transition: Christopher is having trouble moving his chair to the table for art activities. He watches Brandon push his chair to the table but does not speak.	"Brandon, ask Christopher if he would like you to help him with his chair."	Brandon says, "Do you want to sit here beside me?"	Christopher says, "Yes, sit beside Brandon"

Kaitlin that it was nice of her to help Jessie set the table and to share the tea party.

Table 12.2 provides additional examples of contexts, teacher prompts, and anticipated social responses (adapted from Brown, McEvoy, & Bishop [1991]). If EMT is not sufficient to accomplish the desired peer interaction patterns, it may be necessary to implement friendship activities, social integration activities, and/or explicit social skills training.

Both EMT and friendship activities are naturalistic peer interaction interventions that can easily be integrated into inclusive early childhood programs. If, however, they are not sufficient to promote the desired level of peer interactions, plan more structured and intensive procedures such as social integration activities and/or explicit teaching of social skills.

Social Integration Activities

Social integration activities (created through environmental arrangements) are interaction contexts carefully planned to bring children with social interaction difficulties in direct contact daily (for brief periods of time) with peers who are socially responsive and competent. Children with social interaction difficulties are provided with opportunities to 1) observe the socially competent play of their peers, 2) participate in social interactions with their socially competent peers, and 3) establish a positive history of peer interactions (Brown et al., 2001; Jenkins, Odom, & Speltz, 1989). The four components of social integration activities are

- Identification of participating children—groups will typically include one or two children with social interaction difficulties and at least two or three socially responsive and competent children.
- Daily planning of play areas within the classroom.
- Selection of activities that provide multiple opportunities for social interactions and positive play experiences
- Planning, arranging, introducing, and monitoring daily activities.

Specific areas in the classroom in which the social integration activities will take place may change from one day to the next. Identified children are brought to a predetermined area for 5 to 15 minutes of engagement in the social integration activity (essentially a teacher-directed playgroup). Children with social interaction difficulties are placed in close proximity to their socially competent peers every day. All the children soon learn that this playgroup is a regular part of their daily routine, similar to circle time, snacks, and so forth.

Of the play possibilities for the group—functional activities, constructive activities, sociodramatic play, games with rules—sociodramatic play may be most supportive of peer interactions (DeKlyen & Odom, 1989). Whatever activities are selected, it is critical to organize and implement them in such a way as to promote sharing, talking, assisting, and playing among the children. Each day, introduction of the selected activity should include suggestions to the children about how they might structure their play. In some activities, particularly sociodramatic play activities (e.g., making a birthday cake, playing storekeeper, preparing a tea party), it is a good idea to assign roles to the children. In others, it is appropriate to ask the children to decide how they will play with their friends. After introducing and organizing the activity, teachers should withdraw partially and become monitors and supporters. When the children are not playing, talking, sharing, or interacting with one another, the teachers may suggest a play idea, comment on the direction the play is taking, or, when indicated, directly prompt the children to interact with peers other than the ones with whom they have been interacting.

Direct Instruction of Social Skills

Direct instruction of social skills may involve only the children with disabilities, only the socially competent peers of children with disabilities, or both. Planned lessons are scheduled and implemented to teach specific skills. These small-group lessons typically follow a standard format: the adult 1) describes the target skill (e.g., taking turns), 2) prompts two children to model the target skill, and then 3) separates the group into dyads and encourages them to practice the skill (providing one another feedback as to whether they actually performed the skill). After the small-group lesson, an activity is scheduled in which the children will have an opportunity to practice the new skill with others in the group. Initially, the adult stays very near the children to provide prompts and suggestions, moving away only when all the children are consistently demonstrating the skill.

Another type of direct instruction of social skills involves only peers. This approach is called *peer mediated teaching.* Peers are taught to initiate and reciprocate interactions with children with disabilities. Specifically, they are taught how to use social strategies such as establishing eye contact; asking a child to play or share a toy; suggesting play ideas; describing their own or other children's play; organizing play; and sharing, helping, and being responsive to the play of classmates with disabilities (Christopher, Hansen, & Macmillan, 1991; Goldstein, English, Shafer, & Kaczmarek, 1997; Goldstein, Kaczmarek, Pennington, & Shafer, 1992; Odom, McConnell, & Chandler, 1994; Werts et al., 1996).

The third type of direct instruction of social skills involves both children with disabilities and their more socially competent peers. *Buddy skills-training* is an example of this approach. Buddy skills- training teaches social interaction skills to socially competent peers *and* to dyad partners with social interaction difficulties (English, Goldstein, Shafer, & Kaczmarek, 1997). Peers without disabilities are systematically taught a chain of behaviors that includes moving in proximity to children with peer interaction difficulties, saying the children's names and maintaining proximity while talking, and playing with them. There are two types of buddy skills-training: peer training and dyadic training. Peer training includes *sensitivity training* and *strategy-use training.*

In sensitivity training, peers without disabilities are shown videotaped vignettes depicting the types of attention-getting and requesting behaviors that their peers with disabilities might use to initiate communication. The pre-schoolers in the vignettes use unconventional types of communicative behavior such as gesturing and other nonverbal requests for action and attention, vocalization, and speaking unintelligible words or phrases. After each vignette, an adult discusses with the children what they observed and what they thought the child in the tape was trying to do or say.

In the strategy-use training, the children are taught the following "buddy" behaviors:

- Stay near your assigned buddy—stand or sit beside your friend
- Play with your friend—say your buddy's name, establish mutual attention, and talk or suggest playing together
- Talk with your friend—continue to stay close and play and/or talk to him or her

The three strategies can be condensed for the children to a simple mnemonic of "stay-play-talk."

Buddy pairs should be designated. Individual training for the peers with competent social skills consists of five or six sessions (three direct-instruction lessons and two or three practice sessions). The standard procedures to follow in each training session are 1) discussion, 2) adult modeling, 3) guided practice, and 4) independent practice with feedback. Children have mastered the strategies when they are able to perform all three buddy steps without prompts in two consecutive turns.

After peer strategy-use training and practice sessions, dyadic training is conducted with peers without disabilities and children with social interaction difficulties. These training sessions are conducted during classroom activities (e.g., free play, snack, large group). Depending on the needs of the child with disabilities in each dyad, there will be a need for two to four dyadic training sessions. During this training, the peers with disabilities in the dyads are taught a modified version of the stay-play-talk strategy. Most important, they learn to "stay and play" with their buddies. Dyadic sessions continue until the peers with disabilities are able to maintain proximity and interact with their buddies for 4 consecutive minutes in each of three activities in one day.

In the original research, English et al. (1997) assigned peers to a "buddy day" approximately every three days after strategy-use training was completed. After only 7 buddy days over a 12-week period, peers both with and without disabilities showed marked increases in the number of communication acts and social interactions compared with baseline measures.

Supporting Friendships for Children with Autism Characteristics of young children with autism that interfere with the ability to develop peer-related social competence and form friendships are 1) severely restricted social and communication repertoires and 2) difficulties engaging appropriately with toys and other objects. Young children with autism and other significant disabilities need the most intensive intervention. Often, initial social interaction training must focus on careful shaping of basic communication behaviors (e.g., requesting, commenting) using photographs, pictures, or gestures. Concurrently, peers without disabilities are taught to respond to the unconventional communication attempts of their classmates with severe disabilities.

The teacher's role in promoting friendships is to find a suitable social partner, create an environment conducive to positive peer relations, and provide frequent opportunities for children to play together and form mutually regulated friendships. A teacher may serve as an interactive partner, a social coach, or a provider of social opportunities (Danko & Buysse, 2002; Parke & Buriel, 1998). Being an interactive partner means playing with the child in a warm, responsive manner. This provides a model for the child on how to interact with a peer, and it provides opportunities for the child to learn social skills. Social coaching involves giving the child either a direction or the precise words to use to accomplish a social goal. Use social coaching to teach the child how to enter a peer playgroup and/or how to initiate social contacts with possible playmates. Being a provider of social opportunities requires careful attention to potential "social dyads." Notice when children seem to show mutual interest in one another and whom they seem to like. Then arrange play opportunities both within and outside the classroom.

Language and communication abilities and cognitive levels undoubtedly play a role in the development of friendships. When considering a suitable social partner for a child with autism, it is usually a good idea to pair the child with a peer who is slightly younger and perhaps less developmentally advanced in some areas *but who is socially competent.* Because classmates without disabilities often see only the deficit areas of a child with autism, it is important to create opportunities to highlight the special talents of the child (e.g., puzzles, computers, knowledge in a particular area), favorite activities, and favorite characters (e.g., Barney, clowns). Common interests and successful interaction in activities that build on these common interests can lay the groundwork for children to become friends.

FACILITATING AND SUPPORTING COMMUNICATION WITH PEERS

Typically developing children acquire and practice their communicative and social skills through myriad experiences over time and across social contexts (Sameroff & Fiese, 1990). By age 3, they have participated in countless recurring routines in which they have learned to express their intentions, engage in reciprocal interactions, and use social-affective signals. Young children with autism and other severe disabilities need supports to participate in routines and activities with peers in which they can develop and practice interpersonal communication.

Joint Attention and Symbol Use

Two areas are thought to be critical to communication with peers: *joint attention* and *symbol use* (Prizant, Wetherby, Rubin, & Laurent, 2003). Joint attention is the capacity to consider the attentional focus of another person and to draw that attentional focus toward objects and events of mutual interest. This capacity is basic to the emergence of children's communicative and social abilities, to their developing an understanding of the mind, and, possibly, to their ability to have objective thought. Evident in typically developing infants sometime around their first birthday, joint attention underlies a child's ability to coordinate and share attention and emotions, express intentions, and engage in reciprocal social interactions. There is a growing body of research suggesting that a joint attention ability is lacking in most young children with autism and other severe disabilities (Greenspan & Wieder, 1997). These children typically have difficulties with orienting and attending to a social partner, shifting gaze between people and objects, sharing affection or emotional states with another person, following the gaze or the pointing of another person, and drawing the attention of another person to objects or events for the purpose of sharing experiences.

Symbol use is the other area thought to affect communication with peers. This ability is basic to a child's understanding of meaning expressed through gestures, words, and sentences. Young children with autism and other severe disabilities have difficulty learning and using conventional gestures. They also have difficulty learning the conventional meaning of words. The use of challenging behaviors for protesting or establishing social control may be a direct consequence of these limitations.

Social Communication Objectives

Social communication objectives for young children with autism and other severe disabilities may include

- Establishing eye contact with peers
- Looking at peers when they approach or speak
- Reaching out to touch others
- Attending to the gestures and actions of peers
- Holding hands with others
- Engaging in turn taking with peers
- Responding to gestural cues

Each of these skills supports the development of relationships with peers and provides a context or prompt for communication and social exchanges. As noted in Chapter 10, peers without disabilities may be taught how to reinforce and respond to the sometimes subtle social-communication responses of their peers with disabilities. The following are suggestions for teaching social communication skills:

1. *Arrange successful social experiences.* Arrange as many opportunities as possible for successful social experiences with peers who are good language, social, and play models, and be alert to naturally occurring opportunities for these experiences throughout the day. The assumption is that the more peer interactions there are, the more opportunities there will be for children with severe disabilities to acquire and practice language and communication skills. There are two requirements for social experiences to be successful: the activities in which the social experiences take place must be motivating to both of the children involved and there must be instruction of communication strategies for the dyads—the children who lack social communication skills *and* their more competent peers. Use the enhanced milieu teaching (EMT) strategies described above (for facilitation of social behavior) and in Chapter 9 to teach communication in these activities.

2. *Use parallel talk to encourage joint attention.* Parallel talk is providing a running commentary about what the child is doing to support his or her understanding of the behavior of others in the social situation. Parallel talk usually begins with "you" and essentially matches words to actions. For example, Tyler is standing (almost hidden by a bookcase) watching a peer who is moving toy trucks and cars in and out of a small service station. The teacher makes descriptive comments that include the children's names to draw their attention to one another. She says, "You are watching Jason move the cars up and down the garage ramp and you want to play too. You would like to ask Jason to let you put your car on the ramp beside his. You can let Jason know that you want to play with him. Say to Jason, 'May I play too?'" The teacher's comments highlight the action and the toy that are the focus of Tyler's attention. Thus, the parallel talk accompanies and supports the joint attention of Tyler, Jason, and the teacher. Tyler may not be able to imitate the teacher's verbal model, but the two boys look at each other and/or jointly attend to the play activity. The teacher gently facilitates Tyler's participation in the activity, quietly moving away once the boys begin playing.

3. *Provide visual supports.* Augmentative and alternative communication (AAC) is any symbol system that supports or augments speech. It uses sign language, communication boards, photos, pictographs, computer images, or print. Because they use visual language systems (pictures, symbols, or words) to represent concepts, words, or sentences, AAC techniques capitalize on the visual processing abilities of children with autism and other severe disabilities.

In addition to using visual symbols to enhance language comprehension and production in social situations, AAC intervention also uses visual symbols to augment and support the communication of others (Quill, 2000). Use of visual aids reduces the frustration associated with communicative failure in social situations. There is less demand on the child's recall memory because visual information is static and predictable. The child is better able to attend to, organize, and structure information, thus increasing his or her independence because there is decreased reliance on adults.

Low-technology AAC tools, such as picture systems, are simple to develop and inexpensive to produce. The Picture Exchange Communication System (PECS) (Bondy & Frost, 1994) is one example. PECS is similar in some ways to other AAC picture systems. Where it differs is the focus on social exchange. PECS is designed to facilitate and support social communication. Instead of having children point to items in response to an adult request, children are taught to initiate communicative requests by approaching a communication partner and exchanging a pictorial symbol for a desired object and activity. The child learns to communicate to obtain highly motivating objects or events. PECS also includes protocols for expanding communication from single to multiple words and for increasing communicative function from requesting to labeling and commenting. Thus, through a process of six phases, children progress from symbol discrimination to more advanced stages of forming simple sentences with the symbols. Although PECS is primarily used with children who are nonverbal, it can also be used with children who have unintelligible speech, are echolalic, and/or have only a small set of functional words in their repertoire.

SUMMARY

If inclusive environments are to afford the benefits of positive social interactions for children with disabilities, there must be planned and systematic opportunities throughout the day for the children to engage in and practice social and communicative interactions. Brown and colleagues (2001) have provided a social relationship intervention hierarchy that can help teachers plan procedures to enhance the peer-related social competence of young children with disabilities in inclusive settings. Two classroom-wide approaches provide the foundation or first level of the hierarchy: 1) high-quality inclusive preschool programs and 2) *affective interventions* (or antibias activities) and *group friendship activities*. Both are intended to promote positive attitudes and prosocial behaviors. After that come individualized peer interaction interventions: enhanced milieu teaching (EMT) of social behavior, social integration activities, and explicit teaching of social skills. The specific focus of these interventions depends on the individual child and the child's environments. Procedures should be modified and combined as necessary to fit the characteristics of the child and the context.

Missed opportunities for successful social experiences with peers are missed opportunities for learning language and communication skills. Peers in inclusive settings are more than natural partners, they are natural facilitators of language and communication. This chapter has described social interaction intervention procedures to bring about increases (over baseline levels) in 1) cooperative learning and play, 2) social and communication skills, and 3) observational learning. Most important is ensuring that young children with disabilities have *fun*—that they are involved in positive social and communication interactions and play with peers throughout the day, and not just during teaching sessions.

•••••••••••••••••••• **STUDY QUESTIONS** ••••••••••••••••••••

1. Discuss what is entailed in "friendship" for young children.

2. Identify three classroom-wide or large-group-based interventions.

3. Describe the role of social interactions in classrooms based on DAP guidelines.

4. Discuss the rationale for and the basic steps in implementing affective interventions.

5. Describe implementation of group friendship activities.

6. Identify the three approaches to social skills intervention that focus on individual children.

7. Describe the "intrusiveness continuum" of social skills training approaches.

8. Describe the steps for implementing EMT to facilitate social behavior.

9. Describe the four components of social interactions activities.

10. Describe the three approaches to direct instruction of social skills.

11. Define *joint attention* and *symbol use* and discuss their role in social communication.

12. What are social communication objectives for young children with autism and other severe disabilities?

13. Describe three procedures for teaching social communication skills.

13

Environmental Arrangements to Promote Independence

Mary Jo Noonan

• FOCUS OF THIS CHAPTER •

- Age-appropriate independent behavior
- Instructional objectives and lesson plans for independence
- Adaptations and functionally equivalent responses
- Physical development needs, interventions, and strategies for independence
- Communication needs, interventions, and strategies for independence
- Self-help needs, interventions, and strategies for independence

Independent behavior is behavior performed in the presence of naturally oc-curring stimuli. This usually means that the behavior is achieved without the assistance of other people. There are many reasons why children with disabilities may not develop age-appropriate independent behaviors. First, failing to fade instructional prompts may inadvertently teach the children to "always wait for assistance." Second, adults may hold low expectations for children with disabilities and thus may not afford them opportunities to be independ-ent (Stoneman & Rugg, 2004). And third, physical, sensory, or communication needs may interfere with independence. It is important to systematically plan and implement procedures and adaptations that teach independence.

TEACHING INDEPENDENT BEHAVIORS

Independent behavior goals for children with disabilities must be age appropri-ate. For example, 5 minutes of independent play could be a goal for a 1-year-old when placed on a blanket with some toys. Independent requesting might be an appropriate goal for a toddler. The toddler could be taught to point as a way of requesting desired objects, locations, and people. To construct a goal that fos-ters independence, avoid stating performance conditions in which the behavior is initiated or prompted by an adult. Instead, the objective should specify natu-ral conditions under which the skill is needed. Some examples include "When getting dressed in the morning, Sara will choose a T-shirt from the drawer," or "When playing with a friend in the free-play area, Tommy will choose a toy from the shelves." These are more natural conditions than when "given two T-shirts" or "when presented with three toys."

In addition to specifying independence as a performance condition, inde-pendence can be incorporated into the criterion of an objective. For example, when teaching a child to hold a spoon, the criterion might state that the child independently retrieves the spoon if it drops on the tray. Criterion levels for in-dependent behaviors should correspond to the standards or requirements of in-dependence in natural environments. Once objectives have been formulated, the next step is to plan instruction.

Systematic Instruction

Recall that in systematic instruction, instructional prompts are used to help a child learn a correct response. The basic task of teaching is to fade the instruc-tional prompt so that the child responds correctly to the natural prompt. Pro-viding that the performance conditions and criterion specified in the instruc-tional objective are those of independence, when the instructional prompt is faded, the child will be demonstrating an independent response to a naturally occurring stimulus.

To help a child achieve independence, systematic instructional plans should be 1) least intrusive, 2) naturalistic, 3) associated with routines and en-vironmental modifications, and/or 4) designed to promote generalization. *Least intrusive* procedures are those that do not differ from naturalistic learning experiences or interfere with ordinary routines. They have two advantages when teaching independent behavior. First, they are easily eliminated through fading because they are not very noticeable. And second, they are easy for others to implement because they are similar to what people would typically do to help a child.

Naturalistic instruction, particularly enhanced milieu teaching (EMT) (Kaiser, 1993b; Kaiser et al., 1991), was described at length in Chapter 9. Many naturalistic procedures promote independence because the child's behavior is self-initiated rather than adult-prompted. When planning EMT, a specific child behavior can be identified as an *occasion for instruction*. An occasion for instruction may be child behaviors as subtle as a child looking at an object, or as obvious as reaching for a desired object or vocalizing for attention ("Watch me!").

Daily routines provide children with repeated and predictable sequences of events that help them anticipate what comes next. Repetition and anticipation promote learning. For example, a child's morning routine with a baby sitter always begins with the child selecting some toys or books, playing with the sitter for a while, putting the toys/books away, and having a snack. After days or weeks of the routine, the sitter might arrive and be greeted by the child with a book for playtime. When the sitter stops playing and goes to the kitchen to prepare a snack, the child might put the book away, anticipating the snack.

Environmental modifications can be used to provide reminders to help children respond independently. Achieved by physically altering the environment, modifications can range from very intrusive to minimally intrusive. Consider this example: A preschooler is learning to independently distribute napkins and cups at snack time. Once she is reminded to do the task, she usually does so independently. Providing the napkins and cups at her place setting is a natural, nonintrusive prompt for the child to begin distributing the napkins and cups.

Generalization Strategies

Although not always necessary when using naturalistic teaching procedures, including *generalization strategies* in instructional plans will promote independence (these were discussed in detail in Chapter 6). Several generalization procedures (Stokes & Baer, 1977) are well-suited to promoting independence. *Natural contingencies* may be paired with instructional ones to facilitate generalization. Over time, instructional contingencies are faded. *Sufficient exemplar training* promotes independence because it teaches a stimulus class (the group of stimuli that are typically associated with the response). If a preschooler who uses a wheelchair is taught to ask a peer for assistance in maneuvering through a doorway, getting materials that are out of reach, or carrying his lunch tray (*exemplar training*), he is likely to generalize and ask a peer for assistance to retrieve a dropped toy (a response that was not taught). Encountering material from the instructional setting in natural environments (*program common stimuli*) may prompt a new behavior. Finally, self-prompting, a common strategy to *mediate generalization*, facilitates independence across settings and situations because it essentially "goes with" the child wherever he goes.

ADAPTATIONS FOR FUNCTIONAL INDEPENDENCE

White (1980) uses the term *critical function* to distinguish the purpose of a behavior from the physical action used to accomplish it. Crawling, for example, serves the purpose of getting from one place to another—the critical function of mobility. Reaching and vocalizing may serve the purpose of requesting more food—the critical function of expressive communication. A *functionally equivalent* response is a response that accomplishes the same critical function (purpose) as the target behavior, but by another means (Carr & Durand, 1985; Helmshtetter & Durand, 1991). For example, *pointing* is a functionally equivalent response for *grasping* if pointing has the effect of someone giving the child the toy he pointed to (the same effect that would have been achieved if the child could grasp the toy). In general, instructional objectives should focus more on function than form; accomplishing an intended outcome is often more important than a specific behavior or form of behavior (Westling & Fox, 2004).

When a child uses functionally equivalent responses to do a task without assistance, she accomplishes *functional independence*. The following strategies teach an infant or young child to be functionally independent: 1) individualized participation, 2) environmental prompts, 3) learning centers, 4) peer assistance, and 5) prosthetic devices and adaptive equipment.

Individualized Participation

Recall the discussion on group instruction in Chapter 11. Many activities in child care, preschool settings, and early intervention programs are conducted in small- or large-group situations. However, there is no requirement that all children in a group activity participate at the same level or in the same way; participation can be individualized. Consider, for example, using a puppet activity to teach turn taking. Jason, a preschooler with a language delay and hearing impairment, can participate independently by manipulating the puppets while another group member speaks for the puppet.

Environmental Prompts

Another way to help an infant or young child achieve independence is to modify the environment or materials to provide extra clues or reminders. To assist a child to be independent in washing her hands, for example, a series of pictures illustrating task steps can be posted as reminders (Copeland & Hughes, 2000; Klein, Cook, & Richardson-Gibbs, 2001). Color coding (e.g., cubbies, chairs, coats, rug squares, crayon boxes, toothbrushes) is another example of an environmental prompt that allows children to perform independently. An environmental prompt may be permanent (it remains in place) or temporary (it will be faded).

Learning Centers

One purpose of learning centers is to teach children to play without adult assistance. For example, a child care program may have a learning center that includes blocks and other building materials, or a preschool may have a learning center with science materials that change weekly (e.g., "dinosaur week" might include dinosaur coloring books, plastic dinosaur figures and habitats, a dinosaur egg game, a dictionary of dinosaurs, and storybooks about dinosaurs). Learning centers provide opportunities for functional independence because children decide how they want to participate (within clearly established limits), interacting with materials in a manner that suits their interests and skills (Klein et al., 2001).

Peer Assistance

In many situations, peer assistance can help a child be independent (Daigre, Johnson, Bauer, & Smith, 1998). Peers can assist in a wide range of tasks such as helping a child balance while walking, picking up items that a child drops, reminding a child what should be done next, and so on. Although we should be careful not to burden a sibling or young child with too much responsibility for another child, providing assistance in certain situations teaches children to be helpful and considerate. It also encourages empathy and nurturing, important attitudes for children to develop. At the same time, it helps children with disabilities to be independent of adults.

Prosthetic Devices and Adaptive Equipment

Children with physical disabilities sometimes benefit from special compensatory equipment such as a *prosthetic device*—a replacement or adaptation for a missing or nonfunctional limb (Hill, 1999). An artificial leg is a prosthesis for a child who is missing a leg. A splint with a Velcro band that secures a crayon in a child's hand is a prosthesis for a child who is otherwise unable to hold a crayon. If a child is not able to achieve functional independence immediately with the use of a prosthesis, guided practice may be used to teach the child to use the device.

Adaptive equipment refers to specialized furniture and other materials designed to assist individuals with disabilities, usually physical disabilities (Heller, Forney, Alberto, Schwartzman, & Goeckel, 2000). Wheelchairs, walkers, positioning chairs, standers, adjustable tables, modified bicycles, and feeding equipment are examples of adaptive equipment. For many children with special needs, physical support and therapeutically beneficial physical responses obtained with the use of appropriately selected and fitted adaptive equipment result in functional independence.

FUNCTIONAL INDEPENDENCE IN BASIC SKILLS

Disabilities or delays associated with basic skills (gross motor, fine motor, communication, and self-help) may interfere with a child's development of independence in the home, community, play, and child care or school activities. Objectives may need to be formulated as functionally equivalent responses to provide opportunities for independence.

Independence in Gross Motor Skills

Gross motor skills involve large muscle movements. The developmental sequence of gross motor skills includes important developmental skills called *milestones* (e.g., head control, rolling, crawling, sitting, creeping, standing, walking). Movements in and out of these milestones (*transitional movements*) are also important gross motor skills.

Physical Development Difficulties

Motor development is linked to the development of the central nervous system, a process that begins before birth and continues until about age 5. An immature or injured central nervous system is often characterized by delayed motor development, atypical muscle tone, atypical reflexes, postural reaction deficits, and/or compensatory patterns (Pellegrino, 2002). The extent to which these characteristics are present and interfere with typical motor development varies from slight to severe.

Atypical Muscle Tone   Muscle tone, the "resistance to passive movement of a muscle" (Ratliffe, 1998, p. 433), may be too high (*hypertonia* or *spasticity*), too low (*hypotonia* or *flaccidity*), or fluctuating (*athetosis*). Atypical tone may result in too little or too much movement, or movement that is too fast, too slow, or jerky. It also interferes with the development of typical postures and movement patterns and the ability to transition from one position to another (e.g., from creeping to sitting).

Atypical Reflexes   When the central nervous system is injured or immature, these reflexes tend to be atypical in three ways:

1. They *persist* beyond the typical developmental time frame; in typical development these reflexes fade or become integrated with voluntary movement.

2. They are *exaggerated*, easily elicited, and often fully demonstrated; they are *not fleeting* or *partial* as in typical development.

3. They are *obligatory*; once elicited, posture and movement are restricted and bound by the pattern. They are never obligatory in typical development (Pellegrino, 2002).

Postural Reaction Deficits   In young children with motor delays or an injured central nervous system, postural reactions (equilibrium and righting) do not develop or develop incompletely (Pellegrino, 2002). Without righting reactions, there is not a strong physiological urge to establish aligned and upright postures and movements. And without equilibrium reactions that provide balance, typical postural and movement patterns are difficult to attain and maintain.

Compensatory Patterns Many children with motor disabilities do accomplish motor skills, but they may do so through atypical postures called *compensations*. Compensations allow a child to accomplish a useful position, such as holding his head up or sitting, but they restrict movement and block subsequent motor development (Bly, 1983). Examples of compensations include a neck block (holding the head upright by hyperextending the neck and resting the head between elevated shoulders) and a pelvic hip block (sitting by hyperextending the lower spine and using a "frog-legged" position).

Physical Development Intervention Procedures

Motor interventions should be conducted within the context of functional activities. This is called *integrated therapy.* Integrated therapy teaches the purpose of new motor skills and enhances generalization (McWilliam, 1996). Intervention for children with mild physical delays or disabilities will usually target the typical sequences of gross and fine motor skills. For children with severe physical delays or disabilities, the functional use of selected motor skills and adaptive skills will usually be emphasized.

Mild Physical Disabilities Intervention for gross motor skills when mild disabilities are present focuses on teaching the next skill in the developmental sequence and improving postural reactions, particularly the equilibrium (balance) reactions. Physical guidance and activities that encourage the child to practice a skill are common intervention procedures. For example, when a child is beginning to creep (move forward on hands and knees), encouragement is provided by enticing the child to creep toward desired objects held a short distance away. Guided practice assists the child to move her hips and legs back and forth in a creeping pattern. Balance reactions for creeping are encouraged by holding desired toys and objects off to the child's one side, enticing her to lift one arm and reach to the side. Reaching requires the child to shift her weight to maintain the creeping position and avoid falling. If the child is unable to reach to the side, physical guidance to shift her weight is provided.

Severe Physical Disabilities Usually, severe physical disabilities are due to a developmental disorder rather than a delay such as central nervous system injury or a neuromuscular disease. When a severe physical disability is present, the problems of atypical muscle tone, persistent primitive reflexes, delayed or absent postural reactions, and compensatory patterns are likely to characterize motor development. These problems affect the development of functional gross and fine motor skills.

Positioning and carrying procedures are therapeutic techniques that provide stable and aligned posture, typical muscle tone, and inhibit atypical reflexes (Heller et al., 2000). Positions that appear to be opposite or counter to the atypical patterns are usually effective. For example, when a child is placed in his high chair and demonstrates an asymmetrical tonic neck reflex (ATNR), his posture is characterized by too much muscle tone, asymmetry, and excessive extension (his trunk, neck, and head rotate to one side, extremities are extended on his face side, and the opposite extremities flex). This atypical pattern can be prevented or minimized by using pillows, positioning inserts, or a special chair that aligns his body, limbs, and head; flexes his hips, knees, and ankles; and brings his head and shoulders slightly forward. Figure 13.1 illustrates this positioning technique. Appropriate positioning and carrying procedures often facilitate typical movement patterns. This implies that positioning must not be too confining; if a child is *over-positioned*, movement will be restricted and opportunities to attempt and practice new motor skills will not be available.

Using furniture, pillows, or specialized equipment (*adaptive equipment*) for positioning or carrying is called *static positioning*. The devices are fixed in place and cannot be readily adjusted in response to changes in muscle tone or

Figure 13.1. Example of positioning technique to inhibit asymmetrical extensor pattern.

movement or situational demands. Static positioning and carrying procedures, however, provide the child with independence from an adult, and free the adult for activities beyond the reach and confines of holding the child. The alternative to static positioning and carrying is *dynamic positioning* in which an adult's body (instead of equipment) is used to support a child in a desired position. The advantage of dynamic positioning and carrying is that an adult can respond immediately to child and situational needs.

Physical guidance and encouragement techniques that assist the child to accomplish typical postures and movements are called *facilitation* techniques. For example, while assisting with dressing, a father holds his 2-year-old daughter on his lap, helping her to prop herself with her hands on her knees. This position encourages and facilitates head and trunk control (holding her head and trunk upright) and discourages increased muscle tone. As her father helps her put on a T-shirt, he shifts her weight to one side, allowing her to lift her opposite arm into the T-shirt sleeve. As her weight is shifted to one side, she feels the weight bearing through her supporting arm. This *facilitates* an equilibrium reaction in sitting. It also facilitates a righting reaction associated with head and trunk control, encouraging her to realign and maintain her head and trunk upright. Appropriate positioning and carrying procedures (including the use of adaptive equipment) ideally function as facilitation techniques, allowing and encouraging increasingly more independent postures and movement.

Physical and occupational therapists typically have the responsibility of conducting motor evaluations, developing intervention plans, and teaching other team members to implement the plan. Although therapists have expertise in physical development, the team approach is critical to planning motor interventions that address children's movement needs associated with meaningful, functional activities.

Children with physical delays or impairments or neuromotor disabilities may not progress through the typical sequence of physical gross motor development. Motor skill development may be splintered (skills may be skipped), skills may be acquired partially, or they may develop in an atypical fashion (Illingworth, 1983). For example, a child with cerebral palsy may not crawl, but she may learn to scoot backward. When motor delays/disabilities preclude or interfere with independence, functionally equivalent gross motor objectives may be targeted. Several gross motor functions are critical for social and physical independence in home, community, child care, and school environments. These include postural and mobility functions. Table 13.1 presents examples of a few gross motor responses needed by children and some of the critical functions achieved by the motor responses. Note that therapeutic positioning and handling techniques as well as adaptive equipment considerations are included.

Independence in Fine Motor Skills

In the sequence of typical physical development, fine motor skills are refined following the accomplishment of gross motor skills. As previously mentioned, delays in gross motor skills are associated with delays in postural reactions. In

Table 13.1. Examples of gross motor responses important for independence, critical functions, and suggestions for achieving functionally equivalent responses

Gross motor responses	Critical functions	Functional equivalents
Head erect in midline	Visual attending Visual scanning Oral-motor control	Head rests on chair (with or without strap) Head momentarily erect Foam neck brace
Floor and chair sitting	Arms free for fine motor tasks, materials, and toys Upright position for eating and drinking Upright position for adaptive, daily living, and other functional skills	Propped sitting against wall or other surface for floor sitting Kneeling (with/without support or adaptive equipment) Communication of need for access or participation
Walking	Access to locations, materials, and toys Arms free for handling materials Upright position for adaptive, daily living, and other functional skills Participation with peers in movement activities	Wheelchair Walker or cane(s) Knee walking Scooting in sitting position Shoulder bag for carrying materials

turn, delays in postural reactions result in postural instability; that is, difficulty in maintaining proper joint, bone, and overall body alignment and balance (Bly, 1983). The problem of postural instability accentuates the problem of fine motor delays. For example, a preschooler with postural instability in sitting will have difficulty feeding herself because her trunk and shoulders are unsteady and she is continually at risk of falling.

Interventions that improve postural stability result in improved fine motor skills. These interventions can be provided through physical assistance or adaptations. For example, if a child is having difficulty controlling the movement of his toothbrush, he may be guided to spread his feet apart for a more solid base of support. He may also be assisted to hold the edge of the sink for balance. With a steadier base of support and assistance in balance, controlling the movement of his toothbrush is an easier task.

Many fine motor tasks are performed while seated. Postural stability is enhanced when the child is seated in a chair of the proper size (its seat length is the distance from her buttocks to her knees) and she can place her feet flat on the floor or on a footrest. If the child has difficulty sitting upright with her hips at the back of the seat, a wide strap holding her hips in the back of the seat will improve stability. In addition, the table height may be modified to improve postural stability. The table height should be at least a few inches above the height of the child's elbows. For additional support, the table may be raised to a level slightly below the child's armpits.

Fine motor skills are critical for independence in most daily living, adaptive, play, and school skills. If fine motor performance is delayed or impaired, functionally equivalent responses may provide alternatives for accomplishing independence. Examples of important fine motor responses, the critical functions they accomplish, and ideas for functionally equivalent responses are presented in Table 13.2.

Independence in Communication Skills

Infants communicate effectively long before they are able to speak. For example, they spit, purse their lips, gurgle, and smile to indicate their distaste or preference for foods, or they smile and coo to urge a sibling to continue playing. When they begin approximating words, their communication increases in effectiveness and efficiency. Communication becomes a critical tool to meet needs and desires, establish social relationships, participate in family activities, and learn new skills and concepts. Environmental control skills are the foundation of a communication repertoire. For example, an infant who reaches toward his father controls his environment if his father consistently responds by picking him up. Once an initial communication repertoire of environmen-

Table 13.2. Examples of fine motor responses important for independence, their critical functions, and suggestions for achieving functionally equivalent responses

Fine motor responses	Critical functions	Functional equivalents
Reach	Touch and exploration of toys and materials Access to materials and locations	Toys/materials within close proximity Shoulder and trunk stabilization through positioning, handling, or adaptive equipment Attachments (e.g., strings) to eliminate need to reach Prosthetic reaching stick
Grasp	Access to materials Hold and carry materials Play with toys Engage in adaptive, daily living, and other functional skills Indicate choice of objects or materials	Shoulder and trunk stabilization through positioning, handling, or adaptive equipment Adaptive feeding or marking utensils Shoulder bag or adaptive tray to hold and carry materials Materials strapped to hands (e.g., Velcro strap on pen) Materials secured to surface to prevent them from slipping or falling Holding materials with arms, mouth, or feet
Point	Indicate focus of interest Clarify object of communication Indicate desired object or event	Shoulder and trunk stabilization through positioning, handling, or adaptive equipment Whole hand/fist use to indicate/clarify Eye pointing Augmentative communication to indicate/clarify (hand/fist, eye pointing, hand or head switch, and so forth)

tal control skills is established, the young child's repertoire expands: communication becomes more refined and efficient.

Establishing Environmental Control Skills

The infant's earliest efforts to control the environment are simple, nonsymbolic behaviors such as eye contact, pointing, vocalizing, reaching, and touching. There are five phases in the development of environmental control skills:

1. *Attentional interactions:* indicating awareness, recognizing and/or anticipating persons, objects, or events (e.g., smiling in recognition of familiar person)

2. *Contingency interactions:* using simple behaviors to control reinforcing consequences (e.g., playing baby games such as "so big" to maintain interaction with an adult)

3. *Differentiated interactions:* controlling the behavior of others with responses that have socially recognized meanings (e.g., pointing, giving, other nonverbal gestures)

4. *Encoded interactions:* using behaviors that have precise meanings and are understood given the situation—using one- or two-word phrases or sign language in response to environmental stimuli or events (e.g., saying, "ball, Mommy" when a sibling comes into the room holding the ball)

5. *Symbolic interactions:* using behaviors that have precise meanings (e.g., language, pretend play) to communicate, without reliance on the situation to be understood (e.g., saying "Want drink") (Dunst et al., 1987)

Instructional goals are based on the child's communication needs in daily functional activities (derived from assessment strategies described in Chapter 5). The goals build on what a young child is doing and promote the child's development of skills at the next level of environmental control. For example, Timmy's parents indicated that they would like him to express his preferences at mealtimes and when playing with his sister. Presently, Timmy, who is unable to speak due to cerebral palsy, smiles and moves his arms excitedly when he sees his favorite foods and toys. One goal is for Timmy to look at a favorite food or toy for 5 seconds when given two choices. In requiring Timmy to look at a preferred food or toy, Timmy learns that looking controls getting what he wants. This goal moves Timmy from his present phase of awareness to the phase of contingent interactions.

There are five instructional approaches to assist infants and young children in progressing through the phases of environmental control skills: 1) enhance sensitivity, 2) increase opportunities, 3) structure predictable routines, 4) augment input, and 5) modify the environment (Noonan & Siegel, 2003). All five approaches can be used concurrently.

Enhance Sensitivity Learn the ways in which a young child tries to communicate nonsymbolically, and respond immediately when such behaviors are demonstrated. Also respond to the behaviors that *might* be attempts to communicate nonverbally (*infer intent*). This strategy is particularly useful for enhancing parent–child interactions when the child's responses are difficult to detect, inconsistent, or infrequent. For example, Sally's mom notices that Sally stares intently at her when she is enjoying an interaction and wiggles and looks away when she's tired. Mom responds immediately, continuing to talk and play with her when she stares, and ending the interaction and comforting Sally when she wiggles and looks away. As a result of mom's immediate responsiveness, Sally is given control of the length of interactions. In turn, interactions become more satisfying to Sally and her mom.

Increase Opportunities   Be careful not to eliminate a young child's need to communicate by doing everything for him. Increase communication opportunities by altering the environment such as placing things out of reach or delaying expected events. For example, place only two pieces of finger food (slices of an apple) on a toddler's high-chair tray. This will create the need to communicate a request for more food.

Structure Predictable Routines   Help a young child develop expectations by establishing predictable routines such as playing Peekaboo during diapering. When the routine is well-learned, change it or insert a pause to motivate a communication response. For example, hold the diaper above the infant, but don't begin Peekaboo until the infant demonstrates some expectation of the game such as giggling or reaching for the diaper.

Augment Input   Increase the communicative input a child receives by supplementing speech with additional modes. For example, point to photographs while talking to a child, or provide touch cues. The augmentative mode should correspond to the child's level of understanding. Such input may help increase a child's comprehension.

Modify the Environment   Environmental modifications can be used to assist a child to interact with others and to display more alert and responsive behavior. For example, a child may be taken out of his wheelchair and placed on the floor to play at the same level as his peers in the block area of a preschool classroom. Being at eye level with others and having easy access to materials can increase interaction. A child can be assisted to be more alert and responsive by enhancing the sensory qualities of an activity. For example, the visual appeal of a material can be enhanced by giving it a bright background.

Expanding Initial Environmental Control Skills

Once a child is demonstrating environmental control skills with simple, non-symbolic behaviors (e.g., vocalizing for attention, pointing to a desired toy), the next goal is to expand the child's skills to include communication responses serving more uses or functions. Examples of communicative functions ("pragmatics") include requesting, gaining attention, greeting, and protesting. These functions are typically demonstrated first through signals (e.g., specific gestures such as waving "bye-bye," or as a vocalization that communicates, "I'm trying but I need help"). Later, these functions are demonstrated through symbols such as words or sign language.

When the child is using several communicative functions frequently and effectively, communication skills are expanded by increasing complexity. Complexity is increased in two ways. First, the content of what the child talks about can be expanded. Content or meaning is referred to as *semantics*. Children communicate about content such as people, places, events, and objects and about characteristics of people, places, events, and objects. Second, complexity is increased by expanding the structure of communication. The structure or grammar of language is *syntax* and includes such forms as nouns, verbs, and adjectives. Expanding what the child talks about and the structures used to communicate enables the child to communicate more precisely and thus more effectively.

Given the complexity of establishing goals that consider the pragmatic, semantic, and syntactic dimensions of communication, as well as needs related to home and community participation, a team approach is vital. As always, the family's role in decision making is central to the team process. A speech-language pathologist (a professional with expertise in assessing communication needs and planning interventions) is also an important team member.

The formulation of communication goals comes through a combined approach of ecological and developmental assessments. For example, a goal to "initiate requests for desired activities with siblings" may be identified in analyzing family routines. The ecological assessment is also the source for identifying needed vocabulary. In the play activity, for example, learning the names of games may be a vocabulary need.

The level or complexity of the goal is based on the child's present level of performance: syntax and semantics are expanded following developmental sequences. Returning to the example of requesting an activity, the child is using one-word utterances: he's using a grammar that consists of nouns or verbs, and he's talking about actions and people performing actions. A syntactic goal is to use a "noun + verb" form; a semantic goal is use of an "agent + action" expression (e.g., "Tommy + catch").

Alternative Communication Modes Another consideration in formulating communication goals is deciding which communication mode would work best. Augmentative communication includes gestural, pictorial, or symbolic communication systems. Augmentative communication systems are alternative communication systems for some children who are unlikely to ever use speech; for others, the systems supplement and enhance oral communication and are not intended to replace it. Examples of alternative and augmentative systems include American Sign Language; common gestures (e.g., waving at someone to "Come here"); pictures, symbols, or words displayed in a book or on a large surface (communication board); pictures, symbols, or words displayed on an elevated Plexiglas surface for eye pointing (eye-gaze system); and electronic communication boards, some of which "talk" using voice-synthesizer microcomputer technology. Very often the best solution is to combine systems (McCormick & Wegner, 2003). For example, a child taps a bell attached to her wheelchair to call for attention. When someone responds, she points to the picture for "drink" on her communication board, and nods yes when asked if she wants a drink of water. Figure 13.2 illustrates a communication board using line drawings arranged on the tray of a child's wheelchair.

The decision to use an augmentative system and the selection of a system are made by the early intervention team, including the family, speech–language pathologist, teacher or infant specialist, occupational therapist, and physical therapist. As noted throughout this text, parental preference should carry the most weight in decisions about their children. Decisions concerning the selection and use of an augmentative communication system are not one-time decisions. As the child develops and circumstances change, needs and the appropriateness of the system are continually evaluated.

Instructional Procedures   Enhanced mileu teaching (EMT) has been demonstrated to be particularly successful in assisting young children with disabilities to learn and use generalized communication skills (Kaiser, 1993b; Kaiser et al., 1991). As reviewed in Chapter 9, EMT is a hybrid naturalistic approach to communication intervention that includes environmental arrangement, responsive interaction, and milieu teaching (McCormick, 2003c). The procedures are

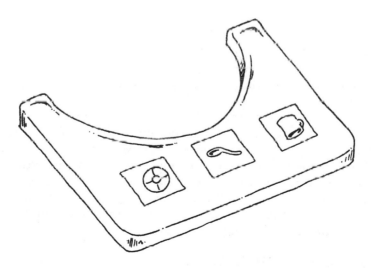

Figure 13.2.   A communication board with line drawings (on a wheelchair tray).

	Date begun: 6/3/05
Child: Joseph K.	Date completed:
Objective: Make request ("Please")	Interventionist(s): Janet Yim
Conditions: When Joseph wants something that is out of reach	
Response: He will say "Please."	
Criterion: So that it is clearly audible, 5 times within 3 days	

Intervention Context	Prompting/Facilitation Techniques	Consequences
Setting(s): At home, at preschool, and in stores or restaurants	Positioning and Handling; Special Equipment/Materials: n/a	Reinforcement: Tell Joseph he can have what he asks for when he says "Please." Give him the item immediately; assist him in using, exploring, or playing with the item if he does not interact with it.
Routine(s)/Activity(ies): During play times at home or preschool, during mealtimes, and while shopping	Environmental Modifications: Place several desired items or toys out of reach but within sight (leave a cup at the edge of the counter, toys on a top shelf of toy shelves, and books on top of an end table).	
Skill Sequence(s): n/a		Corrections: Say "Please," wait 5 seconds, reinforce if correct. If still incorrect or no response, say "Please" and give Joseph the item; do not praise him or interact further.
Occasions for Incidental Intervention: Whenever Joseph focuses on an item for 10 seconds, or whenever Joseph reaches for an item that is beyond his reach	Prompts/Facilitation: Approach Joseph, make eye contact, and ask, "What do you say Joseph?" (wait 5 seconds)	

Figure 13.3. Instructional plan for making request.

well-suited to inclusive settings because they follow the child's lead and instruction is embedded within on-going routines and activities. Figure 13.3 is an instructional plan that illustrates assisting a child in learning to make requests using EMT procedures.

As with gross and fine motor skills, functionally equivalent responses can provide alternatives for accomplishing communication functions when communication delays or impairments are present (McCormick & Wegner, 2003). Table 13.3 lists examples of communication responses, some of the functions accomplished by the responses, and suggestions for functionally equivalent responses. Most of the functionally equivalent responses are skill approximations or communication responses accomplished through *alternative and augmentative communication systems.*

Independence in Self-Help Skills

Self-help skills are personal care skills (e.g., dressing, bathing, brushing teeth, toileting, eating). Sequences of development and the ages at which these skills are acquired by children without disabilities is contained in most developmen-

Table 13.3. Examples of communication responses important for independence, their critical functions, and suggestions for achieving functionally equivalent responses

Communication response	Critical functions	Functional equivalents
Cry or smile	Request/maintain attention of others Greet others Express feelings and emotions Terminate situations	Visual or gestural signal for attention or greeting or to indicate feelings Eye contact to maintain attention of others Touch or hug to express emotion Use of a switch attached to light or call device
Babble	Experiment with or practice elements of speech, language, and oral-motor skills Request/maintain attention of others	Eye contact to maintain attention of others Gestural/physical turn taking during social play Use of switch attached to light or call device
Talk with single words, phrases, or sentences	Practice elements of speech, language, and oral-motor skills Request/maintain attention of others Send specific messages Fulfill needs and desires Express feelings and emotions Engage in social and conversational interactions	Approximations of words, phrases, or sentences Use of gestures, symbols, and/or signs Visual or gestural signal to gain attention or indicate feelings Eye contact to maintain the attention of others "Yes" signaled with head nod when focus of interest/desired object or event is named Activation of switch to indicate words, drawings, pictures, or symbols on a communication board

tal assessment scales such as the *Assessment, Evaluation, and Programming System (AEPS®) for Infants and Children* (Bricker, 2002) and *The Carolina Curriculum for Infants and Toddlers with Special Needs* (3rd ed.) (Johnson-Martin, Attermeier, & Hacker, 2004). This information is useful in determining where to begin instruction and provides information on the age appropriateness of skills.

Many self-help skills are taught using task analysis and the assistance and encouragement procedures described in Chapter 6. For example, in teaching a toddler to wash her hands, a task analysis assessment is first conducted. The steps of the task are delineated as follows:

1. Turn on cold water faucet
2. Wet hands
3. Pick up soap
4. Lather palms

5. Replace soap

6. Lather back of hands

7. Rinse hands

8. Turn water off

9. Pick up towel

10. Dry hands

11. Replace towel

The toddler is helped to wash her hands, and her performance on each step is assessed. If she is unable to perform a step, prompting and motivation procedures are provided to identify teaching strategies that might be included in the instructional plan. The task analysis assessment also helps the teacher or infant specialist determine if the task has unnecessary steps that can be eliminated or combined with others, or if steps are too broad and additional, smaller steps are needed. Following the task analysis assessment, the instructional plan is formulated with the task analysis included (revised according to the assessment results). Prompting and motivation procedures are specified for each step.

If a self-help goal is too difficult, or if it requires participation beyond the child's current abilities, a *partial participation task analysis* may be developed (Snell, 1987). In a partial participation task analysis, steps within the child's capabilities that enable him to participate *meaningfully* are delineated. For example, Snell (1987) described a partial participation task analysis for toothbrushing. The child's participation included opening his mouth for the teacher to brush one quadrant of his teeth, and swallowing a drink of water after each quadrant had been brushed. A child holding his mouth open and swallowing are important steps in assisted toothbrushing that make the task of the adult much easier. Figure 13.4 illustrates an instructional plan for hand washing that includes a partial participation task analysis.

Toileting and feeding are each a complex set of self-help skills that are critical to independence. Therapeutic and specialized instructional procedures for facilitating these skills are drawn from the fields of nursing, psychology, occupational therapy, speech therapy, and physical therapy and are presented here.

Toileting

Toileting comprises several skills: recognizing the need, getting to the bathroom, lowering and raising clothing, getting on and off the toilet, sitting and voiding, wiping, flushing, and washing and drying hands. Among children without disabilities, toileting is typically achieved between 24 and 30 months of age. Toileting is not usually learned earlier than this because the following entry requirements seem to be essential (Farlow & Snell, 2006):

1. The child's schedule of urination and bowel movements occur on a predictable schedule.

	Date begun: 6/6/05
Child: Todd	Date completed:
Objective: Assisted hand washing	Interventionist(s): Selina and Mike

Conditions: Given a request to wash his hands

Response: Todd will assist in washing and drying his hands.

Criterion: 5 consecutive times

Intervention Context	Prompting/Facilitation Techniques	Consequences
Setting(s): At preschool, before lunch At home, before dinner Routine(s)/Activity(ies): 1. Holds one hand up and keeps hand open with fingers apart (adult washes hand with washcloth) 2. Holds other hand up and keeps fingers apart (adult washes hand with washcloth) 3. Holds both hands out with fingers apart (adult dries both hands with towel)	Positioning and Handling; Special Equipment/Materials, Environmental Modifications: Position Todd in his feeder seat. Prompting/Facilitation: Tap hand(s) and say, "Let's wash (or dry) your hand(s)."	Reinforcement: Smile and talk to Todd the entire time he is holding his hand(s) open. Corrections: Shake arm(s) to relax tone. Rub back of hand(s) and gently assist Todd to open his fingers.

Figure 13.4.   Partial participation intervention plan for self-help skill

2. The child remains dry for 1 to 2 hours on a fairly consistent schedule from day to day.
3. The child is at least 2 years old.

Also note that daytime toileting is typically learned before nighttime toileting.

While the child is learning the prerequisites, toileting needs are most easily managed through *timed toileting* (also known as *toilet regulation*). Timed toileting is placing the child on the toilet for a few minutes (not more than 10 minutes) at the times she usually eliminates. If the child uses the toilet, reinforcement is provided. If the child does not eliminate, she is removed from the toilet without any consequences. Timed toileting helps the child learn why and when the toilet is used, and it eases the caretaking task, although accidents may still occur. Timed toileting may also be an appropriate goal for a young child with physical disabilities affecting mobility or fine motor skills that interfere with independence.

Teach children with mild disabilities who are delayed in toileting to recognize the need to use the toilet and to void in it by following a procedure similar to timed toileting. Keep a record of the times the child is dry and wet by checking her diapers frequently (every half hour). Ask her if she needs to use the toilet 5 to 10 minutes before she usually voids. If the child says yes, place her on the toilet for about 5 minutes. Praise her if she eliminates in the toilet; comment that she should try later if she did not use the toilet. Most children with mild delays will learn toileting with this simple procedure.

For children with more severe disabilities, toileting is usually taught by increasing the intake of liquids so that they need to use the toilet more often. This increases the number of teaching opportunities. The toilet-training approach that popularized this procedure is called the *rapid method* and is described in the paperback *Toilet Training in Less than a Day* (Azrin & Foxx, 1974).

Medical clearance should be obtained prior to implementing toilet-training procedures that involve increased fluid intake. Care should be taken not to exceed typical daily water allowances: approximately one to four cups per day for children weighing between 4 and 22 lbs, and approximately four to seven cups per day for children between 22 and 88 lbs (Thompson & Hanson, 1983). A substantial increase in fluids can cause overhydration. Symptoms include nausea, vomiting, muscle twitching, seizures, and coma. Some children have medical conditions for which increased fluid intake is contraindicated (e.g., hypertension or problems of the heart, liver, or kidneys). Fluid intake procedures should *never* be used with children who have epilepsy, hydrocephaly, or a prior spinal injury.

Bedwetting (nocturnal enuresis) is a common among young children. Children are ready to begin nighttime toilet training when they are successful through most of the day with daytime toileting. There are three major types of intervention strategies for nighttime toilet training. The simplest procedure requires that no fluids are provided 1½ to 2 hours before bedtime. Awaken the child a few minutes before the times that he typically voids (most children will only need to use the toilet once during the night) and have him sit on the toilet for 5 minutes. Praise him for a dry bed and for eliminating in the toilet. If his bed is wet, change it without comment. Provide enthusiastic reinforcement in the morning if the child kept his bed dry. Gradually delay the wake-up (10 minute periods) to require that the child stay dry for increasingly longer periods of time.

The second procedure to eliminate nighttime bedwetting uses a *signaling device* placed under the bed sheet that sounds an alarm when the bed is wet. This procedure is most appropriate for children who are at least 5 years of age. When the alarm sounds, awaken the child and help him practice toileting skills (going to the bathroom and using the toilet, changing pajamas and bedding). Provide praise when the child sleeps through the night without wetting the bed.

The third procedure is a rapid bedtime method (Azrin, Sneed, & Foxx, 1973, 1974), much like the daytime rapid training method. The procedure includes increased fluids, use of a signaling device on the bed, hourly checks, toileting practice, and praise for dry bed and eliminating in the toilet. It is not necessary to implement the procedure throughout the entire night; it has been proven effective when used from bedtime until 1 a.m. (Azrin & Besalel, 1979).

Mealtime Skills

Eating and drinking involve a complex set of motor and oral-motor skills. The typical sequence of these skills is described in Table 13.4, which can be used as a guide for determining developmentally appropriate mealtime goals. For infants and young children with mild disabilities, mealtime skills are taught using task analysis and direct instruction described in Chapter 6. For example, drinking from a cup may be task analyzed as follows:

1. Grasp cup
2. Lift cup to mouth
3. Drink a few swallows
4. Return cup to table
5. Release cup

Backwards chaining may be used to teach the task analysis. For instance, assist the child to perform the first four steps, and verbally prompt him to release the cup when it touches the table (the fifth step). When the child is successful with the fifth step, teach the fourth and fifth steps together. As each new combination of steps is learned, add another step until the entire set of steps is acquired. Figure 13.5 is an example of a systematic instructional plan using backwards chaining. It also includes the use of adaptive feeding equipment to assist the child in acquiring independence. Another direct instruction procedure frequently used with self-feeding skills is hand-over-hand assistance. The adult lightly holds the child's hand and assists as necessary (e.g., to hold a spoon, to pick up a cracker).

For young children with severe disabilities, special feeding techniques may be necessary. Occupational, physical, and sometimes speech therapists are the professionals on the early intervention or special education team who collaborate with families to address mealtime concerns. Mealtime intervention plans for young children with severe disabilities may include therapeutic positioning, adaptive equipment, prefeeding techniques, therapeutic feeding techniques, and systematic instruction. The purpose of therapeutic positioning for feeding, eating, and drinking is to make muscle tone typical, inhibit atypical reflexes, and facilitate typical patterns of movement (including oral-motor patterns).

Several goals are particularly critical when positioning a young child for mealtimes. First, the child should be seated and as upright as possible (unless the child is still fed from a bottle or breast). The child's body should be symmetrical and aligned. Usually symmetry and alignment will inhibit atypical postural and tonal patterns. An exception to this may be positioning the child

Table 13.4. Typical development of eating and drinking skills

Age	Skill
Birth	Sucking and swallowing
	Incomplete lip closure
	Unable to release nipple
4 weeks	Opens mouth, waiting for food
	Better lip closure
	Active lip movement when sucking
	Takes cereal from spoon
6 weeks	Pureed fruit from spoon
3 months	Anticipates feeding
4 months	Recognizes bottle, mouth ready for nipple
	Cup feeding may be introduced—very messy but enjoys process
	More control and movement of tongue is handled by child—not by reflexes
	Appetite is more erratic
	Will not consume three full feedings
	Tongue thrust seen more with cup feeding than spoon feeding
5 months	Mouth opens ready for spoon
	Uses hands to draw bottle to mouth but releases when nipple is inserted
	Tongue reversal after spoon removed, ejecting food involuntarily
5 ½ months	Good lip closure
	Overhand grasp with both hands to feed self with cup
6 months	Good control with lips and tongue
	Beginning definite chewing motion by gumming food
7 months	Spoon fed chunky foods
	Feeds self soft foods (banana, vegetables, and so forth)
	Drooling noticed with mouth activity
	Reaches for food with head
8 months	Uses two hands on cup—messy
	Holds own bottle
	Picks up food with thumb and forefinger
	Finger feeds most of food
	Chokes easily when drinking from cup
9 months	Grows impatient when watching meal preparation
	Enjoys chewing
	Likes to finger feed self—messy
	Appetite finicky
10 months	Lateral movement of jaw
	Grasps and brings bottle to mouth
	Food is to be felt, tasted, smeared, and dropped on floor
	Cup feeding still messy—may want to play with it
11 months	Objects if mother tries to help complete feeding
	Can use cup by self
12 months	More choosy about food
	Independent about finishing meal—may dump remaining food on floor
	Lunch is least motivating meal
15 months	Holds cup with fingers—many spills
	Grasps spoon—poor manipulation
	Spoon inverted before insertion
	Shows definite preference for certain foods

Table 13.4.   *(continued)*

Age	Skill
18 months	Drinks from cup well
	Hands empty cup or dish to mother; if she doesn't see—child will drop item
	Chews meat well
	Better control with spoon
21 months	Handles cup well
	Very regimented in eating—wants everything on a routine schedule and presented same way each time
2 years	Can handle small glass with one hand, partially filled
	Moderate spillage from spoon
	Refuses previous favorite food
	Inserts food into mouth without turning over spoon
	Food preference may stem from taste, consistency, or just color
3 years	Minimum spilling from spoon
	Dawdles at mealtime
	Likes to spear food with fork
4 years	Sets table well
	Likes to serve self
	Washes and dries own face and hands
5 years	Appetite may increase, prefers simple food
	Beginning to use knife to spread
	Talkative during meals
	Doesn't always finish meals by self—may need assistance; often asks for help
6 years	Very active; cannot sit still
	Asks for more food than can consume
	Enjoys snacks more than mealtime
	Spills with milk—common at this age
	Breakfast may be most difficult meal
	Not interested in dessert
	May return to finger feeding
7 years	Appetite is less for girls; boys may have tremendous appetite
	May eat formerly disliked dishes
	Interested in desserts
	Use of napkin is spotty
8 years	Girls hold fork in adult fashion; boys hold fork pronated
	Starting to cut with knife
	Shovels food into mouth
	Asks for seconds, even thirds
9 years	Appetite under better control
	Likes to help prepare meals
	Still has difficulty controlling and knowing what to do with napkin
	Difficulty in cutting food to appropriate size, tends to be too big
11 years	Has satisfied feeling after meals
12 years	Bottomless pit—eating constantly
13 years	Appetite more stable
14 years	More like adult balance

From Copeland, M., Ford, L., & Solon, N. (1976). *Occupational therapy for mentally retarded children* (pp. 146–147). Baltimore: University Park Press; reprinted by permission. Data from Gesell and Amatruda (1947), Gesell and Ilg (1946), Ilg and Ames (1955), Rutherford (1971), Smart and Smart (1967), and Spock (1972).

	Date begun: *6/6/05*
Child: *Francie*	Date completed:
Objective: *Scooping*	Interventionist(s): *Mom*

Conditions: *At lunch, when given a plate of ground and sticky food*

Response: *Francie will scoop and eat her lunch.*

Criterion: *Without assistance for 10 minutes, 2 consecutive lunches*

Intervention Context	Prompting/Facilitation Techniques	Consequences
Setting(s): Lunchtime Routine(s)/Activity(ies): 1. *Grasp spoon handle.* 2. *Scoop food onto spoon.* 3. *Raise spoon to mouth.* 4. *Place spoon in mouth and remove food.* 5. *Return spoon to bowl or table.*	Positioning and Handling; Special Equipment/Materials, Environmental Modifications: *Use plate with high rim and small plastic coated spoon.* Prompting/Facilitation: 1. *Point to spoon handle* 2. *(Wait 6 seconds.)* 3. *Model opening your mouth.* 4. *(Wait 6 seconds.)* *Backwards chain: Assist through steps not being taught; prompt and correct current step as noted in this plan.* *(Criterion is 2 consecutive corrects for adding previous step to intervention chain.)*	Reinforcement: *Provide a sip of juice.* Corrections: 1. *Physically assist Francie to grasp and lift spoon.* 2. *Assist Francie to start scooping.* 3. *Physically assist Francie to make correct response.*

Figure 13.5. Intervention plan for feeding skills using backward chaining and adaptive equipment.

with trunk rotation to facilitate relaxation and decrease hypertonicity. The head should be in a slightly forward position with a slight downward tilt for swallowing. Alignment, symmetry, and an upright posture are critical to typical swallowing, the coordination of breathing and swallowing, and preventing food or liquids from passing into the trachea or lungs (aspiration) or choking. Next, the child's feet should be flat on the floor or on a support to provide postural stability. Shoulders and arms should be relaxed and free to move, so that the young child can accomplish hand-to-mouth movements and participate in self-feeding. Occupational and physical therapists on the early intervention or special education team are involved in identifying optimal mealtime position(s) for an infant/young child with neuromotor disabilities.

Therapeutic feeding techniques are strategies to inhibit atypical oral-motor patterns and to facilitate typical oral-motor patterns. Positioning techniques described above are important components of therapeutic feeding techniques.

Prefeeding techniques include rubbing and stroking around and inside the mouth to decrease hypersensitivity, and stretching techniques to facilitate typical tone and movement of the facial muscles. There are also techniques to assist a child with eating and drinking skills such as jaw control, lip closure, tongue control, chewing, and swallowing. An occupational, physical, or speech therapist can recommend and demonstrate appropriate therapeutic prefeeding and feeding techniques.

Infants and young children who need extensive supports for eating and drinking are often at risk for choking. Choking occurs when food or some other object or material obstructs the child's airway. Signs of choking include sudden coughing, gagging, or high-pitched noisy breathing; holding the neck (making the *choking sign*); or bluish lips or skin (American Heart Association, 2004). If the child can cough loudly or speak, the airway is not completely blocked. If the child's breathing is a concern, dial 9-1-1 for emergency assistance. If the child's airway seems to be completely blocked, in addition to calling 9-1-1, administer the Heimlich maneuver (abdominal thrusts). If the Heimlich maneuver is ineffective and the child becomes unresponsive, cardiopulmonary resuscitation (CPR) must be provided (American Heart Association, 2004). Early interventionists and early childhood special educators should receive first aid and emergency care training annually so they can respond competently and quickly to choking and other emergencies that may arise.

For children who are unable to obtain adequate nutrition and hydration orally, feeding tubes (*gavage* feedings) may be used (Heller et al., 2000). A feeding tube is inserted through the abdominal wall (*gastrostomy*), nose (*nasogastric tube*), or mouth (*oralgastric tube*). Food is administered through a gravity method or pump method (kangaroo bag). In the gravity method, food is placed in a large syringe attached to the feeding tube. The syringe is elevated 4 to 5 inches above the child's abdomen if a gastrostomy is used, or 4 to 5 inches above the child's head if a nasogastric or oralgastric tube is used. The food passes slowly through the tube and into the abdomen. Water may be given through the tube after feeding. The pump method is identical to the gravity method, except an electric pump is used to move the food from the bag through the feeding tube. Nasogastric and gastrostomy tubes may be left in place and taped to the skin when not in use. Oralgastric tubes are usually inserted for each feeding and removed afterward.

The insertion of feeding tubes requires special training. Although parents are frequently trained by a nurse or physician to insert the tube, school districts may require that a licensed health care worker (physician or nurse) insert the tube. *Teachers and infant specialists should be aware that there are health concerns associated with feeding tubes.* There is a risk of infection, particularly at the site of a gastrostomy incision, and there is a risk of aspiration when nasogastric or oralgastric feeding tubes are used. Teachers and infant specialists who administer tube feedings should be certain that they receive appropriate training (Heller et al., 2000).

DESIGNING INSTRUCTIONAL PROGRAMS TO PROMOTE INDEPENDENCE

When designing instructional programs to promote independence, be certain that short-term objectives describe behaviors that can be accomplished within 3 or 4 months. In formulating the objectives to foster independence, remember the following pointers: 1) The performance conditions of the objective should be stated as *independent performance conditions*. If adult reminders or prompts do not typically precede the behavior, they should not be included in the conditions of the objective. 2) Whenever possible, the response specified in the objective should be stated as a *general case response*. 3) If the desired response is too difficult for the child to perform independently, consider teaching a *functionally equivalent response* or a response that requires *partial participation*. Another option is to provide *adaptations* or *environmental modifications* that make the task easier or provide assistance to the child. 4) State the criterion for the objective at a level that allows or results in independent performance. It may be necessary to observe others performing the skill to determine the accuracy, fluency, or other response characteristic that best represents the *independent performance criterion.*

Instructional Context

An instructional context that supports and facilitates independence should also be described in the instructional plan. The instructional context specifies where, when, and under what conditions instruction occurs. The following situational variables should be considered to promote independence:

- Conduct instruction in *natural settings* in which the skill would typically occur, and preferably in *more than one* natural setting. This will facilitate generalization.

- Use *naturally occurring routines and activities* as instructional situations, rather than set aside a particular time for instruction. Teaching during naturally occurring routines and activities will help the child recognize when the skill is needed and what purpose it serves.

- Construct *skill sequences* and conduct instruction with more than one skill at a time. Skill sequences teach relationships between behaviors.

- Use EMT procedures and identify child responses that signal the *occasion for instruction*. Using child-determined occasions for instruction is responsive to the interests of the child and provides meaningful and motivating situations for learning.

Contextual strategies to promote independence include environmental supports and instructional techniques that eliminate a child's over-reliance on an adult to accomplish her goals.

Prompting Techniques

It is also critical to select prompting techniques that encourage independence. The following considerations should be addressed:

1. Use *least intrusive procedures*; that is, procedures that do not interfere any more than necessary with the naturally occurring events or interactions. The more instruction interferes with the natural situation, the less likely the child is to generalize the response.

2. Select *naturalistic teaching procedures* such as EMT and time delay. These procedures help children respond independently to the natural prompts present in the environment.

3. Include *generalization techniques* such as sufficient exemplars, common stimuli, or mediation strategies among the prompting/facilitation techniques. In addition to naturalistic teaching procedures, instructional plans should include multiple approaches to facilitate generalization. Independence is greatly enhanced when responses are generalized.

4. If independent performance of the response seems too difficult for the child (the skill is complex, or the skill includes a physical response beyond the child's current abilities), develop *environmental prompts* or *modifications* to make independence a realistic goal. The environmental prompts or modifications may be permanent additions to the environment, or they may be faded as part of the instructional plan.

5. Use *prosthetic devices, special equipment, or therapeutic positioning and handling techniques* to facilitate independent responding when the child has physical or sensory disabilities. Sometimes these accommodations alone will result in independent responding.

6. Consider the use of *peer assistance* to help the child with special needs respond independent of adult assistance. Peer assistance is well-suited to group activities and free-play situations.

After prompting and facilitation strategies have been described, the instructional plan must indicate consequences appropriate to the child's response. There are two specific recommendations for promoting independence that apply to this section of the instructional plan.

First, develop *minimally intrusive* corrections; that is, use corrections that interfere as little as possible. As in the recommendations for prompting and facilitation techniques, the less noticeable the instruction, the more likely the child will generalize and perform the skill independently. Second, use *naturally occurring reinforcers and corrections* whenever possible. If children learn to recognize and use natural contingencies, they will rely less on instructional support and adult assistance. Pairing artificial consequences with natural ones, or exaggerating the natural ones, are simple ways to highlight natural consequences.

These recommendations summarize teaching strategies to consider in planning individualized instruction to promote independence. The examples of instructional plans throughout this chapter illustrate these recommendations. As emphasized in this chapter, independence is not a goal that we *hope* to achieve; it is a goal to actively address through effective intervention strategies.

SUMMARY

This chapter discussed independent skills for meaningful participation in natural settings. Instructional procedures should be least intrusive, naturalistic, incorporated into daily routines, and designed to facilitate generalization. When a child's age or disability limits the extent to which independence can be achieved, goals for functional independence may be appropriate. Functional independence is accomplished by teaching the child equivalent responses or by providing adaptive strategies. Equivalent responses are those that accomplish the same function or purpose of a target behavior. If a child is unable to perform a target behavior due to a disability or delay, it is sometimes possible to teach him the equivalent response. Adaptive strategies include functionally equivalent responses, as well as the use of adaptive equipment and materials. Although independence may seem very difficult for some children to accomplish, particularly if they have multiple or severe challenges, functional independence can almost always be achieved with a bit of creativity and problem solving.

•••••••••••••••••••• **STUDY QUESTIONS** ••••••••••••••••••••

1. Describe appropriate *independent* behavior for 1-, 3-, and 5-year-olds associated with playtime, mealtime, and bathtime.

2. Discuss specific strategies that can be incorporated into systematic instructional plans to help children achieve independence.

3. Define *critical function, functionally equivalent response,* and *functional independence.*

4. Describe how the following strategies can assist children to achieve functional independence: individualized participation, environmental prompts, learning centers, peer assistance, and prosthetic devices and adaptive equipment.

5. Discuss the effects of damage to the central nervous system on muscle tone, reflexes, postural reactions, and motor milestones.

6. What is the purpose of positioning and carrying techniques?

7. Compare and contrast static and dynamic positioning.

8. Identify and discuss three examples of functionally equivalent gross motor responses for children with physical disabilities.

9. Describe the relationship of fine motor development to gross motor development.

10. Identify and discuss three examples of functionally equivalent fine motor responses for children with fine motor needs.

11. Discuss the primary function of communication.

12. List and describe Dunst's five phases in the development of environmental control skills.

13. Describe how you might use the following strategies to help an infant acquire environmental control skills: enhance sensitivity, increase opportunities, structure predictable routines, augment input, and modify the environment.

14. Consider the example of a 4-year-old boy who is reliably using one-word line drawings on his communication board to make requests and to refuse/terminate something. Write

a set of three communication objectives illustrating how you could increase the complexity of this child's communication skills.

15. Identify and discuss three examples of functionally equivalent communication responses for children with communication needs.

16. Describe and contrast a task analysis and a partial participation task analysis.

17. What is the *rapid method* of toilet training? Discuss the pros and cons of teaching independent toileting through this method.

18. Discuss the relationship between physical skills (gross and fine motor) and mealtime skills.

19. Identify and describe the three types of feeding tubes.

14

Transitions

Linda McCormick

- Legal mandates related to transition

- Issues related to the transitions of early childhood: hospital to home, early intervention services to preschool, and preschool to kindergarten

- DEC recommended practices concerning transitions

- Strategies to facilitate successful transitions: hospital to home, early intervention services to preschool, and preschool to kindergarten

- The STEPS model

The concept of transition was popularized initially as a response to the need to facilitate movement of secondary students in special education from school into postschool environments (Wehman, Moon, & McCarthy, 1986; Will, 1984). It soon became evident that the concerns and processes associated with transition have far broader application than postsecondary adjustment. Every person's lifespan is a sequence of transitions or turning points. Transitions always involve change, and even positive transitions that represent achievement of desired goals are stressful because they are marked by greater than usual vulnerability. The stress inherent in transitions may not be avoidable but it can be minimized. The goal for service providers working with infants and young children and their families is to minimize the stress inherent in transitions.

Transition services in early childhood are for the purpose of ensuring that the child and family continue to receive maximum services despite changes within and across programs. Important transitions in the early life of a child with a disability include the move from a hospital to home, to an early intervention program, from infant/toddler services to preschool services, and finally, to elementary school.

Transitions may be horizontal or vertical (Kagan, 1992). Vertical transitions involve movement across environments within the same time frame. For example, a family may move from a hospital neonatal intensive care unit (NICU) to an early intervention program to an inclusive preschool program, and eventually to kindergarten with special education and related services support. Horizontal transitions involve movement across environments across time. For example, the child and family may be involved in multiple activities simultaneously with different support services and in different locations. The child may participate in an inclusive preschool program in the morning, followed by special therapy services in a separate classroom in the afternoon, and, later in the afternoon, child care in another environment.

The IDEA Amendments of 1997 (PL 105-17) addressed the issue of continuity of programs and the importance of a seamless system of services for infants and young children with disabilities and their families. They maintained a distinction between services for infants and toddlers (Part C) and services for preschoolers (Part B), and a distinction (in Part B) between services for preschoolers and those for school-age children. In all cases, transition is identified as an integral component of service delivery to ensure continuity of services and smooth movement between and among programs. Requirements for the age 3 transition plan include designation of a local lead agency, documentation of communication with the family's local education agency 90 days before the child's third birthday, and family involvement. Some states (e.g., Illinois) have state laws requiring transition planning long before that date.

The continuing concerns about transition are reflected in the 2004 IDEA Amendments. Recall from Chapters 1 and 3 that there were several changes in the most recent reauthorization that have relevance to transition. One is the requirement that the family's service coordinator (or another appropriate representative) from the early intervention program must be invited to participate in the IEP meeting when the child transitions to preschool (or kindergarten if the family has opted to continue early intervention services to age 5). Another is the requirement that the team consider the information/materials described in the IFSP when developing the IEP. These requirements are intended to facilitate smooth transition for the family and the child from Part C services to the Part B program.

Because there are no legal mandates for planning the transition from preschool to elementary-age programs, services for this transition vary enormously across states and across agencies and programs within a state. (Sometimes there is absolutely no transition planning and support for 5-year-olds.) After an overview of the important transitions for infants and young children with disabilities and their families, this chapter will consider strategies to make all of the important early childhood transitions as successful as possible.

IMPORTANT TRANSITIONS IN EARLY CHILDHOOD

As noted above, the early childhood period is a time of many transitions for infants and young children with disabilities and their families. Typical transitions are from the NICU to home, to a follow-up clinic, to public or private health care services, to an infant/toddler intervention program, to public or private child care, to preschool, and then to kindergarten.

Hospital to Home

Assuming responsibility for the day-to-day care of a newborn requires enormous adjustments in a family's routine. These adjustments are many times multiplied when the infant is at risk of, or already has, special health care needs. Families are most anxious and vulnerable to stress when the infant with established or biological risk comes home from the hospital. In the NICU the infant was cared for by highly skilled physicians, nurses, social workers, and other support staff. Families are overwhelmed by the need to deal with their infant's basic survival needs.

The concerns that parents face with this first transition include 1) understanding their infant's condition, 2) basic caregiving responsibilities, 3) self-esteem and confidence issues, and 4) decisions about services (Hanline & Deppe, 1990). First, the parents must cope with issues related to understanding their infant's condition (e.g., prematurity, sensory impairment, motor impairment). Their nervousness and apprehension surrounding these issues are compounded by their uncertainly about the survival and future development of their infant and by their feelings of shock, sadness, anger, grief, disappointment, and guilt. When the infant is discharged from the NICU, the parents feel that they have lost their primary emotional supports. They feel abandoned, alone, and isolated. They struggle to come to some understanding of the etiology of their infant's condition, a developmental prognosis for him, and the infant's chances for survival. The goals for early intervention personnel are to help parents 1) establish and maintain contacts with other families of infants with special needs, 2) locate and obtain respite care and child care services (if needed), and 3) locate community-based family support services.

Second, although parents eagerly anticipate the discharge of their infant from the NICU, they are anxious about the transition from the hospital to home. They have many misgivings about their ability to care for their infant, particularly when this is their first child. It is no wonder that parents feel apprehensive about providing for their infant's basic care needs. Many infants are still on a ventilator, gastrointestinal tube feeding, or an apnea monitor when they are discharged from the hospital. In addition, infants with special needs are often fussy and irritable. The parents are faced with assuming the day-to-day care of a very small infant who only days before was cared for by a team of highly skilled medical professionals.

The third concern that parents face has to do with self-esteem and confidence. A premature birth shatters any assumption of controlling the outcomes of pregnancy. The sense of having lost control is heightened during the infant's stay in the NICU because parents are not able to make decisions about the day-to-day care of their child. Understandably, they lose whatever confidence they might have had in themselves as caregivers. The early intervention (EI) service providers must understand and acknowledge the parents' need to regain some control of their lives by making decisions regarding their family and their child.

Finally, the parents must begin making decisions about how they want to participate in community-based support services. Although this may appear to be straightforward, it is not: the problem is more basic and more involved than locating and accessing services. This is the point at which the parents must "go public." They must come to terms with the possibility of developmental delay and the need to allow unfamiliar professionals to enter their lives. If an EI service provider has established a relationship with the family prior to the infant's discharge and supported the transition process, that person is in a good position to help the parents with these decisions.

Early Intervention Services to Preschool

Similar to the hospital-to-home transition, the transition from infant services to preschool involves many decisions about services. At this time many parents are facing especially stressful events related to their child's disabilities. From the initial stages of planning until the preschooler is actually enrolled and attending the new program or programs, this transition brings a whole new set of issues in addition to new roles and responsibilities. The most salient issues associated with this transition are continuity of services, adapting to change, and adjusting to new program expectations. These challenges are especially exigent for families from culturally and linguistically diverse groups. Some issues in relation to transition planning are unique to these families (Bruns & Fowler, 2001).

Preschool to Kindergarten

As noted above, federal and state legislation requires transition plans for children moving from Part C infant and toddler programs into Part B preschool programs, but there is no mandate for transition planning for children moving from preschool Part B programs into general kindergarten or first grade classrooms. This is unfortunate because this transition is a complex one for young children with special needs and their families. There are changes in classroom characteristics (e.g., higher child-to-staff ratios and more large-group instruction) and in teacher expectations (e.g., more autonomy and academic skill acquisition). Families must learn new rules and regulations and how to interact with new teachers, new service personnel, and new institutions.

STRATEGIES TO FACILITATE SUCCESSFUL TRANSITIONS

Transition strategies fall into two categories (with some overlap): those strategies involving communication and collaboration across agencies and programs, and those that specifically prepare the child and the family and the receiving program. The literature describes a consistent set of activities to facilitate communication and collaboration. These activities include 1) visitations across programs; 2) formalized policies and procedures negotiated among agencies; 3) joint training for families and staff; and 4) formalized systems for child referral, evaluation, and placement (Rous, Hemmeter, & Schuster, 1999). Research with the objective of understanding the expectations of teachers in receiving programs is discussed below. Transition planning focuses on preparing the child and the family and on identifying and implementing needed adaptations and supports in the receiving environment.

Hospital to Home

As noted above, the goals for early intervention personnel in the hospital to home transition are to help parents 1) establish and maintain contacts with other families of infants with special needs, 2) locate and obtain respite care and child care services (if needed), and 3) locate community-based family support services. The majority of families receive predischarge hospital training from the hospital NICU staff. This training focuses on the infant's special nutritional needs, operation of specific equipment, and proper positioning. At least one of the family's EI service providers (possibly the service coordinator) should participate in this training with the parents in the transition process.

To be most effective, training to prepare families for discharge should be provided shortly after the infant is admitted to the NICU (Hadden, 2000). Ideally there is considerable repetition because most parents will not recall information unless the same information is repeated often during the time their child is in the hospital. Similarly, they need many opportunities to practice the procedures that they will need to follow when they take the infant home (Sheikh, O'Brien, & McCluskey-Fawcett, 1993). Information should be provided in a verbal format and, whenever possible, parents should be given videotapes and audiotapes as well as books and pamphlets that clearly describe their child's condition and the procedures they will need to implement at home.

Many hospitals use a discharge informational/planning form to ease the hospital-to-home transition (Bruder & Walker, 1990; Hadden, 2000; Meck, Fowler, Chaflin, & Rasmussen, 1995). This form is markedly different from the traditional NICU nursing discharge summaries that tend to be more like a progress report in narrative format with language and symbols that are difficult for nonmedical professionals to interpret. The purpose of the informational/planning form is to encourage and support the sharing of information and needs between families and professionals. It describes the infant's current and future care needs in detail, with space provided for the parents to identify areas of need and topics they would like to have addressed. In addition to information about their infant's condition and care, parents want specific information about a range of developmental issues (e.g., rate of developmental milestones) as well as expectations for the future.

Once the infant is home, the focus of EI support services shifts to 1) helping the parents implement the procedures recommended by the NICU and other medical personnel, 2) answering questions not answered prior to discharge, 3) assisting parents to understand and respond to the infant's social and communication cues, 4) monitoring the infant's developmental progress, and 5) ensuring that the infant's health care needs are met. Many infants continue to require care from medical professionals. The EI care coordinator assists collaboration between the family, the NICU staff, and community health care providers.

What is most helpful during this entire process is support from other families. Only parents who have experienced the same medical issues can really understand what a family is going through during this period. Parent groups are an ideal response. Parents in parent groups can share their knowledge about life with a preterm infant, community services, and disability and offer much-needed reassurances. A number of national and Internet parent-to-parent groups are also available to parents of premature infants (c.f., Parents of Premature Babies, Inc. [Preemie-L]). Parents grow in confidence as they meet their family's changing needs and those of their child.

Early Intervention Program to Preschool

Sensitivity to the needs and fears of the family, careful initial planning, and continued collaboration can avoid interruptions and duplications of services when the child and family transition from early intervention services to preschool. The planning team comprises appropriate EI providers and preschool service providers as well as the family. Specific guidelines for this planning is provided in the DEC Recommended Practices (Bruder & Chandler, 1993; Odom

& McLean, 1996; Sandall, Hemmeter, Smith, & McLean, 2005). The indicators of best practices in the area of transition provided in that document were developed by experts and validated by service providers, parents, administrators, higher education faculty, and researchers.

Two thrusts are evident in the DEC recommended practices: *the importance of family involvement* and *the importance of ongoing evaluation.* The following is a subset of the recommendations:

- Program providers, administrators, and families should allow adequate time for planning and preparation.
- Families must be given information about the components and steps in the transition process, their role in the transition process, and the future service options for their child and family.
- Families must have opportunities to visit potential programs and talk to other families as well as service providers about possible program options.
- EI service providers should be trained to address issues related to transition and how to assist the families in the process.
- EI service providers should be familiar with the tasks, time lines, roles, responsibilities, and related procedures as designated on the interagency transition agreement.
- EI service providers should be familiar with service options and resources within the community and able to make appropriate referrals.
- EI service providers and early childhood education (ECE) and early childhood special education (ECSE) service providers should visit one another's programs and share observations in the transition planning process.
- All involved service providers and family members should determine the transition skills that the child exhibits and those that he will need to learn for the next environment or receiving program.
- EI service providers and family members should facilitate and support acquisition of needed transition skills and address areas of potential difficulties.

The three broad phases of transition are preparation, implementation, and follow-up/evaluation. Each phase has a primary focus on the child and the family.

Preparing the Child for Transition Fowler and Titus (1993) identified four areas that impede the participation of many children when they transition from a home-based EI program to a center-based preschool program. These four areas are 1) separating from parents and home; 2) learning to play with peers and enter a group; 3) following directions, routines, and rules; and 4) having basic safety skills. Teaching and practicing the skills that are expected in the new setting should begin long before transition to the new placement actually occurs. EI service providers and family members should visit the new program to observe daily schedules and activities and identify the social and self-help skills that facilitate participation in daily routines. Also on these visits, family members and service providers in the two programs can discuss program activities and how to best address the differences in expectations between programs. The ecological assessment process described in Chapter 5 can be used to identify expectations of the receiving program, skills that the child will need to participate in daily activities and routines, and needed adaptations and supports. The latter—planning adaptations and supports—is one of the responsibilities of the receiving program.

Preparing the Family for Transition Proactive planning is also advocated for the family (Lazzari & Kilgo, 1989). Most important, parents should be fully informed of their legal rights and responsibilities, and they should have information regarding the preschool classrooms in their district, as well as related services, IEP development, child development expectations, preschool curriculum, and community services (Hanline, 1988). They need to know that professionals recognize and are addressing the differences in service delivery, and they need to be part of the planning process. The inconsistencies in expectations, procedures, and activities between the EI services and the preschool program are stressful for families, especially those from culturally and linguistically diverse groups.

Including parents as partners in the process of identifying skills that the child will need for the next environment and the exchange of information between service providers is critical. Some specific topics for the initial transition planning meetings include 1) a projected date for the transition; 2) the decisions to be made, when they should be made, and who will make them; 3) the family's role in the process; 4) eligibility variables; 5) where to get information about available placement options; and 6) how the child can be prepared for the changes.

Parent preparation workshops are an effective way to prepare families for transition (Noonan & Ratokalau, 1992). Workshops can assist parents to develop the skills needed for the early intervention to preschool transition and for future transitions. Once parents have been provided with education and information and their service-related needs have been identified, the focus shifts to activities (e.g., referrals, visits to possible programs) to meet their identified needs.

Preparing the Receiving Program It is not enough to prepare the child and the family, receiving program staff must also be prepared to facilitate and support the child with disabilities and the family. As noted above, the ecological assessment process described in Chapter 5 can be used to identify needed adaptations and supports in the preschool program.

Both DEC and NAEYC guidelines for transition specifically highlight the importance of communication and cooperation among staff of the sending and receiving programs. It is important for program staff to assess family concerns, preferences, and expectations of the transition process, particularly where culturally and linguistically diverse groups are concerned. The lack of continuity between home and school values and expectations is often confusing to the families, resulting in less involvement and, ultimately, increased stress.

Preschool to Kindergarten

As with other transitions, collaboration and coordination among service providers and administrators is essential for a smooth transition from preschool to kindergarten. Many of the most effective transition practices such as home visits require service providers to commit time outside of general work hours. This undoubtedly explains the finding that practices that require less time commitment are more common. A national survey of kindergarten teachers found that the most frequently used transition practices were sending letters to parents after school started and arranging visits to first grade classrooms (LaParo, Pianta, & Cox, 2000). The least frequently reported transition practices were home visits and meetings to discuss the kindergarten to first grade transition. Generally speaking, teachers did not engage in a large number of unique transition activities for children with special needs. They typically used the same transition practices for children with and without special needs. The transition practices used by kindergarten teachers who had children with special needs in their classes were most often practices that could be used before school started in the fall or those that involved some form of community coordination.

Preparing Children for Kindergarten The earliest work in planning for the transition of children with disabilities from preschool to kindergarten began in the early 1980s with future environment surveys. Vincent et al. (1980) used the term "survival skills" for the list of 84 behaviors generated by her survey of kindergarten teachers. The purpose of identifying and teaching the skills expected in kindergarten settings was to facilitate referral to and maintenance in general education kindergarten.

Several techniques for assessing future environments are evident in the early transition literature: teacher checklists, interviews, and direct observation. For example, McCormick and Kawate (1982) asked kindergarten and first-grade teachers in Hawaii to rate on a checklist the importance of the skills that were generated in the earlier study by Vincent et al. (1980). Items rated as "very important" or "absolutely essential" included the following:

- Working independently (5 items)
- Participating with the group (6 items)
- Following routines (6 items)
- Practicing self-help skills (e.g., taking care of toileting needs) (4 items)
- Following directions (3 items)
- Practicing social/play skills (5 items)
- Communicating functionally (2 items).

McCormick and Kawate compared this list with items on the nine traditional assessment instruments used at that time to determine the extent to which those instruments assessed the behaviors that were of concern to teachers. The results of this comparison indicated that very few of the behaviors that teachers considered important to participation in their classrooms were being assessed by traditional assessment procedures.

Some years later, Hains, Fowler, Schwartz, Kottwitz, and Rosenkoetter (1989) conducted a similar study. They showed kindergarten teachers a list of 153 skills and asked them to indicate the behaviors they considered important for children entering kindergarten. Very few of the skills on their lists (4%) were marked as important. However, observations conducted on the first day of school revealed that teachers expected many more skills than they identified, especially in the areas of following directions, self-help, and social behaviors. Other research in the 1990s that surveyed both preschool and kindergarten teachers confirmed the finding that teachers generally do not consider skills related to academic readiness as critical as those related to independence and participation (Hemmeter & Rous, 1997; Johnson, Gallagher, Cook, & Wong, 1995). There is consensus as to the importance of classroom skills related to independence such as following directions, classroom rules, and routines and participating in group activities.

Two sets of researchers reported their findings from programs that specifically taught survival skills to young children with disabilities (Carta, Atwater, Schwartz, & Miller, 1990; Rule, Fiechtl, & Innocenti, 1990). Both conducted assessments of the behavioral requirements of the kindergarten programs in their communities. Rule and colleagues identified skills in nine areas. They then developed a curriculum and taught the skills to 18 preschool children with disabilities in two child care centers.

In 1995, Le Ager and Shapiro extended this line of research by applying a strategy called template matching to conduct systematic analysis and comparison of child behaviors and environmental variables across settings (Cone, 1987; Hoier, McConnell, & Palley, 1987). In template matching, a "behavioral profile" is developed that includes information about environmental variables in the sending and receiving of educational settings and the performance of persons within those environments. The ecological assessment process described in Chapter 5 is a template-matching approach.

In the Le Ager and Shapiro study, templates were developed to evaluate the differences between the sending (preschool) and the receiving (kindergarten) environments. Activities and teacher behaviors in the preschool environment were altered to align with activities and teacher behaviors in the kindergarten environment. This intervention was effective. At follow-up, kindergarten children who had been involved in the template-matching intervention exhibited fewer competing behaviors and participated more independently in the kindergarten setting than peers in a control group.

The information gained by observing kindergarten classrooms can be extremely helpful in identifying the similarities and differences of the academic, social, and behavioral requirements between those classrooms and preschool settings. However, there is an important caveat that must be set forth in which skills and expectations for the next environment are concerned. These skills must not *at any time* be viewed as prerequisites for placement in the general education setting. The goals and objectives generated by observations of the next environment and ecological assessment provide an essential step in preparing children for transition *and* for identifying initial intervention targets. *The lack of these skills should never, under any circumstances, be used to argue that a child is not ready for transition to a general education setting.*

The STEPS Model   STEPS (Sequenced Transition to Education in the Public Schools) began as a Handicapped Children's Early Education Program (HCEEP) model demonstration program (1984–1987). Subsequently, several outreach grants have continued and expanded the model (Rous et al., 1999). The purpose of STEPS is to formalize a systematic process to facilitate the transition of children from one program or agency to another. This is accomplished by giving administrators, staff, and families the skills to expedite the transition process. There are four major components of the STEPS model being implemented at state and local levels. These include procedures to 1) create an administrative structure that will promote interagency coordination and policy development, 2) increase the ability of families to be actively and effectively involved in the transition process, 3) assist preparation of the child for a new program, and 4) prepare staff to facilitate the transition process.

More specifically, STEPS provides training and technical assistance to state and local personnel in the following areas:

- Developing a communitywide transition system
- Holding effective team meetings
- Developing leadership skills
- Ensuring effective interagency collaboration
- Assessing children's social, behavioral, and functional skills and planning for appropriate intervention
- Ensuring family involvement
- Ensuring effective facilitation and training (adult learning)

STEPS is a model that has demonstrated effectiveness in promoting interagency collaboration at state and local levels. The focus of this collaboration is facilitating transition of young children with special needs and their families from infant/toddler programs to preschool programs and from preschool programs to kindergarten.

SUMMARY

The many transitions in infancy and early childhood—from hospital to home, from early intervention services to preschool, and from preschool to kindergarten—present challenges to children, families, service providers, and programs. The needs and preferences of families from culturally and linguistically diverse groups are especially challenging. This chapter has described the types of early childhood special education transitions and the special challenges inherent in each. A major emphasis has been the importance of communication between service providers in both sending and receiving programs and parents of children with disabilities.

•••••••••••••••••••••••• **STUDY QUESTIONS** ••••••••••••••••••••••

1. Discuss the concept of transition.

2. Contrast the IDEA Part B and Part C provisions related to transition.

3. Discuss parental feelings and concerns when they transition from the hospital to home with an infant with disabilities.

4. Discuss the issues in the transition from early intervention services to preschool and from preschool to kindergarten.

5. What are the goals for service providers in the hospital to home transition?

6. Discuss strategies for preparing parents for the hospital to home transition and support services once the infant is at home.

7. Summarize the DEC Recommended Practices for transition.

8. Describe the three broad phases of transition from early intervention programs to preschool.

9. Describe the preparation of children for kindergarten.

10. What is the STEPS model?

References

Alberto, P.A., & Troutman, A.C. (2002). *Applied behavior analysis for teachers* (6th ed.). Upper Saddle River, NJ: Pearson Education.

Allen, B., & Boykin, A. (1992). African-American children and the educational process: Alleviating cultural discontinuity through prescriptive pedagogy. *School Psychology Review, 21,* 586–596.

Als, H., Lester, B.M., & Brazelton, T.B. (1979). Dynamics of the behavioral organization of the premature infant. In T.M. Field, A.M. Sostek, S. Goldberg, & H.H. Shuman (Eds.), *Infants born at risk* (pp. 173–192). New York: Spectrum.

American Heart Association (n.d.). *Relief of choking in children.* Retrieved November 15, 2004, from http://www.americanheart.org/presenter.jhtml?identifier=3025002

Americans with Disabilities Act (ADA) of 1990, PL 101-336, 42 U.S.C. 12101 *et seq.*

Anderson, L.W. (1976). An empirical investigation of individual differences in time to learn. *Journal of Educational Psychology, 68,* 226–233.

Anderson, S.R., & Spradlin, J.E. (1980). The generalized effects of productive labeling training involving common object classes. *Journal of the Association for the Severely Handicapped, 5,* 143–157.

Asian American Heritage (1995). *A resource guide for teachers, grades k-.* New York: New York City Board of Education, Brooklyn, Office of Multicultural Education.

Au, K. (1980). Participation structures in a reading lesson with Hawaiian children: Finding a culturally appropriate instructional event. *Anthropology and Education Quarterly, 11,* 91–115.

Au, K., & Mason, J. (1981–82). Social organizational factors in learning to read: The balance of rights hypothesis. *Reading Research Quarterly, 17,* 115–152.

Ault, M.J., Gast, D.L., & Wolery, M. (1988). Comparison of progressive and constant time delay procedures in teaching community sign word reading. *American Journal of Mental Retardation, 93*(1), 44–56.

Ayabe, H.I., & Santos, S. (1972). Conceptual tempo and the Oriental American. *Journal of Psychology, 81,* 121–123.

Azrin, N.H., & Besalel, V.A. (1979). *A parent's guide to bedwetting control: A step-by-step method.* New York: Simon & Schuster.

Azrin, N.H., & Foxx, R.M. (1971). A rapid method of toilet training the institutionalized retarded. *Journal of Applied Behavior Analysis, 4,* 89–99

Azrin, N.H., & Foxx, R.M. (1974). *Toilet training in less than a day.* New York: Simon & Schuster.

Azrin, N.H., Sneed, T.J., & Foxx, R.M. (1973). Dry-bed: A rapid method of eliminating bedwetting (enuresis) of the retarded. *Behavior Research and Therapy, 11*, 427–434.

Azrin, N.H., Sneed, T.J., & Foxx, R.M. (1974). Dry-bed training: Rapid elimination of childhood enuresis. *Behavior Research and Therapy, 12*, 147–156.

Baer, D.M. (1970). An age-irrelevant concept of development. *Merrill-Palmer Quarterly, 16*, 238–245.

Bailey, D.B., Jens, K.G., & Johnson, N. (1983). Curricula for handicapped infants. In S.G. Garwood & R.R. Fewell (Eds.), *Educating handicapped infants: Issues in development and intervention* (pp. 387–415). Rockville, MD: Aspen.

Bailey, D.B., & McWilliam, R.A.(1990. Normalizing early intervention. *Topics in Early Childhood Special Education, 10*,(2), 33–47.

Bailey, D.B., & Simeonsson, R.J. (1990). *Family needs survey.* Chapel Hill, NC: University of North Carolina, Frank Porter Graham Child Development Center.

Bambara, L.M., & Warren, S.F. (1993). Massed trials revisited: Appropriate applications in functional skill training. In R.A. Gable & S.F. Warren (Eds.), *Strategies for teaching students with mild to severe mental retardation* (pp. 165–190). Baltimore: Paul H. Brookes Publishing Co.

Bambara, L.M., Warren, S.F., & Komisar, S. (1988). The individualized curriculum sequencing model: Effects on skill acquisition and generalization. *The Journal of the Association for Persons with Severe Handicaps, 13*, 8–19.

Banks, J.A. (1997a). Multicultural education: Characteristics and goals. In J.A. Banks & C.A. McGee Banks (Eds.), *Multicultural education: Issues and perspectives* (3rd ed., pp. 3–31). Needham Heights, MA: Allyn & Bacon.

Banks, J.A. (1997b). *Teaching strategies for ethnic studies* (6th ed.). Needham Heights, MA: Allyn & Bacon.

Banks, J.A., & Banks, C.A.M. (1997). *Multicultural education: Issues and perspectives.* Boston: Allyn & Bacon.

Banks, R.A., Santos, R.M., & Roof, V. (2003). Sensitive family information gathering. *Young Exceptional Children, 6*(2), 11–20.

Barker, R.G. (1968). *Ecological psychology.* Stanford, CA: Stanford University Press.

Barker, R.G., & Gump, P.V. (1964). *Big school, small school.* Stanford, CA: Stanford University Press.

Barrera, I. (1993). Effective and appropriate instruction for all children: The challenge of cultural/linguistic diversity and young children with special needs. *Topics in Early Childhood Special Education, 13*, 461–487.

Barrera, I. (1996). Thoughts on the assessment of young children whose sociocultural background is unfamiliar to the assessor. In S.J. Meisels & E. Fenichel (Eds.), *New visions for the developmental assessment of infants and young children* (pp. 69–84). Washington, DC: ZERO TO THREE: National Center for Infants, Toddlers, and Families.

Barrera, I. (2000). Honoring differences: Essential features of appropriate ECSE services for young children from diverse sociocultural environments. *Young Exceptional Children, 3*(4), 17–24.

Barsch, R.H. (1971). The processing mode hierarchy as a potential deterrent to cognitive efficiency. In J. Hellmuth (Ed.). *Cognitive studies: Deficits in cognition.* New York: Bruner/Mazel.

Bateman, B. (1992). *Writing measurable IEP goals and objectives.* Verona, WI: Attainment Company, Inc.

Bateman, B.D., & Linden, M.A. (1998). *Better IEPs: How to develop legally correct and educationally useful programs* (3rd ed.). Longmont, CO: Sopris West.

Baumgart, D., Brown, L., Pumpian, I., Nisbet, J., Ford, A., & Sweet, M., et al. (1982). The principal of partial participation and individualized adaptations in educational programs for severely handicapped students. *Journal of the Association for Persons with Severe Handicaps, 7*(2), 17–27.

Becker, W., Engelmann, S., & Thomas, D. (1975). *Teaching 2: Cognitive learning and Instruction.* Chicago: Science Research Associates.

Benedict, R. (1934). *Patterns of culture.* Boston: Houghton Mifflin Co.

Bereiter, C., & Engelmann, S. (1966). *Teaching disadvantaged children in the preschool.* Englewood Cliffs, NJ: Prentice-Hall.

Beukelman, D.R., & Mirenda, P. (1992). *Augmentative and alternative communication management of severe communication disorders in children and adults.* Baltimore: Paul H. Brookes Publishing Co.

Bijou, S.W., Peterson, R.F., & Ault, M.H. (1968). A method to integrate descriptive and experimental field studies at the level of data and empirical concepts. *Journal of Applied Behavior Analysis, 1,* 175–191.

Bloom, B. (1964). *Stability and change in human characteristics.* New York: Wiley.

Bly, L. (1983). *The components of normal movement during the first year of life and abnormal motor development.* Chicago: Neurodevelopmental Treatment Association.

Bondy, A.S., & Frost, L.A. (1993). Mands across the water: A report on the application of the picture exchange communication system in Peru. *The Behavior Analyst, 16,* 123–128.

Bondy, A., & Frost, L. (1994). The picture exchange communication system. *Focus on Autistic Behavior 9,* 1–19.

Bowers, C.A. (1984). *The promise of theory: Education and the politics of cultural Change.* New York: Longman.

Brazelton, T.B. (1982). Early intervention: What does it mean? In H.E. Fitzgerald, B.M. Lester, & M.W. Yogman (Eds.), *Theory and research in behavioral pediatrics* (Vol. 1) (pp. 1–34). New York: Plenum.

Bredekamp, S., & Copple, C. (Eds.). (1997). *Developmentally appropriate practice in early childhood programs* (Rev. ed.). Washington DC: National Association for the Education of Young Children.

Bricker, D.D. (1989). *Early intervention for at-risk and handicapped infants, toddlers, and preschool children.* Palo Alto, CA: VORT Corporation.

Bricker, D. (1993). *Assessment, evaluation, and programming system (AEPS®) for birth to three years* (Vol. 1). Baltimore: Paul H. Brookes Publishing Co.

Bricker, D. (1995). The challenge of inclusion. *Journal of Early Intervention, 19,* 179–194.

Bricker, D. (Ed.). (2002). *Assessment, evaluation, and programming system (AEPS®) for infants and children: Vol. 2. AEPS® Test for Birth to Three Years and Three to Six Years.* Baltimore: Paul H. Brookes Publishing Co.

Bricker, D., Bricker, W., Iacino, R., & Dennison, L. (1976). Intervention strategies for the severely and profoundly handicapped child. In N. Haring & L. Brown (Eds.), *Teaching the severely handicapped* (Vol. 1, pp. 277–299). New York: Grune & Stratton.

Bricker, D., & Cripe, J. (1992). *An activity-based approach to early intervention.* Baltimore: Paul H. Brookes Publishing Co.

Bricker, D.D., Cripe, J., & Norstad, S. (1990, October). *Activity-based intervention.* Paper presented at Post Conference Workshop, Council for Exceptional Children Conference, Albuquerque, New Mexico.

Brislin, R.W., Cushner, K., Cherrie, C., & Yong, M. (1986). *Intercultural interactions: A practical guide.* Beverly Hills: Sage Publications.

Bronfenbrenner, U. (1977). Toward an experimental ecology of human behavior. *American Psychologist, 32,* 513–531.

Bronfenbrenner, U. (1979). *The ecology of human development: Experiments by nature and design.* Cambridge, MA: Harvard University Press.

Bronfenbrenner, U. (1992). Ecological systems theory. In R. Vasa (Ed.), *Six theories of child development: Revised formulations and current issues* (pp. 187–248). Philadelphia: Kingsley.

Browder, D.M. (2001). *Curriculum and assessment for students with moderate and severe disabilities.* New York: Guilford Press.

Browder, D., Demchack, M.A., Heller, M., & King, D. (1989). An in vivo evaluation of the use of data-based rules to guide instructional decisions. *Journal of the Association for Persons with Severe Handicaps, 14,* 234–240.

Brown, F., & Holvoet, J. (1982). Effects of systematic peer interaction on the incidental learning of two severely handicapped students. *Journal of the Association for Persons with Severe Handicaps, 7*(4), 19–28.

Brown, F., Holvoet, J., Guess, D., & Mulligan, M. (1980). The individualized curriculum sequencing model (III): Small group instruction. *Journal of the Association for the Severely Handicapped, 5*(4), 352–367.

Brown, L., Branston, M.B., Hamre-Nietupski, S., Pumpian, L., Certo, N., & Gruenewald, L. (1979). A strategy for developing chronological age-appropriate and functional curricular content for severely handicapped adolescents and young adults. *Journal of Special Education, 13,* 81–90.

Brown, W.H., & Odom, S.L. (1995). Naturalistic peer interventions for promoting preschool children's social interactions. *Preventing School Failure, 39,* 38–42.

Brown, W.H., McEvoy, M.A., & Bishop, N. (1991). Incidental teaching of social behavior. *Teaching Exceptional Children, 24*(1), 35–38.

Brown, W.H., Odom, S.L., & Conroy, M.A. (2001). An intervention hierarchy for promoting young children's peer interactions in natural environments. *Topics in Early Childhood Special Education, 21,* 162–175.

Brown, W.H., Odom, S.L., Li, S., & Zercher, C. (1999). Ecobehavioral assessment in inclusive early childhood programs: A portrait of preschool inclusion. *The Journal of Special Education, 33,* 138–153.

Brown, W.H., Ragland, E.U., & Bishop, J.N. (1989). A naturalistic teaching strategy to promote young children's peer interactions. *Teaching Exceptional Children 21,* 8–10.

Brown, W.H., Ragland, E.U., & Fox, J.J. (1988). Effects of group socialization procedures on the social interactions of preschool children. *Research in Developmental Disabilities, 9,* 359–376.

Brown, W.H., McEvoy, M.A., & Bishop, N. (1991). Incidental teaching of social behavior. *Teaching Exceptional Children, 24,* 35–38.

Bruder, M.B. (1997). The effectiveness of specific educational/developmental curricula for children with established disabilities. In M.J. Guralnick (Ed.), *The effectiveness of early intervention* (pp. 523–548). Baltimore: Paul H. Brookes Publishing Co.

Bruder, M.B. (2000a). Family centered early intervention: Clarifying our values for the millennium. *Topics in Early Childhood Special Education, 20,* 105–115.

Bruder, M.B. (2000b). The Individualized Family Service Plan (IFSP). *ERIC ED Digest* #E605. Arlington, VA: ERIC Clearinghouse of Disabilities and Gifted Education.

Bruder, M.B. (2001). Inclusion of infants and toddlers. In M.J. Guralnick (Ed.), *Early childhood inclusion* (pp. 203–228). Baltimore: Paul H. Brookes Publishing Co.

Bruder, M.B., & Chandler, L.K. (1993). Transition: DEC recommended practices. In Council for Exceptional Children, Division for Early Childhood, *DEC recommended practices: Indicators of quality in programs for infants and young children with special needs and their families* (pp. 96–106). Reston, VA: Council for Exceptional Children.

Bruder, M.B., & Walker, L. (1990). Discharge planning: Hospital to home transitions for infants. *Topic in Early Childhood Special Education, 9*(4), 26–42.

Bruner, J.S. (1960). *The process of education.* New York: Vintage.

Bruner, J. (1975). The ontogenesis of speech acts. *Journal of Child Language, 2,* 1–19.

Bruner, J. (1977). Early social interaction and language acquisition. In H. Schaffer (Ed.), *Studies in mother-infant interaction* (pp. 271–289). New York: Academic Press.

Bruns, D.A., & Fowler, S.A. (2001). *Transition is more than a change in services: The need for a multicultural perspective.* Champaign, IL: Early Childhood Research Institute on Culturally and Linguistically Appropriate Services, University of Illinois at Urbana-Champaign. Retrieved on September 11, 2004, from http://clas.uiuc.edu/tech report/tech4.html

Bunce, B. (2003). Children with culturally diverse backgrounds. In L. McCormick, D.F. Loeb, & R.L Schiefelbusch (Eds.), *Supporting children with communication difficulties in inclusive settings: School based language intervention* (pp. 367–407). Boston: Allyn & Bacon.

Butterfield, R.A. (1983). The development and use of culturally appropriate curriculum for American Indian students. *Peabody Journal of Education, 61,* 50–66.

Caldwell, B.M., & Bradley, R.H. (1984). *Home observation for measurement of the environment (HOME).* Little Rock, AR: University of Arkansas at Little Rock, Center for Research on Teaching and Learning.

Cameron, M.J., Maguire, R.W., & Maguire, M. (1998). Lifeway influences on challenging behaviors (pp. 273–288). In J.K. Luiselli & M. J. Cameron (Eds.), *Antecedent control: Innovative approaches to behavioral support.* Baltimore: Paul H. Brookes Publishing Co.

Capone, A., & Hull, K. (1994, June). *Discipline-Free IEP Workshop Presentation.* Kansas Inservice Training System (KITS), First Summer Institute, Lawrence, Kansas: University of Kansas, Department of Special Education.

Carr, E.G. (1977). The motivation of self-injurious behavior: A review of some hypotheses. *Psychological Bulletin, 84,* 800–816.

Carr, E.G., Carlson, J.I., Langdon, N.A., Magito-McLaughlin, D., & Yarbrough, S.C. (1998). Two perspectives on antecedent control: Molecular and molar. In J.K. Luiselli & M.J. Cameron (Eds.), *Antecedent control: Innovative approaches to behavioral support* (pp. 3–28). Baltimore: Paul H. Brookes Publishing Co.

Carr, E.G., & Durand, V.M. (1985). Reducing behavior problems through functional communication training. *Journal of Applied Behavior Analysis, 18,* 111–126.

Carr, E.G., Levin, L., McConnachie, G., Carlson, J.L., Kemp, D.C., & Smith, C.E. (1994). *Communication-based intervention for problem behavior: A user's guide for producing positive change.* Baltimore: Paul H. Brookes Publishing Co.

Carr, E.G., Reeve, C.E., & Magito-McLaughlin, D. (1996). Contextual influences on problem behavior in people with developmental disabilities. In L.K. Koegel, R.L. Koegel, & G. Dunlap (Eds.), *Positive behavioral support: Including people with difficult behavior in the community* (pp. 403–423). Baltimore: Paul H. Brookes Publishing Co.

Carr, E.G., Robinson, S., & Palumbo, L.W. (1990). The wrong issue: Aversive vs. nonaversive treatment. The right issue: Functional vs. nonfunctional treatment. In A.C. Repp & N.N. Singh (Eds.), *Perspectives on the use of nonaversive and aversive interventions for persons with developmental disabilities* (pp. 361–380). Sycamore, IL: Sycamore.

Carta, J.J., Atwater, J.B., Schwartz, I.S., & Miller, P.A. (1990). Applications of ecobehavioral analysis to the study of transitions across early education settings. *Education and Treatment of Children, 13,* 298–315.

Carta, J.J., Schwartz, I.S., Atwater, J.B., & McConnell, S.R. (1991). Developmentally appropriate practice: Appraising its usefulness for young children with disabilities. *Topics in Early Childhood Special Education, 11,* 1–20.

Castenada, A. (1976). Cultural democracy and the educational needs of Mexican American children. In R.L. Jones (Ed.), *Mainstreaming and the minority child.* Reston, VA: Council for Exceptional Children.

Chandler, L. (1998). Promoting positive interaction between preschool-age children during free play: The PALS Center. *Young Exceptional Children, 1*(3), 14–19.

Charlop-Christy, M.H., Carpenter, M., Le, L., LeBlanc, L.A., & Kellet, K. (2002). Using the Picture Exchange Communication System (PECS) with children with autism: Assessment of PECS acquisition, speech, social-communication behavior, and problem behavior. *Journal of Applied Behavior Analysis, 35,* 213–231.

Charner, K. (1993). *The giant encyclopedia of theme activities for children 2 to 5: Over 600 favorite activities created by teachers and for teachers.* Beltsville, MD: Gryphon House.

Chen, Y.J., & McCollum, J.A. (2001). Taiwanese mothers' perspectives of parent-infant interaction with children with Down Syndrome. *Journal of Early Intervention, 24,* 252–265.

Children's Defense Fund. (1998). *The state of America's children: Yearbook 1998.* Washington, DC: Author. ERIC Document Reproduction Service No. ED 418 794.

Christensen, C.M. (1992). Multicultural competencies in early intervention: Training professionals for a pluralistic society. *Infants and Young Children, 4*(3), 49–63.

Christopher, J., Hansen, D., & Macmillan, V. (1991). Effectiveness of a peer-helper intervention to increase children's social interactions. *Behavior Modification, 15*(1), 2–50.

Chung, D.K. (1992). Asian cultural commonalities: A comparison with mainstream American culture. In S.M. Furuto, R. Biswas, D.K. Chung, K. Murase, & R. Ross-Sheriff (Eds.), *Social work practice with Asian Americans* (pp. 27–44). Thousand Oaks, CA: Sage Publications.

Collier, C. (2000). *Separating difference from disability: Assessing diverse learners.* Vancouver, WA: Cross Cultural Developmental Education Services.

Collins, B.C., Gast, D.L., Ault, M.J., & Wolery, M. (1991). Small group instruction: Guidelines for teachers of students with moderate to severe handicaps. *Education and Training in Mental Retardation, 26,* 18–32.

Cone, J.D. (1987). Intervention planning using adaptive behavior instruments. *The Journal of Special Education, 21,* 127–148.

Copeland, M., Ford, L., & Solon, N. (1976). *Occupational therapy for mentally retarded children.* Baltimore: University Park Press.

Copeland, S.R., & Hughes, C. (2000). Acquisition of a picture prompt strategy to increase independent performance. *Education and Training in Mental Retardation and Developmental Disabilities, 35,* 294–305.

Correa, V., & Tulbert, B. (1991). Teaching culturally diverse students. *Preventing School Failure, 35*(3), 20–25.

Cripe, J.W., & Venn, M.L. (1997). Family guided routines for early intervention services. *Young Exceptional Children, 1*(1), 18–26.

Cristophel, D. (1990). The relationships among teacher immediacy behaviors, student motivation, and learning. *Communication Education, 39,* 335–345.

Csapo, M. (1981). Comparison of two prompting procedures to increase response fluency among severely handicapped learners. *Journal of the Association for the Severely Handicapped, 6*(1), 39–47.

Cummins, J. (1984). *Bilingualism and special education: Issues in assessment and pedagogy.* Clevedon Avon, England: Multilingual Matters.

Daigre, I.R., Johnson, L.J., Bauer, A.M., & Smith, D. A. (1998). Developing an inclusive, prosocial curriculum. In L.J. Johnson, M.J. Montagne, P.M. Elgas, & A.M. Bauer (Eds.), *Early childhood education: Blending theory, blending practice* (pp. 173–186). Baltimore: Paul H. Brookes Publishing Co.

D'Amato, J. (1981). *Power in the classroom.* Paper presented at the annual meeting of the American Anthropological Association, Los Angeles.

Damen, L. (1987). *Culture learning: The fifth dimension in the language classroom.* Reading, MA: Addison-Wessley.

Daniels, M. (1994). The effect of sign on hearing children's language. *Communication Education, 43,* 291–298.

Danko, C.D., & Buysse, V. (2002). Thank you for being a friend. *Young Exceptional Children 6*(1), 2–9.

Darnell, R. (1979). *Reflections on Cree interactional etiquette: Educational implications*(Working Papers in Sociolinguistics No. 57). Austin, TX: Southwestern Educational Development Laboratory.

Davis, C.A., & Brady, M.P. (1993). Expanding the utility of behavioral momentum with young children: Where we've been, where we need to go. *Journal of Early Intervention, 17,* 211–223.

Davis, C.A., Brady, M.P., Hamilton, R., McEvoy, M.A., & Williams, R.E. (1994). Effects of high-probability requests on the social interactions of young children with severe disabilities. *Journal of Applied Behavior Analysis, 17,* 619–637.

Davis, C.A., Brady, M.P., Williams, R.E., & Hamilton, R. (1992). Effects of high-probability requests on the acquisition and generalization of responses to requests in young children with behavior disorders. *Journal of Applied Behavior Analysis, 25,* 905–916.

Davis, C.A., & Reichle, J. (1996). Variant and invariant high-probability requests: Increasing appropriate behaviors in children with emotional-behavioral disorders. *Journal of Applied Behavior Analysis, 19,* 471–482.

Dawson, G., & Osterling, J. (1997). Early intervention in autism. In M.J. Guralnick (Ed.), *The effectiveness of early intervention* (pp. 307–326). Baltimore: Paul H. Brookes Publishing Co.

Day, H.M. (1987). Comparison of two prompting procedures to facilitate skill acquisition among severely mentally retarded adolescents. *American Journal of Mental Deficiency, 91,* 366–372.

DeKlyen, M., & Odom, S.L. (1989). Activity structure and social interactions with peers in developmentally integrated play groups. *Journal of Early Intervention, 13,* 342–352.

Denney, M.K., Singer, G.H.S., Singer, J., Brenner, M.E., Okamoto, Y., & Fredeen, R.M. (2001). Mexican immigrant families' beliefs and goals for their infants in the neonatal intensive care unit. *JASH, 26,* 148–157.

Dentler, R.A., & Hafner, A.L. (1997). *Hosting newcomers: Structuring educational opportunities for immigrant children.* New York: Teachers College Press.

Dinnebeil, L.A., Hale, L.M., & Rule, S. (1996). A qualitative analysis of parents' and service coordinators' descriptions of variables that influence collaborative relationships. *Topics in Early Childhood Special Education, 16,* 322–347.

Division for Early Childhood Task Force on Recommended Practices. (1993). *DEC recommended practices: Indicators of quality in programs for infants and young children with special needs and their families.* Reston, VA: Council for Exceptional Children.

Division for Early Childhood (DEC). (1998, April). *Position statement on interventions for challenging behavior.* Denver, CO: Author.

Division for Early Childhood (DEC). (1999). *Concept paper on the identification of and intervention with challenging behavior.* Reston, VA: Council for Exceptional Children.

Dunlap, G., & Conroy, M. (2003). Positive behavior support for young children with challenging behavior. In G. Dunlap, M. Conroy, L. Kern, G. DuPaul, J. VanBrakle, & P. Strain, et al. (Eds.), *Research synthesis on effective intervention procedures: Executive summary* (Chapter 1). Tampa, FL: University of South Florida, Center for Evidence-Based Practice: Young Children with Challenging Behavior.

Dunlap, G., DePerczel, M., Clarke, S., Wilson, D., Wright, S., & White, R., et al. (1994). Choice making to promote adaptive behavior for students with emotional and behavioral challenges. *Journal of Applied Behavior Analysis, 27,* 505–518.

Dunst, C.J. (1981). *Infant learning.* Allen, TX: DLM/Teaching Resources.

Dunst, C.J. (1997). Conceptual and empirical foundation of family-centered practice. In R. Illback, C. Cobb, & J.H. Joseph (Eds.), *Integrated services for children and families: Opportunities for psychological practice* (pp. 75–91). Washington, DC: American Psychological Association.

Dunst, C.J. (2001). Participation of young children with disabilities in community learning activities. In M.J. Guralnick (Ed.), *Early childhood inclusion* (pp. 307–333). Baltimore: Paul H. Brookes Publishing Co.

Dunst, C.J., Bruder, M.B., Trivette, C.M., Raab, M., & McLean, M. (2001). Natural learning opportunities for infants, toddlers, and preschoolers. *Young Exceptional Children, 4*(3), 18–25.

Dunst, C.J., Cooper, C.S., Weeldreyer, J.C., Snyder, K.D., & Chase J.J. (1988). Family needs scale. In C.J. Dunst, C.M. Trivette, & A.G. Deal. (Eds.), *Enabling and empowering families: Principles and guidelines for practice.* Cambridge, MA: Brookline Books.

Dunst, C.J., Cushing, P.J., & Vance, S.D. (1985). Response-contingent learning in profoundly handicapped infants: A social systems perspective. *Analysis and Intervention in Developmental Disabilities, 5,* 33–47.

Dunst, C.J., Hamby, D., Trivette, C.M., Raab, M., & Bruder, M.B. (2000). Everyday family and community life and children's naturally occurring learning opportunities. *Journal of Early Intervention, 23,* 151–164.

Dunst, C.J., Johanson, C., Trivette, C., & Hamby, D. (1991). Family-oriented early intervention policies and practices: Family-centered or not? *Exceptional Children, 58,* 115–126.

Dunst, C.J., Lesko, J.J., Holbert, K.A., Wilson, L.L., Sharpe, K.L., & Liles, R.F. (1987). A systematic approach to infant intervention. *Topics in Early Childhood Special Education, 7*(2), 19–37.

Dunst, C.J., & Paget, K. (1991) Parent-professional partnerships and family empowerment. In M. Fine (Ed.), *Collaboration with parents of exceptional children* (pp. 25–44). Brandon, VT: Clinical Psychology.

Dyer, K., Dunlap, G., & Winterling, V. (1990). The effects of choice making on the serious problem behaviors of students with developmental disabilities. *Journal of Applied Behavior Analysis, 23,* 515–524.

Edmiaston, R., Dolezal, V., Doolittle, S., Erickson, C., & Merritt, S. (2000). Developing individualized education programs for children in inclusive settings: A developmentally appropriate framework. *Young Children, 55*(4), 36–41.

Education for All Handicapped Children Act of 1975, PL 94-142, 20 U.S.C. 1400 *et seq.*

Elgas, P.M., & Lynch, E. (1998). Group structures. In L.J. Johnson, M.J. LaMontagne, P. Elgas, & A.M. Bauer (Eds.), *Early childhood education: Blending theory, blending practice* (pp. 187–199). Baltimore: Paul H. Brookes Publishing Co.

English, K., Goldstein, H., Shafer, K., & Kaczmarek, L. (1997). Promoting interactions among preschoolers with and without disabilities: Effects of a buddy skills-training program. *Exceptional Children, 63,* 229–243.

Epstein, M.H., Hallahan, D.P., & Kauffman, J.M. (1975). Implications of the reflectivity-impulsivity dimension for special education. *Journal of Special Education, 9,* 11–25.

Erickson, F., & Mohatt, G. (1982). Cultural organization of participation structures in two classrooms of Indian students. In G. Spindler (Ed.), *Doing the ethnography of schooling: Educational anthropology in action* (pp. 132–174). New York: Holt, Rinehart & Winston.

Esmailka, W., & Barnhardt, C. (1981). *The social organization of participation in three Athabaskan cross-cultural classrooms.* Fairbanks, AK: University of Alaska Center for Cross Cultural Studies. (ERIC Document Reproduction Service No. ED 231 571).

Falvey, M., Brown, L., Lyon, S., Baumgart, D., & Schroeder, J. (1980). Strategies for using cues and correction procedures. In W. Sailor, B. Wilcox, & L. Brown (Eds.), *Methods of instruction for severely handicapped students* (pp. 109–133). Baltimore: Paul H. Brookes Publishing Co.

Farlow, L.J., & Snell, M.E. (2006). Teaching basic self-care skills. In M.E. Snell & F. Brown (Eds.), *Instruction of students with severe disabilities* (6th ed., pp. 328–374). Upper Saddle River, NJ: Prentice-Hall.

Favazza, P.C., La Roe, J., Phillipsen, L., & Kumar, P. (2000). Representing young children with disabilities in classroom environments. *Young Exceptional Children, 3*(3), 2–8.

Favazza, P.C., & Odom, S.L. (1997). Promoting positive attitudes of kindergarten-age children toward people with disabilities. *Exceptional Children, 63,* 405–418.

Fowler, S.A., & Titus, P.F. (1993). Handling transitions. In P.J. Beckman & G.B. Boyes (Eds.), *Deciphering the system: A guide for families of young children with disabilities* (pp. 101–116). Cambridge, MA: Brookline.

Franklin, M.E. (1992). Culturally sensitive instructional practices for African-American learners with disabilities. *Exceptional Children, 59,* 115–122.

Frea, W., Craig-Unkefer, L., Odom, S.L., & Williams, D. (1999). Differential effects of structured social integration and group friendship activities for promoting social interaction with peers. *Journal of Early Intervention, 22,* 230–242.

French, J.E. (2000). Itard, Jean-Marc-Gaspard. In A.E. Kazdin (Ed.), *Encyclopedia of psychology.* Oxford: Oxford University Press.

Friend, M. (2000). Myths and misunderstandings about professional collaboration. *Remedial and Special Education, 21,* 130–132.

Friend, M., & Cook, L. (1996). *Interactions: Collaboration skills for school professionals* (2nd ed.). New York: Longman.

Frost, L.A., & Bondy, A.S. (1994). *The picture exchange communication system training manual.* Cherry Hill, NJ: Pyramid Educational Consultants.

Gallimore, R., Boggs, J.W., & Jordan, C. (1974). *Culture, behavior, and education: A study of Hawaiian-Americans.* Beverly Hills: Sage.

Gesell, A., & Amatruda, C.S. (1947). *Developmental diagnosis* (2nd ed.). New York: Paul B. Hoeber.

Gesell, A., & Ilg, F.L. (1946). *Youth: The years from ten to sixteen.* New York: Harper & Row.

Glendenning, N.J., Adams, G.L., & Sternberg, L. (1983). Comparison of prompt sequences. *American Journal of Mental Deficiency, 88,* 321–325.

Gold, M.W. (1980). *Try another way. Training manual.* Champaign, IL: Research Press.

Goldenberg, C. (2004). Literacy for all children in the increasingly diverse schools of the United States. In N. Unrau & R. Ruddell (Eds.), *Theoretical models and processes of reading* (5th ed., pp. 1636–1666). Newark, DE: International Reading Association.

Goldenberg, C., & Gallimore, R. (1991). Local knowledge, research knowledge, and educational change: A case study of first-grade Spanish reading improvement. *Educational Researcher, 20*(8), 2–14.

Goldfarb, W. (1945). Psychological deprivation in infancy and subsequent adjustment. *American Journal of Orthopsychiatry, 15,* 247–255.

Goldfarb, W. (1949). Rorschach test differences between family reared, institution reared, and schizophrenic children. *American Journal of Orthopsychiatry, 19,* 624–633.

Goldfarb, W. (1955). Emotional and intellectual consequences of psychologic deprivation in infancy: A re-evaluation. In P.H. Hoch & J. Zubin (Eds.), *Psychopathology of childhood* (pp. 29–44). New York: Grune & Stratton.

Goldstein, H., English, K., Shafer, K., & Kaczmarek, L. (1997). Interaction among preschoolers with and without disabilities: Effects of across-the-day peer intervention. *Journal of Speech, Language, and Hearing Research, 40,* 33–48.

Goldstein, H., Kaczmarek, L., Pennington, R., & Shafer, K. (1992). Peer-mediated intervention: Attending to, commenting on, and acknowledging the behavior of preschoolers with autism. *Journal of Applied Behavior Analysis, 25,* 289–305.

Goodenough, F., & Maurer, K. (1961). The relative potency of the nursery school and the statistical laboratory in boosting IQ. In J. Jenkins & D. Paterson (Eds.), *Studies in individual differences.* New York: Appleton-Century-Crofts.

Goodenough, W.H. (1981). *Culture, language, and society* (2nd ed.). Menlo Park, CA: Benjamin/Cummings.

Goodman, J.R. (1992). *When slow is fast enough: Educating the delayed preschool child.* New York: Guilford Press.

Goodman, J.R., & Bond, L. (1993). The individualized education program: A restrospective critique. *Journal of Special Education, 26,* 408–422.

Greenbaum, P. (1983). *Nonverbal communications between American Indian children and their teachers.* Lawrence, KS: Native American Research Associates. (ERIC Document Reproduction Service No. ED 239 804).

Greenspan, S., & Meisels, S.J. (1996). Toward a new vision for the developmental assessment of infants and young children. In S.J. Meisels & E. Fenichel (Eds.), *New visions for the developmental assessment of infants and young children* (pp. 11–26). Washington, DC: ZERO TO THREE: National Center for Infants, Toddlers, and Families.

Greenspan, S.I., & Wieder, S. (1997). Developmental patterns and outcomes in infants and children with disorders in relating and communicating: A chart review of 200 cases of children with autism spectrum diagnoses. *Journal of Developmental and Learning Disorders, 1,* 87–141.

Greenspan, S.I., & Wieder, S. (1999). A functional developmental approach to autism spectrum disorder. *Journal of the Association for Persons with Severe Handicaps, 24,* 147–161.

Greenspan, S.I., Wieder, S., & Simons, R. (1998). *The child with special needs: Encouraging intellectual and emotional growth.* Cambridge, MA: Perseus.

Greismann, Z. (1990). Medically fragile children. *West's Education Law Reporter, 61*(2), 403–408.

Grisham-Brown, J., & Hemmeter, M.L. (1998). Writing IEP goals and objectives: Reflecting an activity-based approach to instruction for young children with disabilities. *Young Exceptional Children, 3*(1), 2–10.

Grossman, H. (1995). *Special education in a diverse society.* Boston: Allyn & Bacon.

Guess, D., Horner, D., Utley, B., Holvoet, J., Maxon, D., Tucker, D., & Warren, S. (1978). A functional curriculum sequencing model for teaching the severely handicapped. *AAESPH Review, 3,* 202–215.

Guess, D., & Noonan, M.J. (1982). Curricula and instructional procedures for severely handicapped students. *Focus on Exceptional Children, 14,* 1–12.

Guralnick, M.J. (1997). Second-generation research in the field of early intervention. In M.J. Guralnick (Ed.), *The effectiveness of early intervention* (pp. 3–20). Baltimore: Paul H. Brookes Publishing Co.

Guralnick, M.J. (2001). Framework for change in early childhood inclusion. In M.J. Guralnick (Ed.), *Early childhood inclusion* (pp.1–35). Baltimore: Paul H. Brookes Publishing Co.

Gutierrez-Clellen, V.F. (1996). Language diversity: Implications for assessment. In S.F. Warren & J. Reichle (Series Eds.) & K.N. Cole, P.S. Dale, & D.J. Thal (Vol. 6, Eds.), *Communication and language intervention series: Vol. 6. Assessment of communication and language* (pp. 29–56). Baltimore: Paul H. Brookes Publishing Co.

Hadden, D.S. (2000). The long anticipated day: Strategies for success when a premature infant comes home from the neonatal intensive care unit. *Young Exceptional Children 3*(2), 21–27.

Hagopian, L.P., Rush, K.S., Lewin, A.B., & Long, E.S. (2001). Evaluating the predictive validity of a single stimulus engagement preference assessment. *Journal of Applied Behavior Analysis, 34,* 475–485.

Hains, A. H., Fowler, S.A., Schwartz, I.S., Kottwitz, E., & Rosenkoetter, S. (1989). Planning school transitions: Family and professional collaboration. *Early Childhood Research Quarterly, 4,* 75–88.

Hains, A.H., Lynch, E.W., & Winton, P.J. (2000). *Moving towards cross-cultural competence in lifelong personnel development: A review of the literature* (CLAS Technical Report #3). Champaign, IL: University of Illinois at Urbana-Champaign, Early Childhood Research Institute on Culturally and Linguistically Appropriate Services, retrieved February 27, 2001, from http://clas.uiuc.edu/techreport/tech3.html

Hale-Benson, J.E. (1986). *Black children: Their roots, culture and learning styles* (Rev. ed.). Baltimore: Johns Hopkins University Press.

Hale-Benson, J.E. (1990). Visions for children: African-American early childhood education programs. *Early Childhood Research Quarterly, 5,* 199–213.

Halle, J.W. (1982). Teaching functional language to the handicapped: An integrative model of natural environment teaching techniques. *Journal of the Association for the Severely Handicapped, 7*(4), 29–37.

Halle, J., Marshall, A., & Spradlin, J. (1979). Time delay: A technique to increase language use and facilitate generalization in retarded children. *Journal of Applied Behavior Analysis, 12,* 431–439.

Hancock, T.B., & Kaiser, A.P. (2002). The effect of trainer-implemented Enhanced Milieu Teaching on the social communication of children with autism. *Topics in Early Childhood Special Education, 22*(1), 39–54.

Haney, M., & Cavallaro, C.C. (1996). Using ecological assessment in daily program planning for children with disabilities in typical preschool settings. *Topics in Early Childhood Special Education, 16,* 76–81.

Hanley, G.P., Iwata, B.A., Thompson, R.H., & Lindberg, J.S. (2000). A component analysis of "stereotypy as reinforcement" for alternative behavior. *Journal of Applied Behavior Analysis, 33,* 285–297.

Hanline, M.F. (1988). Making the transition to preschool: Identification of parent needs. *Journal of the Division for Early Childhood, 12,* 98–107.

Hanline, M.F., & Deppe, J. (1990). Discharging the premature infant: Family issues and implications for intervention. *Topics in Early Childhood Special Education, 9*(4), 15–25.

Hanson, M.J. (2004). Ethnic, cultural, and language diversity in service settings. In E.W. Lynch & M.J. Hanson (Eds.), *Developing cross-cultural competence: A guide for working with children and families* (3rd ed., pp. 3–18). Baltimore: Paul H. Brookes Publishing Co.

Hanson, M.J., & Lynch, E.W. (1989). *Early intervention: Implementing child and family services for infants and toddlers who are at-risk or disabled.* Austin, TX: Pro-Ed.

Hanson, M.J., & Zercher, C. (2001). The impact of cultural and linguistic diversity in inclusive preschool environments. In M.J. Guralnick (Ed.), *Early childhood inclusion: Focus for change* (pp. 413–432). Baltimore: Paul H. Brookes Publishing Co.

Hanson, M.J., Gutierrez, S., Morgan, M., Brennan, E.L., & Zercher, C. (1997). Language, culture, and disability: Interacting influences on preschool inclusion. *Topics in Early Childhood Special Education, 17,* 307–337.

Hanson, M.J., Wolfberg, P., Zercher, C., Morgan, M., Gutierrez, S., Barnwell, D., & Beckman, P.J. (1998). The culture of inclusion: Recognizing diversity at multiple levels. *Early Childhood Research Quarterly, 13,* 185–209.

Haring, N., Liberty, K., & White, O. (1981). *Final report: Field initiated research studies of phases of learning and facilitating instructional events for the severely/profoundly handicapped.* (U. S. Department of Education, Contract No. G007500593) Seattle: University of Washington: College of Education.

Harris, S.L., & Delmolino, L. (2002). Applied behavior analysis: Its application in the treatment of autism and related disorders in young children. *Infants and Young Children, 14*(3), 11–17.

Harrison, P.J., Lynch, E.W., Rosander, K., & Borton, W. (1990). Determining success in interagency collaboration. An evaluation of processes and behaviors. *Infants and Young Children, 3,* 69–78.

Harry, B. (1992). Developing cultural self-awareness: The first step in values clarification for early interventionists. *Topics in Early Childhood Special Education, 12,* 333–350.

Harry, B. (1998). Parental visions of "una vida normal/a normal life": Cultural variations on a theme. In L.J. Meyer, H.S. Park, M. Grenot-Scheyer, I.S. Schwartz, & B. Harry (Eds.), *Making friends: The influences of culture and development* (pp. 47–62). Baltimore: Paul H. Brookes Publishing Co.

Harry, B. (2002). Trends and issues in serving culturally diverse families of children with disabilities. *Journal of Special Education, 36*(3), 131–138.

Hart, B. (1982). So that teachers can teach: Assigning roles and responsibilities. *Topics in Early Childhood Special Education, 2*(1), 1–8.

Hart, B.M., & Risley, T.R. (1968). Establishing the use of descriptive adjectives in the spontaneous speech of disadvantaged preschool children. *Journal of Applied Behavior Analysis, 1,* 109–120.

Hart, B.M., & Risley, T.R. (1975). Incidental teaching of language in the preschool. *Journal of Applied Behavior Analysis, 8,* 411–420.

Hart, B.M., & Rogers-Warren, A.K. (1978). Milieu teaching approaches. In R.L. Schiefelbusch (Ed.), *Bases of language intervention* (Vol. 2, pp. 193–235). Baltimore: University Park Press.

Heflin, L.J., & Alberto, P.A. (2001). Establishing a behavioral context for learning for students with autism. *Focus on Autism and Other Developmental Disabilities, 16,* 93–101.

Heller, K.W., Forney, P.E., Alberto, P.A., Schwartzman, M.N., & Goeckel, T.M. (2000). *Meeting physical and health needs of children with disabilities: Teaching student participation and management.* Belmont, CA: Wadsworth.

Helmstetter, E., & Durand, V. M. (1991). Nonaversive interventions for severe behavior problems. In L.H. Meyer, C.A. Peck, & L. Brown (Eds.), *Critical issues in the lives of people with severe disabilities* (pp. 559–600). Baltimore: Paul H. Brookes Publishing Co.

Hemmeter, M.L., & Kaiser, A.P. (1994). Enhanced milieu teaching: Effects of parent-implemented language intervention. *Journal of Early Intervention, 18,* 269–289.

Hemmeter, M.L., & Ostrosky, M. (2003). Classroom preventive practices. In G. Dunlap, M. Conroy, L. Kern, G. DuPaul, J. VanBrakle, P. Strain, et al. (Eds.), *Research synthesis on effective intervention procedures: Executive summary* (Chapter 4). Tampa, FL: University of South Florida, Center for Evidence-Based Practice: Young Children with Challenging Behavior.

Hemmeter, M.L., & Rous, B. (1997). *Teachers' expectations of children transitioning into kindergarten or ungraded primary programs: A national survey.* Paper presented at the Division of Early Childhood Conference, New Orleans, LA.

Herr, J., & Larson, Y.L., (2003). *Creative resources for the early childhood classroom* (4th ed.). Albany, NY: Delmar.

Hestenes, L., & Carroll, D.E. (2000). The play interactions of young children with and without disabilities: Individual and environmental influences. *Early Childhood Research Quarterly, 15,* 229–246.

Heward, W.L., Courson, F.H., & Narayan, J.S. (1989). Using choral responding to increase active student response during group instruction. *Teaching Exceptional Children, 21*(3), 72–75.

Hill, J.L. (1999). *Meeting the needs of students with special physical and health care needs.* Upper Saddle River, NJ: Merrill/Prentice Hall.

Hilliard, A.S. (1989). Teachers and cultural styles in a pluralistic society. *NEA Today, 7*(6), 65–69.

Hirayama, K.K. (1985). Asian children's adaptation to public schools. *Social Work in Education, 7,* 213–230.

Hoier, T.S., McConnell, S., & Palley, A.G. (1987). Observational assessment for planning and evaluating educational transitions: An initial analysis of template matching. *Behavioral Assessment, 9,* 5–19.

Holland, J.G., & Skinner, B.F. (1961). *The analysis of behavior.* New York: McGraw-Hill.

Holvoet, J., O'Neil, C., Chazdon, L., Carr, D., & Warner, J. (1983). Hey, do we really have to take data? *Journal of the Association for the Severely Handicapped, 8*(3), 56–70.

Horn, E., Lieber, J., Li, S., Sandall, S., & Schwartz, I. (2000). Supporting young children's IEP goals in inclusive settings through embedded learning opportunities. *Topics in Early Childhood Special Education, 20,* 208–223.

Horner, R.H., Albin, R.W., Todd. A.W., & Sprague, J.R. (2006). Positive behavior support for individuals with severe disabilities. In M.E. Snell & F. Brown (Eds.), *Instruction of students with severe disabilities* (6th ed., pp. 206–250). Upper Saddle River, NJ: Prentice-Hall.

Horner, R., Day, M., Sprague, J., O'Brien, M., & Heathfield, L. (1991). Interspersed requests: A nonaversive procedure for reducing aggression and self-injury during instruction. *Journal of Applied Behavior Analysis, 24*, 265–278.

Horner, R.H., Dunlap, G., Koegel, R.L., Carr, E.G., Sailor, W., Anderson, J., et al. (1990). Toward a technology of "nonaversive" behavioral support. *Journal of the Association for Persons with Severe Handicaps, 15*, 125–132.

Horner, R.H., & Day, H.M. (1991). The effects of response efficiency on functionally equivalent competing behavior. *Journal of Applied Behavior Analysis, 24*, 719–732.

Horner, R.H., & McDonald, R.S. (1982). Comparison of single instance and general case instruction in teaching a generalized vocational skill. *Journal of the Association for the Severely Handicapped, 7*(3), 7–20.

Horner, R.H., Sprague, J.R., O'Brien, M., & Heathfield, L.T. (1990). The role of response efficiency in the reduction of problem behaviors through functional equivalence training: A case study. *Journal of the Association for Persons with Severe Handicaps, 15*, 91–97.

Horner, R.H., Sprague, J., & Wilcox, B. (1982). General case programming for community activities. In B. Wilcox & G.T. Bellamy (Eds.), *Design of high school programs for severely handicapped students* (pp. 61–98). Baltimore: Paul H. Brookes Publishing Co.

Hoyson, M., Jamieson, B., & Strain, P. (1984). Individualized group instruction of normally developing and autistic-like children: The LEAP curriculum model. *Journal of the Division for Early Childhood, 8*, 157–172.

Humphrey, G. (1962). Introduction. In J.M.G. Itard (Au.). *The wild boy of Aveyron.* New York: Appleton-Century-Crofts.

Hundert, J., Mahoney, B., Mundy, F., & Vernon, M.L. (1998). A descriptive analysis of developmental and social gains of children with severe disabilities in segregated and inclusive preschools in southern Ontario. *Early Childhood Research Quarterly, 13*, 49–65.

Hunt, J.M. (1961). *Intelligence and experience.* New York: Ronald Press.

Ilg, F.L., & Ames, L.B. (1955). *Child behavior.* New York: Harper & Row.

Illingworth, R.S. (1983). *The development of the infant and young child: Abnormal and normal* (8th ed.). New York: Churchill Livingstone.

Individuals with Disabilities Education Act (IDEA) of 1990, PL 101-476, 20 U.S.C. §§ 1400 *et seq.*

Individuals with Disabilities Education Act (IDEA) Amendments of 1997, PL 105-17, 20 U.S.C. §§ 1400 *et seq.*

Individuals with Disabilities Education Improvement Act (IDEA) of 2004, PL 108-446, 20 U.S.C. §§ 1400 *et seq.*

Irving Independent School District v. Tatro, 468 U.S. 883, 104 S. Ct. 3371, 82 L. Ed. 2nd 664 (1984).

Iwata, B.A., Dorsey, M.F., Slifer, K.J., Bauman, K.E., & Richman, G.S. (1982). Toward a functional analysis of self-injury. *Analysis and Intervention in Developmental Disabilities, 2*, 3–20.

Janney, R., & Snell, M.E. (2000). *Teachers' guides to inclusive practices: Behavioral support.* Baltimore: Paul H. Brookes Publishing Co.

Janney, R., & Snell, M.E. (2005). *Teachers' guides to inclusive practices: Modifying schoolwork* (2nd ed.). Baltimore: Paul H. Brookes Publishing Co.

Jenkins, J.R., Odom, S.L., & Speltz, M.L. (1989). Effects of social integration on preschool children with handicaps. *Exceptional Children, 55*, 420–428.

Johnson, D. (1971). Black kinesics: Some non-verbal communication patterns in black culture. *Florida Reporter, 9*, 1–2.

Johnson, D., & Johnson, R. (1975). *Learning together and alone: Cooperation, competition, and individualization.* Englewood Cliffs, NJ: Prentice Hall.

Johnson, R., & Johnson, D. (1981). Building friendships between handicapped and nonhandicapped students: Effects of cooperative individualistic instruction. *American Educational Research Journal, 18,* 415–423.

Johnson, D., & Johnson, R. (1983). The socialization and achievement crisis: Are cooperative learning experiences the solution? In L. Bickman (Ed.), *Applied Psychology Annual 4* (pp. 159–164). Beverly Hills, CA: Sage.

Johnson, D., & Johnson, R. (1986). Mainstreaming and cooperative learning strategies. *Exceptional Children, 52*(6), 553–561.

Johnson, D.W., & Johnson, R.T. (1989). *Cooperation and competition: Theory and Research.* Edina, MN: Intraction.

Johnson, L.J., Gallagher, R.J., Cook, M.J., & Wong, P. (1995). Critical skills for kindergarten: Perceptions of kindergarten teachers. *Journal of Early Intervention, 19*(4), 315–327.

Johnson, L.J., Pugach, M.C., & Hammitte, D.J. (1988). Barriers to effective special education consultation. *Remedial and Special Education, 9*(6), 41–47.

Johnson-Martin, N.M., Attermeier, S.M., & Hacker, B.J. (2004). *The Carolina Curriculum for infants & toddlers with special needs* (3rd ed.). Baltimore: Paul H. Brookes Publishing Co.

Jordan, C., & Tharp, R.G. (1979). Culture and education. In A.J. Marsella, R.G. Tharp, & T. Ciborowski (Eds.), *Perspectives in cross-cultural psychology* (pp. 265–285). New York: Academic.

Jordan, C., Tharp, R.G., & Vogt, L. (1985). *Compatibility of classroom and culture: General principles with Navajo and Hawaiian instances* (Working Paper). Honolulu: Kamehameha Schools/Bishop Estate, Center for the Development of Early Education.

Jung, L.A. (2003). More is better: Maximizing natural learning opportunities. *Young Exceptional Children, 6*(3), 21–26.

Kagan, S. (1992). The strategic importance of linkages and transition between early childhood programs and early elementary school. In *Sticking together: Strengthening linkages and the transition between early childhood education and early elementary school* (Summary of a National Policy Forum). Washington, DC: U.S. Department of Education.

Kaiser, A.P. (1993a). Functional language. In M. Snell (Ed.), *Instruction of students with severe disabilities* (4th ed., pp. 347–370). New York: Macmillan.

Kaiser, A.P. (1993b). Parent-implemented language intervention. In A.P. Kaiser & D.B. Gray (Eds.), *Enhancing children's communication: Vol. 2. Research foundations for intervention* (pp. 63–84). Baltimore: Paul H. Brookes Publishing Co.

Kaiser, A. (2000). Teaching functional communication skills. In M.E. Snell & F. Brown (Eds.). *Instruction of students with severe disabilities* (5th ed., pp. 453–491). Columbus, Ohio: Merrill.

Kaiser, A, Hendrickson, J., & Alpert, K. (1991). Milieu language teaching: A second look. In R. Gable (Ed.), *Advances in mental retardation and developmental disabilities* (Vol. I, pp. 63–92). London: Kingsley.

Kaiser, A., Ostrosky, M.M., & Alpert, K. (1993). Training teachers to use environmental arrangement and milieu teaching with nonvocal preschool children. *Journal of the Association for Persons with Severe Handicaps, 18,* 188–199.

Kalyanpur, M., & Harry, B. (1999). *Culture in special education: Building reciprocal family-professional relationships.* Baltimore: Paul H. Brookes Publishing Co.

Kamps, D., Walker, D., Maher, J., & Rotholz, D. (1992). Academic and environmental effects of small group arrangements in classrooms for students with autism and other developmental disabilities. *Journal of Autism and Developmental Disorders, 22,* 277–293.

Kanner, L. (1943). Autistic disturbances of affective contact. *Nervous Child, 2,* 217–250.

Kanner, L. (1967). Medicine in the history of mental retardation. *American Journal of Mental Deficiency, 72*(2), 165–170.

Kazdin, A.E. (1977). Assessing the clinical or applied importance of behavior change through social validation. *Behavior Modification, 1,* 427–452.

Kazdin, A.E. (2001). *Behavior modification in applied settings* (6th ed.). Belmont, CA: Wadsworth/Thomson.

Kennedy, C.H., & Souza, G. (1995). Functional analysis and treatment of eye-poking. *Journal of Applied Behavior Analysis, 28,* 27–37.

Kennedy, C.H., Itkonen, T., & Lindquist, K. (1995). Comparing interspersed requests and social comments as antecedents for increasing student compliance. *Journal of Applied Behavior Analysis, 28,* 97–98.

Kern, L., & Dunlap, G. (1998). Curricular modifications to promote desirable classroom behavior. In J.K. Luiselli & M.J. Cameron (Eds.), *Antecedent control: Innovative approaches to behavioral support* (pp. 289–307). Baltimore: Paul H. Brookes Publishing Co.

Key, M.R. (1975). *Paralanguage and kinesics: Nonverbal communication.* Metuchen, NJ: Scarecrow.

Kilgo, J.L., Johnson, L., LaMontagne, M., Stayton, V., Cook, M., & Cooper, C. (1999). Importance of practices: A national study of general and special early childhood educators. *Journal of Early Intervention, 22,* 294–305.

Kirk, S. (1958). *Early education of the mentally retarded.* Urbana: University of Illinois Press.

Kitano, M. (1983). Early education for Asian-American children. In O.N. Saracho & B. Spodek (Eds.), *Understanding the multicultural experience in early childhood education* (pp. 45–66). Washington, DC: National Association for the Education of Young Children.

Klein, M.D., Cook, R.E., & Richardson-Gibbs, A.M. (2001). *Strategies for including children with special needs in early childhood settings.* Albany, NY: Delmar.

Koegel, L.K., Koegel, R.L., Harrower, J.K., & Carter, C.M. (1999). Pivotal response intervention I: Overview of approach. *JASH, 24,* 174–185.

Koegel, R. (1987). A natural language teaching paradigm for nonverbal autistic children. *Journal of Autism and Developmental Disabilities, 17,* 189–200.

Koegel, R.L., & Koegel, L.K. (2006). *Pivotal response treatments for autism: Communication, social, & academic development.* Baltimore: Paul H. Brookes Publishing Co.

Koegel, R.L., & Rincover, A. (1974). Treatment of psychotic children in a classroom environment: I. Learning in a large group. *Journal of Applied Behavior Analysis, 7,* 45–49.

Koegel, R.L., Carter, C.M., & Koegel, L.K. (1998). Setting events to improve parent-teacher coordination and motivation for children with autism. In J.K. Luiselli & M.J. Cameron (Eds.), *Antecedent control: Innovative approaches to behavioral support* (pp. 167–186). Baltimore: Paul H. Brookes Publishing Co.

Kohler, F.W., & Strain, P.S. (1997). Merging naturalistic teaching and peer-based strategies to address the IEP objectives of preschoolers with autism: An examination of structural and child behavior outcomes. *Focus on Autism and Other Developmental Disabilities, 12*(4), 196–206.

Kohler, F.W., Strain, P.S., Maretsky, S., & DeCesare, L. (1990). Promoting positive and supportive interactions between preschoolers: An analysis of group-oriented contingencies. *Journal of Early Intervention, 14,* 327–341.

Krantz, P.L, & Risley, T.R., (1977). Behavior ecology in the classroom. In K.D. O'Leary & S. O'Leary (Eds.), *Classroom management: The successful use of behavior management* (pp. 60–82). Elmsford, NY: Pergamon.

Krashen, S.D. (1982). *Principles and practices in second language acquisition.* Elmsford, NY: Pergamon.

Krashen, S.D., & Terrell, T.D. (1983). *The natural approach: Language acquisition in the classroom.* Elmsford, NY: Pergamon.

Ladson-Billings, G. (1994). *The dreamkeepers: Successful teachers of African-American Children.* San Francisco: Jossey-Bass.

Lalli, J.S., Casey, S., & Kates, K. (1995). Reducing escape behavior and increasing task completion with functional communication training, extinction, and response chaining. *Journal of Applied Behavior Analysis, 28,* 261–268.

LaParo, K.M., Pianta, R.C., & Cox, M.J. (2000). Teachers' reported transition practices for children transitioning into kindergarten and first grade. *Exceptional Children, 67*(1), 7–20.

Laturnau, J. (2001). *Standards-based instruction for English language learners.* Honolulu, HI: PREL. Also available at www.prel.org/products/pc_/standards-based.pdf and www.prel.org/products/pc_/standards-based.htm

Lazzari, A.M., & Kilgo, J.L. (1989). Practical methods for supporting parents in early transitions. *Teaching Exceptional Children, 22*(1), 40–43.

Le Ager, C., & Shapiro, E.S. (1995). Template matching as a strategy for assessment of and intervention for preschool students with disabilities. *Topics in Early Childhood Special Education, 15,* 187–218.

Leith, S., & Slentz, K. (1984). Successful teaching strategies in selected Northern Manitoba schools. *Canadian Journal of Native Education, 12,* 24–30.

LeLaurin, K.D., & Risley, T.R. (1972). The organization of day care environments: "Zone" versus "man-to-man" staff assignments. *Journal of Applied Behavior Analysis, 5,* 225–232.

Lieber, J., Beckman, P.J., Hanson, M.J., Janko, S., Marquart, J.M., Horn, E., & Odom, S.L. (1997). The impact of changing roles on relationships between professionals in inclusive programs. *Early Education and Development, 8,* 67–82.

Lipka, J. (1990). Integrating cultural form and content in one Yup'ik Eskimo classroom: A case study. *Canadian Journal of Native Education, 17,* 18–32.

Lipsky, D.K., & Gartner, A. (1997). *Inclusion and school reform: Transforming America's classrooms.* Baltimore: Paul H. Brookes Publishing Co.

Losardo, A., & Bricker, D. (1994). Activity-based intervention and direct instruction: A comparison study. *American Journal of Mental Retardation, 98,* 744–765.

Losardo, A., & Notari-Syverson, A. (2001). *Alternative approaches to assessing young children.* Baltimore: Paul H. Brookes Publishing Co.

Lovaas, O.I. (1987). Behavioral treatment and normal educational and intellectual functioning in young autistic children. *Journal of Consulting and Clinical Psychology, 55,* 3–9.

Lovaas, O.I. (2002). *Teaching individuals with developmental delays: Basic intervention techniques.* Austin, TX: Pro-Ed.

Lovaas, O.I., Koegel, R.L., & Schreibman, L. (1979). Stimulus overselectivity in autism: A review of research. *Psychological Bulletin, 86,* 1236–1254.

Lovaas, O.I., & Schreibman, L. (1971). Stimulus overselectivity of autistic children in a two stimulus situation. *Behaviour Research and Therapy, 9,* 305–310.

Lucyshyn, J.M., Horner, R.H., Dunlap, G., Albin, R.W., & Ben, K.R. (2002). Positive behavior support with families. In J.M. Lucyshyn, G. Dunlap, & R.W. Albin (Eds.), *Families and positive behavior support: Addressing problem behavior in family contexts* (pp. 3–43). Baltimore: Paul H. Brookes Publishing Co.

Luiselli, J.K., & Cameron, M.J. (1998). *Antecedent control: Innovative approaches to behavioral support.* Baltimore: Paul H. Brookes Publishing Co.

Lynch, E.W. (2004). Developing cross-cultural competence. In E.W. Lynch & M.J. Hanson (Eds.), *Developing cross-cultural competence: A guide for working with children and families* (3rd ed.) (pp. 41–80). Baltimore: Paul H. Brookes Publishing Co.

Lynch, E.W., & Hanson, M.J. (Eds.). (2004). Changing demographics: Implications for training in early intervention. *Infants and Young Children, 6*(1), 50–55.

Lynch, E.W., & Struewing, N.A. (2002). Children in context. *Young Exceptional Children Monograph Series No. 4,* 83–96.

Lyon, S., & Lyon, G. (1980). Team functioning and staff development: A role release approach to providing integrated educational services for severely handicapped students. *Journal of the Association for the Severely Handicapped, 5*(3), 250–263.

McCathren, R.B., & Watson, A.L. (2001). Facilitating the development of intentional communication. In M. Ostrosky & S. Sandall (Eds.), Teaching strategies: What to do to support young children's development. *Young Exceptional Children Monograph Series No. 3* (25–35). DEC/CEC.

McClannahan, L.E., & Krantz, P.J. (1993). The Princeton Child Development Institute. In S.L. Harris & J.S. Handleman (Eds.), *Preschool education programs for children with autism* (pp. 107–126). Austin, TX: Pro-Ed.

McCollum, J.A., & Stayton, V.D. (1985). Infant/parent interaction: Studies and intervention guidelines based on the SIAI Model. *Journal of the Division for Early Childhood, 9*(2), 125–135.

McCormick, L. (2003a). Policies and practices. In L. McCormick, D.F. Loeb, & R.L. Schiefelbusch (Eds.), *Supporting children with communication difficulties in inclusive settings: School-based language intervention* (2nd ed., pp.155–188). Boston: Allyn & Bacon.

McCormick, L. (2003b). Ecological assessment and planning. In L. McCormick, D.F. Loeb, & R.L. Schiefelbusch (Eds.), *Supporting children with communication difficulties in inclusive settings: School-based language intervention* (2nd ed., pp. 235–257). Boston: Allyn & Bacon.

McCormick, L. (2003c). Language intervention in the inclusive preschool. In L. McCormick, D.F. Loeb, & R.L. Schiefelbusch (Eds.), *Supporting children with communication difficulties in inclusive settings: School-based language intervention* (2nd ed., pp. 333–366). Boston: Allyn & Bacon.

McCormick, L., & Feeney, S. (1995). Modifying and expanding activities for children with disabilities. *Young Children, 50*(4), 10–17.

McCormick, L., & Goldman, R. (1979). The transdisciplinary model: Implications for service delivery and personnel preparation for the severely and profoundly handicapped. *AAESPH Review, 4,* 152–161.

McCormick, L., & Kawate, J. (1982). Kindergarten survival skills: New directions for preschool special education. *Education and Training of the Mentally Retarded, 17,* 247–252.

McCormick, L., & Noonan, M.J. (1996). A "can do" inventory for 3–year–olds. *Teaching Exceptional Children, 28*(4), 4–9.

McCormick, L., & Noonan, M.J. (2002). Ecological assessment and planning. *Young Exceptional Children Monograph # 4* (47–60). Division for Early Childhood (DEC) of the Council for Exceptional Children. Longmont, CO: Sopris West.

McCormick, L., Noonan, M.J., & Heck, R. (1998). Variables affecting interaction and task engagement in inclusive preschool classrooms. *Journal of Early Intervention, 21,* 160–167.

McCormick, L., & Wegner, J. (2003). Supporting augmentative communication. In L. McCormick, D.F. Loeb, & R.L. Schiefelbusch (Eds.), *Supporting children with communication difficulties in inclusive settings: School-based language intervention* (2nd ed., pp. 435–459). Boston: Allyn & Bacon.

McEachin, J.J., Smith, T., & Lovaas, O. I. (1993). Long-term outcome for children with autism who received early intensive behavioral treatment. *American Journal of Mental Retardation, 97*(4), 359–372.

McGee, G.G., Daly, T., Izeman, S.G., Mann, L.H., & Risley, T.R. (1991). Use of classroom materials to promote preschool engagement. *Teaching Exceptional Children, 12*(4), 44–47.

McLean, M., & Crais, E.R. (1996). Procedural considerations in assessing infants and preschoolers with disabilities. In M. McLean, D.B. Bailey, Jr., & M. Wolery (Eds.), *Assessing infants and preschoolers with special needs* (pp. 46–68). Columbus, OH: Charles E. Merrill.

McMaster, K.N., & Fuchs, D. (2002). Effects of cooperative learning on the academic achievement of students with learning disabilities: An update of Tateyama-Sniezek's review. *Learning Disabilities Research and Practice, 17,* 107–117.

McWilliam, R.A. (1991). Targeting teaching at children's use of time. *Teaching Exceptional Children, 23*(4), 42–43.

McWilliam, R.A. (1992). *Family-centered intervention planning: A routines based approach.* Tucson, AZ: Communication Skill Builders/Psychological Associates.

McWilliam, R.A. (1996a). Implications for the future of integrating specialized services. In R.A. McWilliam (Ed.), *Rethinking pull-out services in early intervention: A professional resource* (pp. 343–372). Baltimore: Paul H. Brookes Publishing Co.

McWilliam, R.A. (Ed.). (1996b). *Rethinking pull-out services in early intervention: A professional resource.* Baltimore: Paul H. Brookes Publishing Co.

McWilliam, R.A. (1996c). Service delivery issues in center-based early intervention. In R.A. McWilliam (Ed.), *Rethinking pull-out services in early intervention: A professional resource* (pp. 3–26). Baltimore: Paul H. Brookes Publishing Co.

McWilliam, R.A. (2000). Recommended practices in interdisciplinary models. In S. Sandall, M.E. McLean, & B.J. Smith (Eds.), *DEC recommended practices in early intervention/early childhood special education* (pp. 47–52). Denver, CO: Division of Early Childhood (DEC) of the Council for Exceptional Children (CEC).

McWilliam, R.A., Wolery, M., & Odom, S.L. (2001). Instructional perspectives in inclusive school classrooms. In M.J. Guralnick (Ed.), *Early childhood inclusion: Focus on change* (pp. 503–727). Baltimore: Paul H. Brookes Publishing Co.

Meck, M., Fowler, S., Claflin, K., & Rasmussen, L. (1995). Mothers' perceptions of their NICU experience one and seven months after discharge. *Journal of Early Intervention, 19,* 288–301.

Meltzer, L.J. (1994). Assessment of learning disabilities: The challenge of evaluating cognitive strategies and processes underlying learning. In G.R. Lyon (Ed.), *Frames of reference for the assessment of learning disabilities: New views of measurement issues* (pp. 571–606). Baltimore: Paul H. Brookes Publishing Co.

Mesibov, G.B. (1993). Treatment outcome is encouraging. *American Journal of Mental Retardation, 97,* 379–380.

Mesibov, G.B. (2005). *What is TEACCH?* Retrieved May 23, 2005, from University of North Carolina at Chapel Hill, Division TEACCH Web site: http://www.teacch.com

Messick, S. (1976). *Individuality in learning: Implications of cognitive style and creativity for human development.* San Francisco: Jossey-Bass.

Michnowicz, L.L., McConnell, S.R., Peterson, C.A., & Odom, S.L. (1995). Social goals and objectives of preschool IEPs: A content analysis. *Journal of Early Intervention, 19,* 273–282.

Miles, M., & Miles, C. (1993). Education and disability in cross-cultural perspective: Pakistan. In S.J. Peters (Ed.), *Education and disability in cross-cultural perspective* (pp.167–235). New York: Garland.

Miller, R. (1996). *The developmentally appropriate inclusive classroom in early education.* Albany, NY: Delmar.

Mindes, G. (2000). *Building character: Five enduring themes for a stronger early childhood curriculum.* Upper Saddle River, NJ: Pearson Education.

Minke, K.M., Bear, G.G., Deemer, S.A., & Griffin, S.M. (1996). Teachers' experiences with inclusive classrooms: Implications for special education reform. *The Journal of Special Education, 30,* 152–186.

Montessori, M. (1964). *The Montessori method.* New York: Schocken.

Mount, B. (1992). *Person centered planning: Promises and precautions.* New York: Graphic Futures.

Mount, B. (1994). Benefits and limitations of personal futures planning. In V.J. Bradley, J.W. Ashbough, & B.C. Blaney (Eds.), *Creating individual supports for people with developmental disabilities* (pp. 97–108). Baltimore: Paul H. Brookes Publishing Co.

Mulligan, M., Guess, D., Holvoet, J., & Brown, F. (1980). The individualized curriculum sequencing model (1): Implications from research on massed-, distributed-, or spaced-trial training. *Journal of the Association for the Severely Handicapped, 5*(4), 325–336.

Mullis, L. (2002). Natural environments: A letter from a mother to friends, families, and professionals. *Young Exceptional Children, 5*(3), 21–24.

Murphy, M., & Vincent, L.J. (1989). Identification of critical skills for success in day care. *Journal of Early Intervention, 13,* 221–229.

Napier, R.W., & Gershenfeld, M.K. (1993). *Groups: Theory and experience* (5th ed.). Boston: Houghton Mifflin.

Neef, N.A., Iwata, B.A., & Page, T.J. (1977). The effects of known item-interspersal on acquisition and retention of spelling and sight-reading words. *Journal of Applied Behavior Analysis, 10,* 738.

Neilsen, S.L., & McEvoy, M.A. (2004). Functional behavioral assessment in early education settings. *Journal of Early Intervention, 26,* 115–131.

Nieto, S. (2000). *Affirming diversity: The sociopolitical context of multicultural education* (3rd ed.). New York: Addison Wesley Longman.

Noddings, N., & Shore, P.J. (1984). *Awakening the inner eye: Intuition in education.* New York: Teachers College Press.

Noonan, M.J., & Kilgo, J. (1987). Transition services for early age individuals with severe mental retardation. In R. Ianacone & R. Stodden (Eds.), *Transition issues and directions* (pp. 25–37). Reston, VA: Council for Exceptional Children.

Noonan, M.J., & Ratokalau, N.B. (1992). Project PPT: the Preschool Preparation and Transition project. *Journal of Early Intervention, 15,* 390–398.

Noonan, M.J., Ratokalau, N.B., Lauth-Torres, L., McCormick, L., Esaki, C.A., & Claybaugh, K.W. (1992). Validating critical skills for preschool success. *Infant-Toddler Intervention, 2*(3), 187–202.

Noonan, M.J., & Siegel, E.B. (2003). Special needs of students with severe disabilities and autism. In L. McCormick, D.F. Loeb, & R.L. Schiefelbusch (Eds.), *Supporting children with communication difficulties in inclusive settings: School-based language intervention* (pp. 409–433). Boston: Allyn & Bacon.

Nordquist, V.M., Twardosz, S., & McEvoy, M.A. (1991). Effects of environmental reorganization in classrooms for children with autism. *Journal of Early Intervention, 15,* 135–152.

North Carolina at Chapel Hill, Division TEACCH Web site: http://www.teacch.com

Northup, J. (2000). Further evaluation of the accuracy of reinforcer surveys: A systematic replication. *Journal of Applied Behavior Analysis, 33,* 335–338.

Northup, J., George, T., Jones, K., Broussard, C., & Vollmer, T. (1996). A comparison of reinforcer assessment methods: The utility of verbal and pictorial choice procedures. *Journal of Applied Behavior Analysis, 29,* 201–212.

Notari-Syverson, A.R., & Shuster, S. L. (1995). Putting real-life skills into IEP/IFSPs for infants and young children. *Teaching Exceptional Children. 27*(2), 29–32.

Odom, S.L. (2000). Preschool inclusion: What we know and where we go from here. *Topics in Early Childhood Special Education, 20,* 20–27.

Odom, S.L., McConnell, S.R., & Chandler, L.K. (1994). Acceptability and feasibility of classroom-based social interaction interventions for young children with disabilities. *Exceptional Children, 60,* 226–236.

Odom, S.L., & McLean, M.E. (Eds.) (1996). Early intervention /early childhood special education: Recommended practices. Austin, TX: Pro-Ed.

Odom, S.L., Zercher, C., Li, S., Marquart, J., & Sandall, S. (1998, May). *Social relationships of preschool children with disabilities in inclusive settings.* Paper presented at the Conference on Research Innovations in Early Intervention, Charleston, SC.

Ogbu, J.U. (1991). Immigrant and involuntary minorities in comparative perspective. In M. Gibson & J.U. Ogbu (Eds.), *Minority status and schooling: A comparative study of immigrant and involuntary minorities* (pp. 3–33). New York: Garland.

O'Neill, R.E., Horner, R.H., Albin, R.W., Sprague, J.R., Storey, K., & Newton, J.S. (1997). *Functional assessment and program development for problem behavior: A practical handbook*. Pacific Grove, CA: Brooks/Cole.

Pace, G.M., Ivancic, M.T., Edwards, G.L., Iwata, B.A., & Page, T.J. (1985). Assessment of stimulus preference and reinforcer value with profoundly retarded individuals. *Journal of Applied Behavior Analysis, 18*, 249–255.

Palincsar, A.S., Brown, A.L., & Campione, J.C. (1994). Models and practices of dynamic assessment. In E. Wallach & K. Butler (Eds.), *Language learning disabilities in school-age children and adolescents* (pp. 132–144). New York: Macmillan.

Parents of Premature Babies, Inc. (Preemie-L) (n.d.). Retrieved July 18, 2005, from http://www.preemie-l.org/

Park, J., Turnbull, A.P., & Park, H. (2001). Quality of partnerships in service provision for Korean American parents of children with disabilities: A qualitative inquiry. *JASH, 26*, 158–170.

Parke, R.D., & Buriel, R. (1998). Socialization in the family: Ethnic and ecological perspectives. In W. Damon & N. Eisenberg (Eds.), *Handbook of child psychology, Vol. 3: Social, emotional, and personality development* (5th ed., pp. 463–552). New York: John Wiley & Sons.

Peck, C.A. (1995). Some further reflections on the difficulties and dilemmas of inclusion. *Journal of Early Intervention, 19*, 197–199.

Peck, C.A., Furman, G.C., & Helmstetter, E. (1993). Integrated early childhood programs: Research on implementation of change in organizational contexts. In C.A. Peck, S.L. Odom, & D.D. Bricker (Eds.), *Integrating young children with disabilities in community programs: Ecological perspectives on research and implementation* (pp. 187–205). Baltimore: Paul H. Brookes Publishing Co.

Pelco, L.E., & Reed-Victor, E. (2003). Understanding and supporting differences in child temperament: Strategies for early childhood environments. *Young Exceptional Children, 3*(3), 2–11.

Pellegrino, L. (2002). Cerebral palsy. In M.L. Batshaw (Ed.), *Children with disabilities* (5th ed., pp. 443–466). Baltimore: Paul H. Brookes Publishing Co.

Peterson, N. (1987). *Early intervention for handicapped and at-risk children*. Denver: Love Publishing.

Peterson, S.L., Bondy, A.S., Vincent, Y., & Finnegan, C. S. (1995). Effects of altering communicative input for students with autism and no speech: Two case studies. *Augmentative and Alternative Communication, 11*, 93–100.

Philips, S.U. (1976). Some sources of cultural variability in the regulation of talk. *Language in Society, 5*, 81–95.

Philips, S.U. (1983). *The invisible culture*. New York: Longman.

Piaget, J. (1952). *The origins of intelligence in children*. New York: International Universities Press.

Piaget, J. (1954). *The construction of reality in the child*. New York: Basic Books.

Piazza, C.C., Fisher, W.W., Hagopian, L.P., Bowman, L.G., & Toole, L. (1996). Using a choice assessment to predict reinforcer effectiveness. *Journal of Applied Behavior Analysis, 29*, 1–9.

Presler, B., & Routt, M.L. (1997). Inclusion of children with special health care needs in early childhood programs. *Dimensions in Early Childhood, 5*, 26–31.

Pretti-Frontczak, K.L., Barr, D.M., Macy, M., & Carter, A. (2003). Research and resources related to activity-based intervention, embedded learning opportunities, and routines-based instruction: An annotated bibliography. *Topics in Early Childhood Special Education, 23*, 310–325.

Pretti-Frontczak, K., & Bricker, D. (2004). *An activity-based approach to early intervention* (3rd ed.). Baltimore: Paul H. Brookes Publishing Co.

Prizant, B.M., Wetherby, A.M., Rubin, E., & Laurent, A.C. (2003). The SCERTS model: A transactional, family-centered approach to enhancing communication and socioemotional abilities of children with Autism Spectrum Disorder. *Infants and Young Children, 16*(4), 296–316.

Putnam, J.W., Rynders, J.E., Johnson, R., & Johnson, D. (1989). Collaborative skill instruction for promoting positive interactions between mentally handicapped and nonhandicapped children. *Exceptional Children, 55*(6), 550–557.

Quill, A.K. (2000). *Do-Watch-Listen-Say: Social and communication intervention for children with autism.* Baltimore: Paul H. Brookes Publishing Co.

Rainforth, B., & York, U. (1991). Handling and positioning. In E.P. Orlove & D. Sobsey (Eds.), *Educating children with multiple disabilities: A transdisciplinary approach* (2nd ed., pp. 79–119). Baltimore: Paul H. Brookes Publishing Co.

Rainforth, B., York, J., & MacDonald, C. (1992). *Collaborative teams for students with severe disabilities.* Baltimore: Paul H. Brookes Publishing Co.

Ramirez, M., & Castenada, A. (1974). *Cultural democracy, bicognitive development and education.* New York: Academic Press.

Ratliffe, K.T. (1998). *Clinical pediatric physical therapy: A guide for the physical therapy team.* St. Louis: Mosby.

Reinhiller, H. (1996). Coteaching: New variations on a not-so-new practice. *Teacher Education and Special Education, 19,* 34–48.

Repp, A., & Horner, R.H. (Eds.) (1999). *Functional analysis of problem behavior: From effective assessment to effective support.* Belmont, CA: Wadsworth.

Rogers-Warren, A., & Warren, S.F. (1980). Mands for verbalization: Facilitating the display of newly taught language. *Behavior Modification, 2,* 361–382.

Rogoff, G., & Wertsch, J. (Eds.) (1984). *Children's learning in the Zone of Proximal Development.* San Francisco: Jossey Bass.

Romski, M.A., & Sevcik, R.A. (1993). Language learning through augmented means: The process and its products. In S.F. Warren & J. Reichle (Eds.), *Enhancing children's communication: Vol. 2. Communication and language intervention series.* Baltimore: Paul H. Brookes Publishing Co.

Rosegrant, T., & Bredekamp, S. (1992). Planning and implementing transformational curriculum. In S. Bredekamp & T. Rosegrant (Eds.), *Reaching potentials: Appropriate curriculum and assessment for young children, Vol. 1* (pp. 66–91). Washington, DC: NAEYC.

Rosenkoetter, S.E., & Squires, S. (2000). Writing outcomes that make a difference for children and families. *Young Exceptional Children, 4*(1), 2–8.

Rotholz, D.A. (1987). Current considerations on the use of one-to-one instruction with autistic students: Review and recommendations. *Education and treatment of children, 10,* 271–278.

Rous, B., Hemmeter, M.L., & Schuster, J. (1999). Evaluating the impact of the STEPS model on development of community-wide transition systems. *Journal of Early Intervention, 22,* 38–50.

Rowe, M.B. (1974). Wait time and rewards as instructional variables: Their influence on language, logic, and gate control. Part 1: Wait time. *Journal of Research in Science Teaching, 11,* 81–97.

Rubin, K.H., & Howe, H. (1985). Toys and play behaviors: An overview. *Topics in Early Childhood Special Education, 5*(3), 1–9.

Rule, S., Fiechtl, B.J., & Innocenti, M.S. (1990). Preparation for transition to mainstreamed post-preschool environments: Development of a survival skills curriculum. *Topics in Early Childhood Special Education, 9*(4), 78–90.

Rule, S., Losardo, A., Dinnebeil, L., Kaiser, A., & Rowland, C. (1998). Translating research on naturalistic instruction into practice. *Journal of Early Intervention, 21,* 283–293.

Rutherford, F.W. (1971). *You and your baby.* New York: Signet Books.

Sailor, W., & Guess, D. (1983). *Severely handicapped students: An instructional design.* Boston: Houghton Mifflin.

Sainato, D.M., & Carta, J.J. (1992). Classroom influences on the development of social competence in young children with disabilities. In S.L. Odom, S.R. McConnell, & M.A. McEvoy (Eds.), *Social competence of young children with disabilities: Issues and strategies for intervention* (pp. 93–109). Baltimore: Paul H. Brookes Publishing Co.

Sainato, D.M., & Morrison, R.S. (2001). Transition to inclusive environments for young children with disabilities. In M.J. Guralnick (Ed.), *Early childhood inclusion* (pp. 293–306). Baltimore: Paul H. Brookes Publishing Co.

Sainato, D.M., Strain, P.S., Lefebvre, D., & Rapp, N. (1987). Facilitating transition time with handicapped preschool children: A comparison between peer-mediated and antecedent prompt procedures. *Journal of Applied Behavior Analysis, 20,* 285–291.

Salend, S.J. (2001). *Creating inclusive classrooms: Effective and reflective practices* (4th ed.). Columbus, OH: Merrill/Prentice Hall.

Salend, S.J., & Salinas, A. (2003). Language differences or learning difficulties: The work of the multidisciplinary team. *Teaching Exceptional Children, 35*(4), 36–43.

Sameroff, A.J., & Chandler, M.J. (1975). Reproductive risk and the continuum of caretaking causality. In F.D. Horowitz, M. Hetherington, S. Scarr-Salapatek, & G. Siegel (Eds.), *Review of child development research* (Vol. 4, pp. 187–244). Chicago: University of Chicago Press.

Sameroff, A., & Fiese, B. (1990). Transactional regulation and early intervention. In S. Meisels & J. Shonkoff (Eds.), *Handbook of early childhood intervention* (pp. 119–149). Cambridge, England: Cambridge University Press.

Sandall, S., Hemmeter, M.L., Smith, B.J., & McLean, M.E. (Eds.) (2005). *DEC recommended practices: A comprehensive guide for practical application in early intervention/early childhood special education.* Missoula, MT: Division for Early Childhood (DEC), Council for Exceptional Children (CEC).

Sandall, S., McLean, M., & Smith, J. (Eds.) (2000). *DEC recommended practices in early childhood special education.* Longmont, CO: Sopris West.

Santos, R.M. (2001). Using what children know to teach them something new: Applying high-probability procedures in the classroom and at home. In M. Ostrosky & S. Sandall (Eds.), Teaching strategies: What to do to support young children's development. *Young Exceptional Children Monograph Series No. 3* (71–80). DEC/CEC.

Santos, R.M., & Lignugaris/Kraft, B. (1999). The effects of direct questions on preschool children's responses to indirect requests. *Journal of Behavioral Education, 9*(3/4) 193–210.

Saunders, R.R., & Saunders, M.D. (1998). Supported routines. In J.K. Luiselli & M.J. Cameron (Eds.), *Antecedent control: Innovative approaches to behavioral support* (pp. 245–272). Baltimore: Paul H. Brookes Publishing Co.

Schertz, H.H., & Odom, S.L. (2004). Joint attention and early intervention with autism: A conceptual framework and promising approaches. *Journal of Early Intervention, 27,* 42–54.

Schiller, P., & Hastings, K. (1998). *The complete resource book: An early childhood curriculum with over 2000 activities and ideas!* Beltsville, MD: Gryphon House.

Schiller, P., & Phipps, P. (2002). *The complete daily curriculum for early childhood: Over 1200 easy activities to support multiple intelligences and learning styles.* Saint Paul, MN: Consortium.

Schön, D.A. (1983). *The reflective practitioner: How professionals think in action.* New York: Basic Books.

Schopler, E., Short A., & Mesibov, G. (1989). Relation of behavioral treatment to normal educational functioning: Comment on Lovaas. *Journal of Consulting and Clinical Psychology, 57,* 162–164.

Schwartz, I.S., & Baer, D.M. (1991). Social validity assessments: Is current practice state of the art? *Journal of Applied Behavior Analysis, 24,* 189–204.

Schwartz, I.S., Billingsley, F.F., & McBride, B.M. (1998). Including children with autism in inclusive preschools: Strategies that work. *Young Exceptional Children, 1*(2), 19–26.

Schwartz, I.S., Garfinkle, A.N., & Bauer, J. (1998). The picture exchange communication system: Communicative outcomes for young children with disabilities. *Topics in Early Childhood Special Education, 18*, 144–159.

Schwartz, I.S., & Olswang, L.B. (1996). Evaluating child behavior change in natural settings: Exploring alternative strategies for data collection. *Topics in Early Childhood Special Education, 16*, 82–101.

Schwartz, I.S., Sandall, S.R., McBride, B.J., & Boulware, G.L. (2004). Project DATA (Developmentally Appropriate Treatment for Autism): An inclusive school-based approach to educating young children with autism. *Topics in Early Childhood Special Education, 24*, 156–168.

Seibert, J.M., Hogan, A.P., & Mundy, P.C. (1982). Assessing interactional competencies: The Early Social-Communication Scales. *Infant Mental Health Journal, 3*, 244–258.

Seibert, J.M., Hogan, A.P., & Mundy, P.C. (1987). Assessing social and communication skills in infancy. *Topics in Early Childhood Special Education, 7*(2), 38–48.

Shade, B.J. (1982). Afro-American cognitive style: A variable in school success. *Review of Educational Research, 52*, 219–244.

Shade, B.J. (1994). Understanding the African-American learner. In E.R. Hollins, J.E. King, & W.C. Hayman, *Teaching diverse populations: Formulating a new knowledge base* (pp. 175–189). Albany, NY: State University of New York Press.

Shade, B.J., Kelly, C., & Oberg, M. (1997). *Creating culturally responsive classrooms.* Washington, DC: American Psychological Association.

Shearer, M.S., & Shearer, D.E. (1979). The Portage Project: A model for early childhood education. *Portage project readings.* Portage, WI: Portage Project.

Sheikh, L., O'Brien, M., & McCluskey-Fawcett, K. (1993). Parent preparation for the NICU-to-home transition: Staff and parent perceptions. *Children's Health Care, 22*(3), 227–239.

Sheldon, K. (1996). "Can I play too?" Adapting common classroom activities for young children with limited motor abilities. *Early Childhood Education Journal, 11*, 115–120.

Shonkoff, J.P., & Phillips, D.A. (Eds.). (2000). *From neurons to neighborhoods: The science of early childhood development.* Washington, DC: National Academy Press.

Siegel, B. (2000). Behavioral and educational treatments for autism spectrum disorders. *The Advocate, 33*, 22–25.

Siegel, D.J. (1999). *The developing mind: Toward a neurology of interpersonal experience.* New York: The Guilford Press.

Singleton, K.C., Schuster, J.W., & Ault, M.J. (1995). Simultaneous prompting in a small group instructional arrangement. *Education and Training in Mental Retardation and Developmental Disabilities, 30*, 218–230.

Skeels, H.M. (1966). Adult status of children with contrasting early life experiences. *Monographs of the Society for Research in Child Development, 31*, (Serial No. 105).

Skeels, H.M., & Dye, H. (1939). A study of the effects of differential stimulation on mentally retarded children. *Proceedings and Addresses of the American Association on Mental Deficiency 44*, 114–136.

Skinner, B.F. (1938). *The behavior of the organism.* Englewood Cliffs, NJ: Prentice Hall.

Skrtic, T.M. (1991). *Behind special education: A critical analysis of professional culture and school organization.* Denver, CO: Love Publishing.

Skrtic, T.M. (1995). Deconstructing/reconstructing the professions. In T.M. Skrtic (Ed.), *Disability and democracy: Reconstructing (special) education for postmodernity* (pp. 3–62). New York: Teachers College Press.

Slavin, R., DeVies, D., & Edwards, K. (1983). *Cooperative learning.* New York: Longman.

Smart, M.S., & Smart, R.C. (1967). *Children: Development and relationships.* New York: The Macmillan Co.

Smith, B.J., & Rapport, M.J. (2001). Public policy in early childhood inclusion. In M.J. Guralnick (Ed.), *Early childhood inclusion* (pp. 49–58). Baltimore: Paul H. Brookes Publishing Co.

Smith, G., & Rose, D. (1993). *Administrator's policy handbook for preschool main-streaming.* Cambridge, MA: Brookline Books.

Snell, M.E. (1987). *Systematic instruction of persons with severe handicaps.* Columbus, OH: Merrill.

Snell, M.E., & Brown, F. (2006a). Development and implementation of educational programs. In M.E. Snell & F. Brown (Eds.), *Instruction of students with severe disabilities* (6th ed., pp. 111–169). Upper Saddle River, NJ: Prentice Hall.

Snell, M.E., & Brown, F. (2006b). *Instruction of students with severe disabilities* (6th ed.). Upper Saddle River, NJ: Prentice Hall.

Snell, M.E., & Gast, D.L. (1981). Applying time delay procedure to the instruction of the severely handicapped. *Journal of the Association for Persons with Severe Handicaps, 6*(3), 3–14.

Sobsey, D., & Wolf-Schein, E.G. (1991). Sensory impairments. In F.P. Orelove & D. Sobsey (Eds.), *Educating children with multiple disabilities: A transdisciplinary approach* (2nd ed., pp. 119–154). Baltimore: Paul H. Brookes Publishing Co.

Spitz, R.A. (1945). Hospitalism: An inquiry into the genesis of psychiatric conditions in early childhood. *Psychoanalytic Study of the Child* (Vol. 1), 53–74. New York: International Universities Press.

Spitz, R.A. (1946a). Anaclitic depression: An inquiry into the genesis of psychiatric conditions in early childhood, II. *Psychoanalytic Study of the Child* (Vol. 2), 313–342. New York: International Universities Press.

Spitz, R.A. (1946b). Hospitalism: A follow-up report on investigation described in Vol. 1, 1945. *Psychoanalytic Study of the Child* (Vol. 2), 113–117. New York: International Universities Press.

Spock, B.J. (1972). *Baby and child care* (Rev. ed.). New York: Simon & Schuster.

Stokes, T.F., & Baer, D.M. (1977). An implicit technology of generalization. *Journal of Applied Behavior Analysis, 10,* 349–367.

Stokes, T.F., & Osnes, P.G. (1988). The developing applied technology of generalization and maintenance. In R.H. Horner, G. Dunlap, & R.L. Koegel (Eds.), *Generalization and maintenance: Life style changes in applied settings* (pp. 5–19). Baltimore: Paul H. Brookes Publishing Co.

Stoneman, Z., & Rugg, M.E. (2004). Partnerships with families. In S.R. Hooper & W. Umansky (Eds.), *Young children with special needs* (4th ed., pp. 90–117). Upper Saddle River, NJ: Pearson Education.

Strain, P.S. (1990). Least restrictive environment for preschool children with handicaps: What we know, what we should be doing. *Journal of Early Intervention, 14,* 291–296.

Strain, P.S. (1995). The challenge of inclusion: Points well-taken and related challenges. *Journal of Early Intervention, 19,* 195–197.

Strain, P.S. (1999). Sometimes there is more to a baseline than meets the eye. *Journal of Early Intervention, 22,* 109–110.

Strain, P.S., McGee, G.G., & Kohler, G.W. (2001). Inclusion of children with autism in early intervention environments. In M.J. Guralnick (Ed.), *Early childhood inclusion* (pp. 337–363). Baltimore: Paul H. Brookes Publishing Co.

Strain, P.S., Wolery, M., & Izeman, S. (1998). Considerations for administrators in the design of service options for young children with autism and their families. *Young Exceptional Children, 1*(2), 8–16.

Sugai, G., Horner, R.H., & Sprague, J. (1999). Functional assessment-based behavior support planning: Research-to-practice-to-research. *Behavioral Disorders, 24,* 223–227.

Super, C., & Harkness, S. (1982). The development of affect in infancy and early childhood. In D. Wagner & H. Stevenson (Eds.), *Cultural perspectives on child development* (pp.1–119). San Francisco: W. H. Freeman.

Super, C., & Harkness, S. (1986). The developmental niche: A conceptualization at the interface of child and culture. *International Journal of Behavioral Development, 9,* 545–569.

Taubman, M., Brierley, S., Wishner, J., Baker, D., McEachin, J., & Leaf, R. (2001). The effectiveness of a group discrete trial instructional approach for preschoolers with developmental disabilities. *Research in Developmental Disabilities, 22,* 205–219.

Taylor, S.J. (1988). Caught in the continuum: A critical analysis of the principle of the least restrictive environment. *Journal of the Association for Persons with Severe Handicaps, 3,* 41–45.

Tharp, R.G. (1989). Psychocultural variables and constants: Effects on teaching and learning in schools. *American Psychologist, 44,* 349–359.

Tharp, R.G., & Gallimore, R. (1988). *Rousing minds to life: Teaching, learning, and schooling in social context.* New York: Cambridge University Press.

Tharp, R.G., & Yamauchi, L.A. (1994). *Effective instructional conversation in Native American classrooms.* (Educational Practice Report No. 10). Santa Cruz, CA, and Washington, DC: National Center for Research on Cultural Diversity and Second Language Learning.

Thompson, R.A. (2001). Development in the first years of life. *The Future of Children, 11*(1), 21–33.

Thompson, T., & Hanson, R. (1983). Overhydration: Precautions when treating urinary incontinence. *Mental Retardation, 21,* 139–143.

Thorp, E. (1997). Increasing opportunities for partnerships with culturally and linguistically diverse families. *Intervention in School and Clinic, 32,* 261–269.

Thousand, J.S., & Villa, R.A. (2000). Collaborative teaming: A powerful tool in school restructuring. In R.A. Villa & J.S. Thousand (Eds.), *Restructuring for caring and effective education: Piecing the puzzle* (pp. 254–292). Baltimore: Paul H. Brookes Publishing Co.

Thousand, R.A., & Thousand, J.S. (Eds.). (2000). *Restructuring for caring and effective education: Piecing the puzzle.* Baltimore: Paul H. Brookes Publishing Co.

Touchette, P.E. (1971). Transfer of stimulus control: Measuring the moment of transfer. *Journal of the Experimental Analysis of Behavior, 15,* 347–354.

Turbiville, V.P., Turnbull, A.P., Garland, C.W., & Lee, I.M. (1996). Development and implementation of IFSPs and IEPs: Opportunities for empowerment. In S.L. Odom & M.E. McLean (Eds.), *Early intervention/early childhood special education: Recommended practices* (pp. 77–100). Austin, TX: PRO-ED.

Turnbull, A.P., Summers, J.A., & Brotherson, M.J. (1983). *Working with families with disabled members. A family systems approach.* Lawrence, KS: University of Kansas Press.

Twardosz, S., Norquist, V.M., Simon, R., & Botkin, D. (1983). The effect of group affection activities on the interaction of socially isolate children. *Analysis and Intervention in Developmental Disabilities, 13,* 311–338.

U.S. Bureau of the Census. (1996). U.S. Census Bureau: The official statistics [On-line]. Available: http://www.census.gov/ [1998, October 28].

U.S. Department of Education, National Center for Education Statistics. (1999). *Teacher quality: A report on the preparation and qualifications of public school teachers.* NCES 1999–080. Washington, DC: NCES.

Van Tatenhove, G.M. (1987). Teaching power through augmentative communication: Guidelines for early intervention. *Journal of Childhood Communication Disorders, 10,* 185–199.

Vandercook, T., York, J., & Forest, M. (1989). The McGill Action Planning System (MAPS): A strategy for building the vision. *Journal of the Association for Persons with Severe Handicaps, 14,* 205–215.

Vincent, L.J., Salisbury, C., Walter, G., Brown, P., Gruenewald, L.J., & Powers, M. (1980). Program evaluation and curriculum development in early childhood special education: Criteria of the next environment. In W. Sailor, B. Wilcox, & L. Brown (Eds.), *Methods of instruction for severely handicapped students* (pp. 308–328). Baltimore: Paul H. Brookes Publishing Co.

Walker, H., & Hops, H. (1976). Increasing academic achievement by reinforcing direct academic performance and/or facilitative nonacademic responses. *Journal of Educational Psychology, 68,* 218–225.

Warren, S.F., Yoder, P.J., Gazdag, G.E., Kim K., & Jones, H.A. (1993). Facilitating prelinguistic communication skills in young children with developmental delay. *Journal of Speech and Hearing Research, 36,* 83–97.

Weeks, M., & Gaylord-Ross, R. (1981). Task difficulty and aberrant behavior in severely handicapped students. *Journal of Applied Behavior Analysis, 14,* 449–463.

Wehman, P., Moon, M.S., & McCarthy, P. (1986). Transition from school to adulthood for youth with severe handicaps. *Focus on Exceptional Children, 10*(5), 1–12.

Weikart, D.P., Rogers, L., Adcock, C., & McClelland, D. (1971). *The cognitively oriented curriculum.* Washington, DC: National Association for the Education of Young Children.

Werts, M.G., Caldwell, N.K., & Wolery, M. (1996). Peer modeling of response chains: Observational learning by students with disabilities. *Journal of Applied Behavior Analysis, 29,* 53–66.

Westby, C.E. (1985). Learning to talk-talking to learn. In C.S. Simon (Ed.), *Communication skills and classroom success* (pp. 181–218). San Diego: College-Hill.

Westling, D., & Fox, L. (2004). *Teaching students with severe disabilities* (3rd ed.). Upper Saddle River, NJ: Prentice Hall.

Whalen, C., Schuster, J.W., & Hemmeter, M.L. (1996). The use of unrelated instructive feedback when teaching in a small group instructional arrangement. *Education and Training in Mental Retardation and Developmental Disabilities, 31,* 188–202.

White, O.R. (1980). Adaptive performance objectives: Form versus function. In W. Sailor, B. Wilcox, & L. Brown (Eds.), *Methods of instruction for severely handicapped students* (pp. 47–69). Baltimore: Paul H. Brookes Publishing Co.

White, S., & Tharp, R.G. (1988, April). *Questioning and wait time: A cross-cultural analysis.* Paper presented at the annual meeting of the American Educational Research Association, New Orleans.

Wicker, A.W. (1979). Ecological psychology: Some recent and prospective developments. *American Psychologist, 34,* 755–765.

Widaman, K.F., & Kagan, S. (1987). Cooperativeness and achievement: Interaction of student cooperativeness with cooperation versus competitive classroom organization. *Journal of School Psychology, 25,* 355–365.

Will, M. (1984). *OSERS programming for the transition of youth with disabilities: Bridges from school to working life.* Washington, DC: U.S. Department of Education, Office of Special Education and Rehabilitative Services.

Winterton, W.A. (1976). *The effect of extended wait-time on selected verbal response characteristics of some Pueblo Indian children.* Unpublished doctoral dissertation, University of New Mexico, Albuquerque.

Winton, P.J., McCollum, J.A., & Catlett, C. (Eds.). (1997). *Reforming personnel preparation in early intervention.* Baltimore: Paul H. Brookes Publishing Co.

Winzer, M., & Mazurek, K. (1998). *Special education in multicultural contexts* (2nd ed.). Upper Saddle River, NJ: Prentice Hall.

Witkin, H.A., Moore, C.A., Goodenough, D.R., & Cox, P.W. (1977). Field-dependent and field-independent cognitive styles and their educational implications. *Review of Educational Research, 47,* 1–64.

Wolery, M. (1994). Implementing instruction for young children with special needs in early childhood classrooms. In M. Wolery & J.S. Wilbers (Eds.), *Including children with special needs in early childhood programs* (pp. 151–166). Washington, DC: National Association for the Education of Young Children (NAEYC).

Wolery, M. (1996). *Using assessment information to plan intervention programs.* In M.E. McLean, D.B. Bailey, & M. Wolery (Eds.), Assessing infants and preschoolers with special needs (2nd ed.) (pp. 491–518). Englewood Cliffs, NJ: Prentice Hall.

Wolery, M. (2000). Recommended practices in child-focused interventions. In S. Sandall, M.E. McLean, & B.J. Smith, (Eds.), *DEC recommended practices in early intervention/early childhood special education* (pp. 29–37). Denver, CO: Division of Early Childhood (DEC) of the Council for Exceptional Children (CEC).

Wolery, M. (2001). Embedding constant time delay procedures in classroom activities. In M. Ostrosky & S. Sandall (Eds.), Teaching strategies: What to do to support young children's development. *Young Exceptional Children Monograph Series No. 3* (81–90). DEC/CEC.

Wolery, M. (2004). Using assessment information to plan intervention programs. In M. McLean, M. Wolery, & D.B. Bailey (Eds.), *Assessing infants and preschoolers with special needs* (3rd ed.). Columbus, OH: Pearson.

Wolery, M., Anthony, L., & Heckathorn, J. (1998). Transition-based teaching: Effects on transitions, teachers' behaviors, and children's learning. *Journal of Early Intervention, 21*, 117–131.

Wolery, M., Ault, M.J., & Doyle, P.M. (1992). *Teaching students with moderate and severe disabilities: Use of response prompting strategies.* White Plains, NY: Longman.

Wolery, M.R., & Dyk, L. (1984). Arena assessment: Description and preliminary social validation data. *JASH, 9,* 231–235.

Wolery, M., McWilliam, R.A., & Bailey, D.B. (2005). *Teaching infants and preschoolers with disabilities* (3rd ed.). Upper Saddle River, NJ: Pearson Prentice Hall.

Wolf, M.M. (1978). Social validity: The case for subjective measurement or How applied behavior analysis is finding its heart. *Journal of Applied Behavior Analysis, 11,* 203–214.

Yamall, P. (2000). Current interventions in autism—a brief analysis. *The Advocate, 33,* 25–27.

Yamauchi, L.A., & Tharp, R.G. (1995). Culturally compatible conversations in Native American classrooms. *Linguistics and Education, 7,* 349–367.

Zanolli, K., Daggett, J., & Adams, T. (1996). Teaching preschool age autistic children to make spontaneous initiations to peers using priming. *Journal of Autism and Developmental Disorders, 26,* 407–422.

Zirpoli, S.B. (1995). Designing environments for optimal behavior. In T. Zirpoli (Ed.), *Understanding and affecting the behavior of young children* (pp. 123–149). Englewood Cliffs, NJ: Merrill.

Index

Page numbers followed by *f* indicate figures; those followed by *t* indicate tables.

in time delay schedules, 127
see also Direct instruction
Co-teaching model of inclusion, 15
see also Partnerships; Teams
Council for Exceptional Children (CEC), *see*
Division for Early Childhood (DEC),
Council for Exceptional Children
CPR, *see* Cardiopulmonary resuscitation
Credibility problems of teams, 33
Crisis management plans, 222, 223t, 234
Criterion-referenced tests, 52–54, 53t
Critical functions, 290, 296t, 297t, 303t
Critical periods, *see* Sensitive periods
Cross-cultural competence, 36–37, 40, 42,
226
see also Cultural considerations
Cues
with children with autism, 178–179
concrete cues, 164, 166t
contextual cues, 164, 166t
for decreasing challenging behaviors,
236–237
definition, 126
in time delay procedures, 202
see also Prompts
Cultural considerations
case examples, 165–168
challenging behaviors, perceptions of,
223–224, 233–234
cognitive processes, 154–157, 159t
cross-cultural competence, 36–37, 40, 42,
226
cultural diversity, implications of, 36
cultural reciprocity, 42–44, 226
cultural relativity, 103
culturally compatible education, 152–158,
159t, 160, 165–168
culturally relevant instruction, 16–17, 152
culture, defined, 35, 152
English as a second language (ESL),
160–165, 166t
family-centered intervention, 19
functional assessment interviews, 226–227
influence of culture on behavior, 35
involuntary minorities, 157
motivation, 157–158
in naturalistic curriculum model, 90–91
parenting practices, 40–42, 83
portfolio assessments, 117
social organization, 158
sociolinguistics, 153–154, 159t
special education, culture of, 37–40
transitions to preschool, 320
Culture in Special Education (Kalyanpur &
Harry), 37–38

Curricula
for children with autism, 173–174
definition, 78
naturalistic model, 82–91
traditional models, 78–82, 81t
Curriculum-based assessment, *see* Criterion-
referenced tests

Daily activities
in ecological assessment, 104–105,
106f–107f
general self-help skills, 302–304, 305f
mealtime skills, 307, 308t–309t, 310–311,
310f
toileting, 304–307
see also Routines; Schedules, daily
DAP, *see* Developmentally appropriate
practices
Data collection
in ecological assessment, 110, 111f, 112
graphing methods, 146–148, 148f
monitoring systematic instruction,
143–148, 147f, 148f
portfolio assessments, 113–117
positive behavior support (PBS), 242
quantitative versus qualitative data, 112
time delay procedures, 203
Deafness, children with, 211–213
DEC, *see* Division for Early Childhood
(DEC), Council for Exceptional
Children
Delay schedules, 126–127, 129, 201–204
Delayed reinforcement, 241
Destructive behaviors, 220
Development
brain development research, 8
eating and drinking skills, 308t–309t
motor development problems, 292–293
Developmental curriculum model, 78–79,
81t
Developmental, Individual-Difference,
Relationship-Based (DIR) intervention
model, 183, 188
Developmental psychology, 4
Developmental quotient (DQ), 5
Developmental stage model of intervention,
52–54
Developmental-cognitive curriculum model,
79–80, 81t
Developmentally appropriate practices
(DAP), 85, 104, 109, 271
Developmentally delayed children
under Education of the Handicapped Act
Amendments of 1986, 10